Leon Kelly

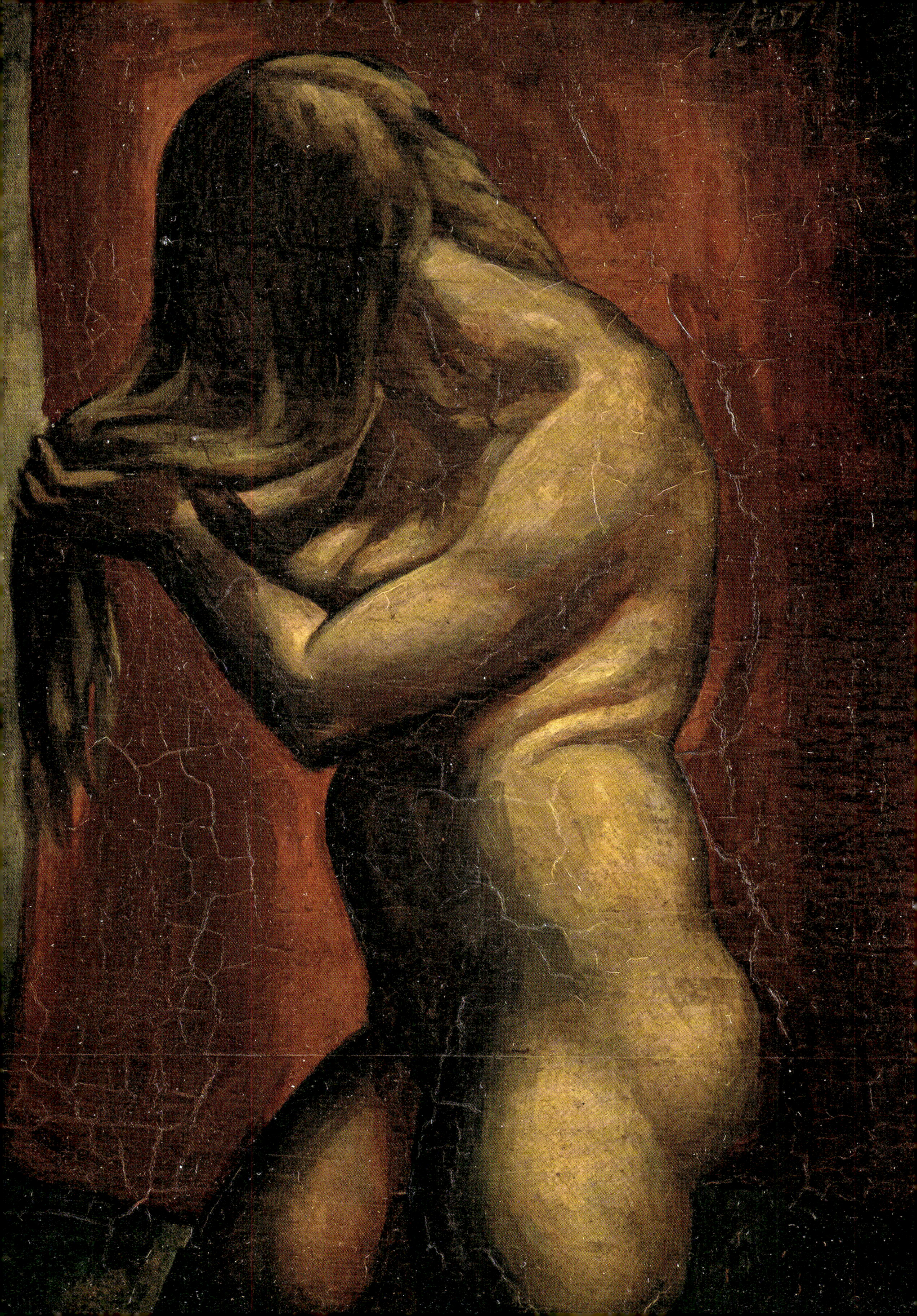

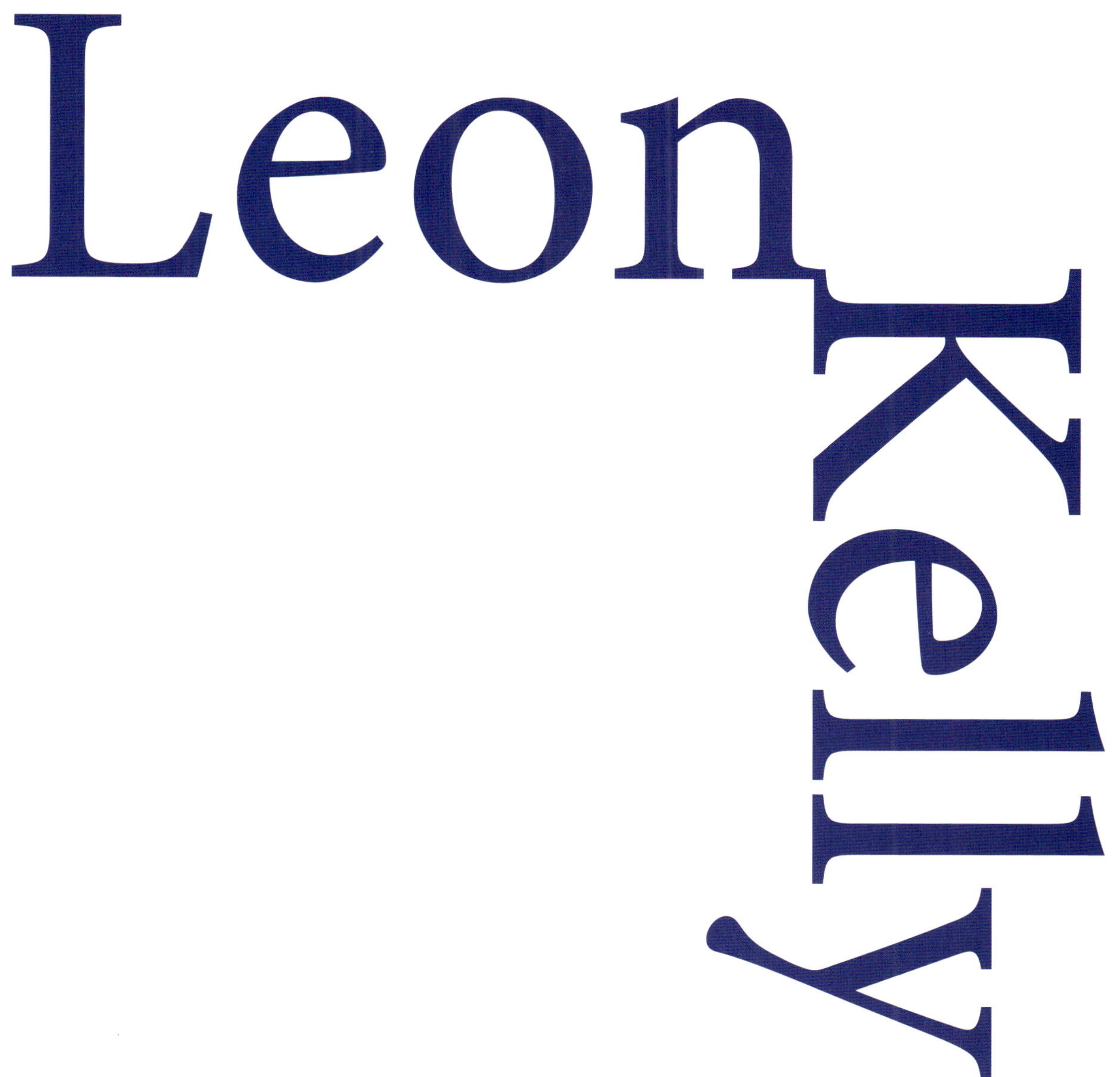

Beyond Surrealism

The Gerd and Helga Plewig Collection

HIRMER

Text by Uwe Jourdan

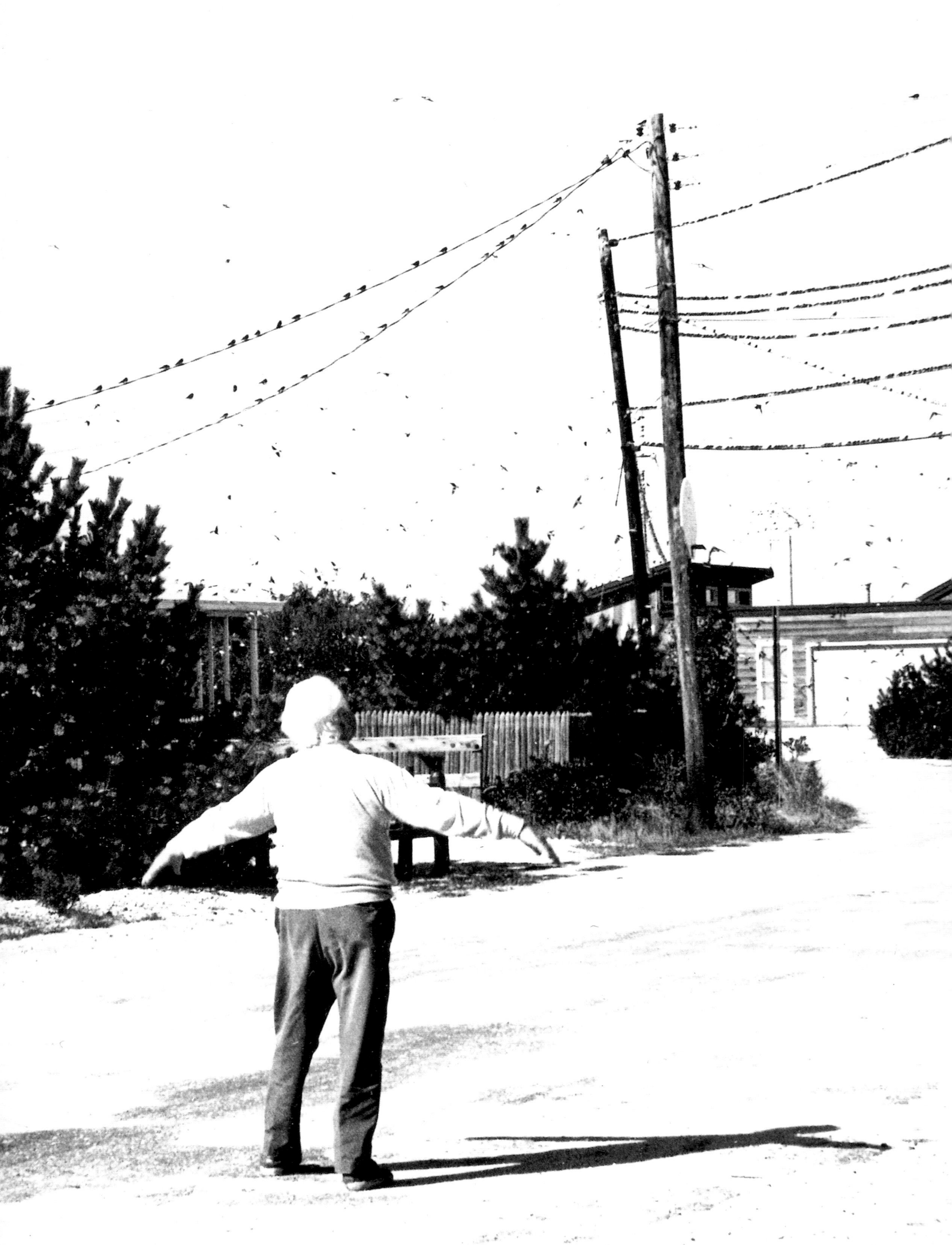

Contents

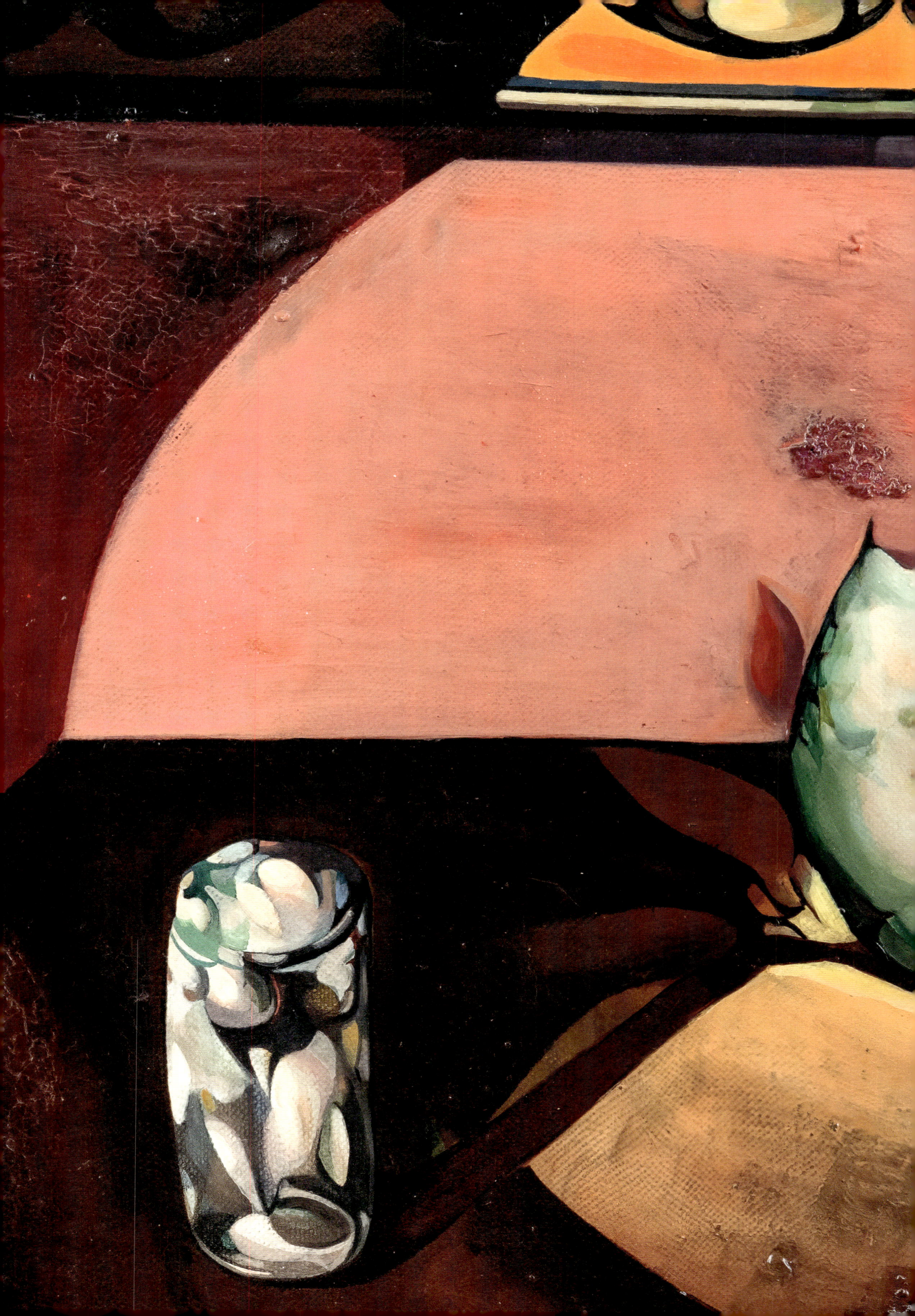

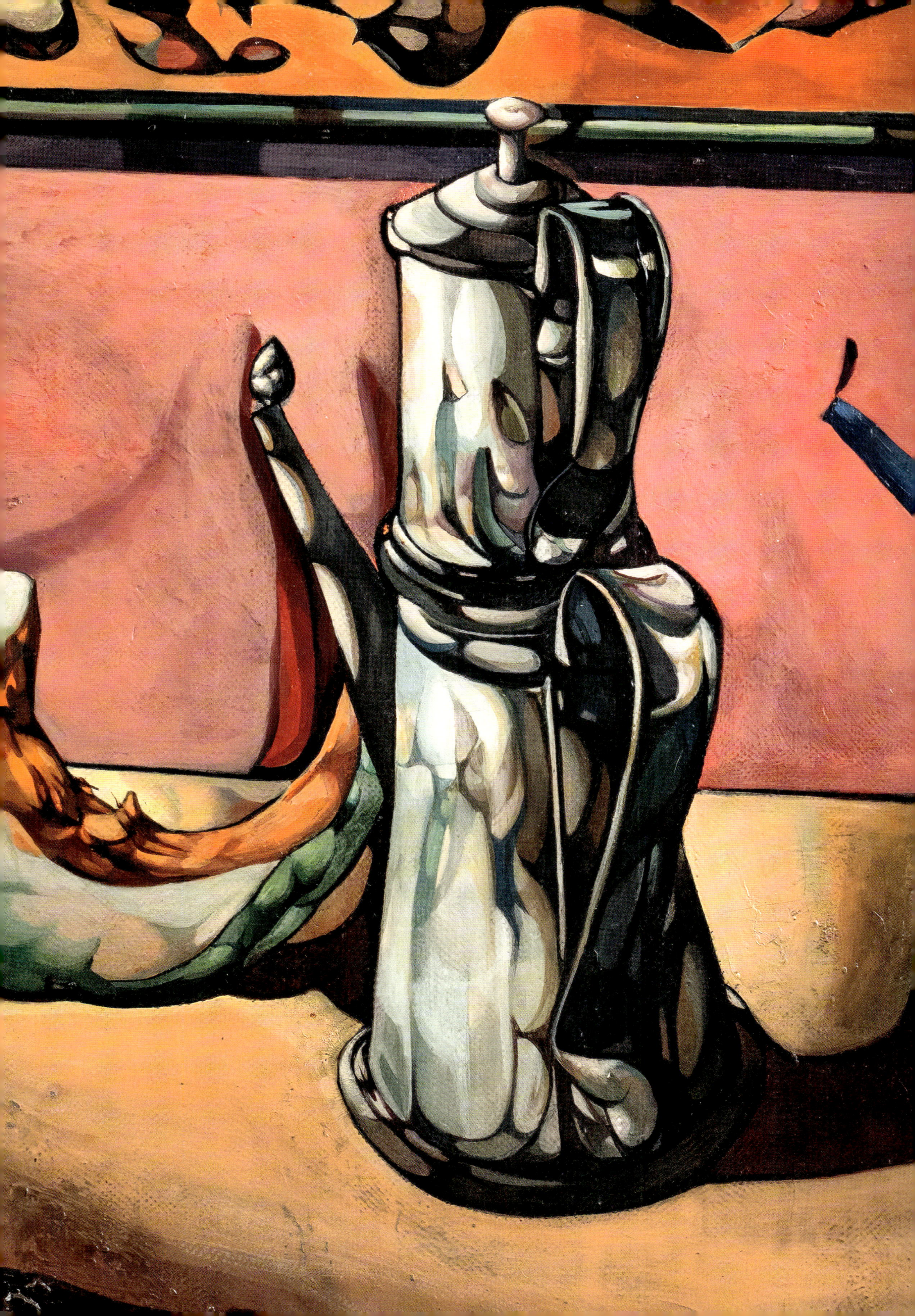

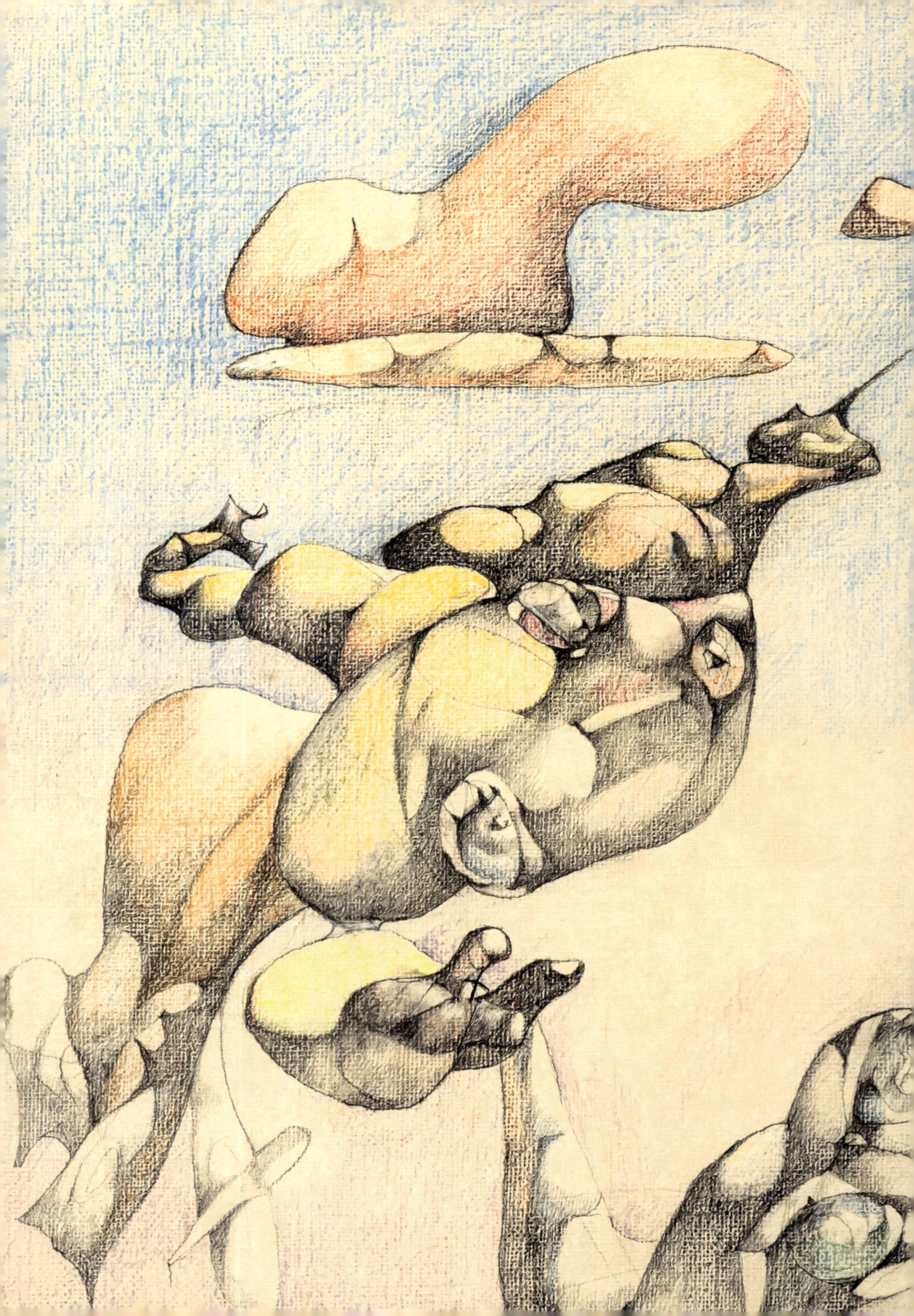

Serendipity

Gerd Plewig

Encountering an artist, almost completely unknown to Europeans, on a small remote island off the Atlantic coast of New Jersey, USA, one who touched our lives, remains one of the happiest moments in our lives. The story began in 1967, when I qualified for an American Working Permit for medicine, receiving a grant to work for a year in the United States through the Ventnor Foundation in New Jersey. After working in the suburbs of Philadelphia, serendipity introduced me to an eminent researcher and dermatologist at the University of Pennsylvania in Philadelphia, Professor Albert Montgomery Kligman, MD, PhD, Dr. h.c. He offered me a position with him for two years, from 1967 to 1969. His family owned a summer house in the marsh landscape inOceana Drive, Long Beach Island, a remote, twenty-nine kilometer long – but only up to 800 meters wide – island off the Atlantic coast of New Jersey, about 6,560 kilometers away from my home in Munich, Germany. This is where my mentor invited me to spend occasional weekends to discuss our research results. It was the beginning of a life-long friendship between our families.

Kligman invited my wife Helga and me to spend our honeymoon in 1976 with them, during the best time for a vacation, in September, and then every year thereafter. Serendipity was when the hosts mentioned to us in 1978 that across from their house in Oceana Drive, in the next street, Pompano Drive, lived a famous artist and painter.

Let's go and meet him. This was Leon Kelly, now in his late seventies, who lived alone in the typical wooden house, with a garage that had been turned into a storage room for his works. Leon Kelly was not active as an artist anymore, he lived by himself, distant from family and friends, except for his next-door neighbors, who occasionally looked after him, and his dedicated friend Helen Silvermaster, an executive in a construction, land developing, and dredging company. She took care of his immediate needs, helping him to live from the sparse income from the paintings he sold. Sidney Rothman, a gallerist in Barnegat Light, Long Beach Island, regularly offered works by Kelly.

Helga and I visited him over the next few years. Leon seemed to enjoy our friendship. One day he mentioned that about a hundred of his paintings were stored in a warehouse in New York City. On a paper he wrote the address and a note stating that the two of us were permitted to see his works. When we rang the bell at the New York warehouse, the person in charge told us that Leon's daughter had decided that no other person should be admitted to the stored works. Evidently, she had put her father under her tutelage. Our last visit to Leon was in September 1981, shortly before his death in October 1982. Helen Silvermaster accompanied us while we visited him to buy some paintings.

Serendipity means finding something unexpectedly. The word is derived from the old Persian term for Ceylon, known today as Sri Lanka. The fairy tale "The Three Princes of Serendip" closes with a happy ending. Horace Walpole introduced the word serendipity into the English-speaking world. Leon Kelly entered our personal world by sheer luck.

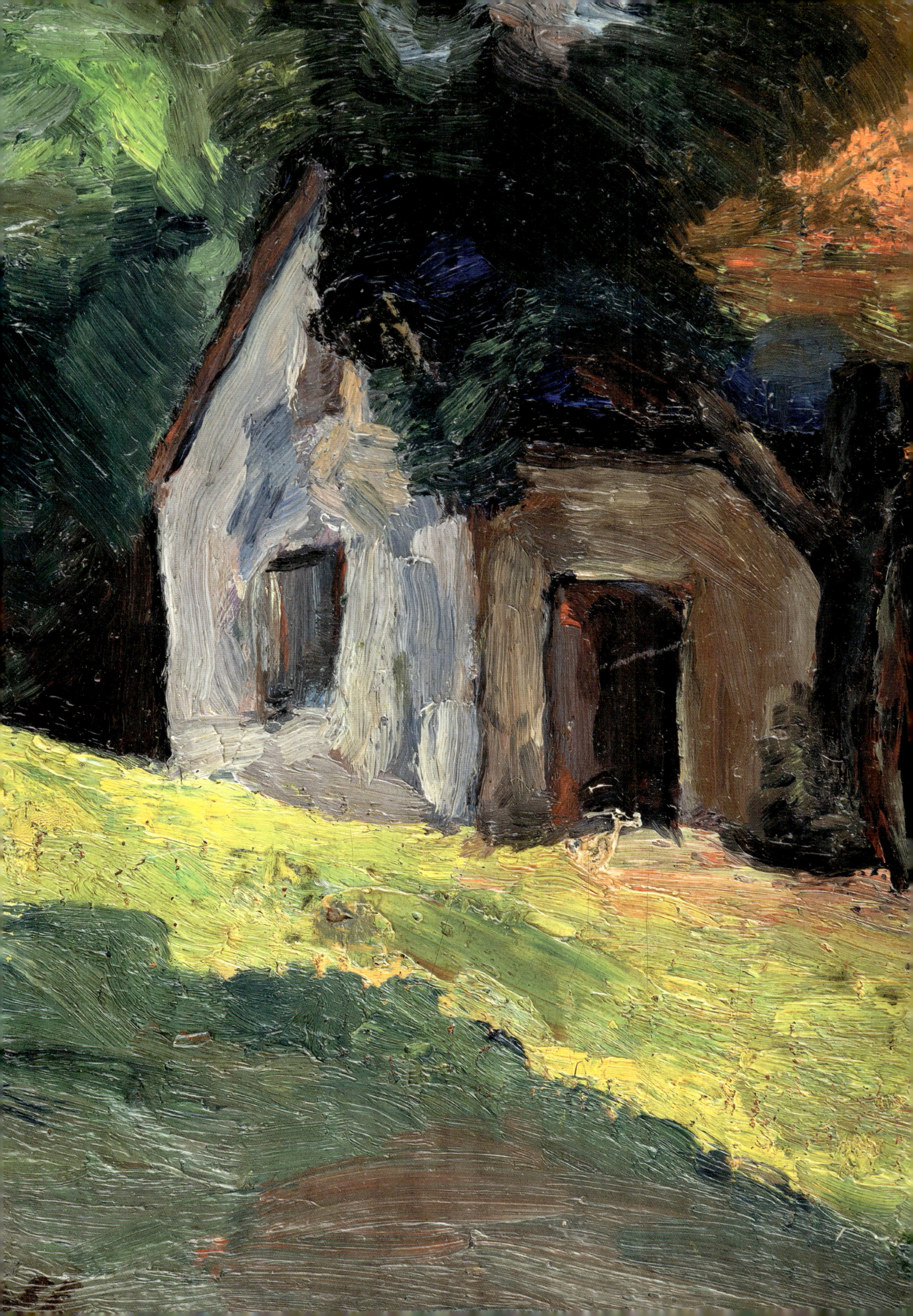

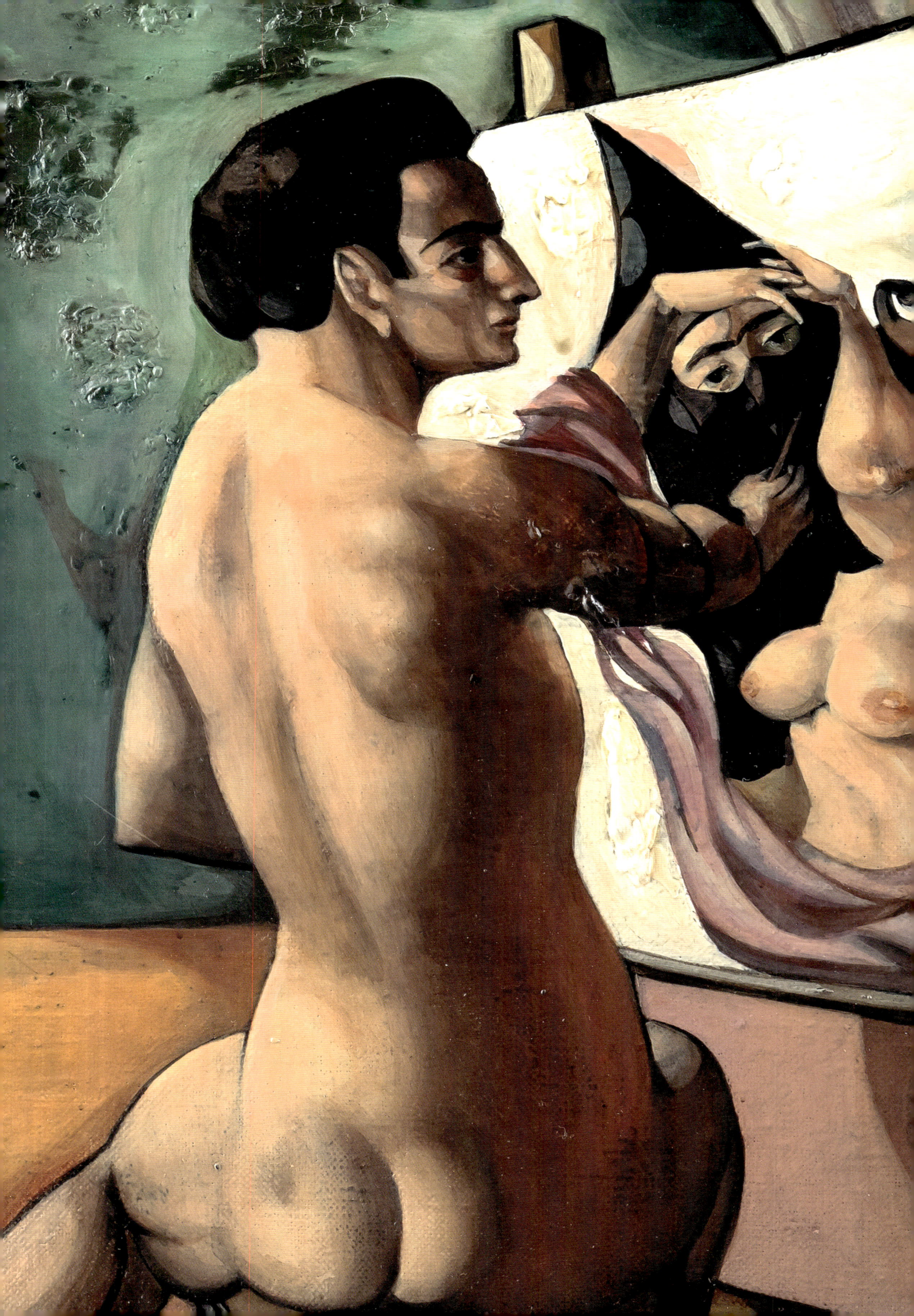

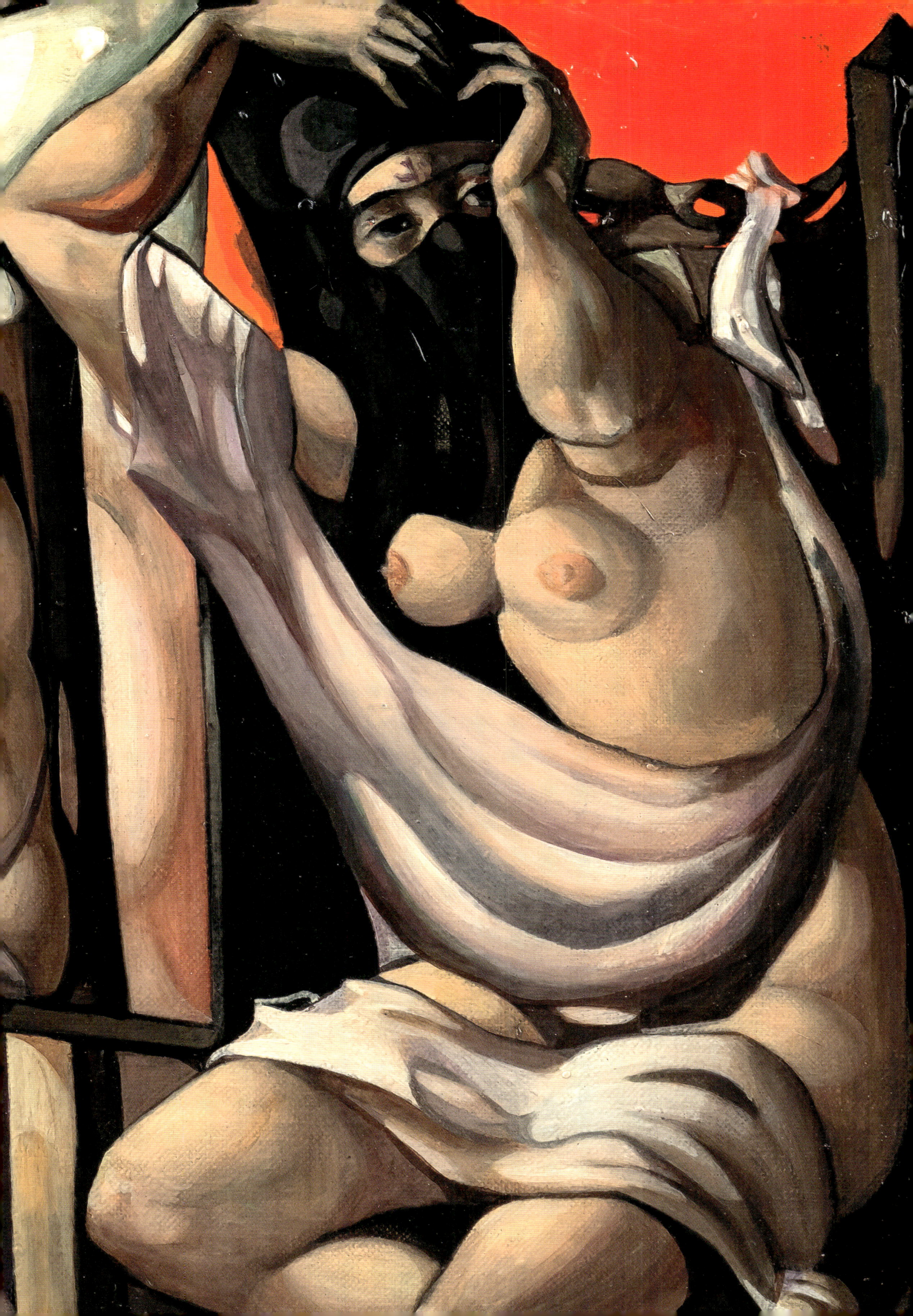

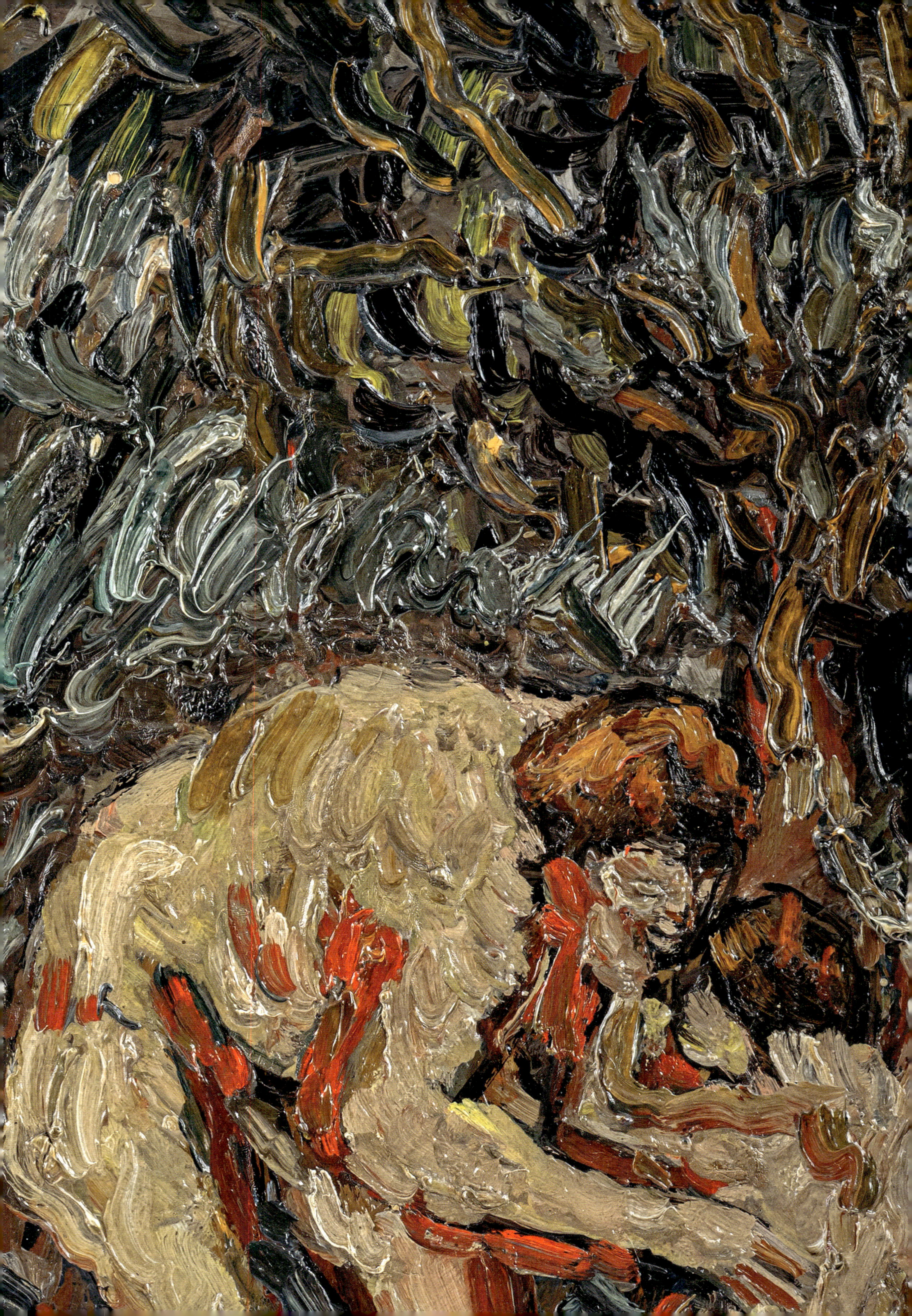

Beyond Surrealism

Uwe Jourdan

Leon Kelly has been considered an American representative of surrealism, at least since the early 1940s, when he was inspired by the surrealists who had fled Europe. The collection of over a hundred works from all periods of Kelly's oeuvre presented in this book offers a new opportunity to trace his artistic development, at the same time making clear that the attribution to surrealism must be viewed more nuancedly. After the years spent in Paris, where he came into contact with the current trends of modernism and at the same time studied the Old Masters in the museums, Kelly found his way via Cubism and Realism to surrealism, which served as the springboard for the more personal direction he embarked on.

"As for my own work, in the future I do not know if I could fit into any group or 'ism,' because of having worked alone for so long," observed Leon Kelly in a letter to the gallerist Julian Levy in 1958 (Sawin/Naumann, p. 100). Although he admitted that what he produced in these years was the result of his intensive contact with surrealism, he nevertheless distanced himself from it.

In his celebrated painting "The Plateau of Chess" from 1945—very much in the style of Salvador Dalí's landscapes—Leon Kelly bid farewell to surrealism, whose revolutionary ideas he had never fully embraced.

In 1924, amid the wreckage of the Great War, French poet André Breton railed against the values of the world as it was and could never again be, one ruled by realism and rationality. “The mere word ‘freedom’ is the only one that still excites me,” stated Breton in his Surrealist Manifesto.

It is therefore worth noting that the last major exhibition dedicated to Kelly was held in 2008 under the title “Leon Kelly - An American Surrealist.”

In the spring of 1946, Kelly took a teaching job at the Brooklyn Museum School. Here he discovered their collection of Peruvian textiles, the impact of which changed his artistic direction for the next several years. Kelly had determined that American artists had been under the influence of Europe for too long and was searching for another visual tradition closer to the American experience. He found it in the textiles and began to study Peruvian civilization and art.

When Kelly died in 1982, he had spent half of his life living and working on a sandy strip off the coast of New Jersey, many years of which were spent in seclusion and solitude. While the New York art scene celebrated New Abstraction, he turned away from it and continued to explore his own artistic path. In his technical perfection, acquired through decades of drawing, he differed tremendously from the prevailing zeitgeist (*Champêtre Royal – Lunar Personages at Lunch* can be regarded as the ultimate masterpiece in his work as a draftsman).

After his last solo exhibition at the Iolas Gallery in New York, “Paintings 1955–1972,” the recluse went silent and completed his last major work, *Bathers at Loveladies*.

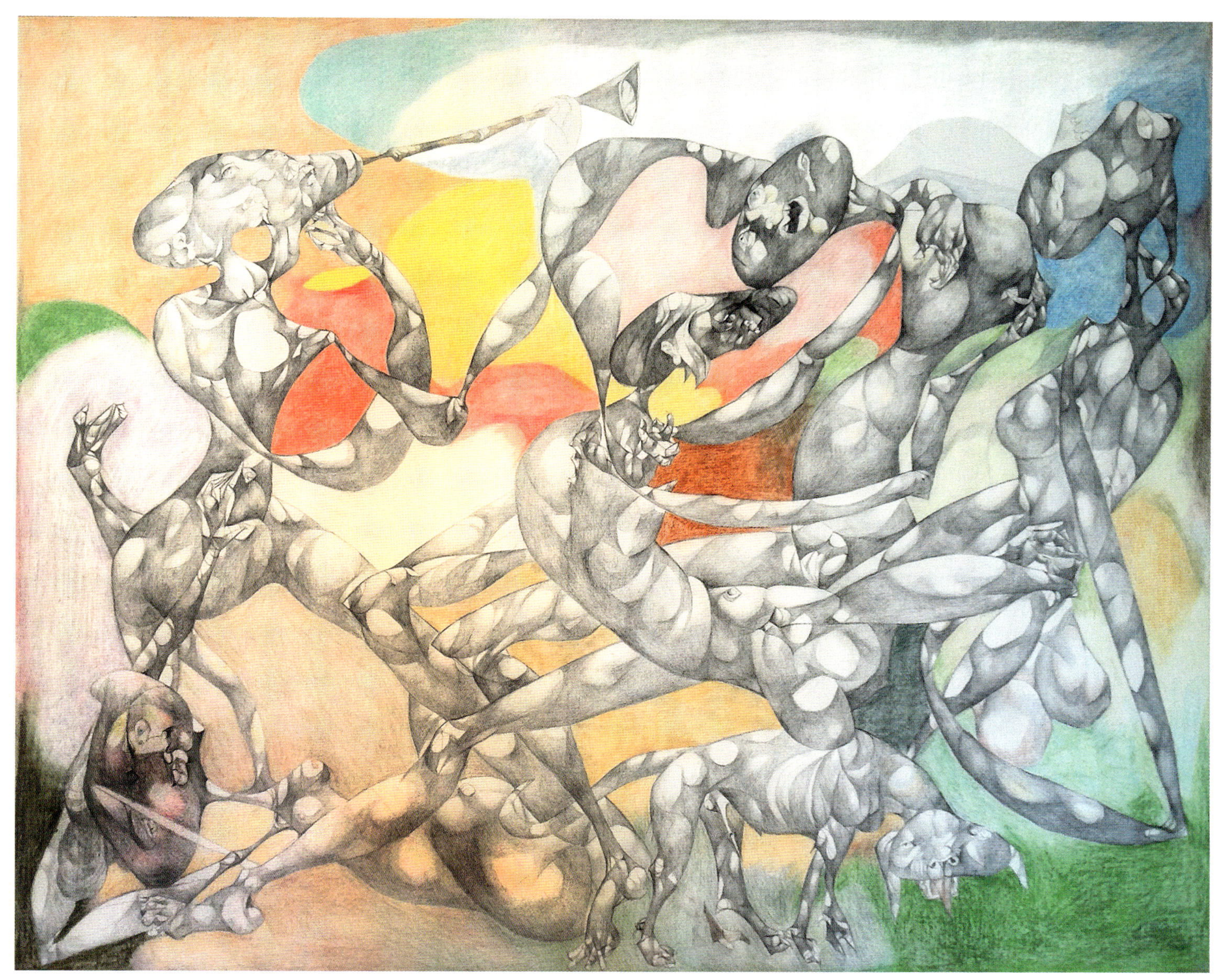

Leon Kelly, *Champêtre Royal – Lunar Personages at Lunch*, 1963, 185 × 216 cm, Conté crayon and crayons on canvas, private collection, courtesy Francis M. Naumann Fine Art, New York

Around 150 works by Leon Kelly have been offered at American auctions in recent decades. Although his works are represented in important museums (Metropolitan Museum of Art, New York; Museum of Modern Art, New York; Philadelphia Museum of Art; Tel Aviv Museum of Art), the prices for his works by no means reflect the significance of this artist and the uniqueness of his work.

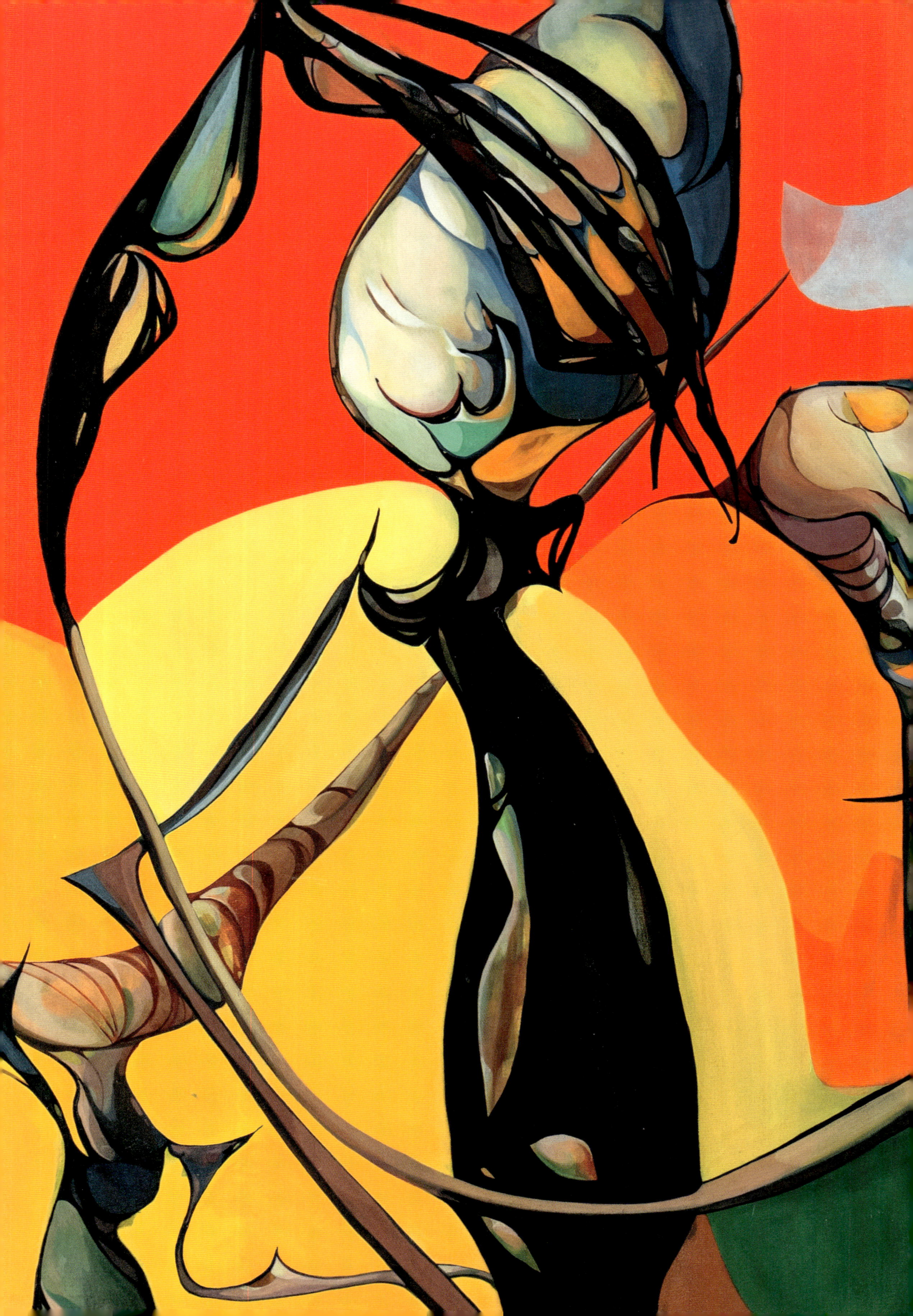

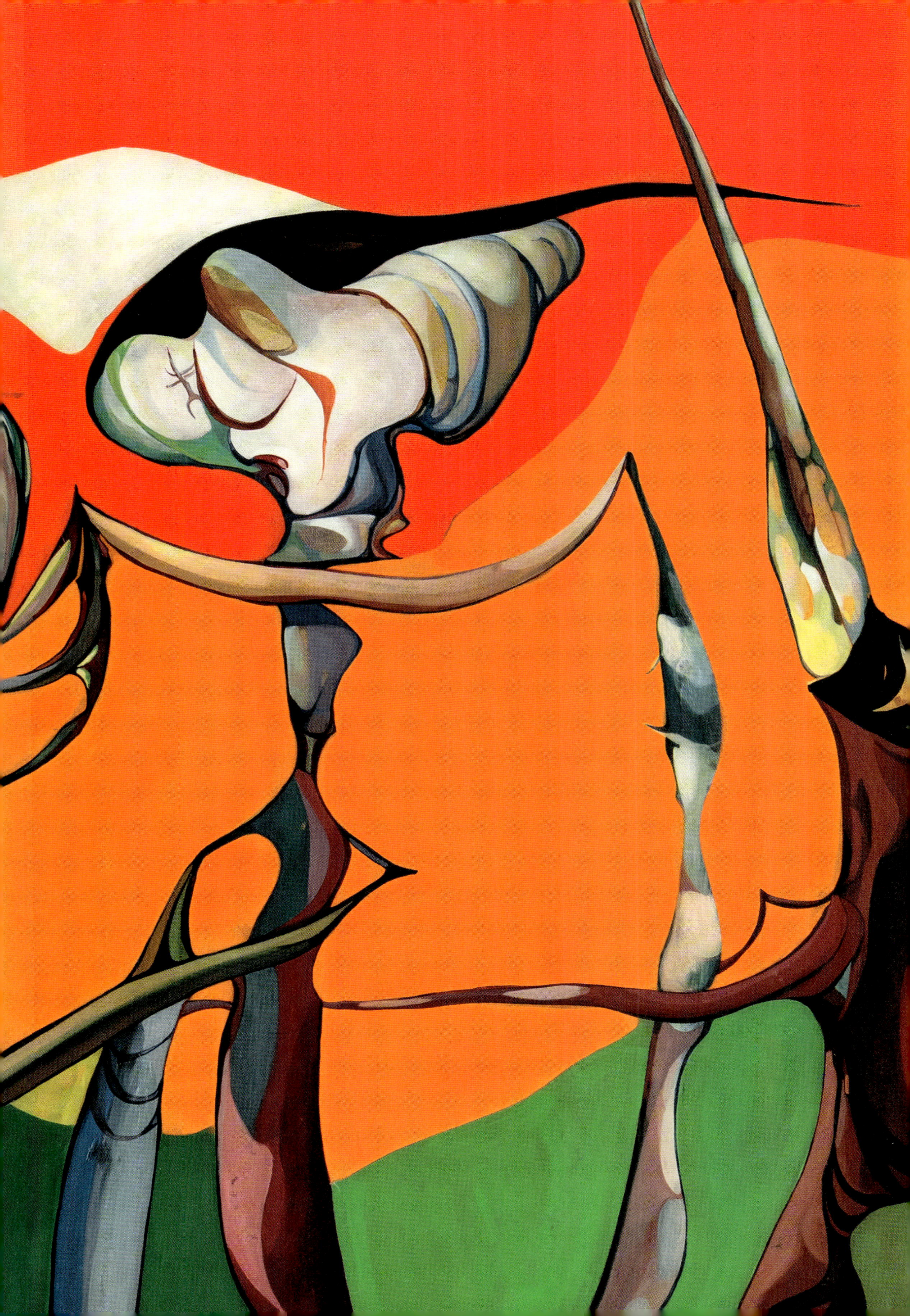

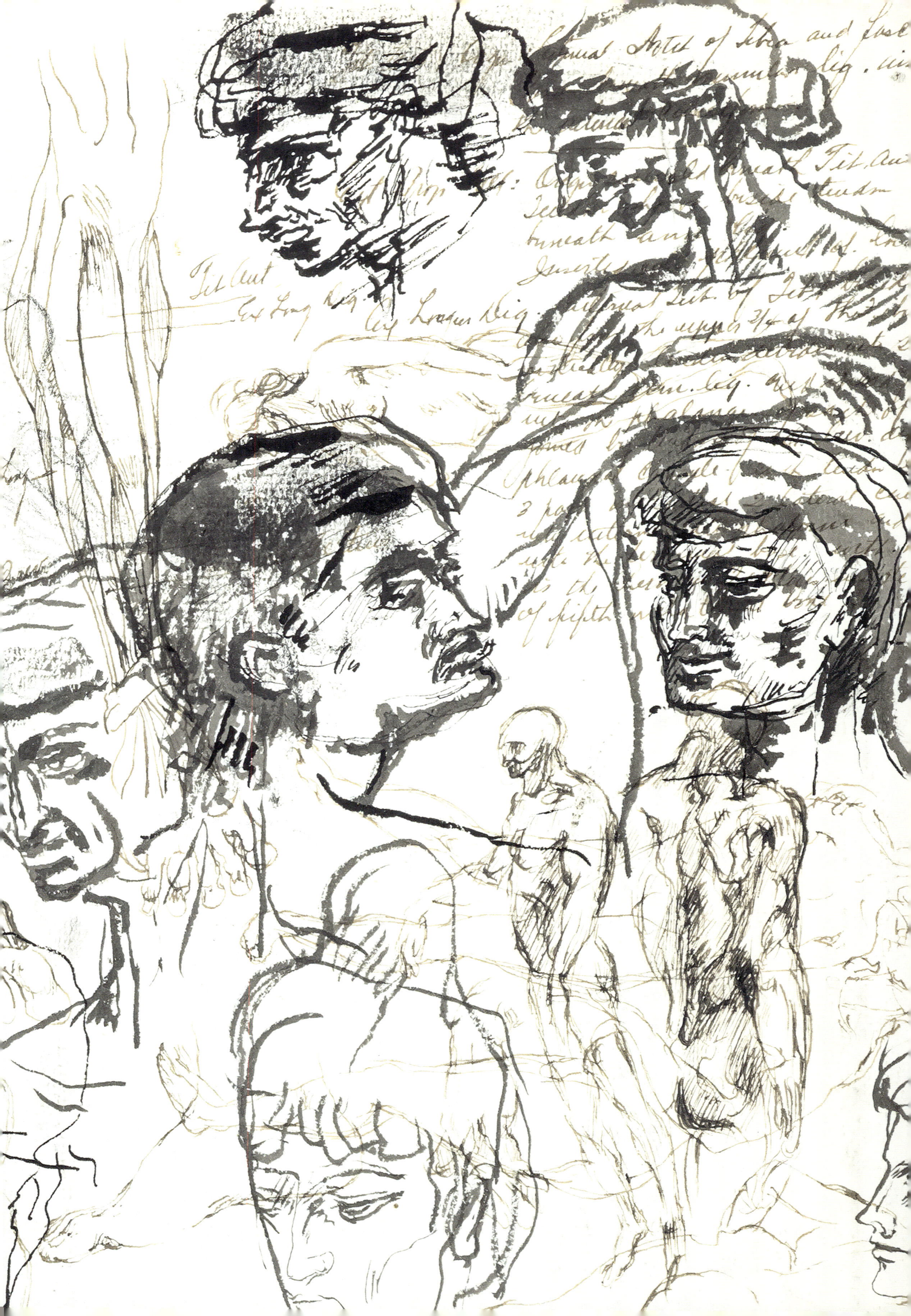

In His Own Words

The Art of Leon Kelly ...

I think of art as a force. Painting is a good way to isolate that force so that the painter as well as the layman, too, can see it, eventually understand it, recognize it as the vital part of art of all ages, and finally use it in their lives. That force is wrapped into every great master's work, no matter when or where they live, by whom they are influenced, or what their subject is.

I like to develop shapes based on the unfamiliar forms I see, and to assemble them to create the balance, depth, rhythm, and contrast I find in nature. I am interested in the new vision that is both revealed and implied by inventions of science such as the microscope, the camera, and the telescope. I am involved with all the strata of humanity and with all animal life. I study insects, their wings and construction; all the visible world interests me. Then, too, there is the internal vision of the painting. That is personal. That is elusive, always beyond.

Return and Departure Paintings

All of these canvases were painted during my association with Julien Levy and are in the Julien Levy Collection. My studio is located on a small island off the coast of southern New Jersey. At times the island is completely immersed in fog, giving the impression that sea, sky, space are one and that the island is a platform in infinite space. These paintings relate to the extreme feeling of nostalgia experienced by the continual arrival and departure of people, animals, and birds.

The wind and the sea sweep away the imprints of their marks on the sand. They seem to appear as a thin thread, and as they approach, they become strangely close and inflated. As they depart, they again diminish to a thick and invisible thread.

Insects

Many of these paintings are also in the Julien Levy Collection. They are of imaginary insects and their relation in feeling and meaning to people. They are closely connected to the extreme delicacy of construction of the human nervous system. Insects that seem to be the psychological skeleton of human sensations.

Birds

The silent and mystical relationship of birds to the elements. They come and go like the spiritual counterparts of human beings, or like the first trial of a new soul. Down from infinite space to stand for a moment like strange messengers, or like a glance at a face in a mirror that will never be seen again.

I like to develop shapes based on the unfamiliar forms I see, and assemble them to create the balance, depth, rhythm and contrast I find in nature. How to transpose the form that is floating in the mind, that has been drifting for a million years on a remote pellicle or film, and then fix it by the rules art has devised for affixing form.

I am beginning to feel an entirely new existence related to objects. An intense realization of the living force beyond the appearance. The force common to all things, the living quality aside from the habits or superficial facets of the object. In recent drawings my interest is to try to define an expression of the evasive inner spirit of man and objects in their momentary relationships.

The equation in my own forms of the revelation of one man or object or a group, from the waves that appear and quickly disappear; the result of the sensation or realization of psychological contact with a real or subconscious event.

After several trips to the reservations of the Plains and Pueblo Indians, and to Mexico, I felt the influence of an indigenous culture would be an interesting and important thing to integrate in my expression. The subject matter of pre-Columbian textiles and artifacts (particularly Peruvian and Ecuadorian) appealed very much to me because of their beauty of rare color and texture and their inspiration and light [...]. Not only did my work become involved with aspects of the textiles and artifacts, but I also based it upon a poetic version of the religion, industry, politics, and general life of the people of that period, as well as I could understand it. In 1953 I went to Spain and Africa and since then the source of inspiration of my work has been from that area. My contact with the people of Morocco and Spain is an entirely personal one. I believe the feeling is more fluid since it is directly from a living source and that the general color tonality has changed. I was quite influenced by the silence of moving people and the physical invisibility of the individual, nearly always wrapped in cloths and veils [...]. In 1954–55 I started on a group of paintings relating to the moon. I have used the moon in a symbolic shape as the head of the figure in *Girl Standing Behind the Moon* and also in *Meeting the Moon Man*. The small still life paintings of flowers and plants of the moon are imaginary versions of plants and flowers that have drifted to earth. Subjects and themes may vary in painting, but it is really the beauty of painting itself that is of primary concern.

The recent paintings and drawings do sometimes project the idea of a sensation of turmoil, even of conflict perhaps. There is a reflection of an inner agony, not

alone, the agony of my own frustration and the environment of my existence, but there is an agony in my figures that is a common denominator for all living things.
I watch the mantis crush the cricket and the gangster annihilate another human being on the street. It seems like the same poetry of destruction and the same souls scream all through nature, from plants to kings. I am aware that the public asks for a clean painting of a clean H-bomb. Perhaps they want relief, which is fair.

Personally, I believe I have a strong shot of the chemical that makes hermits and monks, but I wish that I did not, for I am torn within by a tenderness and compassion for fellow man in general. The happiness of others is a great joy to me. Also, I suppose I do much internal writhing over the biological unity of all natural forms in their strange and frightening process of transition and transformation, together with the flying sparks that might be souls in the endless shifting of their position from one capsule to another, whether that capsule be a man or an ant […] every surface of nature is in transition and flight, from the microscopic to the cosmos in general, and I think it all must be bathed in the emotional sea within the artist.

The nearest 1 ever got to a group or movement was while you had your gallery. I could not evaluate myself well enough to determine whether I had a connection or not. […] I am sure that what I am doing now, to date, is a result of this very strong contact with surrealism. […] As for my own work, in the future I do not know if I could fit into any group or "ism" because of having worked alone for so long. […] The public feels they have been poked the wrong way for quite some time by the new paintings in spite of the fact [that] the paintings

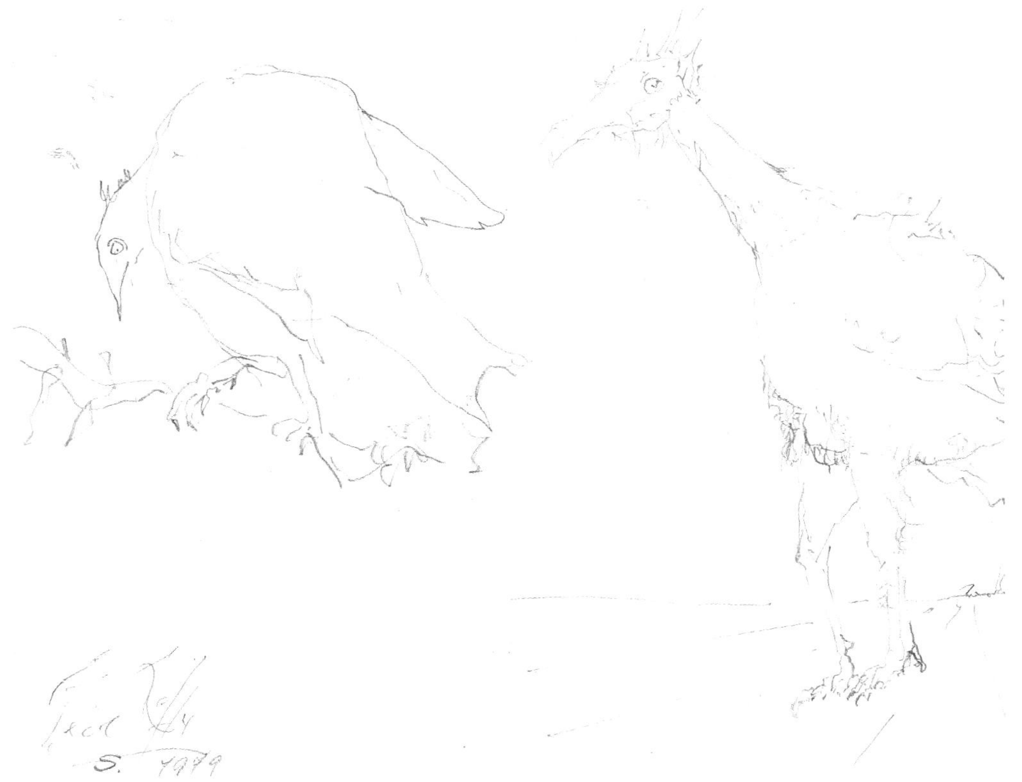

Leon Kelly, *No title (Birds)* [detail], pencil, signed and dated 1979, 28 × 231.5 cm, Plewig Collection

were not aimed at them. The present abstract school is a desire to rectify this disagreement to some extent, but nearly all the paintings need an LP record to go with them in the form of emotional analysis.

Influence of Indian Cultures

Pre-Incaic and pre-Columbian influence of the Andean area. Megalithic period, the fortress of Sacsayhuamán, Ollantaytambo, Cuzco. The walls of Cuzco and remains of architecture throughout the area. In 1947 I spent considerable time in the Brooklyn Museum, New York, in careful examination of the Peruvian textiles and fabrics preserved in the collection. I became influenced by the beauty and delicacy of the methods of fabrications and the poetry of the themes woven in the textiles. I felt the great purity of expression in these fragments of textiles. They seemed to retain a spiritual beauty of expression and a living quality that I had never before experienced in artifacts. This mystic realization became a point of departure for my work. Not only did I find the textiles and fabrics inspiring but also the mosaics of feathers incorporated in the varied forms of garments, pottery designs, and the goldwork of the Quimbaya. My paintings and drawings since 1947 have been based on the theme of the rituals of this ancient civilization in a purely imaginary and contemporary style. The imaginary figures used as subjects were the mystic priest, the prince, the virgin textile weavers of the religious cult, birds, and architecture. In contemplating the mystic quality of the pre-Columbian era I tried to bring into my work the absence of the element of time existing between that period and ours. I desired to give the personages used as subjects in the paintings and drawings a timeless quality, that the spirit embodied in the subjects was static and timeless. The mystic priest and others were not constructed in the conventional human form, but constructed in a way as though made of soft wax, plastic, and capable of fluid change and equilibrium. The head of the mystic priest seems to be wrapped in textiles, nerves, and wires of light. His head is sometimes enclosed in a trellis defining the symbol of his unique spiritual relation to society. He is impregnable in the trellis. The prince is usually standing and he is mainly preoccupied with birds of an imaginary character. He is often given the attitude of rigidity and he may hold a spear or staff. The external beauty of birds are of interest but he is mainly concerned with the spirit within the bird, which is a part of all living things, human, animal, and vegetation.

Both the prince and the priest are involved in the magic work of the weavers of textiles. I have used this theme many times in my drawings, which I have kept in an antique silver tone on very fine rag handmade paper, in order to convey the feeling of the precious quality corresponding with my thoughts of the ancient culture. In the latter part of 1951 I abandoned the association of thought with the ancient culture and have used themes dealing with actual living personalities and events, which has suffused an entirely new quality into my work. I believe that the poetic understanding of ancient people revealed through their artifacts has been of importance in a way that has given me an entirely new understanding of living people, events, and objects.

One of my motives for evolving hypothetical figures and objects was for technical reasons. I did not wish to become absorbed in the technical treatment of actual physical resemblances and the formalized methods of modeling form and textures together with the observation of surface details of infinite variety. My figures are not restricted to any given color or convention of form and therefore become solid, harmonious, and living in their own right. At present I do not forget their living counterpart.

Visits to western and southwestern United States between 1939 and 1949. Visits to the pueblos of New Mexico, San Ildefonso, Santa Domingo, Cochiti, and others throughout the area. Visits to the Laboratory of Anthropology at Santa Fe. Great admiration for the work of the Hopi potter Nampeyo, whose works are in the Museum of Santa Fe and the Laboratory of Anthropology. Visits to the Arapaho and Shoshone in the state of Wyoming. Examination of petroglyphs in Wyoming and New Mexico. I have lived for short periods of time on the Indian reservations. Study of the work of Indian cultures in the Trocadero and Louvre in Paris, the Metropolitan Museum, Brooklyn Museum, American Museum of Natural History, and Heye Foundation in New York. Alaskan Indians and Eskimos, Montclair Museum, Montclair, New Jersey, University of Pennsylvania Museum, Philadelphia.

During the years 1941–1945 I was associated with the Julien Levy Gallery in New York City. I had four one-man shows of paintings and drawings at the gallery. My work was represented in an exhibition of the group of painters represented by the Julien Levy Gallery. Ernst, Tanguy, Delvaux, Magritte, Chirico, Matta, Berman, Tanning, Cornell, Dali, Tchelitchew, Duchamp, Campigli. Several of these painters I had known years before in Europe. During this period of association with the gallery my work took on some of the influences of the other painters, which

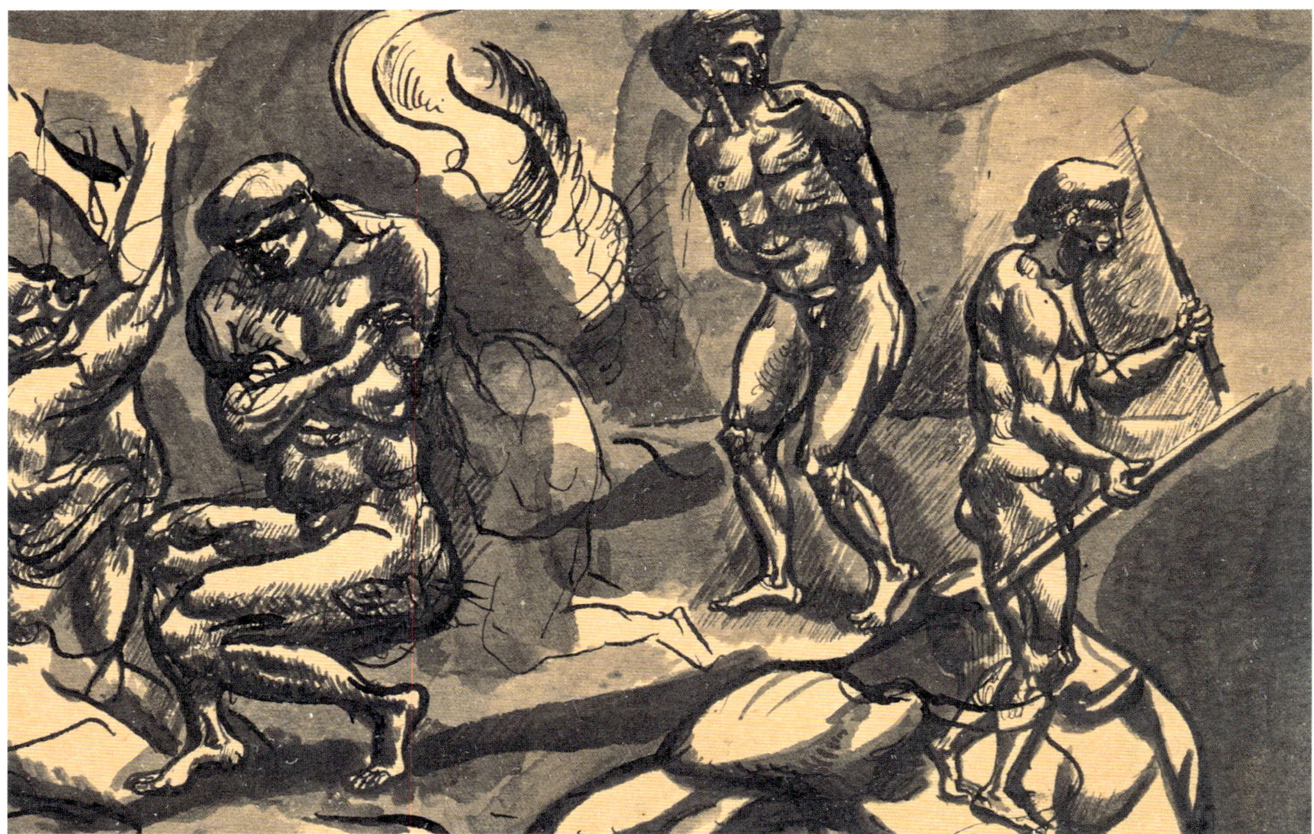

Leon Kelly, *Untitled* (Detail)
Ink, 13 × 17 cm

I suppose is unavoidable to some extent. It is no doubt due to these exhibitions that my work has been grouped with surrealism. I believe now that my work has either become disassociated with surrealism or gone a step further. I think that I have been able to realize to some extent the description of an inner living quality that is the counter-balance of objects and people. The word spiritual is not fitting since it might tend to convey an idea of religion connected with the objects in my painting. I am not interested in projecting any kind of religious thought.

In 1947, after spending much time in contact with the textiles of pre-Columbian Peru, I found in them what seemed to me to be a unique quality similar to the quality of a living thing, aside from the conventional subject matter depicted. The color relations, light, geometry, and beauty of craft seemed to me to have captured something entirely beyond the description of the pictorial scene. That evasive sensation of life was evident to me in the form of power which seemed unrelated to any time. Since then I have been desirous of instilling this feeling in my own work. It is a mysterious quality and it must have been behind the hands of Titian while he painted the *Man with a Glove*. It is from this period that I believe my work departed from the category of surrealism. It is not a prac-tice to resort to the past for inspiration. I feel that all that is contained in past work is about me in a living form, objects, vegetation, and people. Chronological difference does not seem to be of great importance. In 1949 I had the opportunity of examining many drawings on pottery by Nampeyo. Here it appeared to me that this unusual quality of reality or life itself seemed to be contained in them. In my own work I desire to remain within the confines of my own contemporary scheme and to evolve the pictorial imagery close to my own existence. I want the elements in my work to be presented with that positive quality of architecture and that the geometry of the canvas be severely connected with the subject. Perhaps this is the result of long admiration for the Italian school of painting and architecture. Also I think it is because I wish to give this evidently nebulous thought a very positive form and realism. I do not want to lose sight of the living quality that is beneath the maze of complex patterns in our existence. We feel that someone is knocking at a door beyond our sensitivity. We strain for the message. Or perhaps an invisible sacred bird is perched on our shoulder. It is the unknown and unseen things perhaps that desire to evolve into a painted reality. I am beginning to feel this very much about objects in general. It is a force perhaps strictly related to the objects and beyond the realm of optical vision. The force identical to each thing, aside from the superficial or relegated purpose of the object or animal.

There is a still life by Zurbaran in St. Louis of which I have a photograph. Beyond the beauty of painted surfaces, apart from the kind of fruit, which is well depicted, there is a power that has been extremely well realized in this painting. It is as though a strange combination of figures has been struck, giving the same sensation that is felt in the presence of a living thing. There is a small portrait in the National Gallery in Washington, DC, that affects me in the very same way. And it is this feeling that has so impressed me in the ancient Peruvian textiles. I have never actually touched one of the textiles, but I feel that it could be like the sensation of touching a person. It is much of the beauty of these textiles that I have desired to bring into my own work.

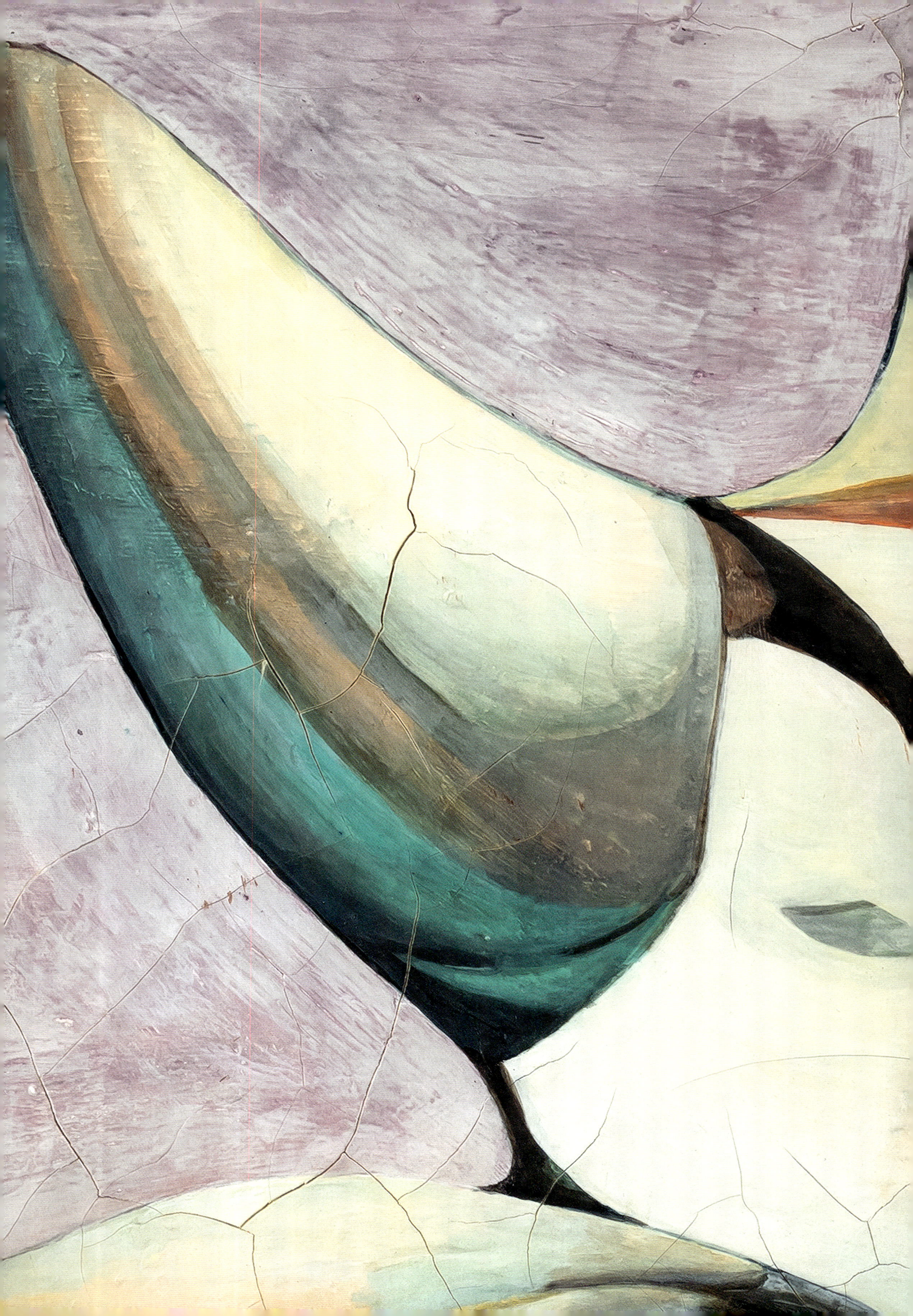

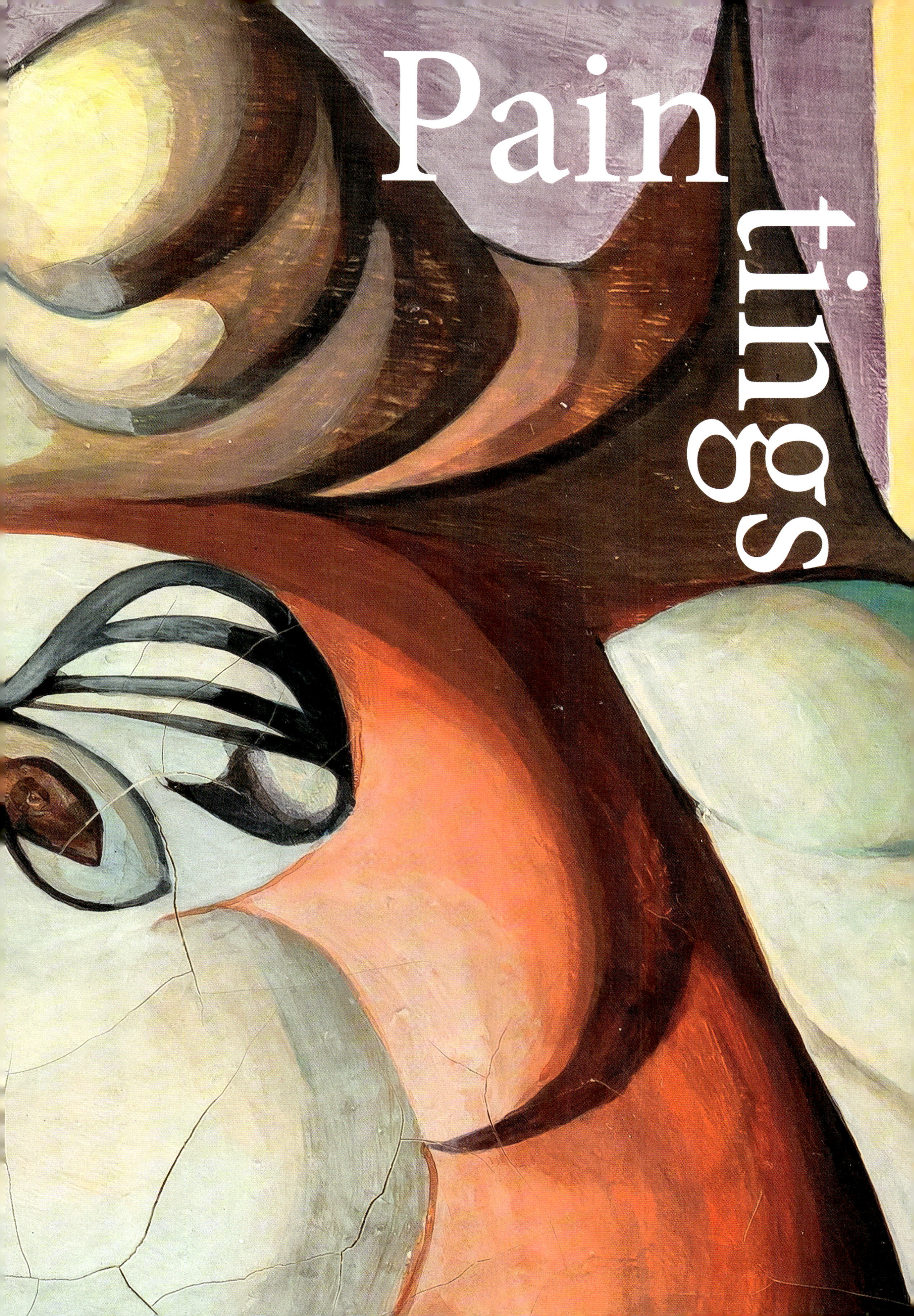

Pain tings

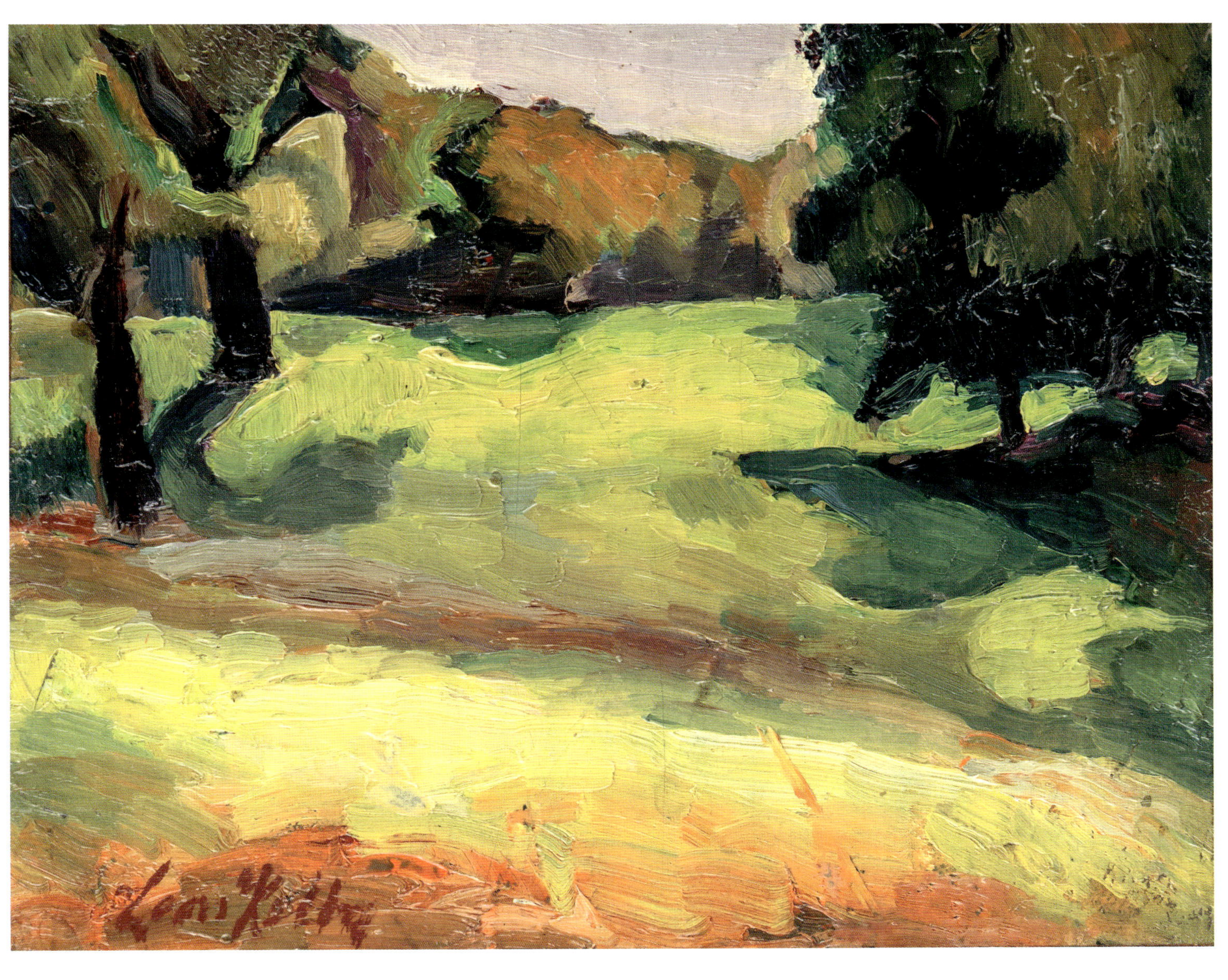

1
Landscape, 1920
Oil on cardboard, 20.5 × 25.5 cm

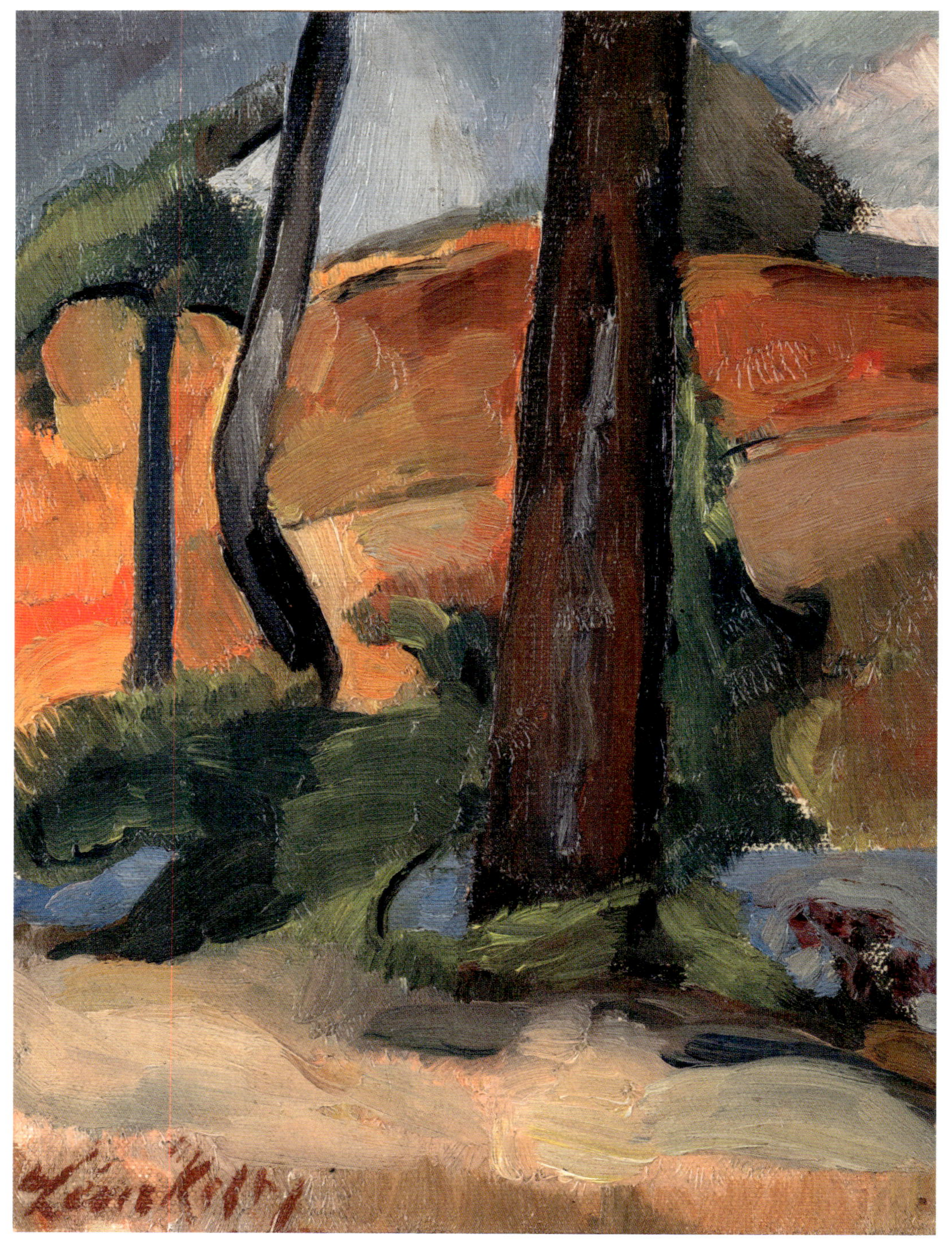

2
Trees Landscape, 1921
Oil on canvas, 25 × 19 cm

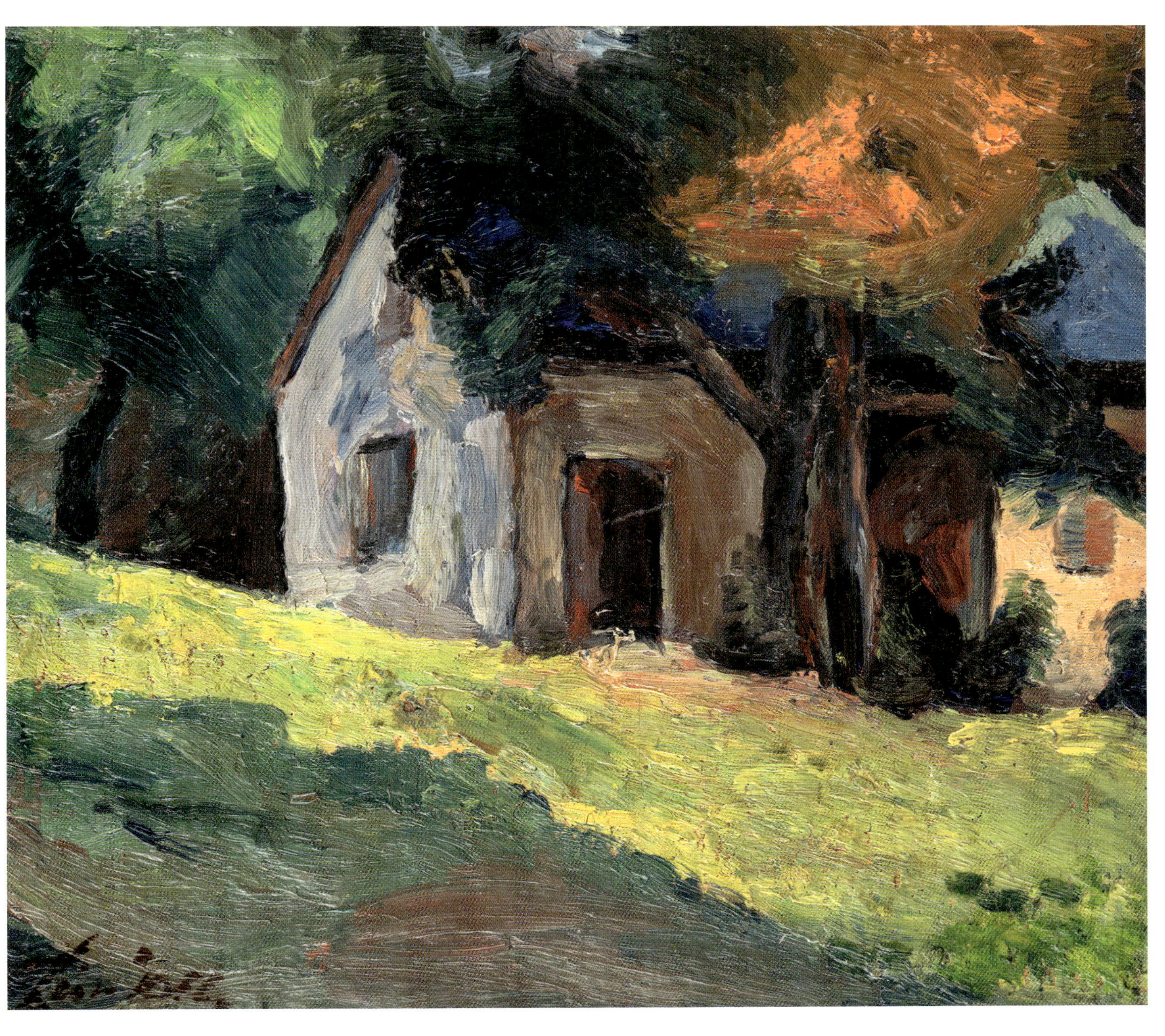

3
Landscape and Barn, 1922
Oil on cardboard, 23 × 26.5 cm

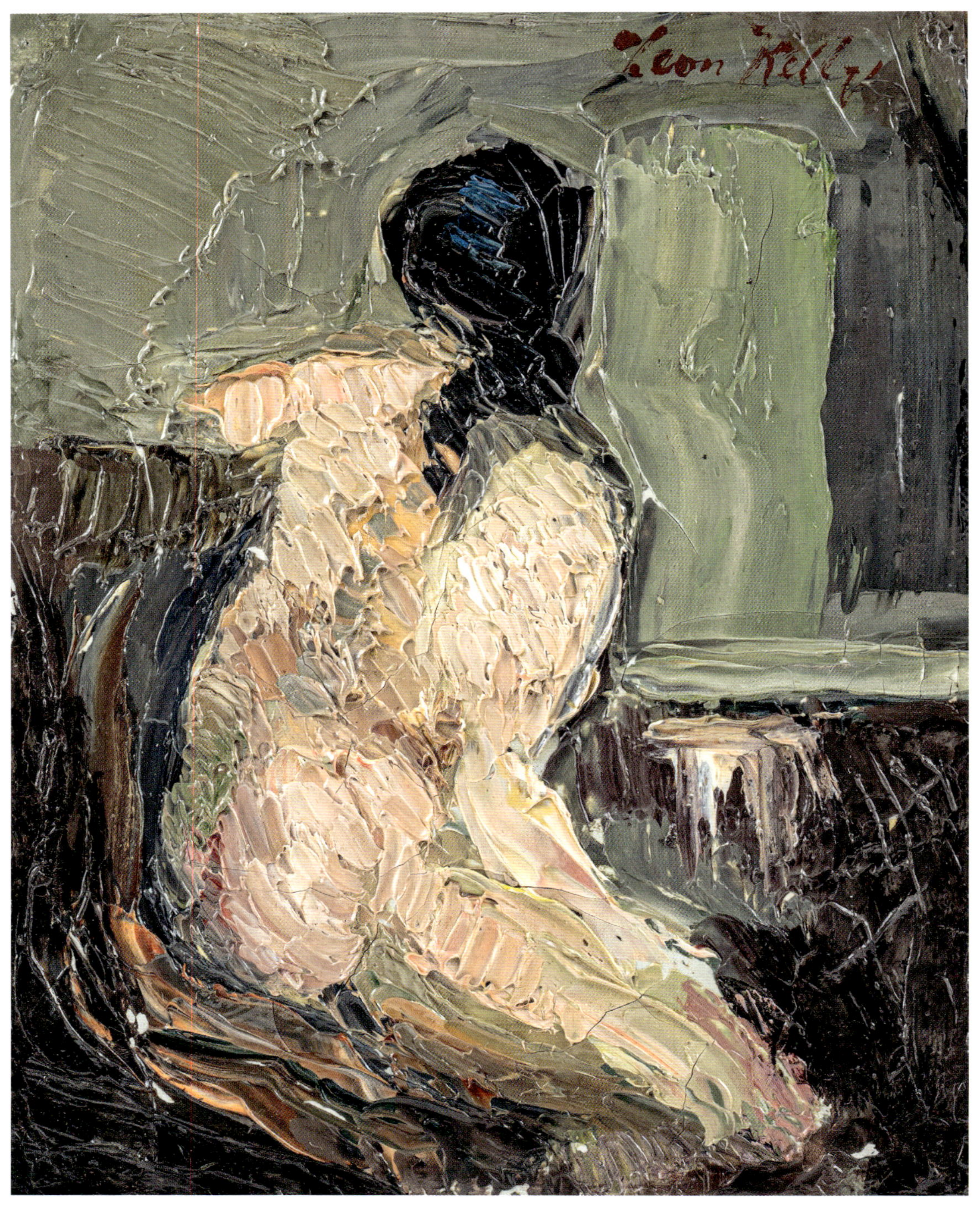

4
Seated Nude, 1923
Oil on canvas on cardboard, 21.5 × 18.5 cm

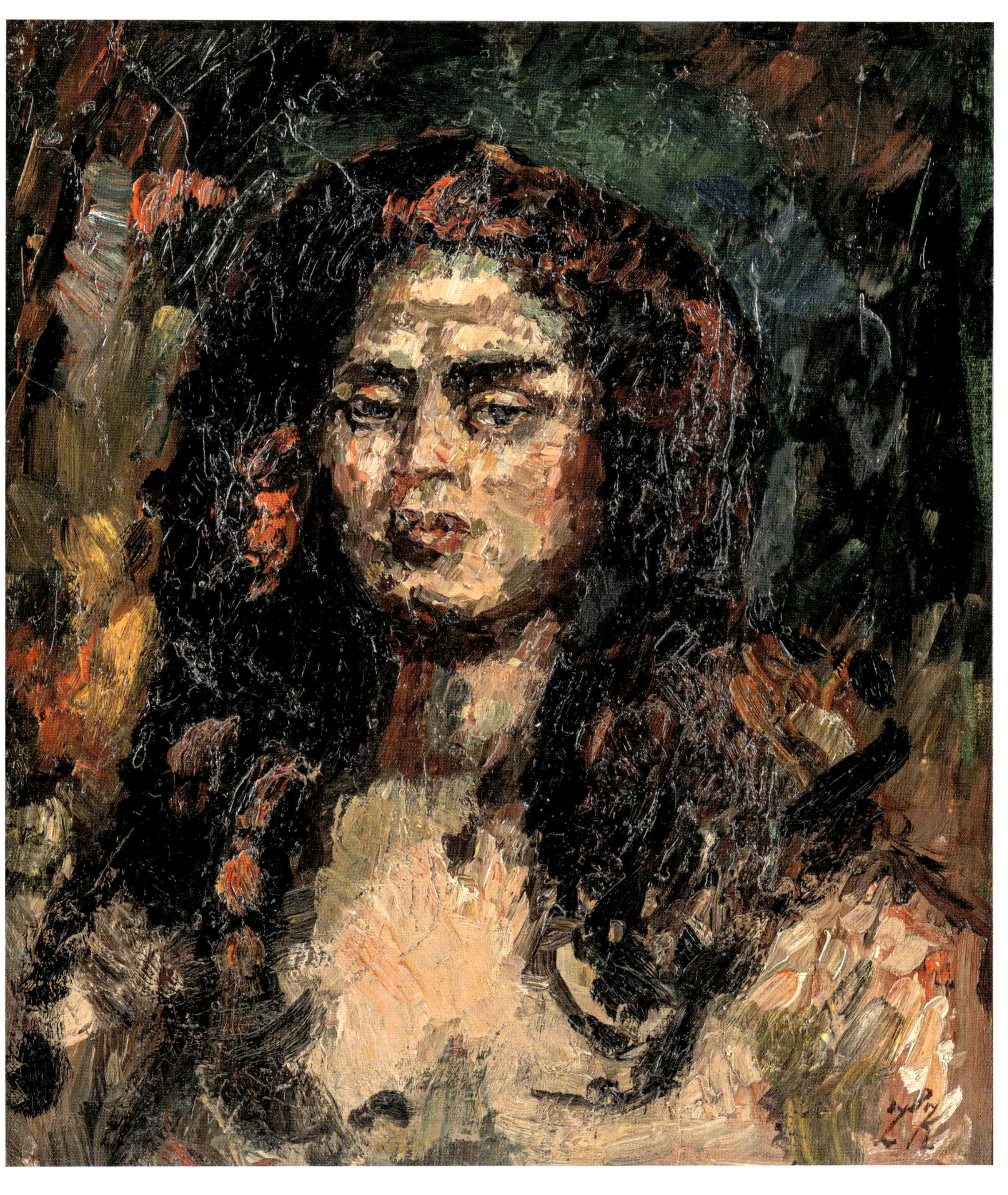

5
Head of a Young Girl, 1924
Oil on canvas on board, 46 × 37.5 cm

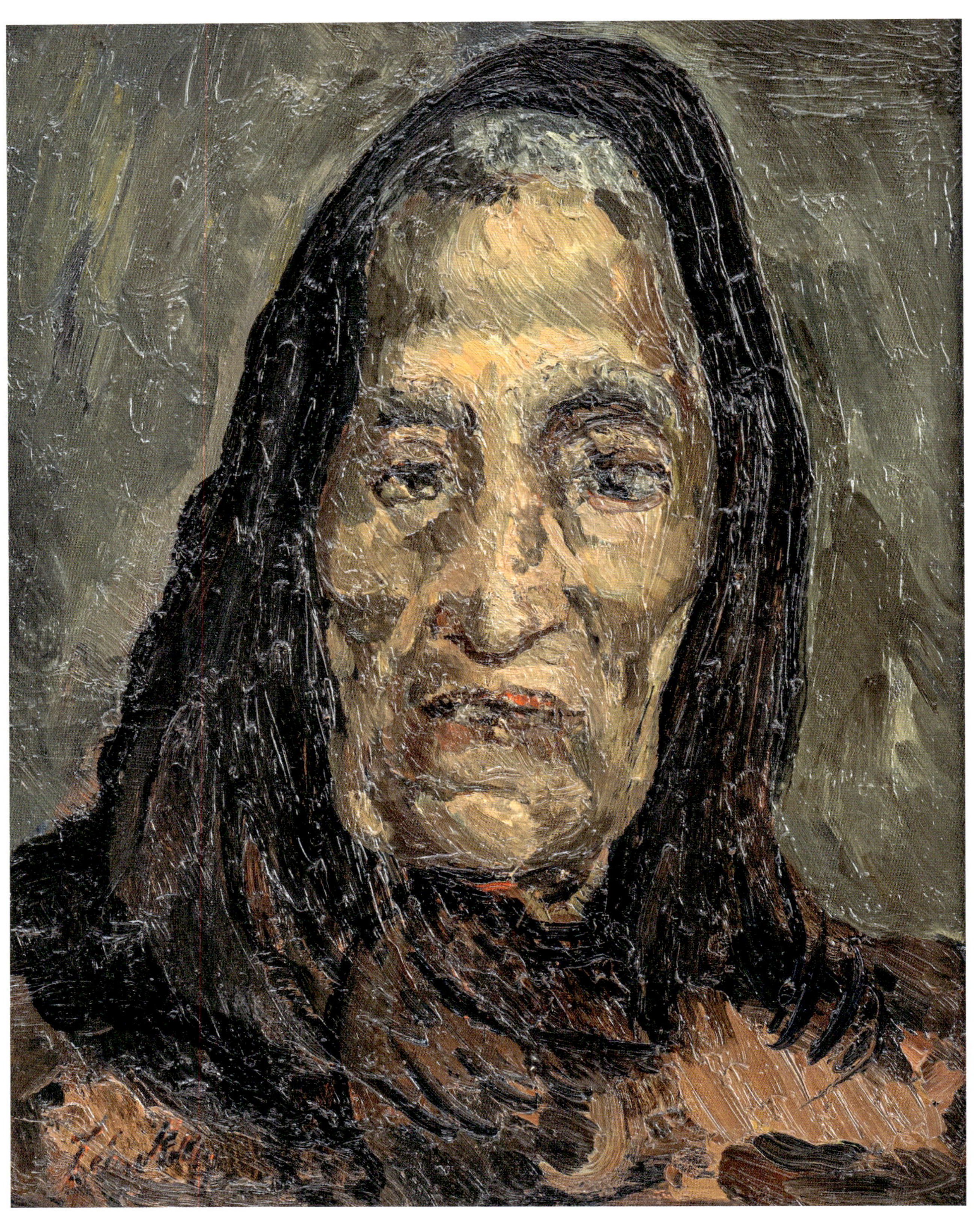

6
Old Italian Woman, 1924
Oil on board, 41 × 33 cm

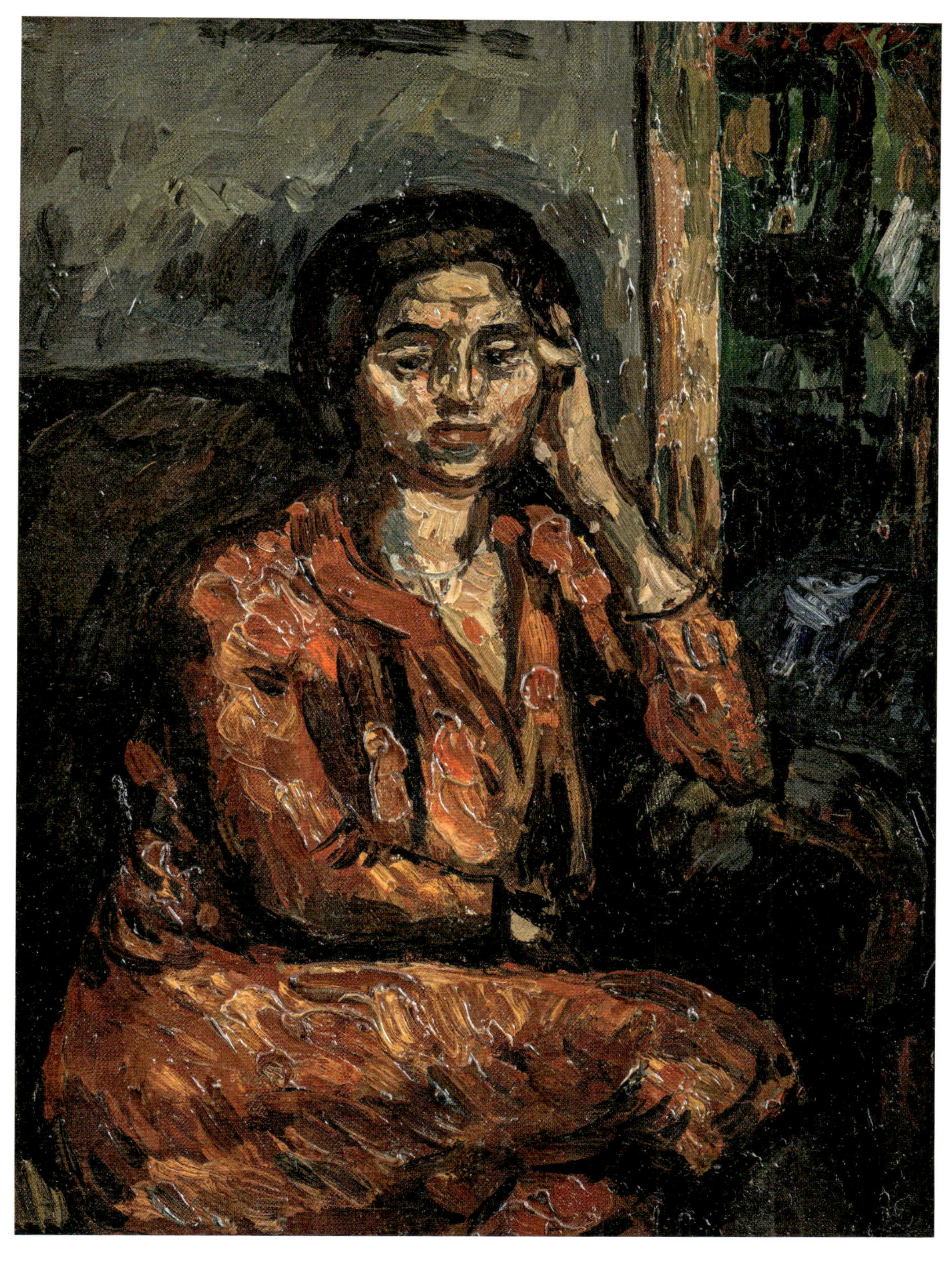

7
Portrait, 1925
Oil on cardboard, 30 × 21.5 cm

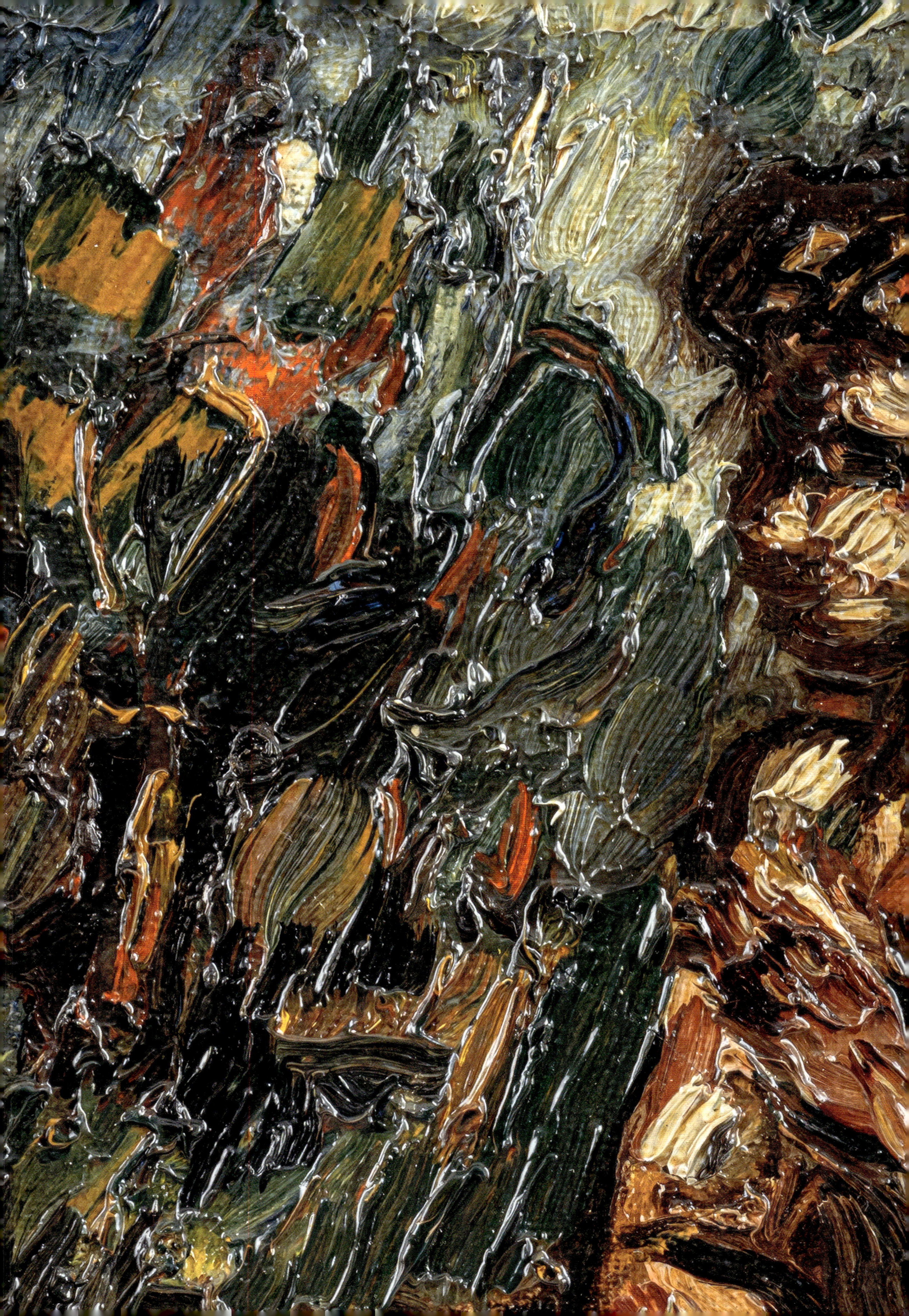

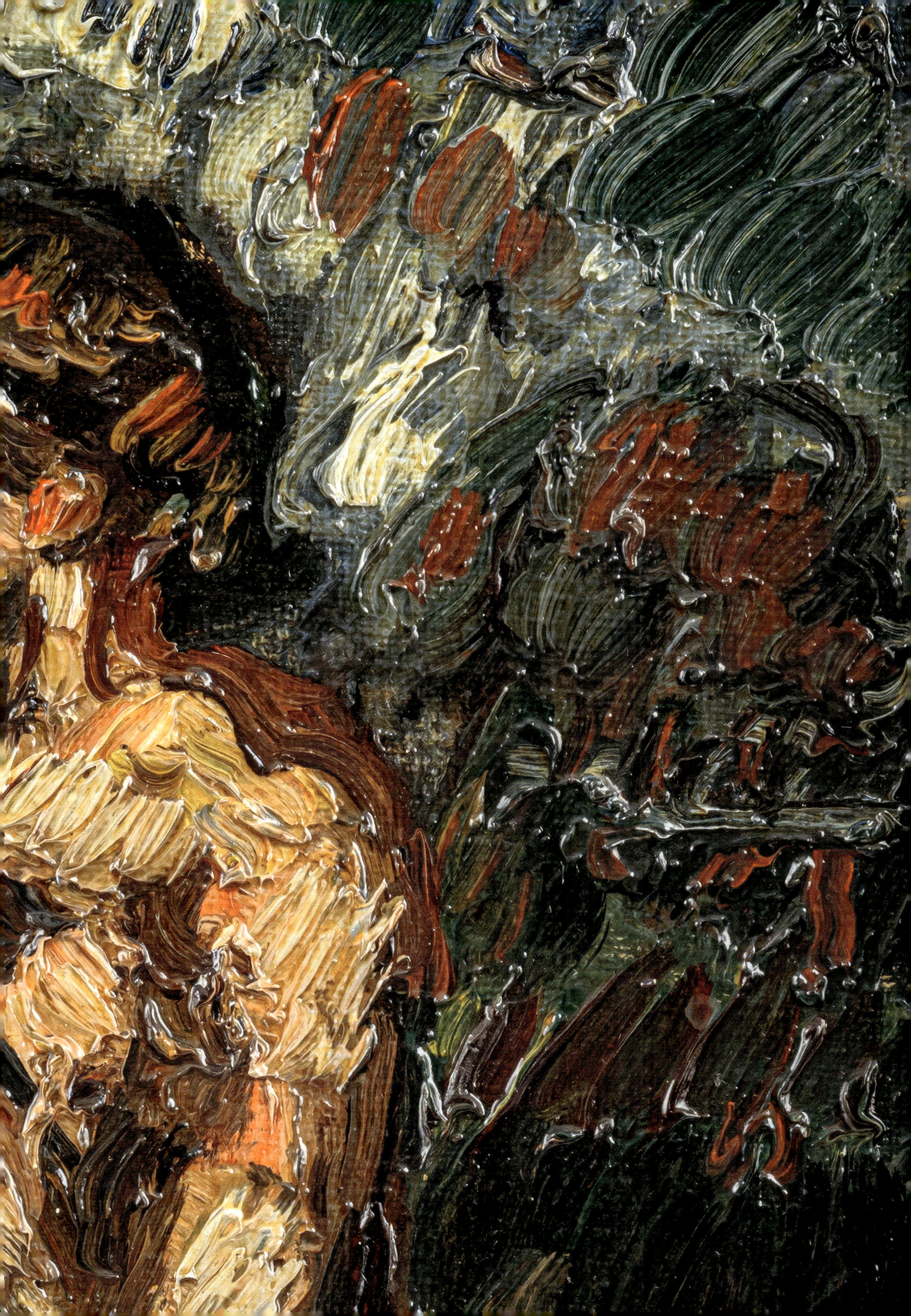

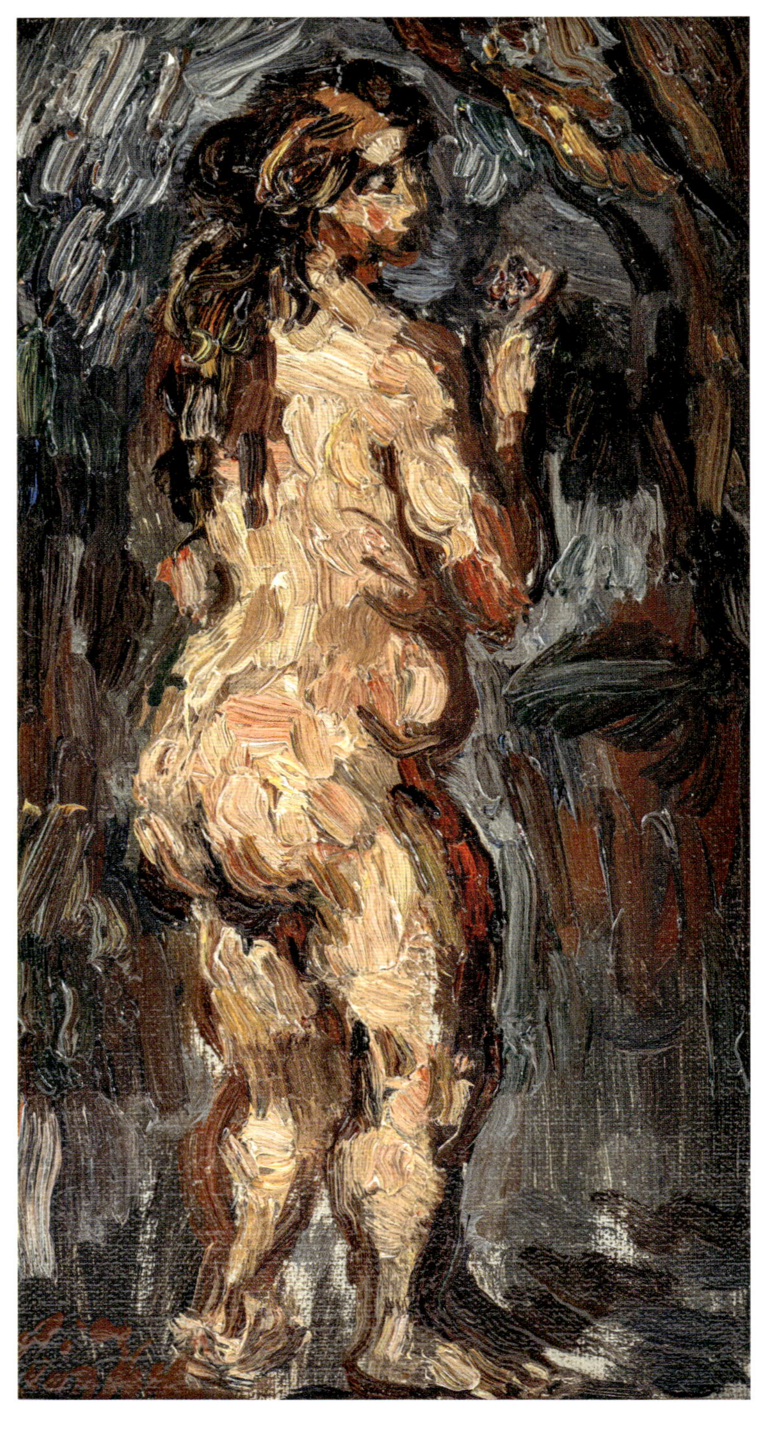

8
Landscape with Standing Nude
Oil on cardboard, 23 × 12 cm

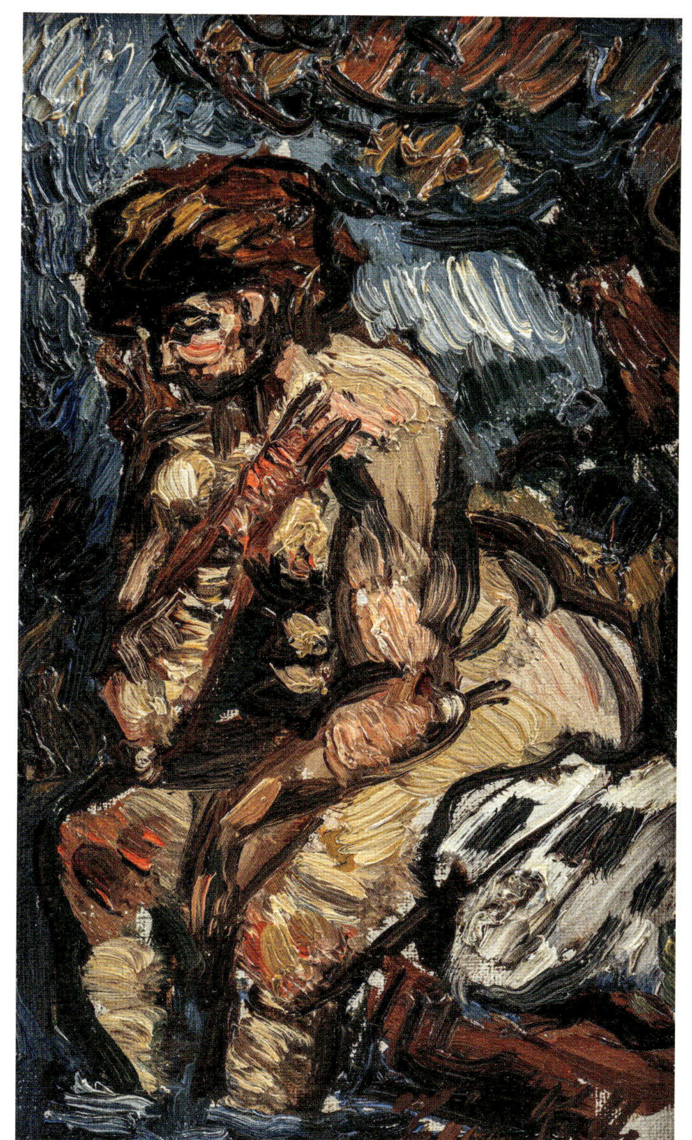

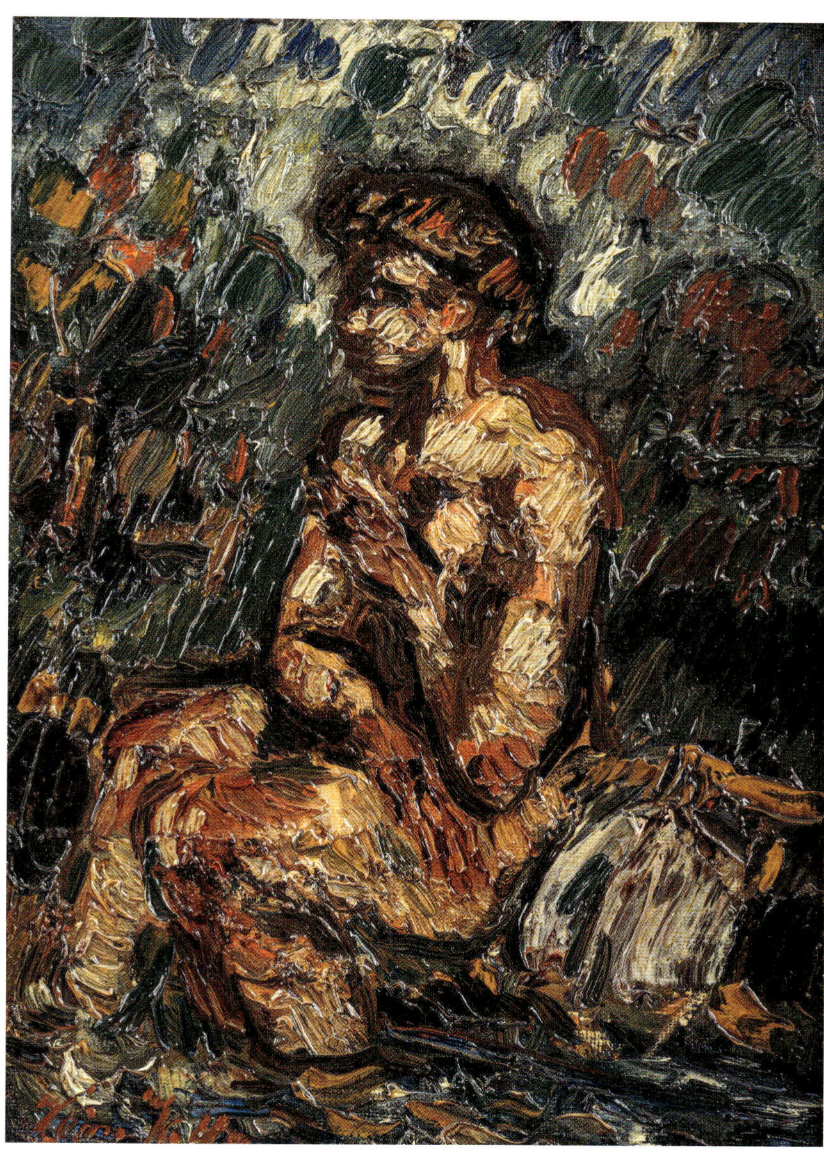

9
Landscape with Seated Bather
Oil on board, 22 × 12 cm

10
Bather, 1925
Oil on canvas on cardboard, 33 × 24 cm

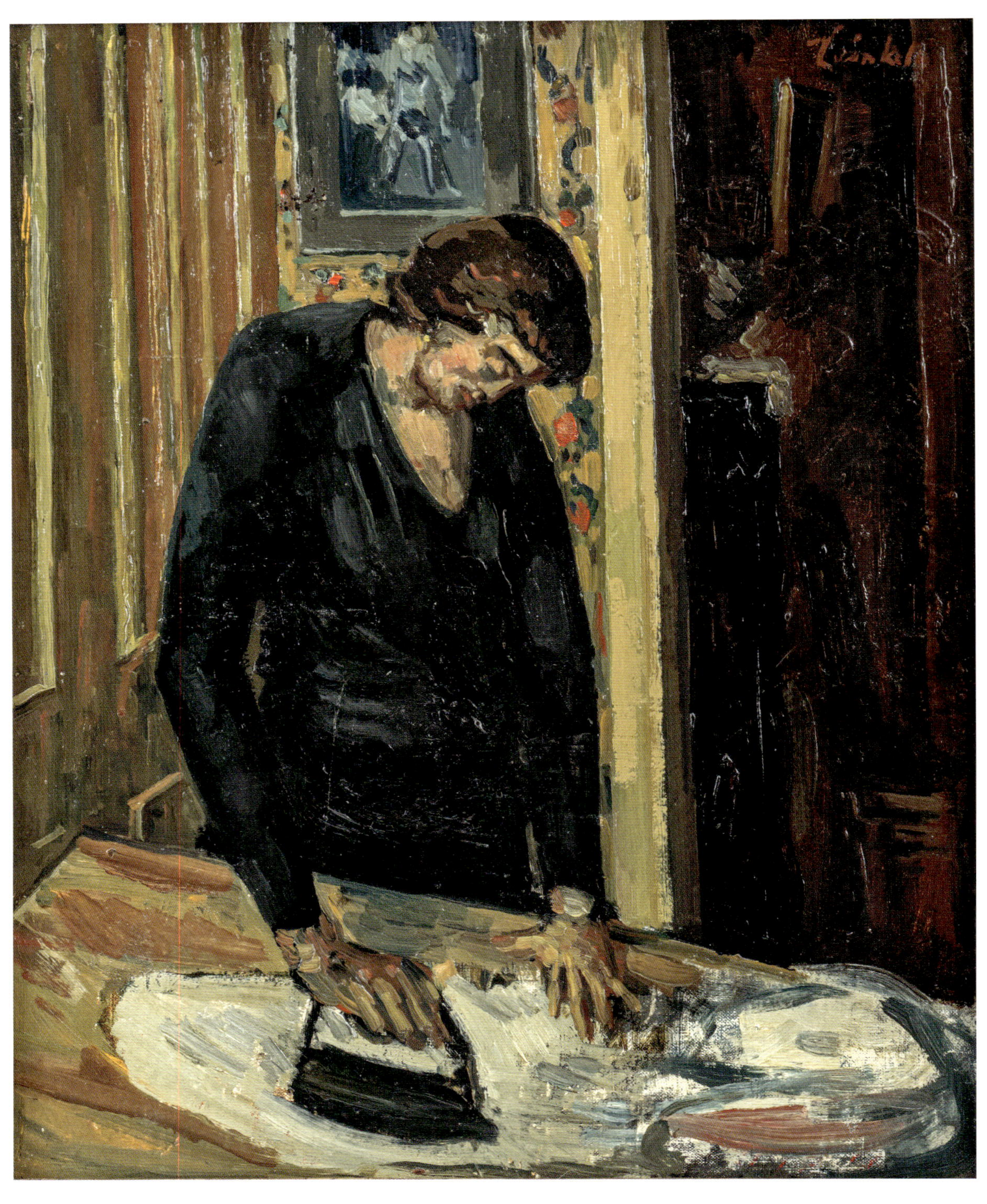

11
Woman Ironing, 1925
Oil on canvas on cardboard, 46.5 × 38 cm

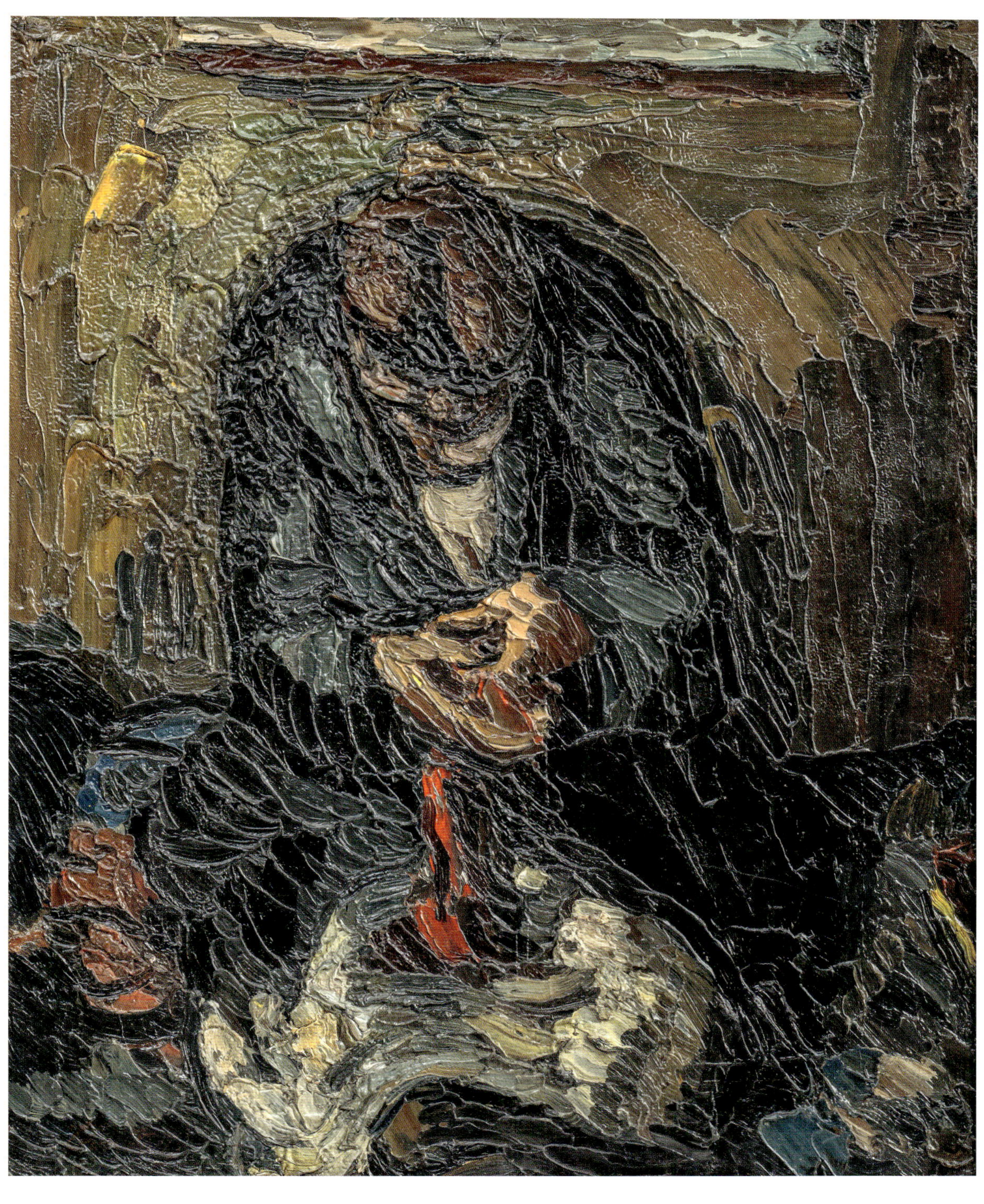

12
Henriette / The Seamstress, 192(?)
Oil on canvas on cardboa-d, 48 × 38 cm

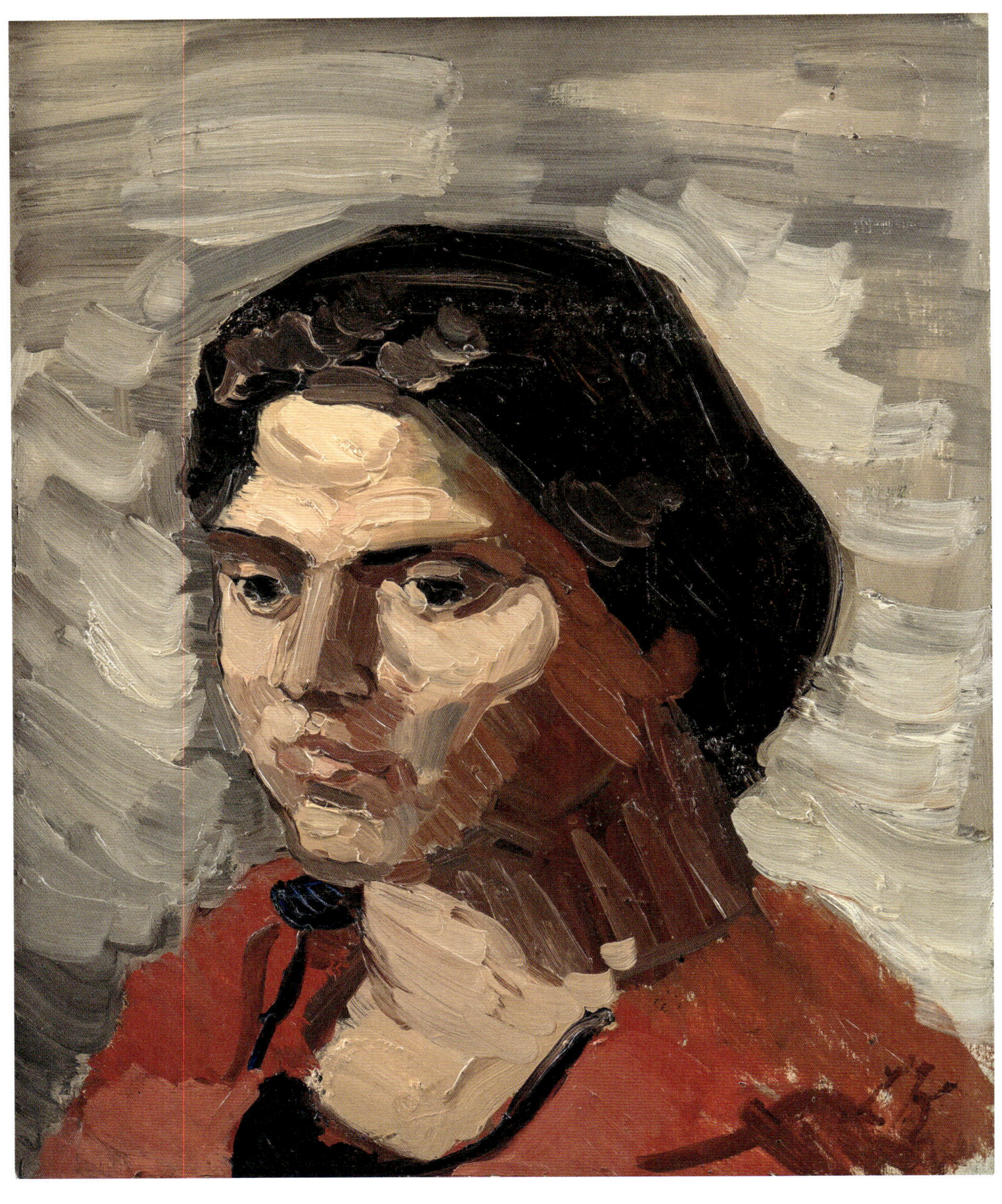

13
Head of a Young Girl / Henriette, 1926
Oil on board, 45.5 × 38 cm

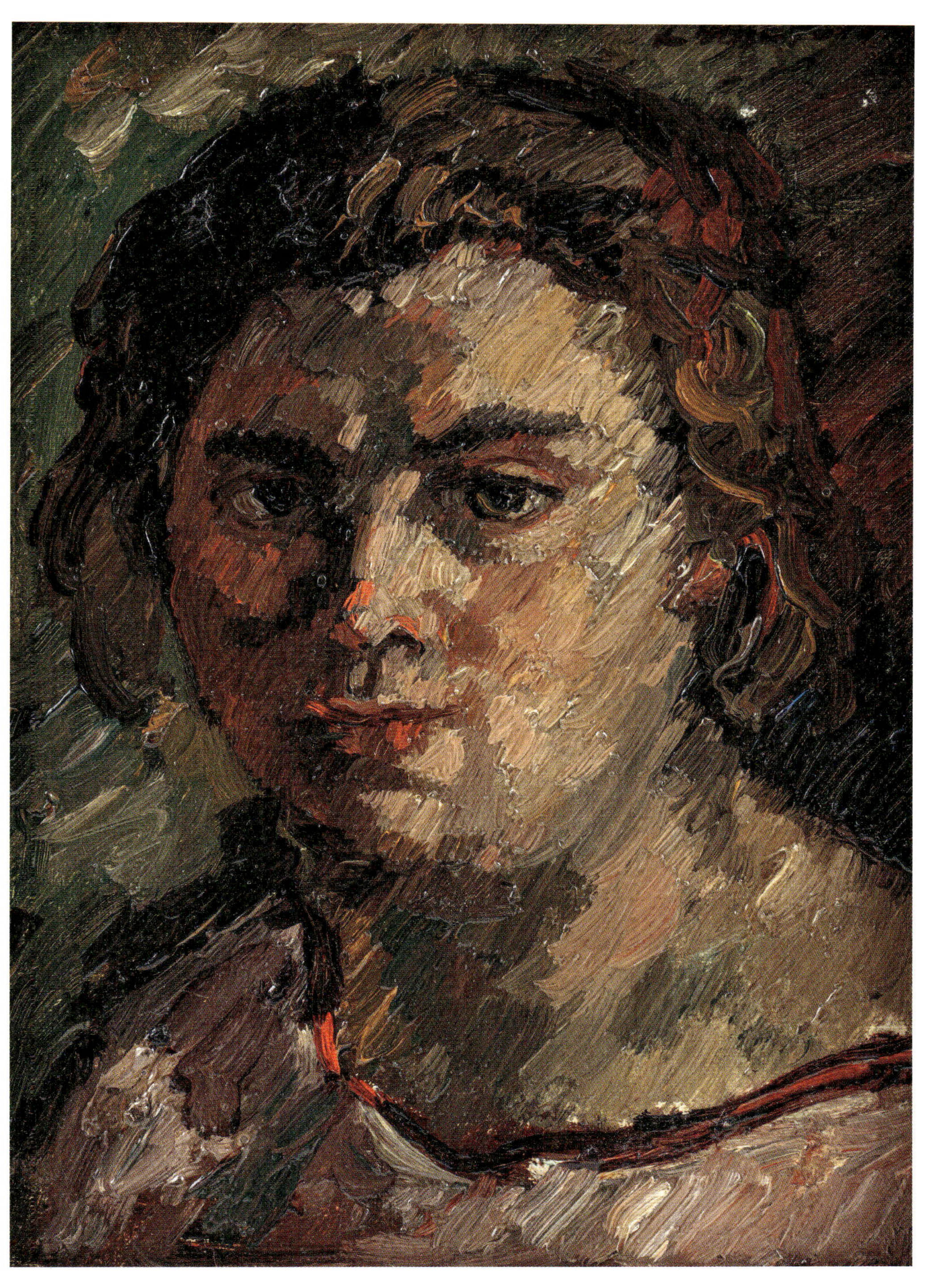

14
Head Henriette, 1927
Oil on cardboard, 21 × 15 cm

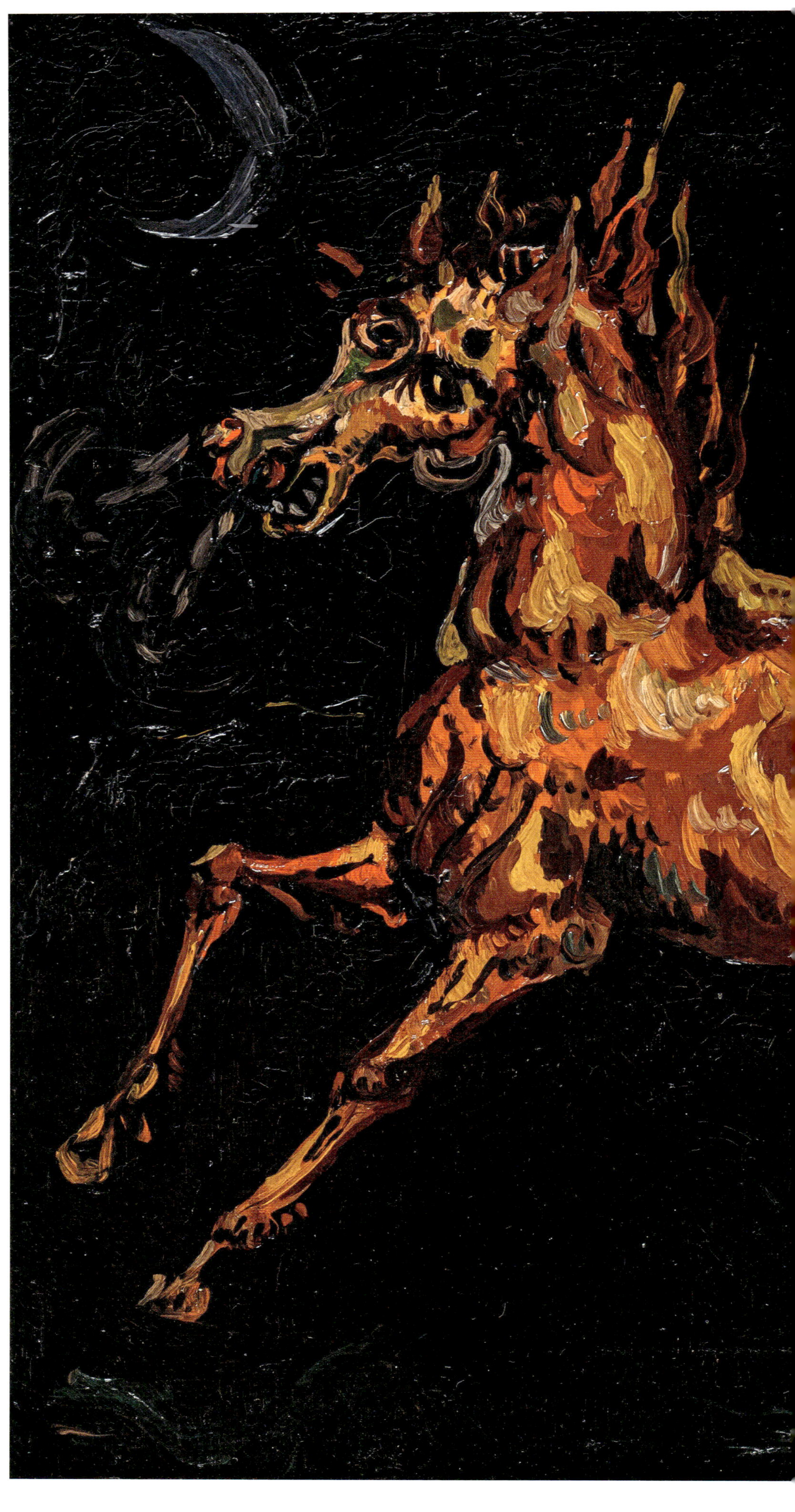

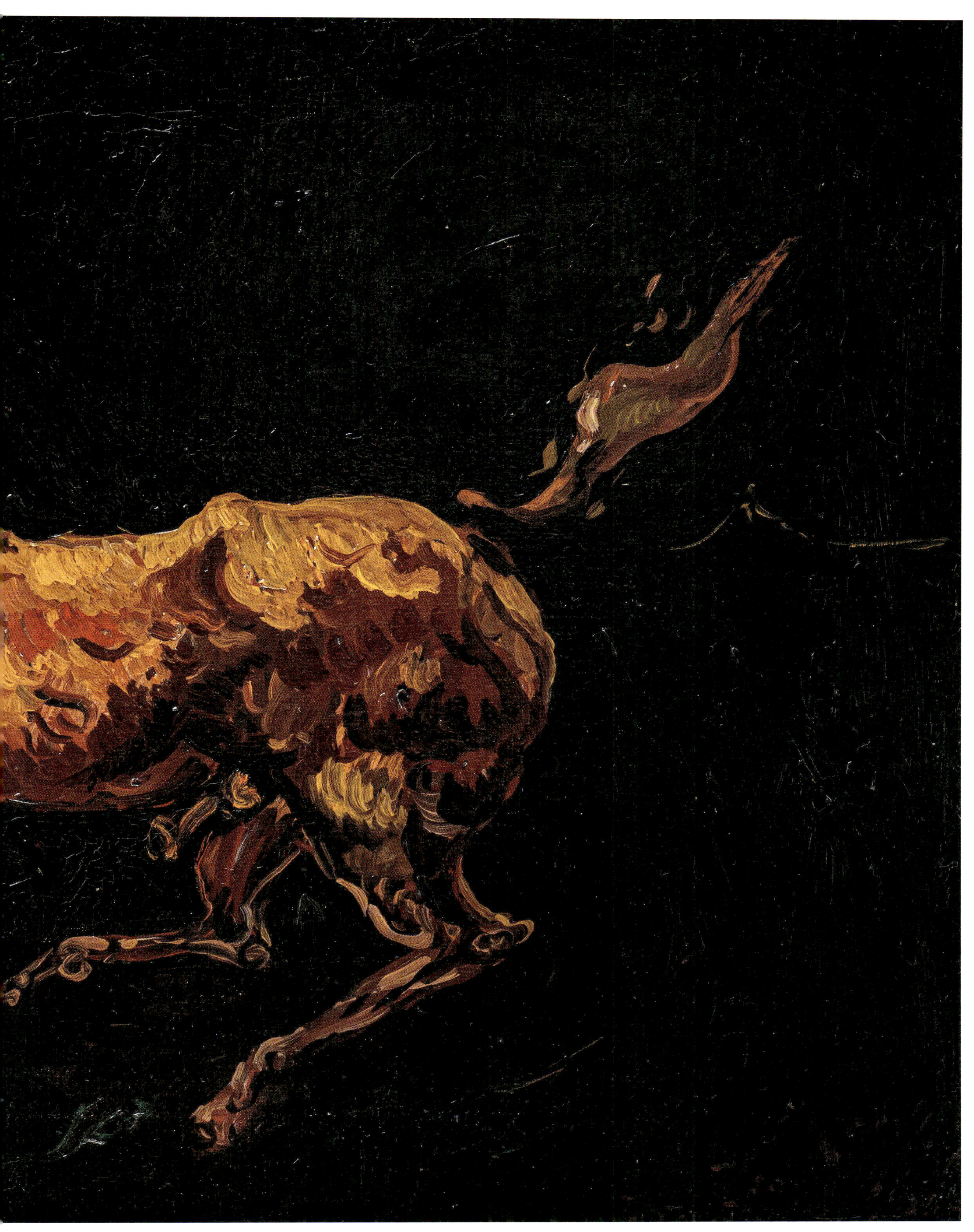

15
Untitled (Horse), 1940
Oil on canvas, 38 × 50.5 cm

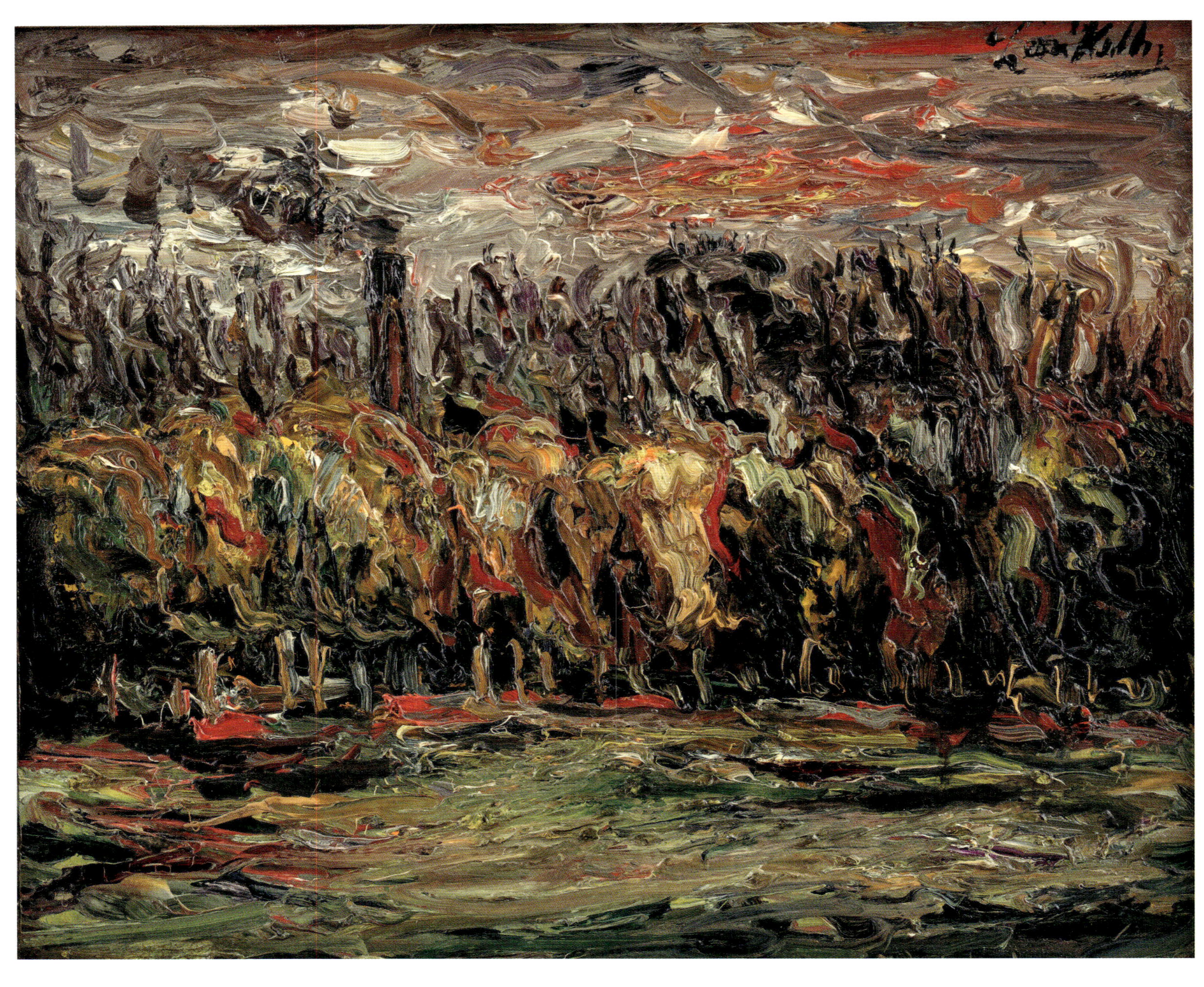

16
Autumn Landscape, 1926
Oil on board, 38 × 45.5 cm

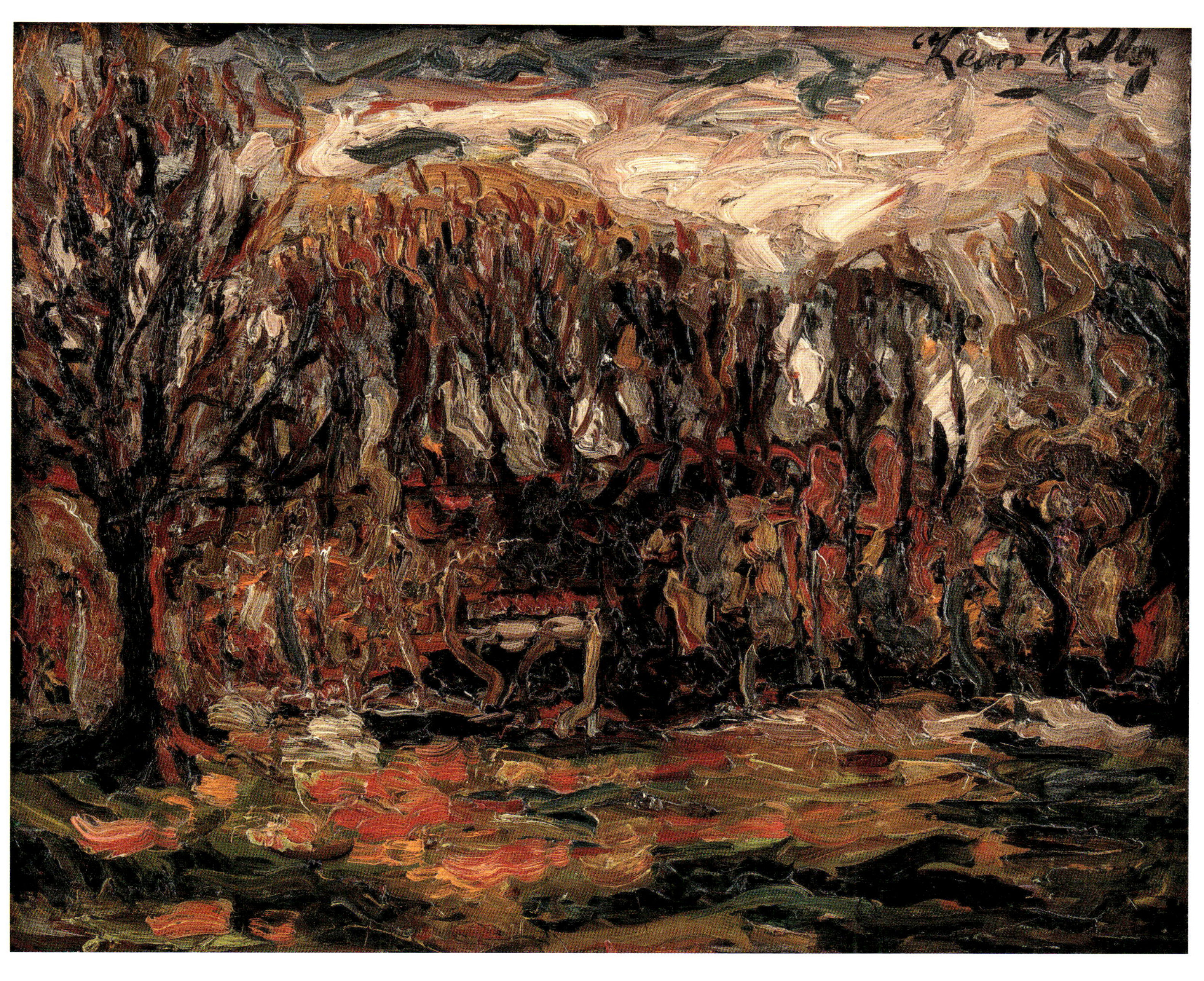

17
Autumn Landscape near Paris, 1926
Oil on board, 38 × 45.5 cm

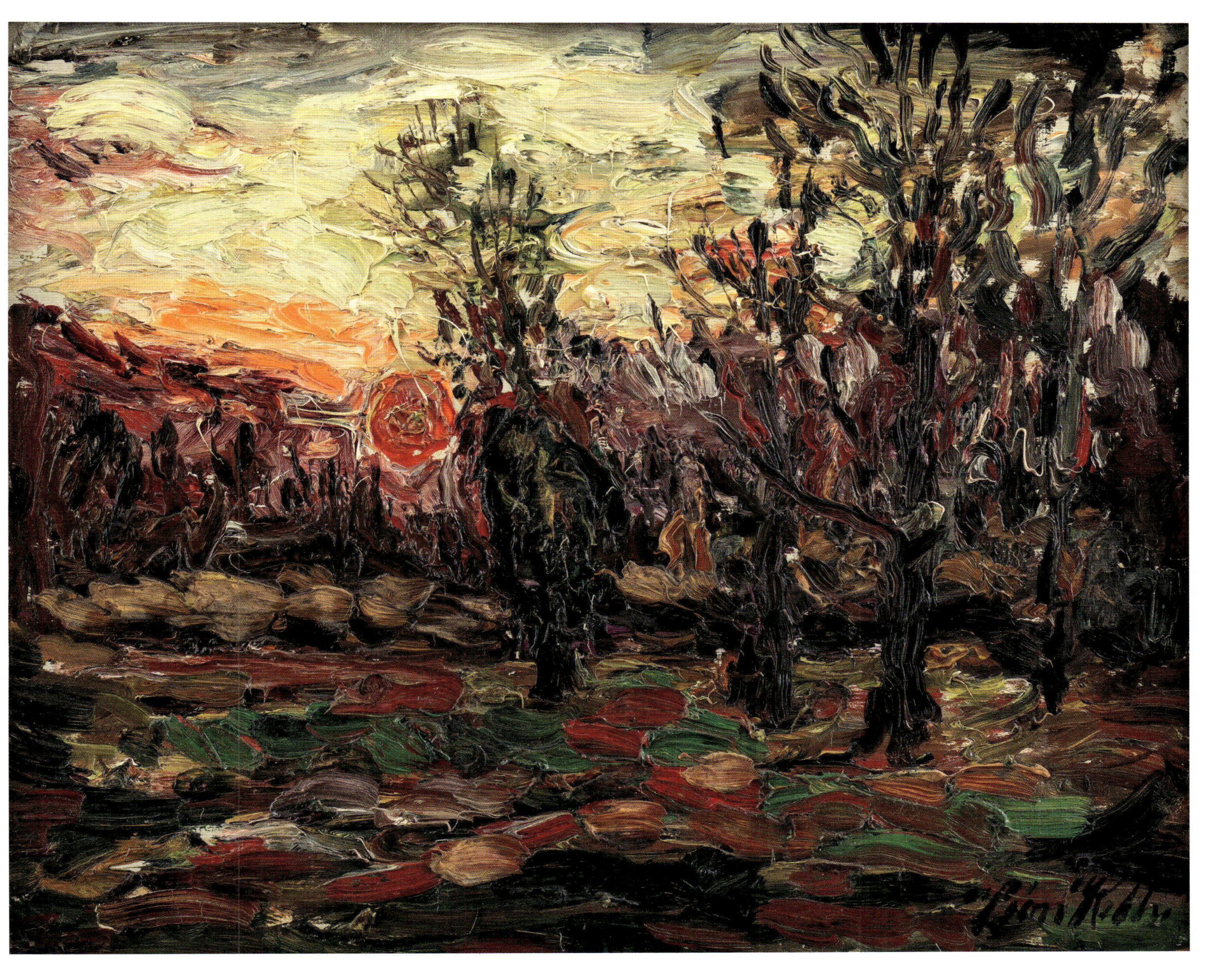

18
Landscape with Sunset, 1926
Oil on board, 38 × 45.5 cm

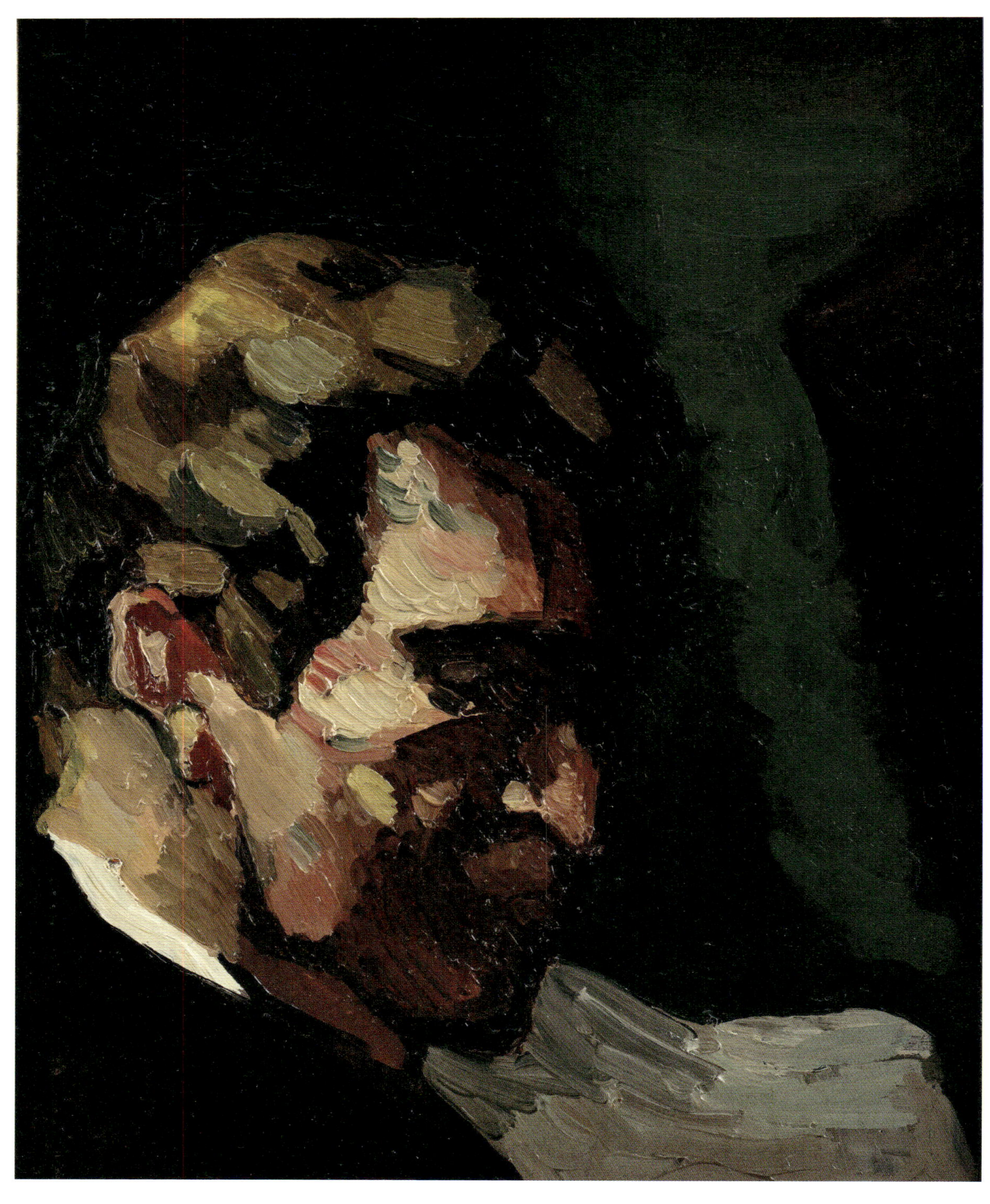

19
Portrait of Matthew Sharpe, 1927
Oil on board, 40 × 32 cm

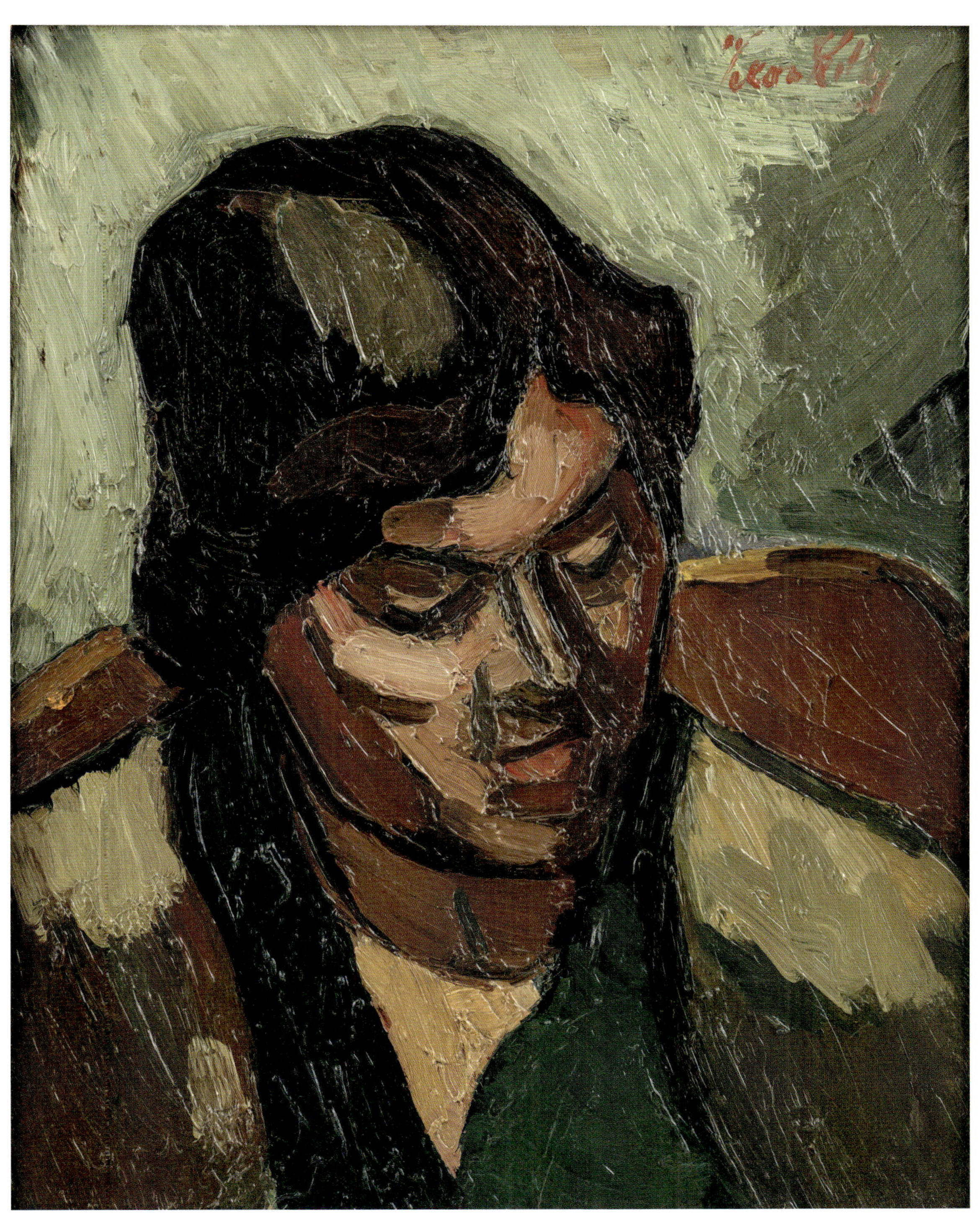

20
Portrait of Henriette with a Green Scarf, 1928
Oil on board, 40.5 × 33 cm

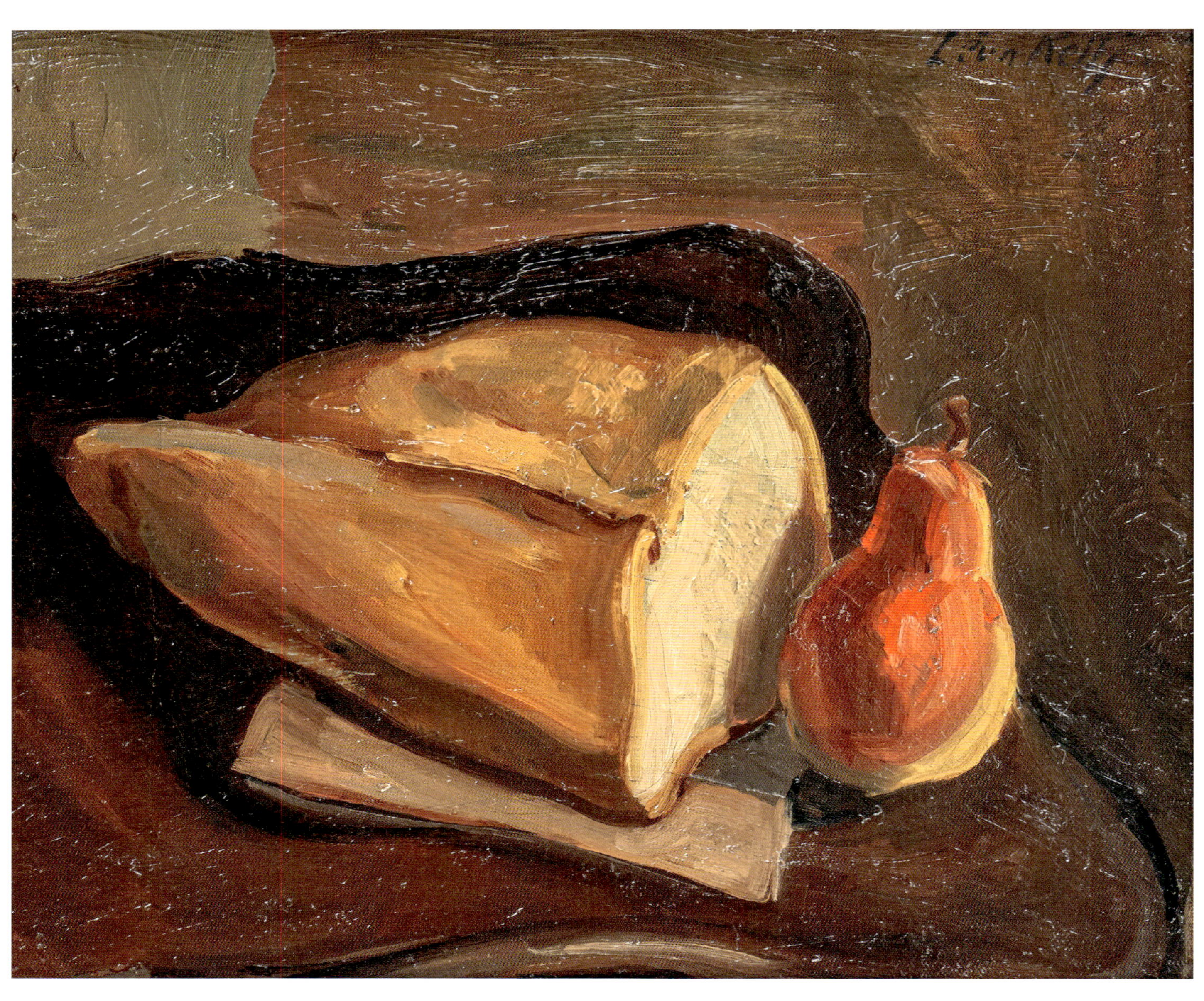

21
Bread and a Pear, 1930
Oil on canvas, 26 × 31 cm

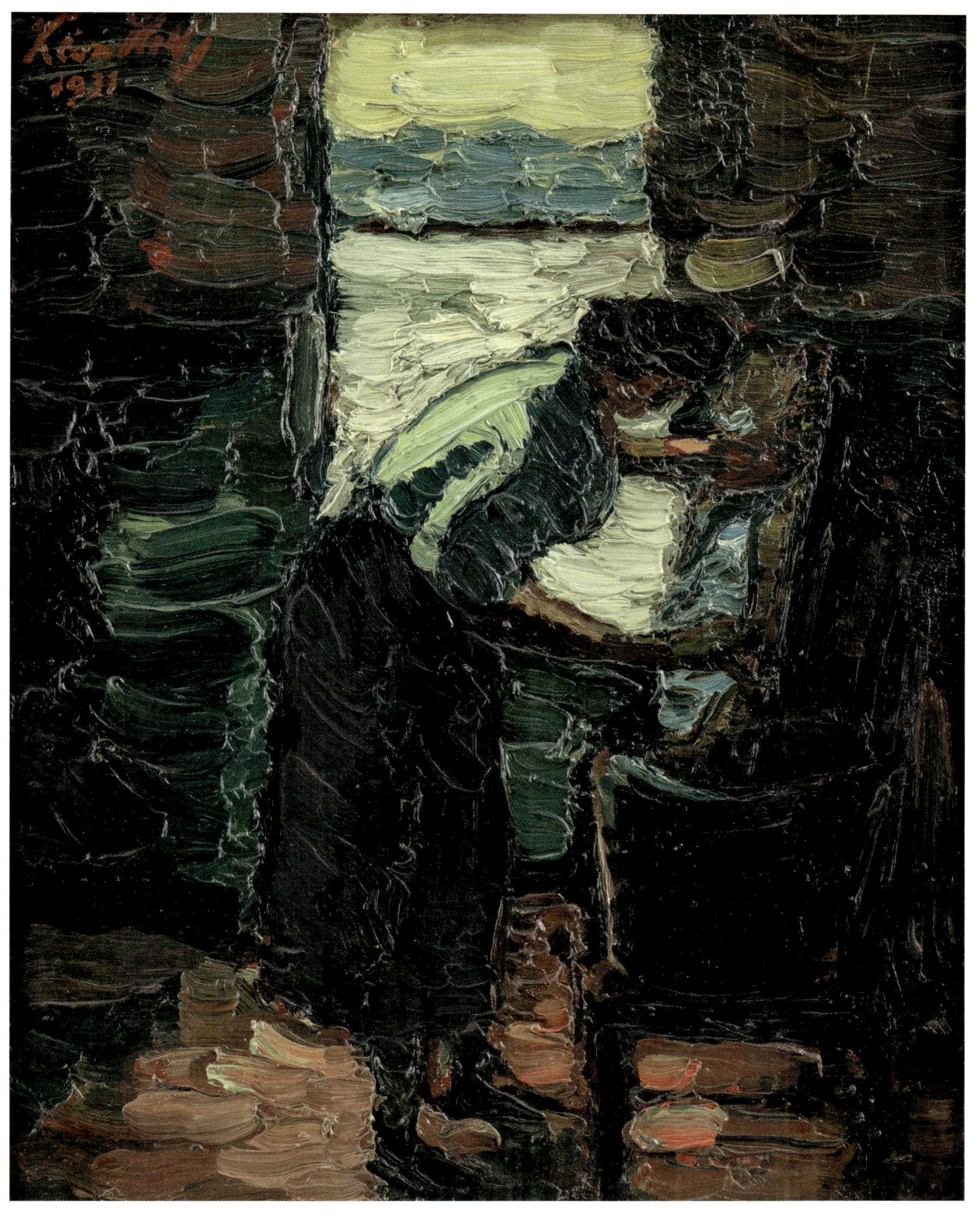

22
The Laundress, 1931
Oil on board, 43 × 34 cm (compare no. 98, p. 165)

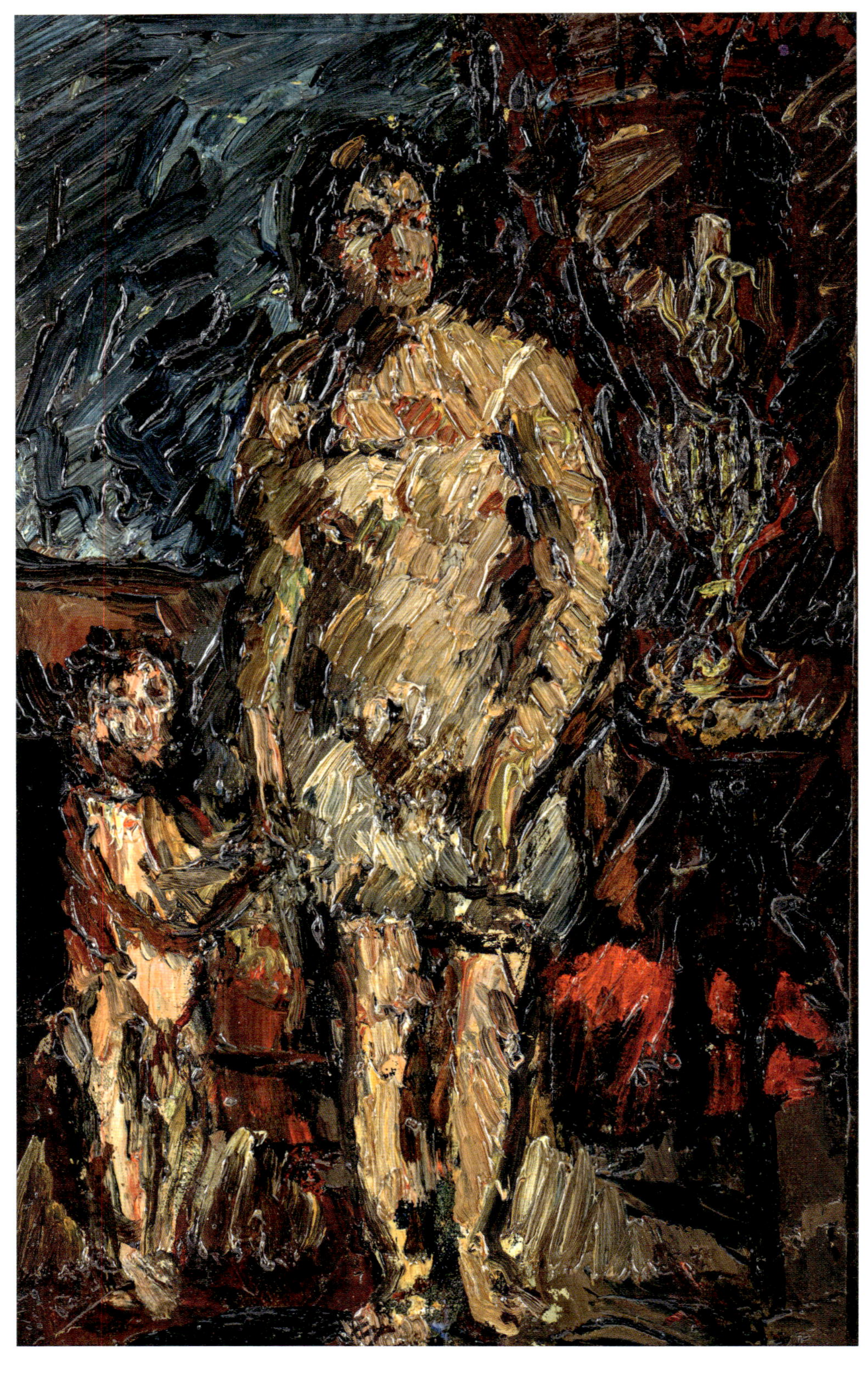

23
Woman Leading a Child, 1926
Oil on cardboard, 42 × 27.5 cm

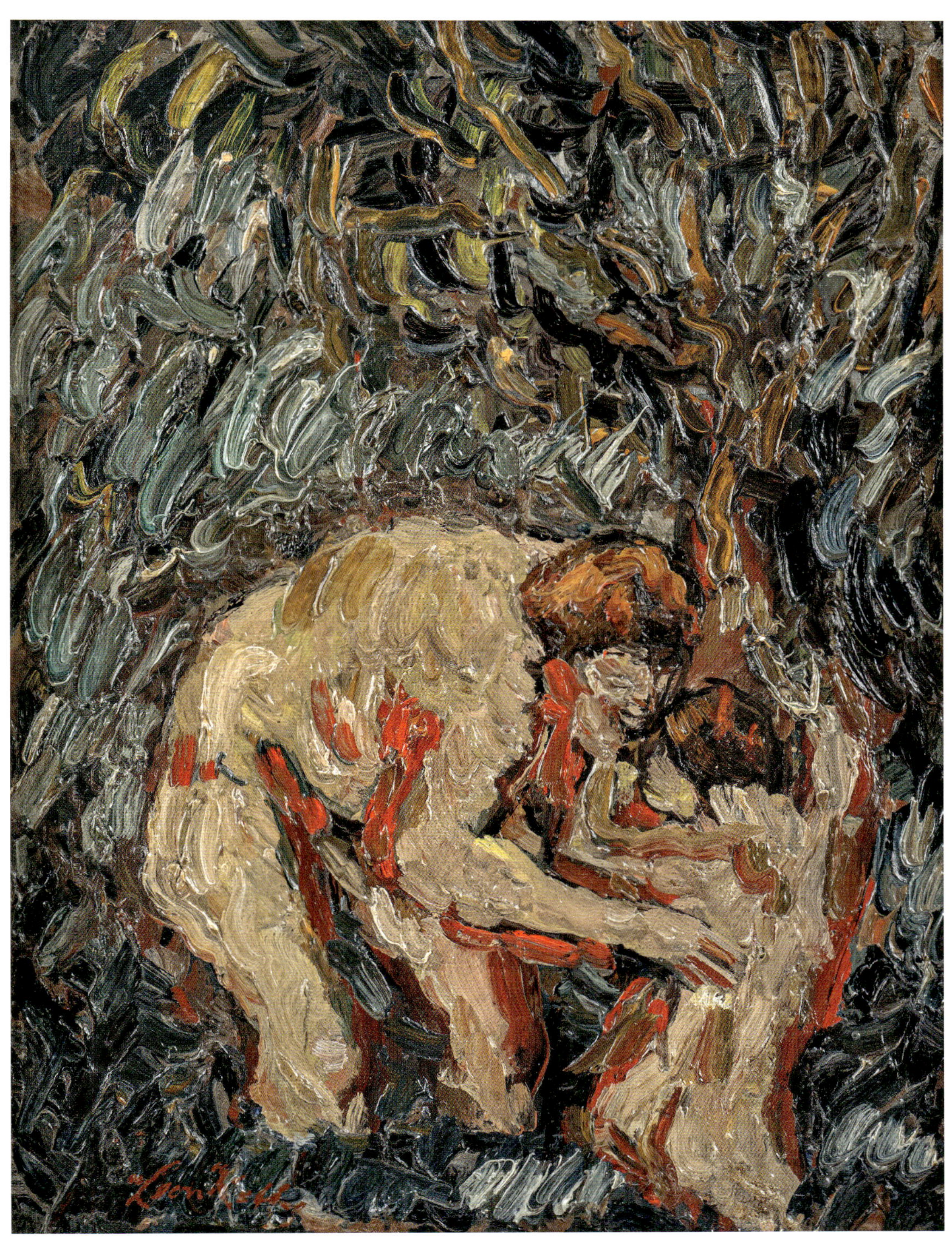

24
Femme bagnant son enfant/Woman Bathing, 1929
Oil on canvas on board, 32.5 × 24.5 cm

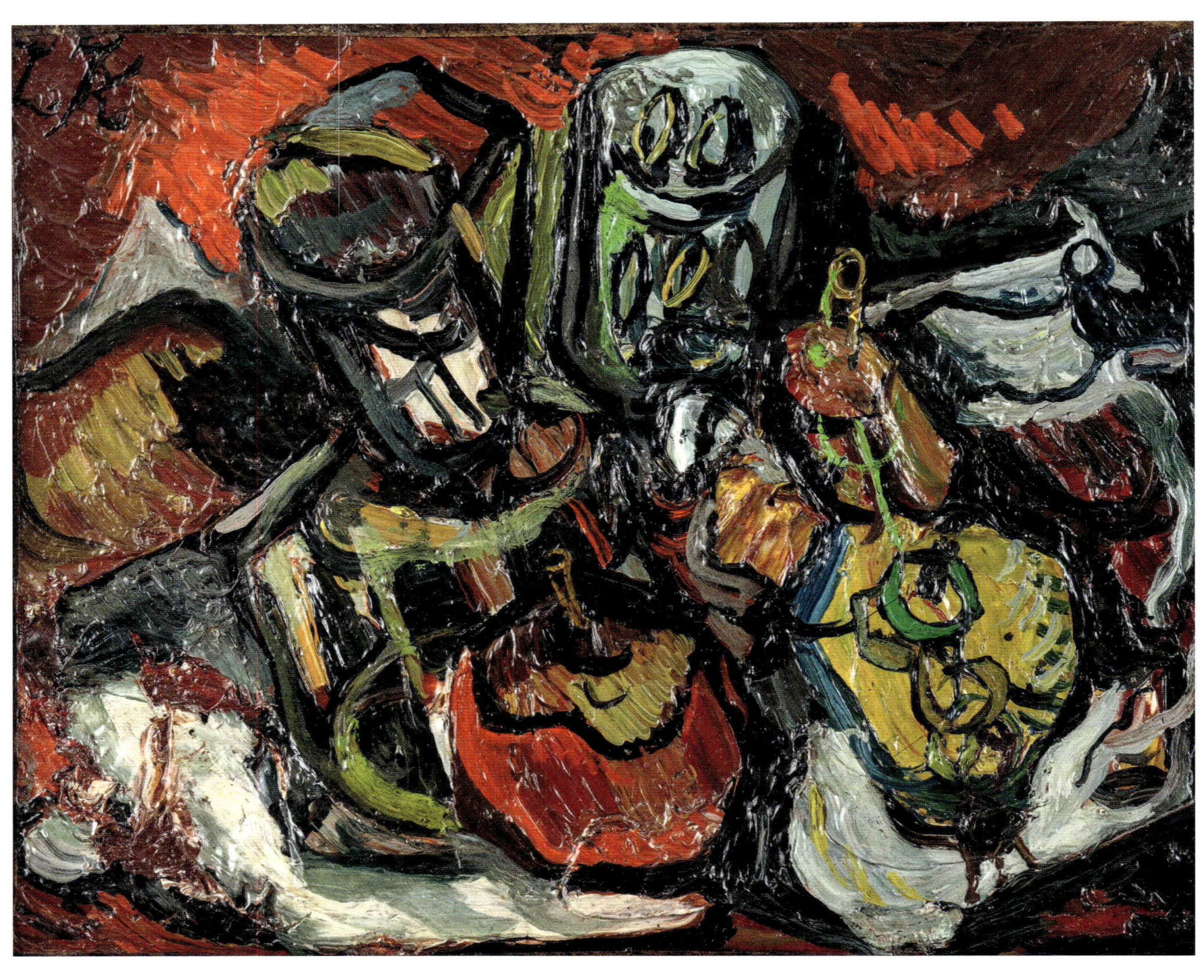

25
Fruit and Glasses, 1930
Oil on cardboard, 20.5 × 25.5 cm

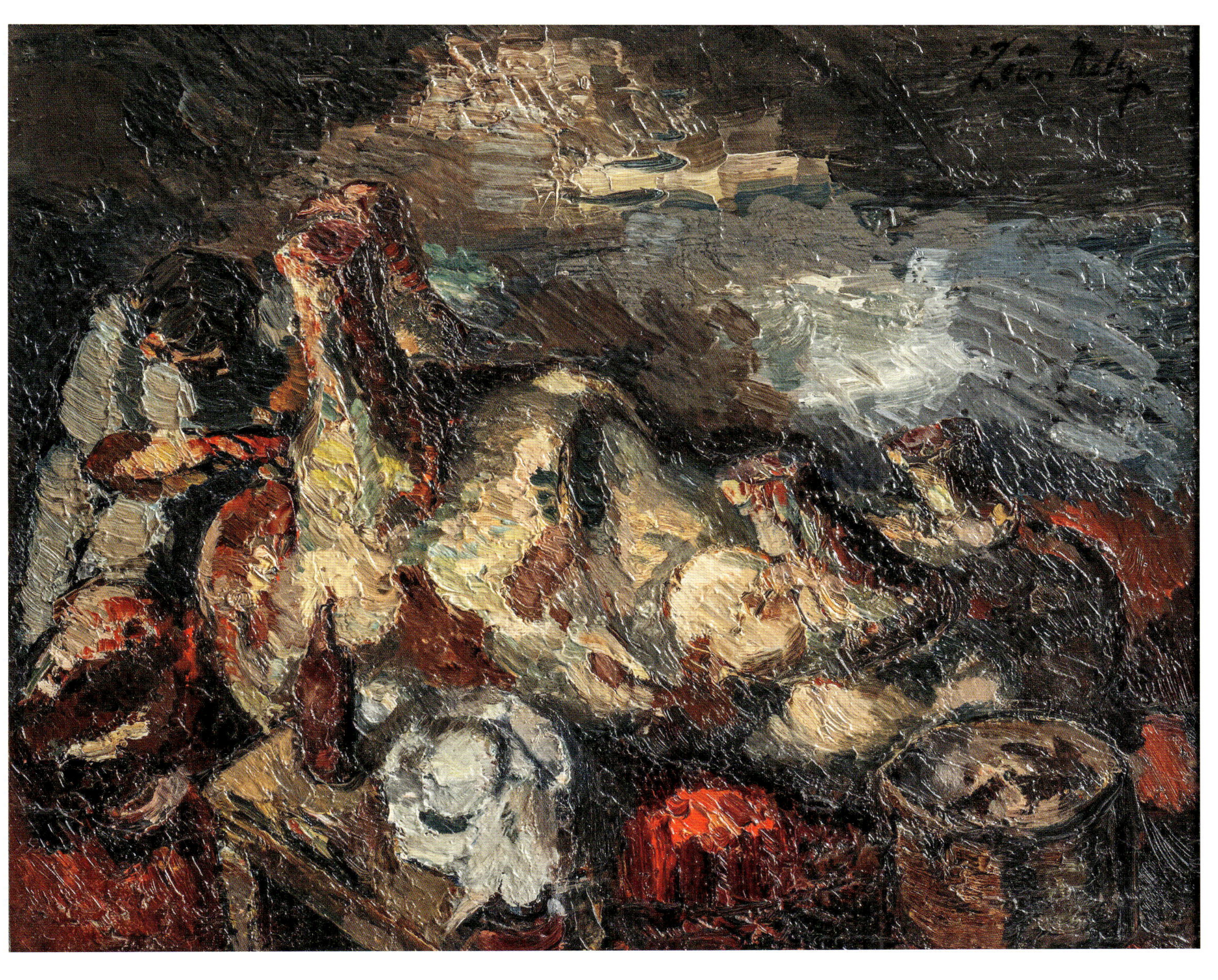

26
The Abattoir, 1927
Oil on board, 33.5 × 41 cm

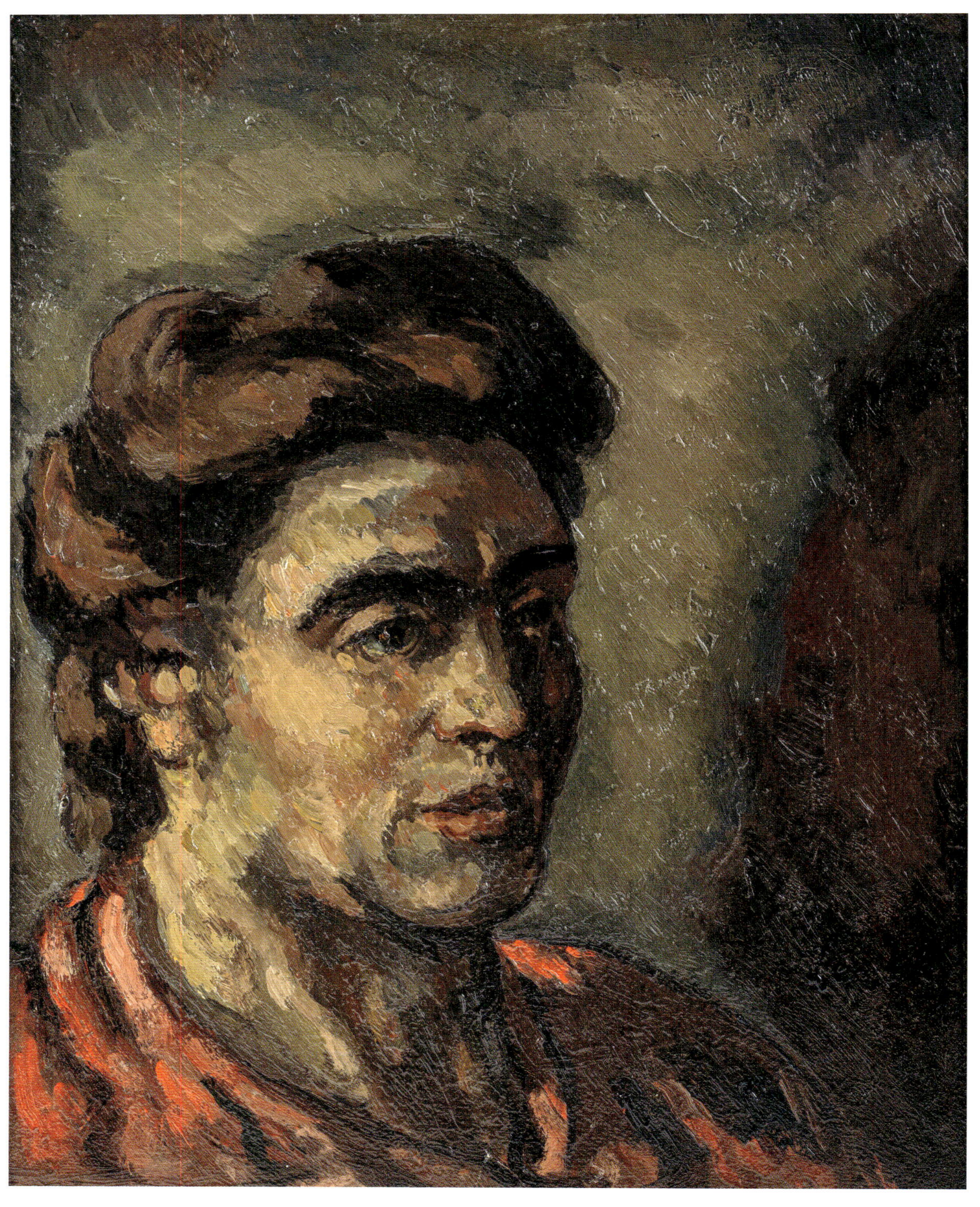

27
Portrait Henriette, 1930
Oil on board, 41 × 33 cm

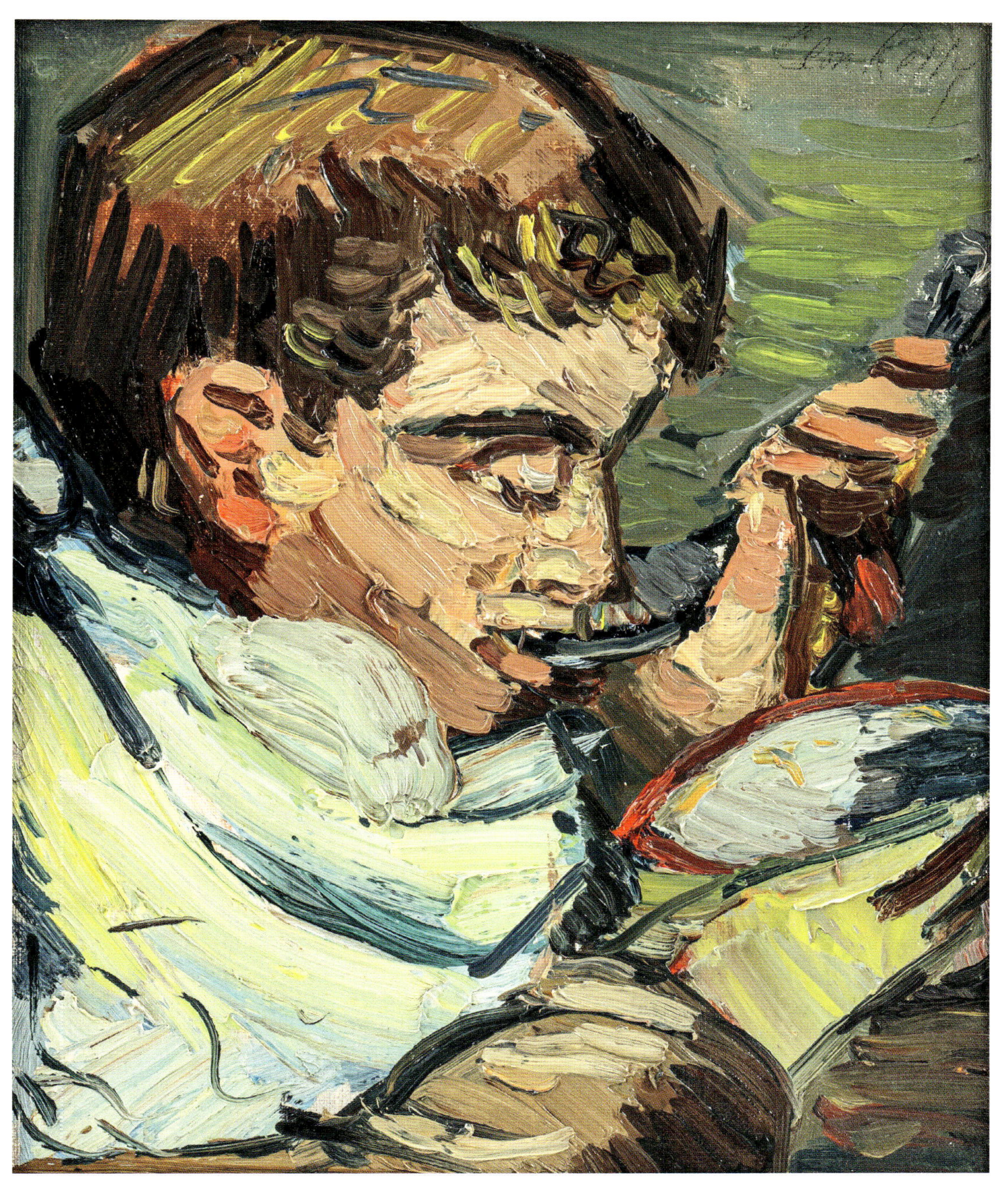

28
A Child Eating Soup, 1930
Oil on canvas on cardboard, 34.5 × 29.5 cm

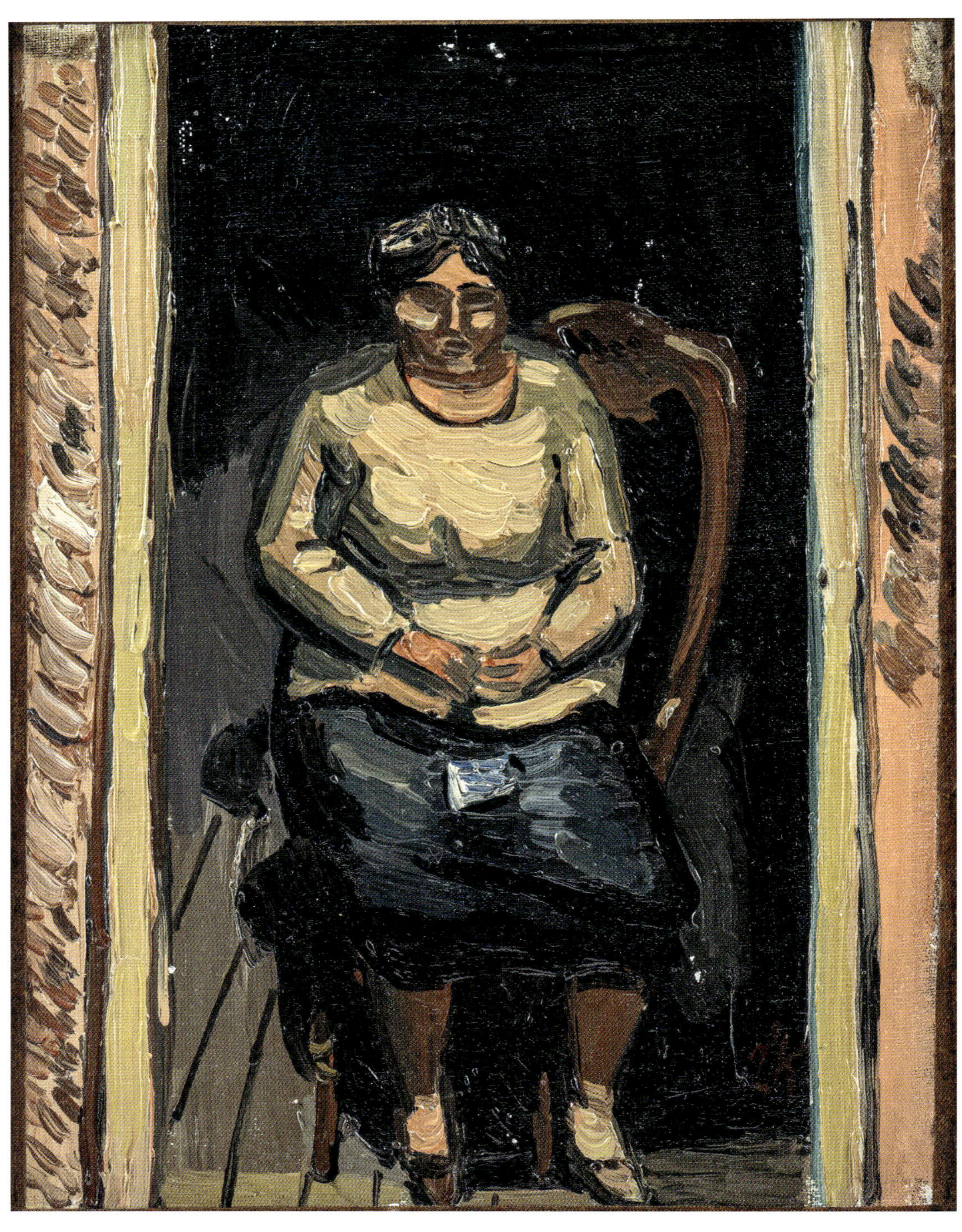

29
Figure Seated in Doorway, 1930
Oil on canvas on cardboard, 30 × 22.5 cm

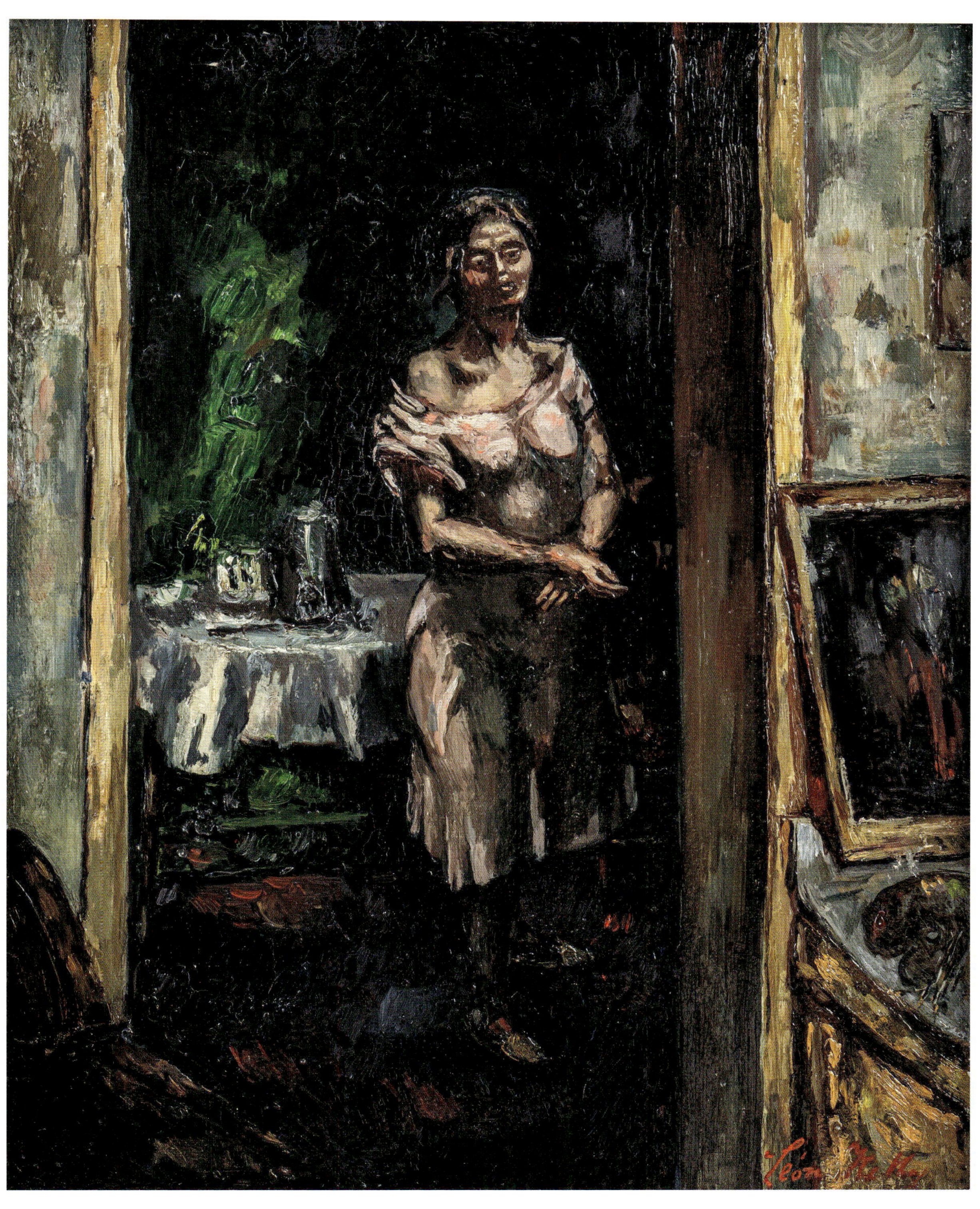

30
Henriette in the Doorway, 1930
Oil on board, 41 × 33 cm

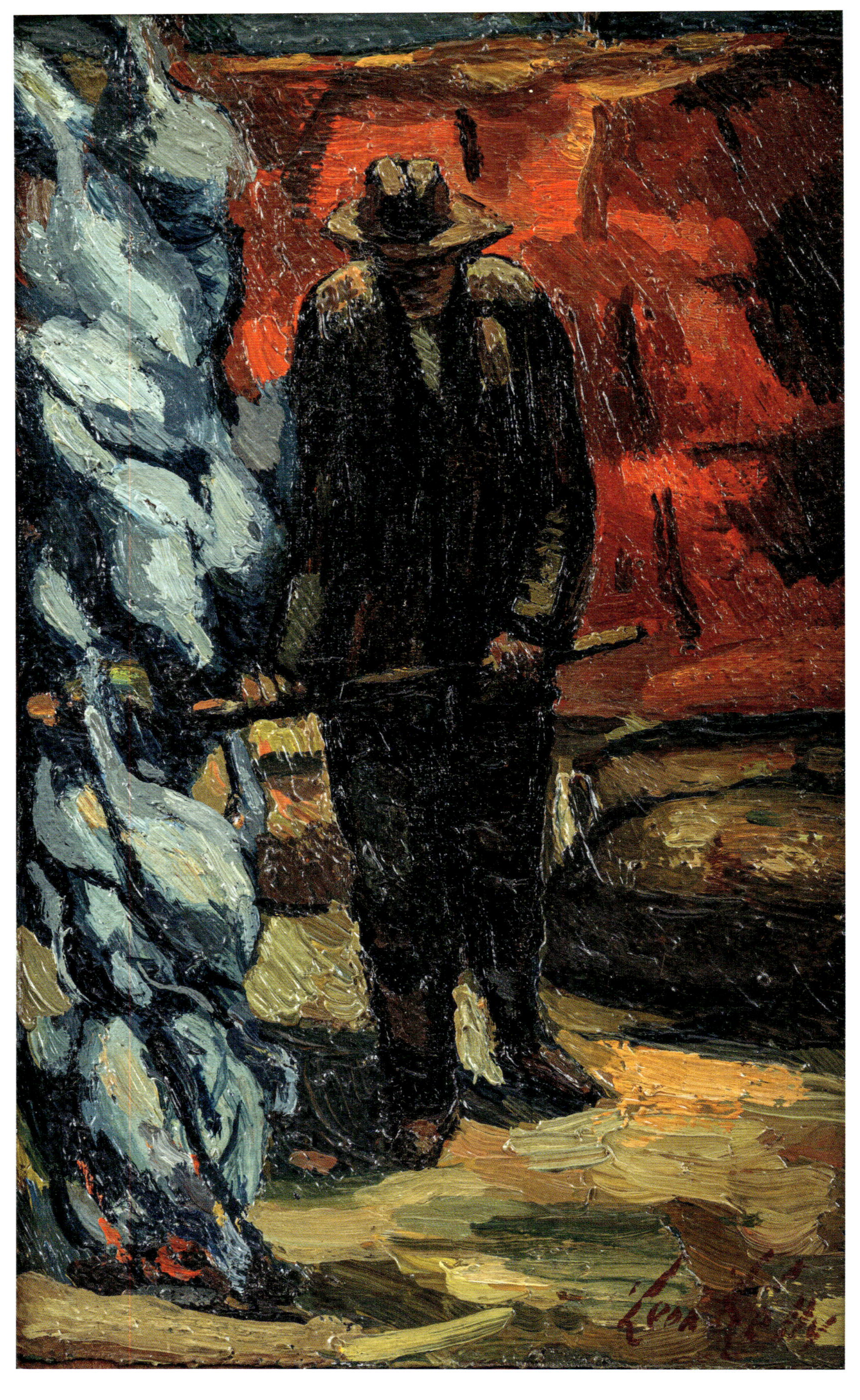

31
Man Burning Leaves, 1930
Oil on board, 30 × 18.5 cm

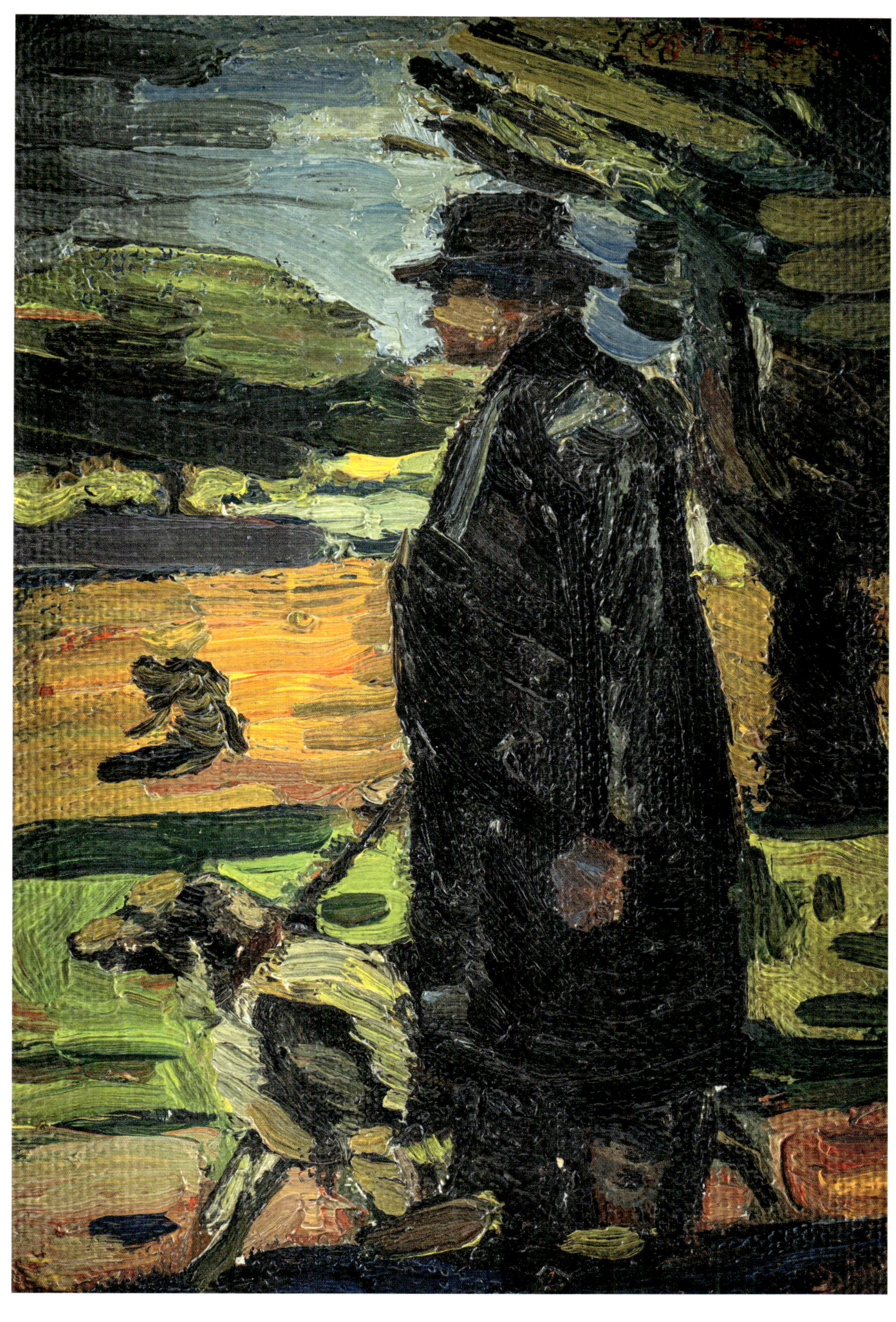

32
Self-Portrait with Dog, 1930
Oil on canvas, 24 × 16.5 cm

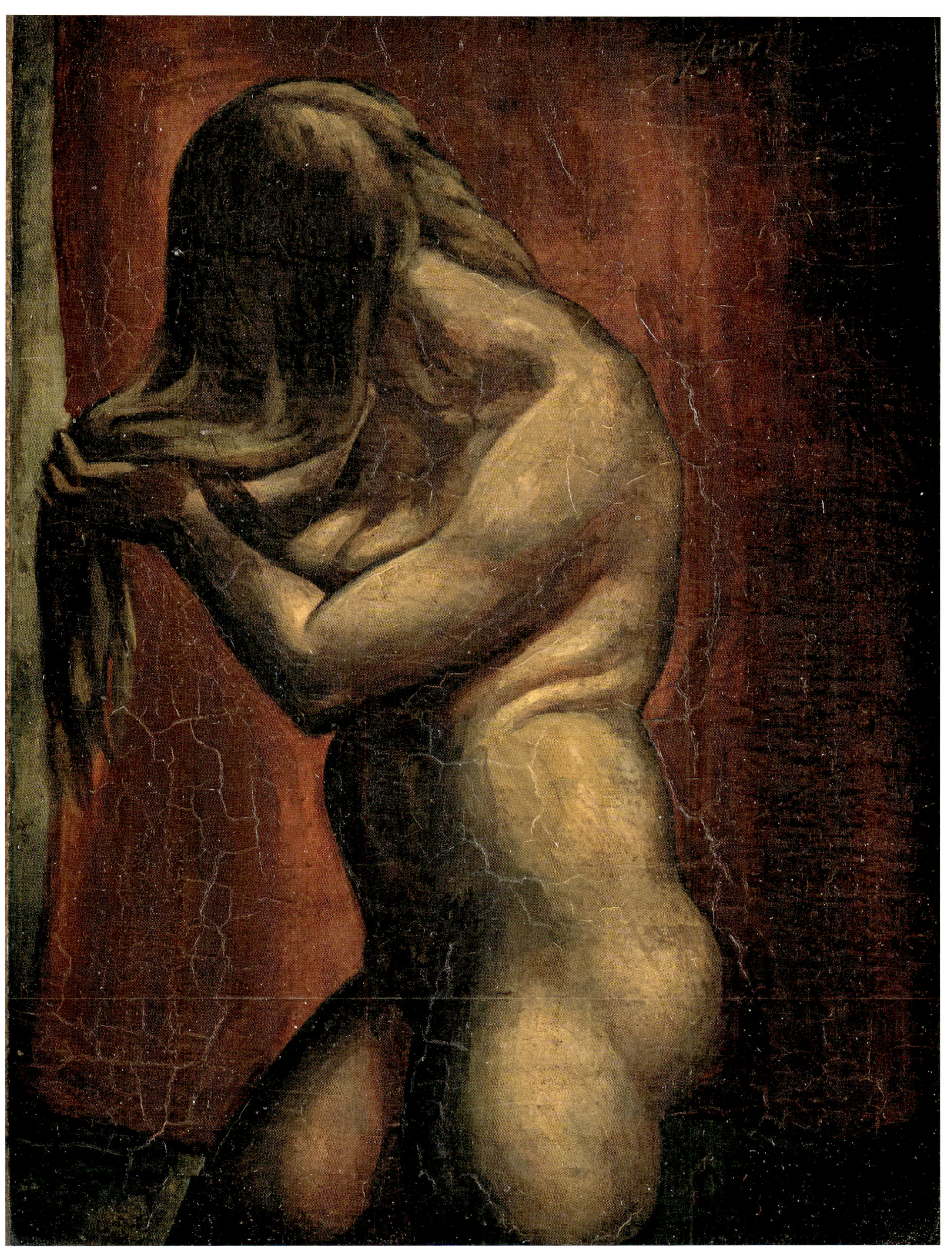

33
Untitled (Female Nude), ca. 1966
Oil on board, 24 × 18 cm

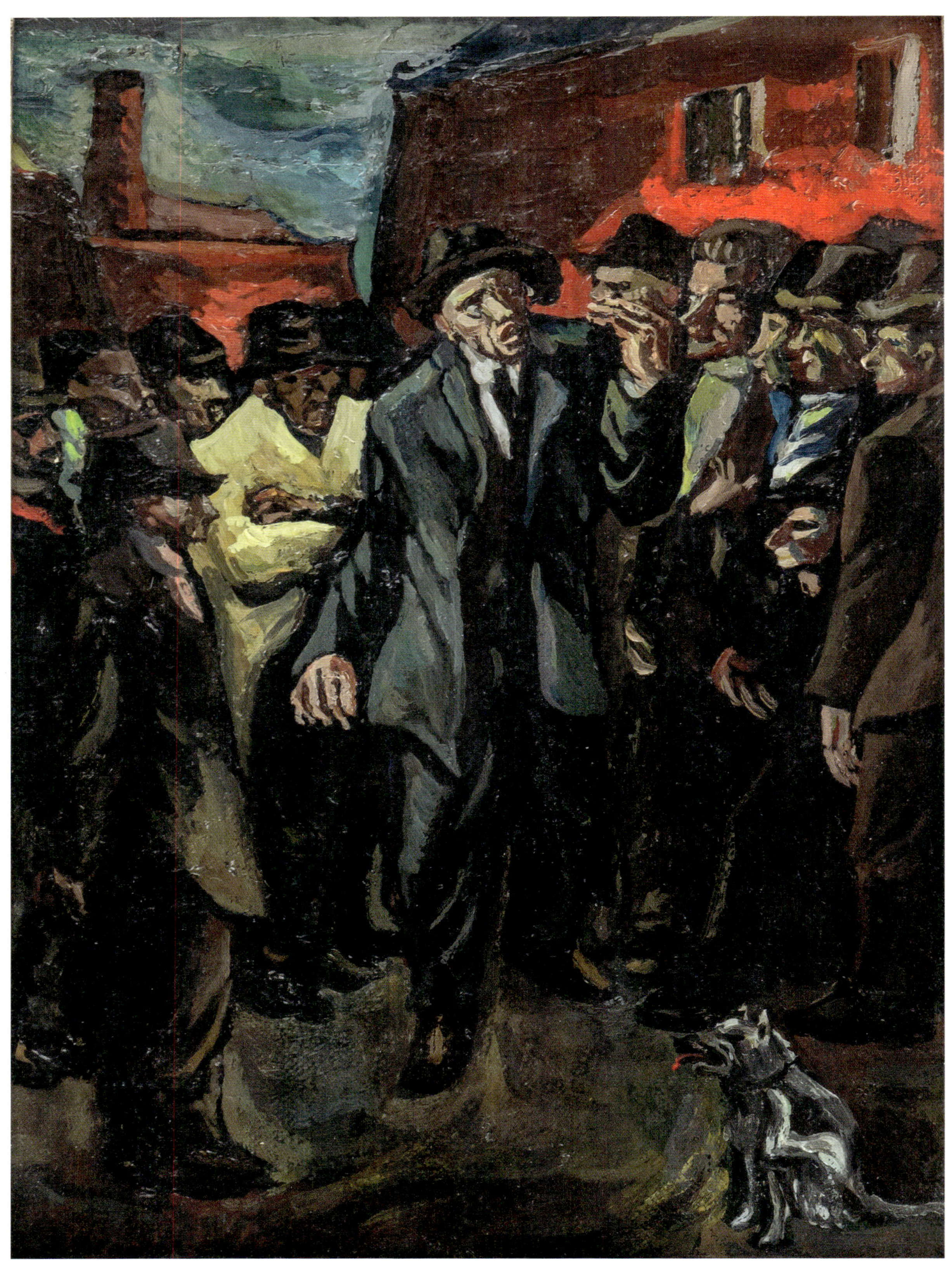

34
Labor Agitator, 1930
Oil on canvas, 29 × 22 cm

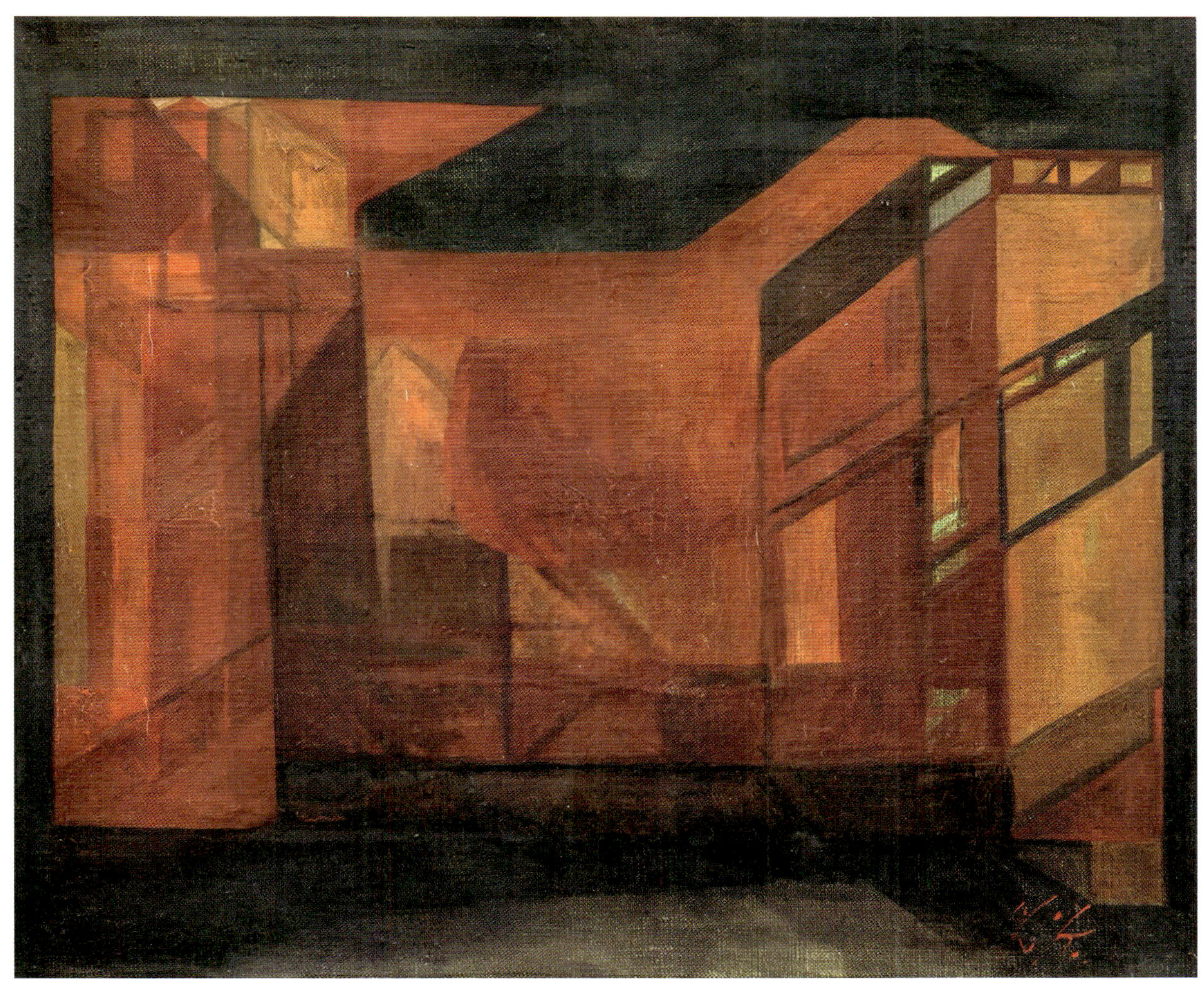

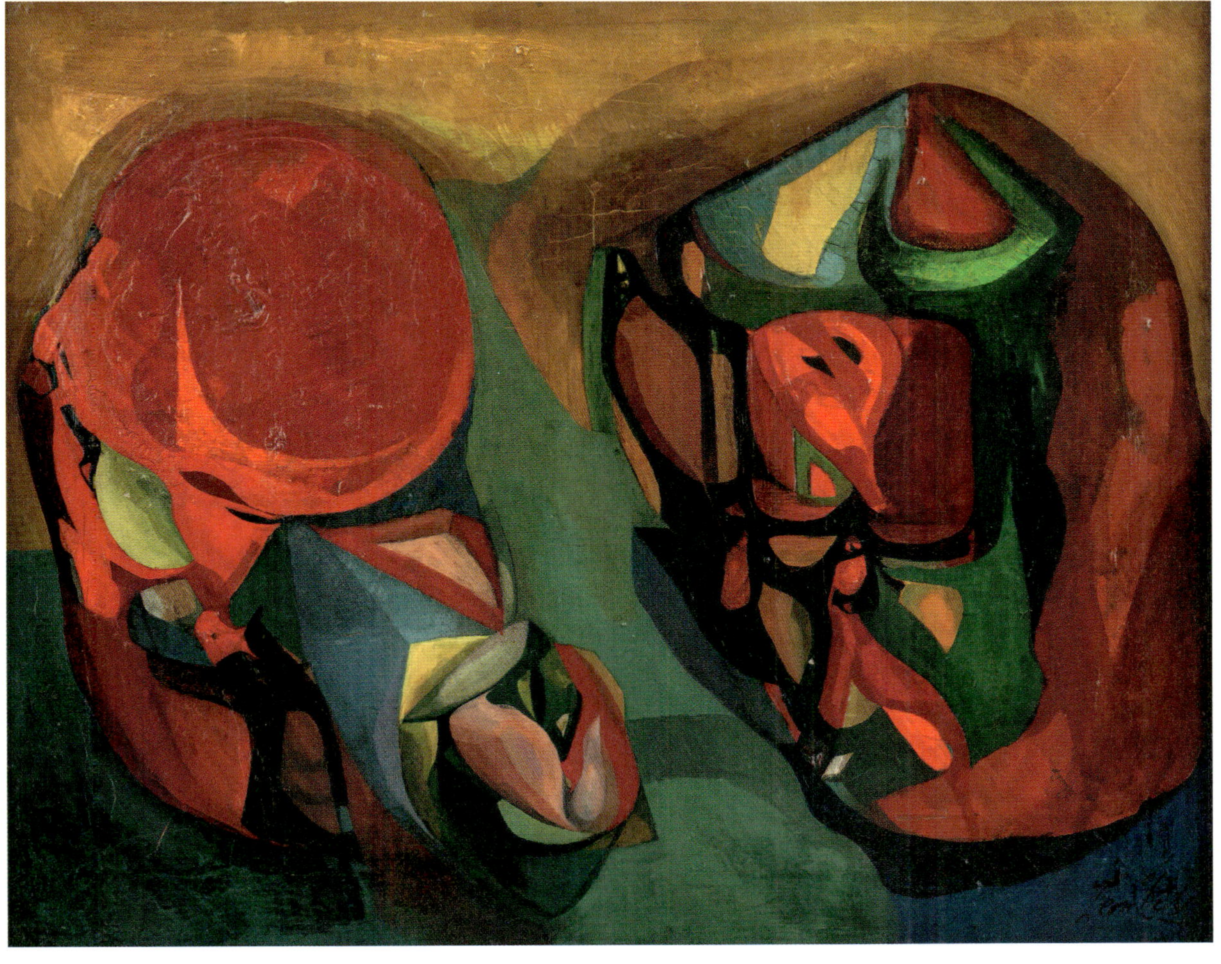

35
Construction of a Garage, 1937
Oil on canvas, 25.5 × 30.5 cm

36
Visit to a Temple, 1938
Oil on canvas, 40.5 × 51 cm (cf. fig. 133, p. 214)

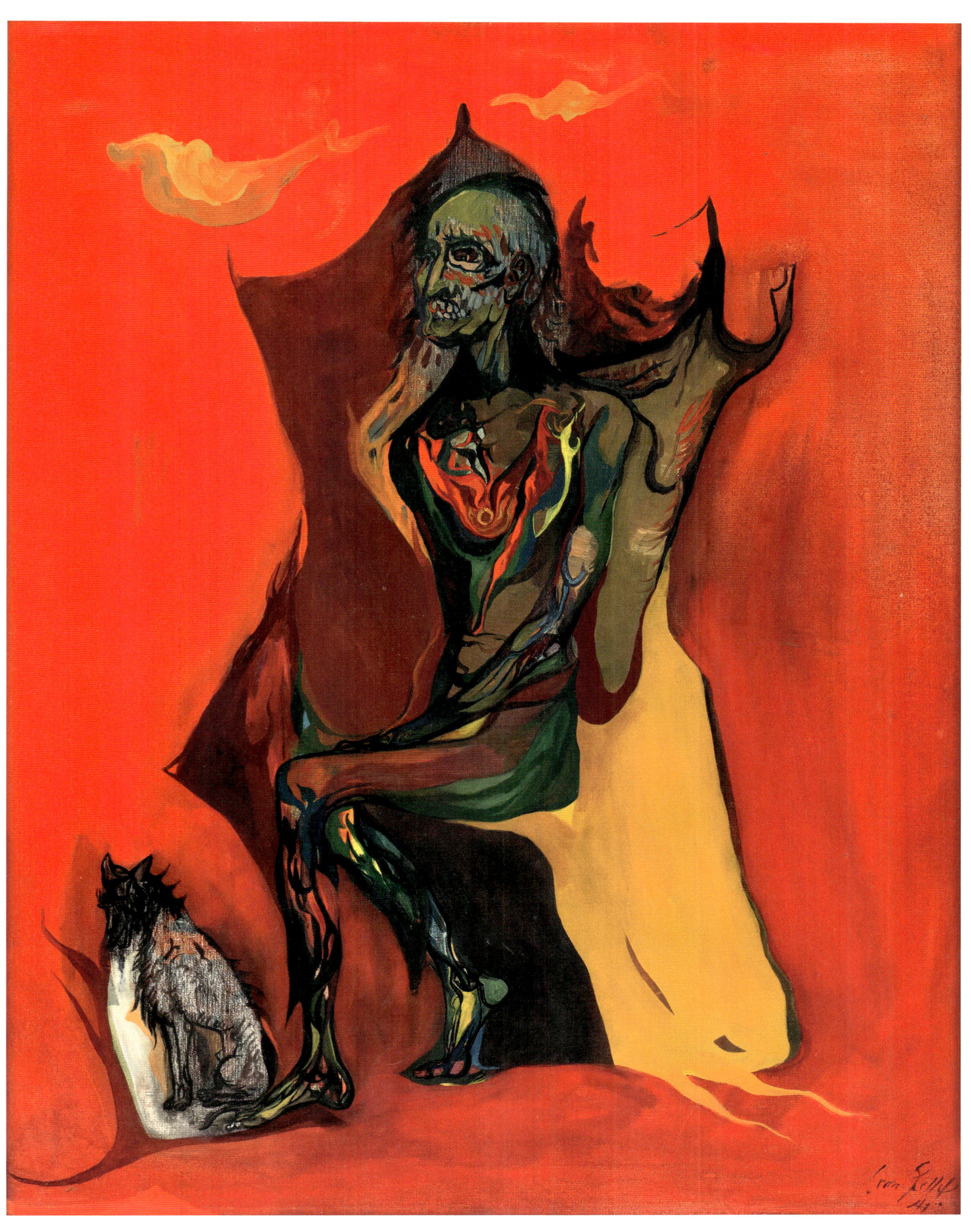

37
Mendicant, 1941
Oil on canvas, 76 × 61 cm

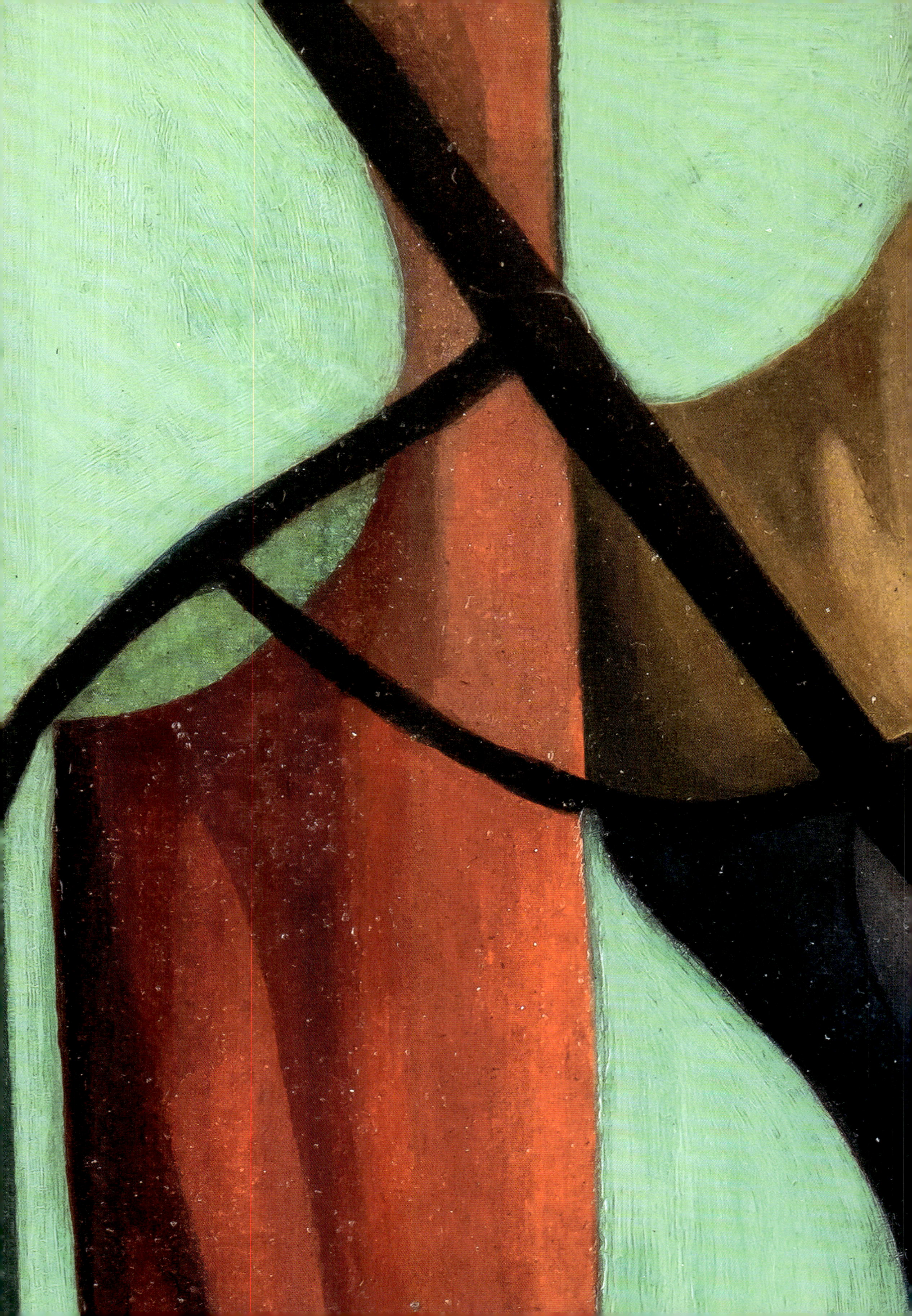

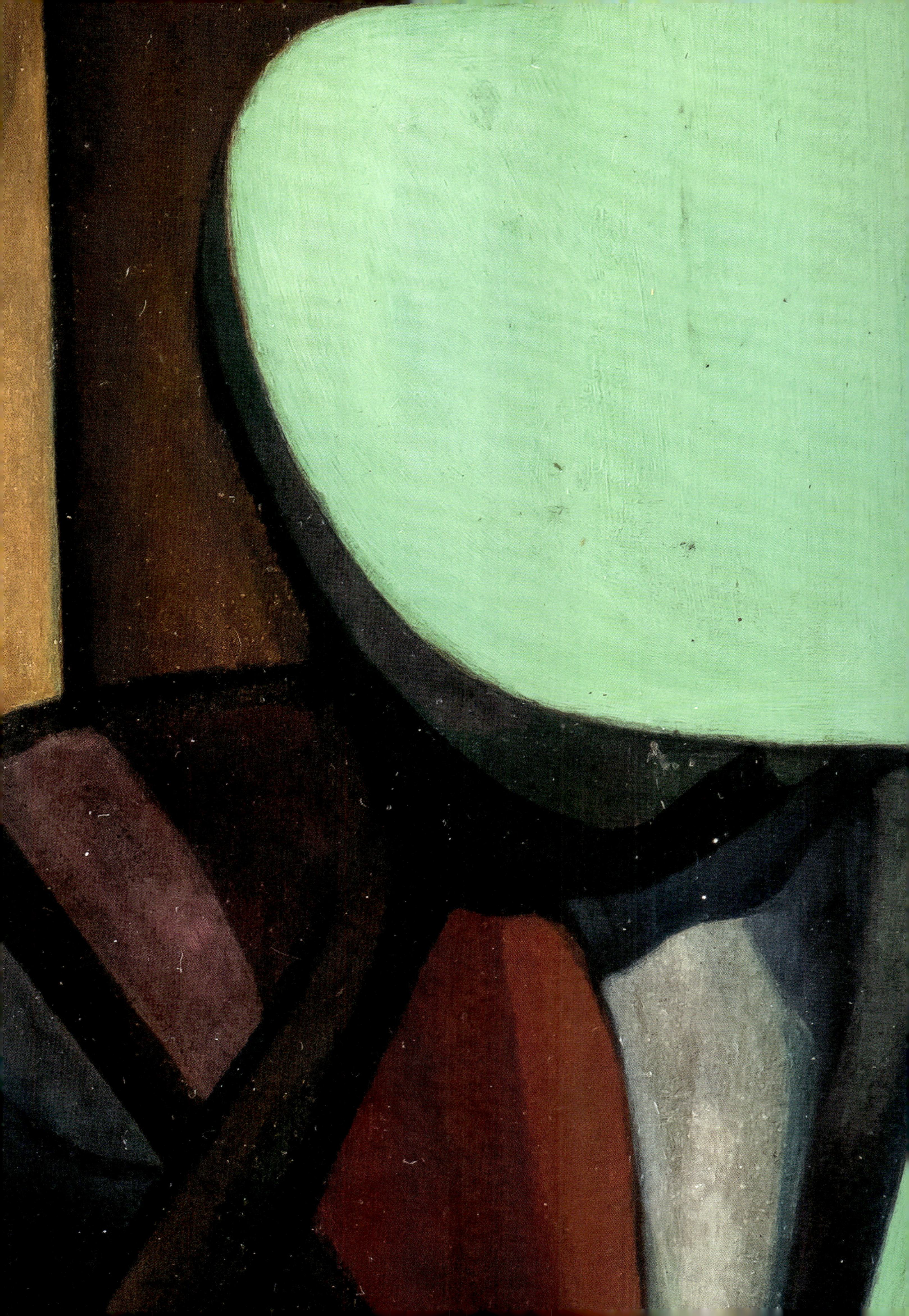

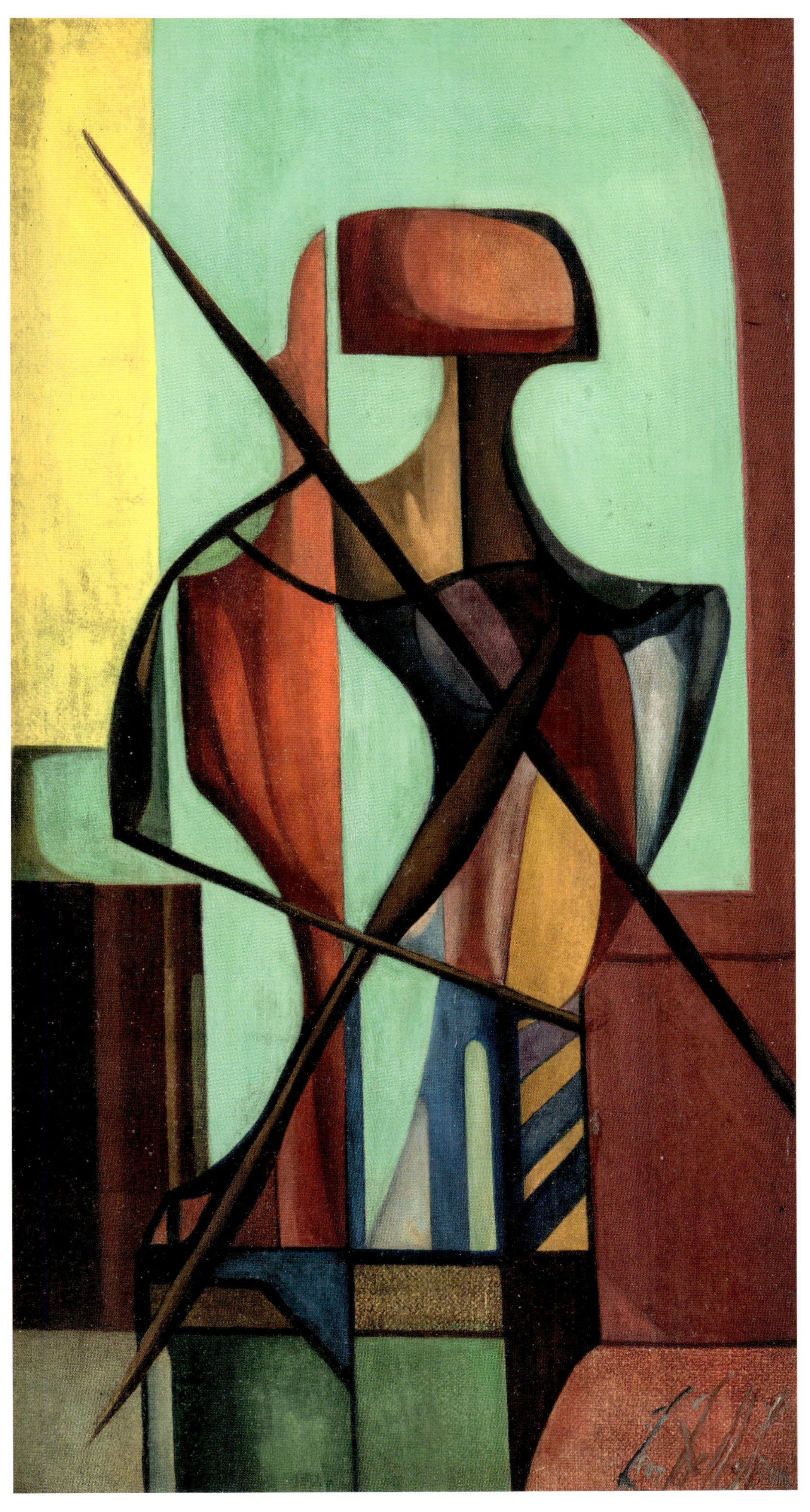

38
Hunter with a Bird, 1949
Oil on canvas, 38 × 20.5 cm

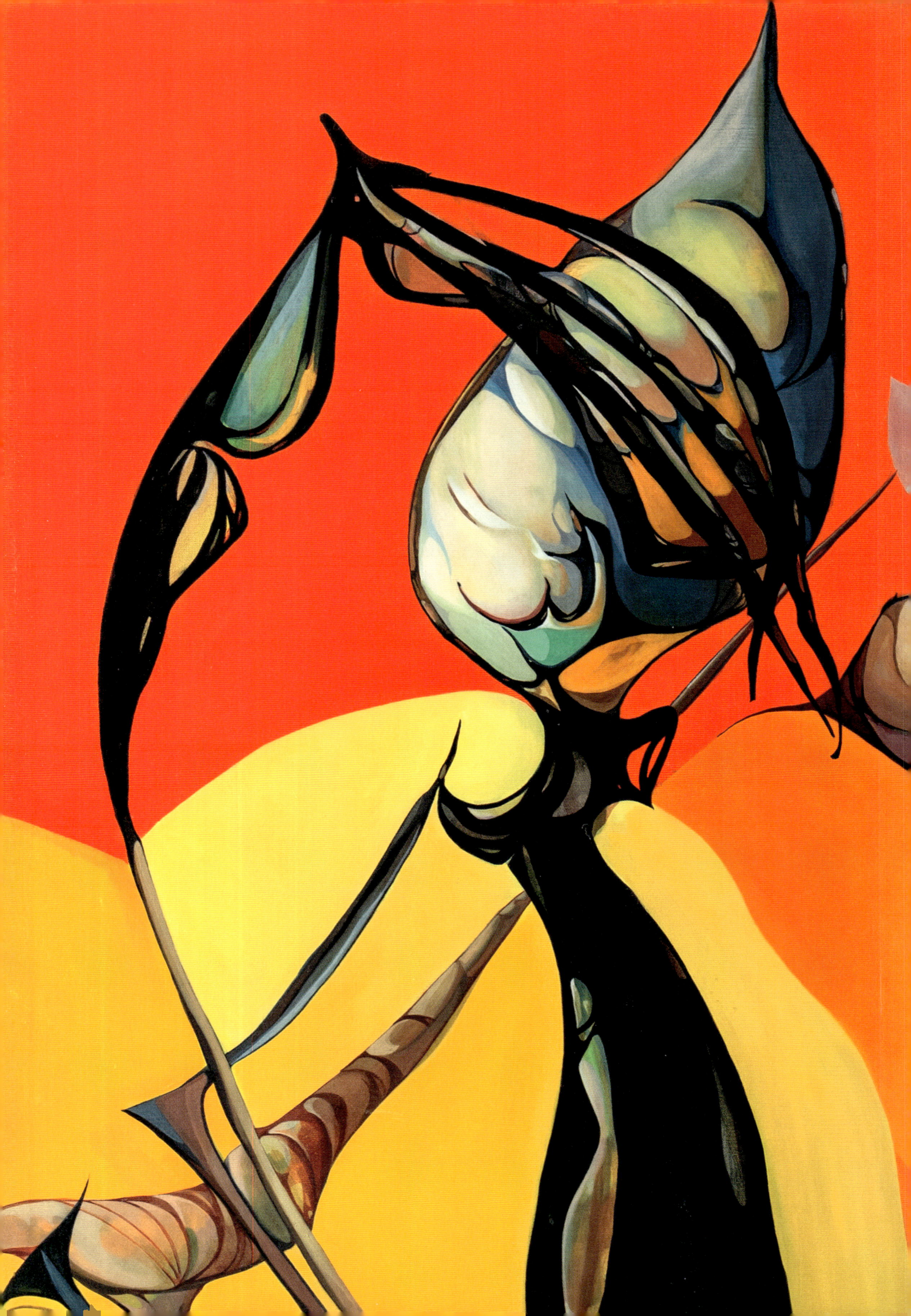

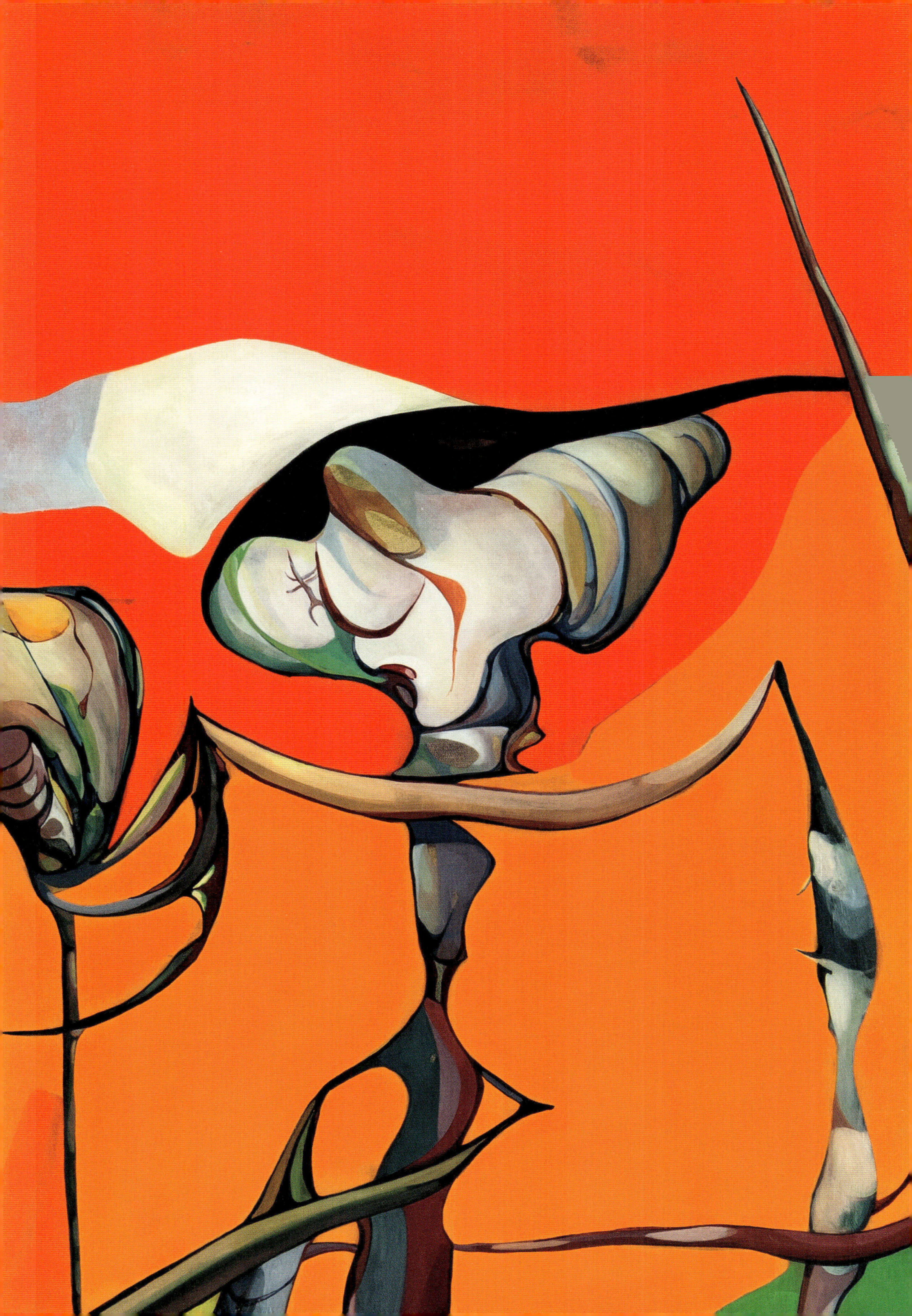

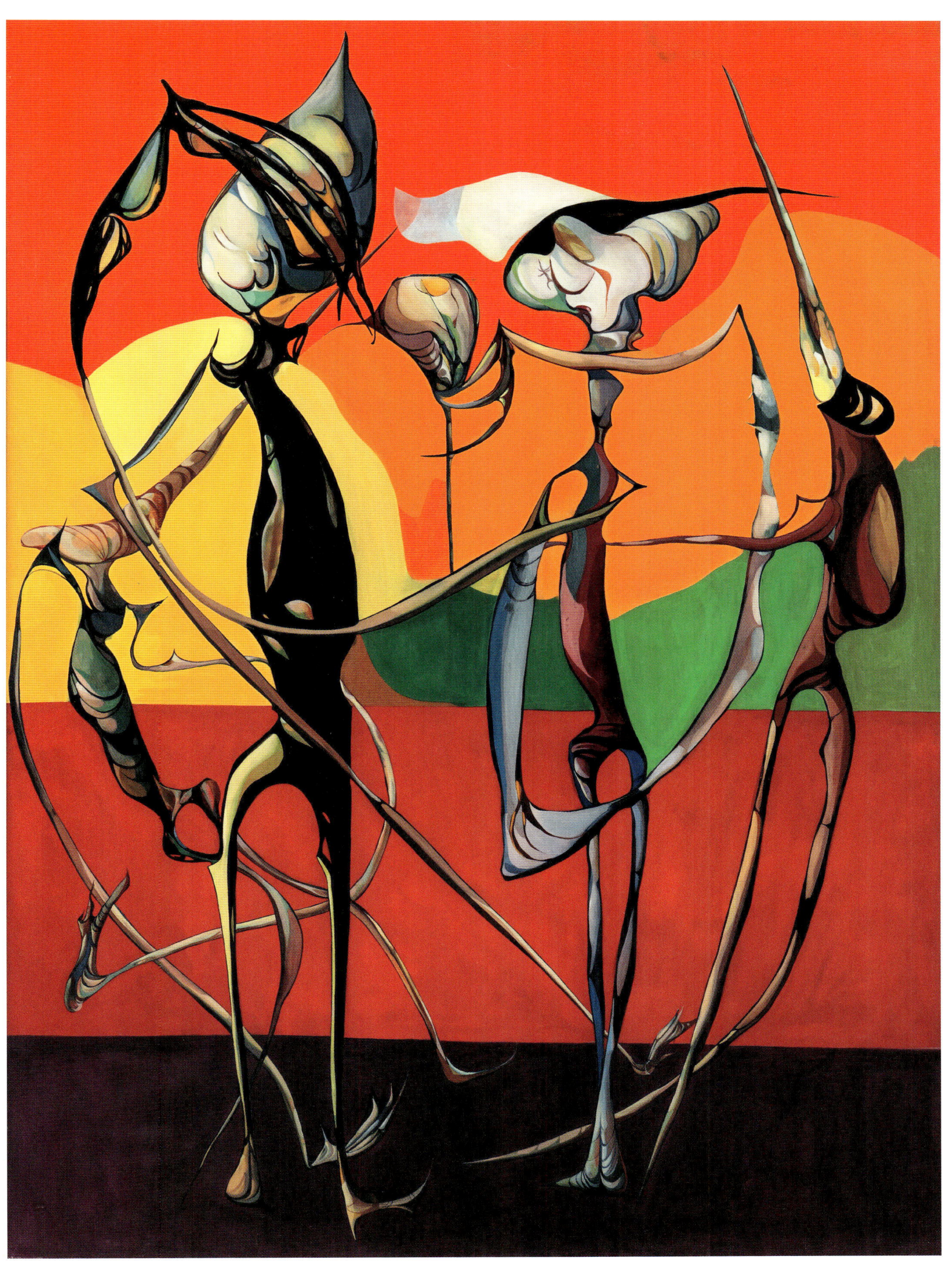

39
The Ritual, 1954
Oil on canvas, 183 × 134 cm

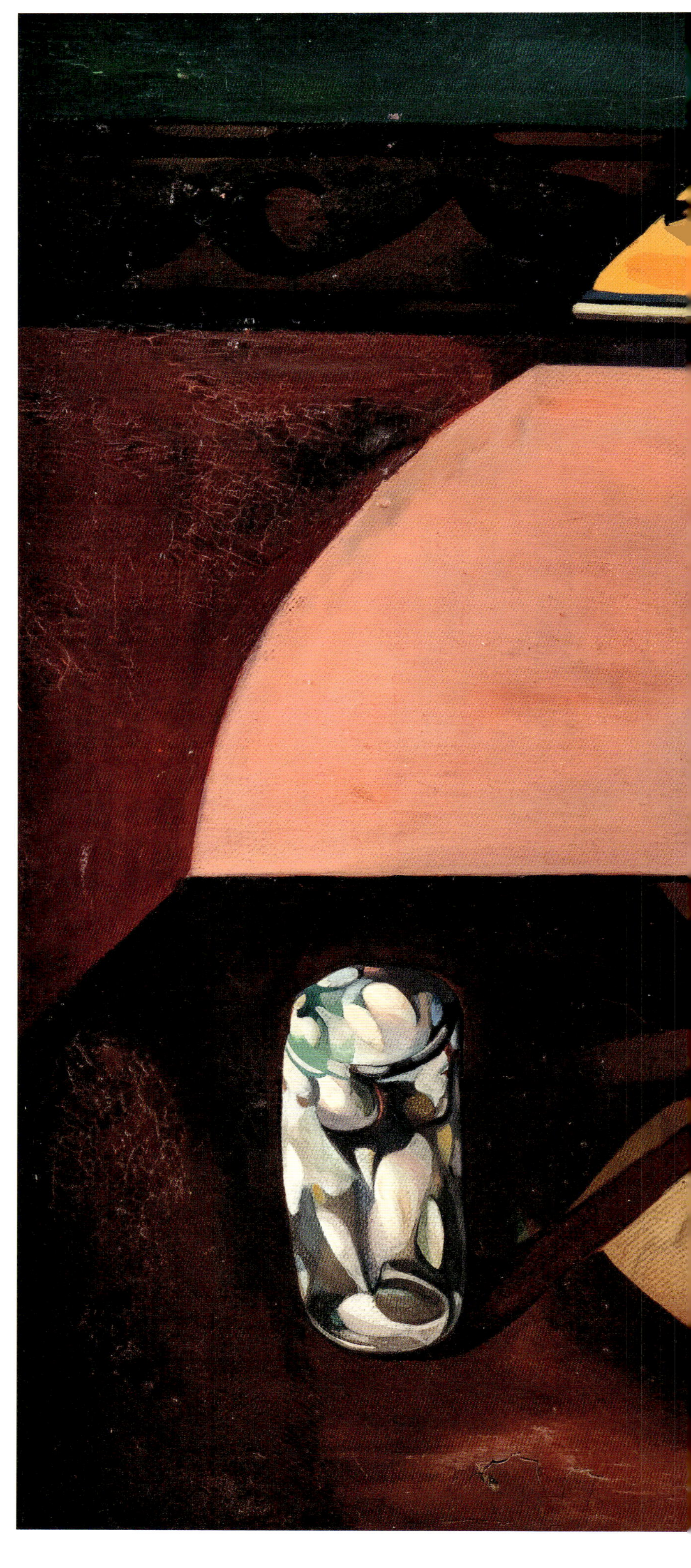

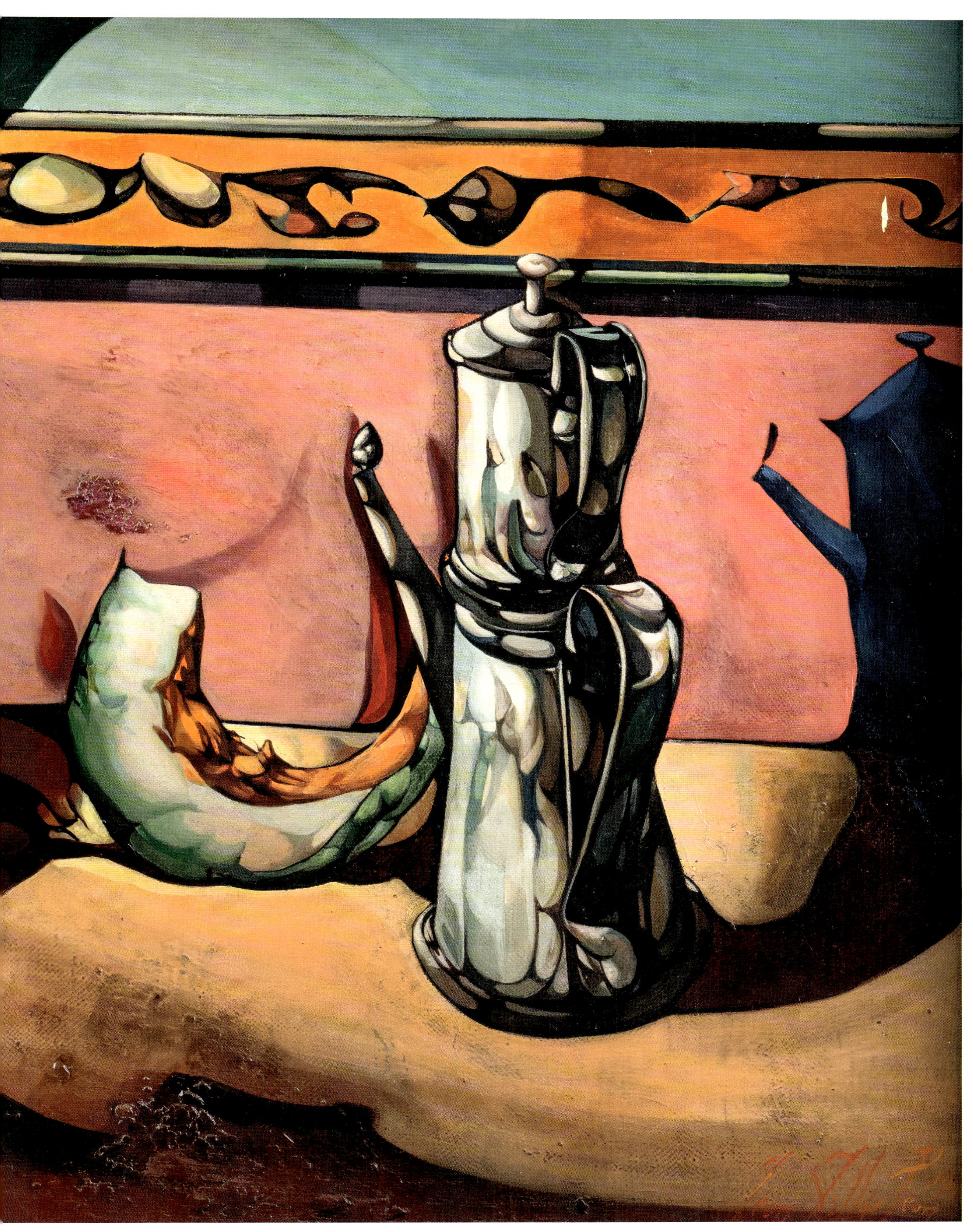

40
The Solitary Glass, 1961
Oil on canvas, 52 × 66 cm

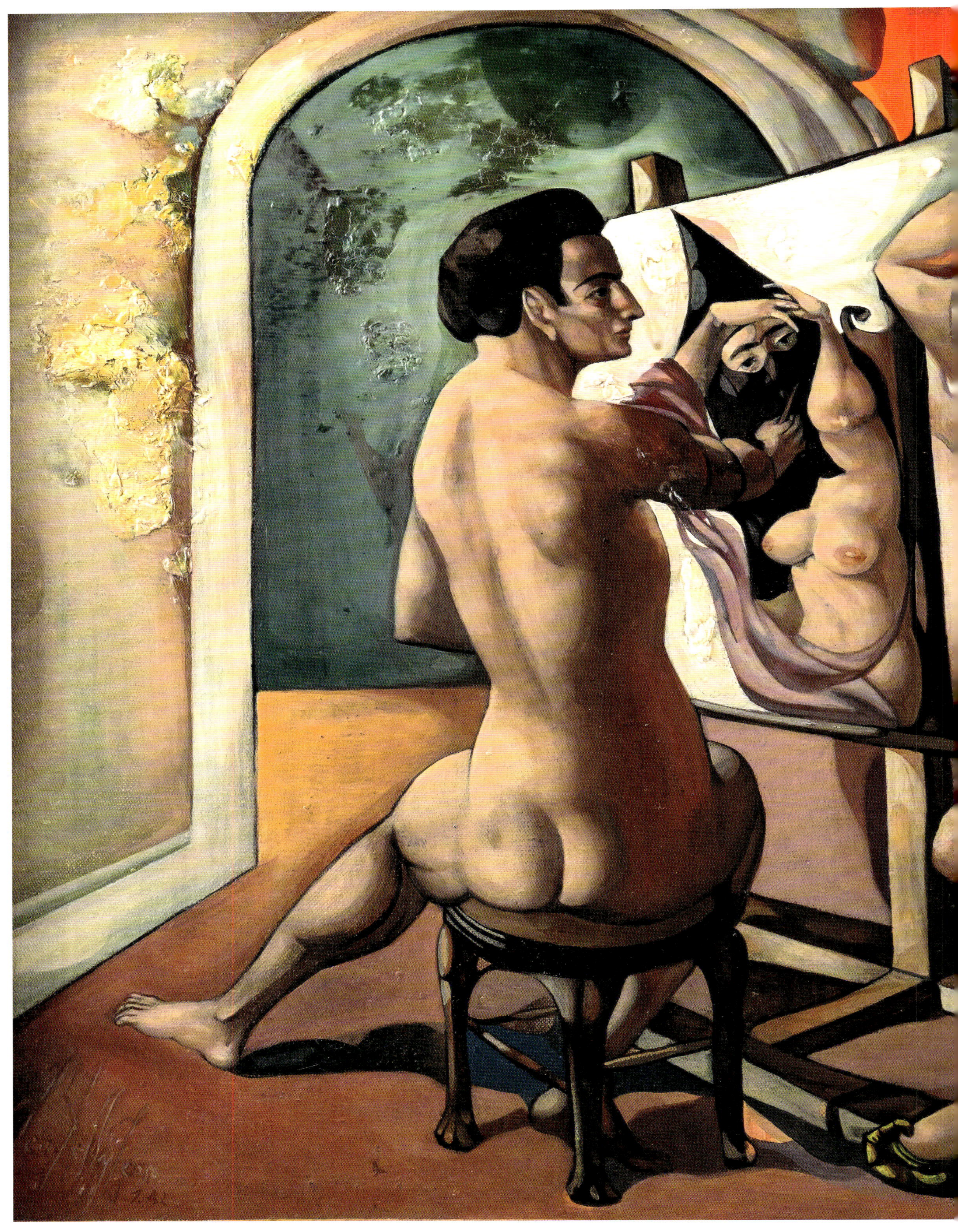

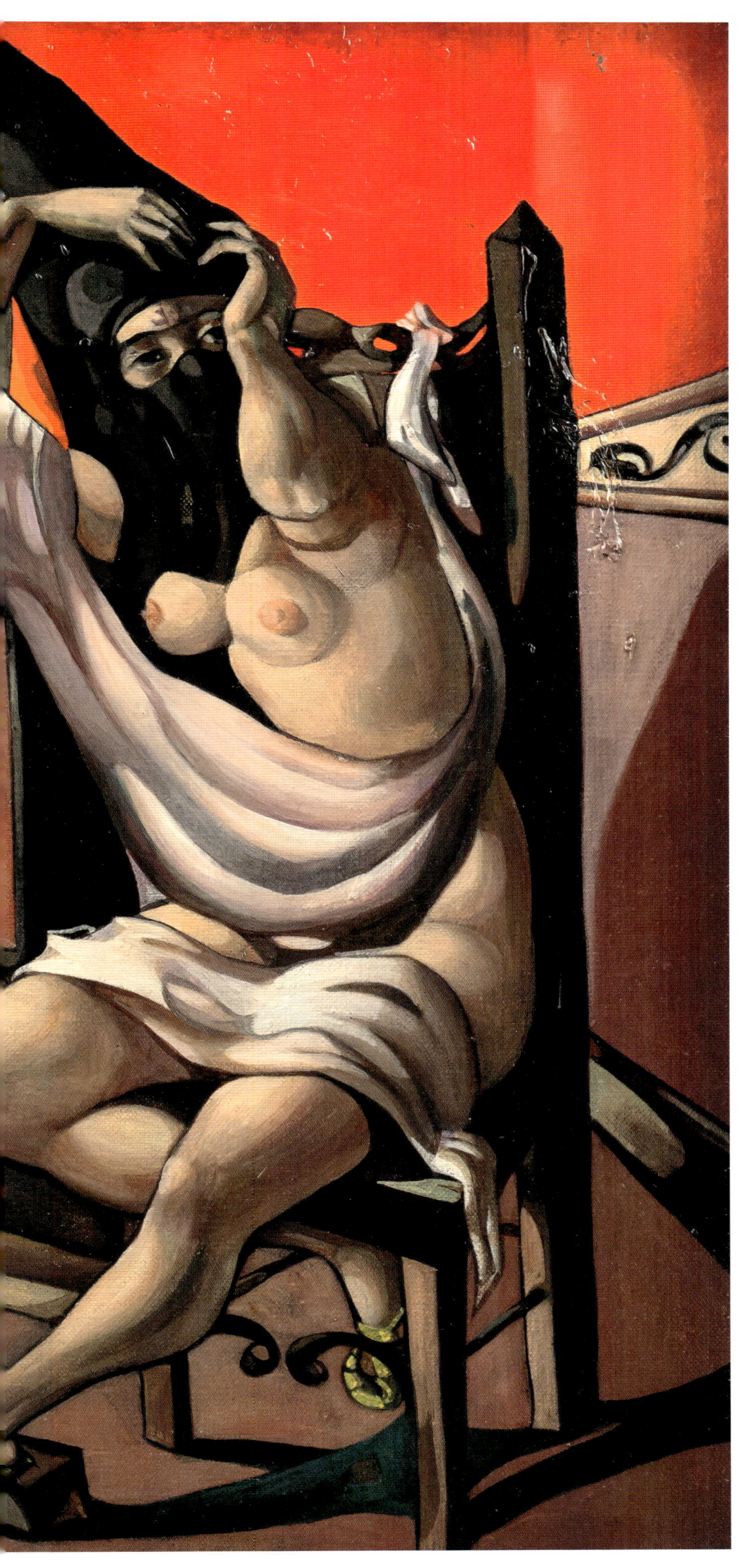

41
The Levantine Model, 1962
Oil on canvas, 40.5 × 50.5 cm

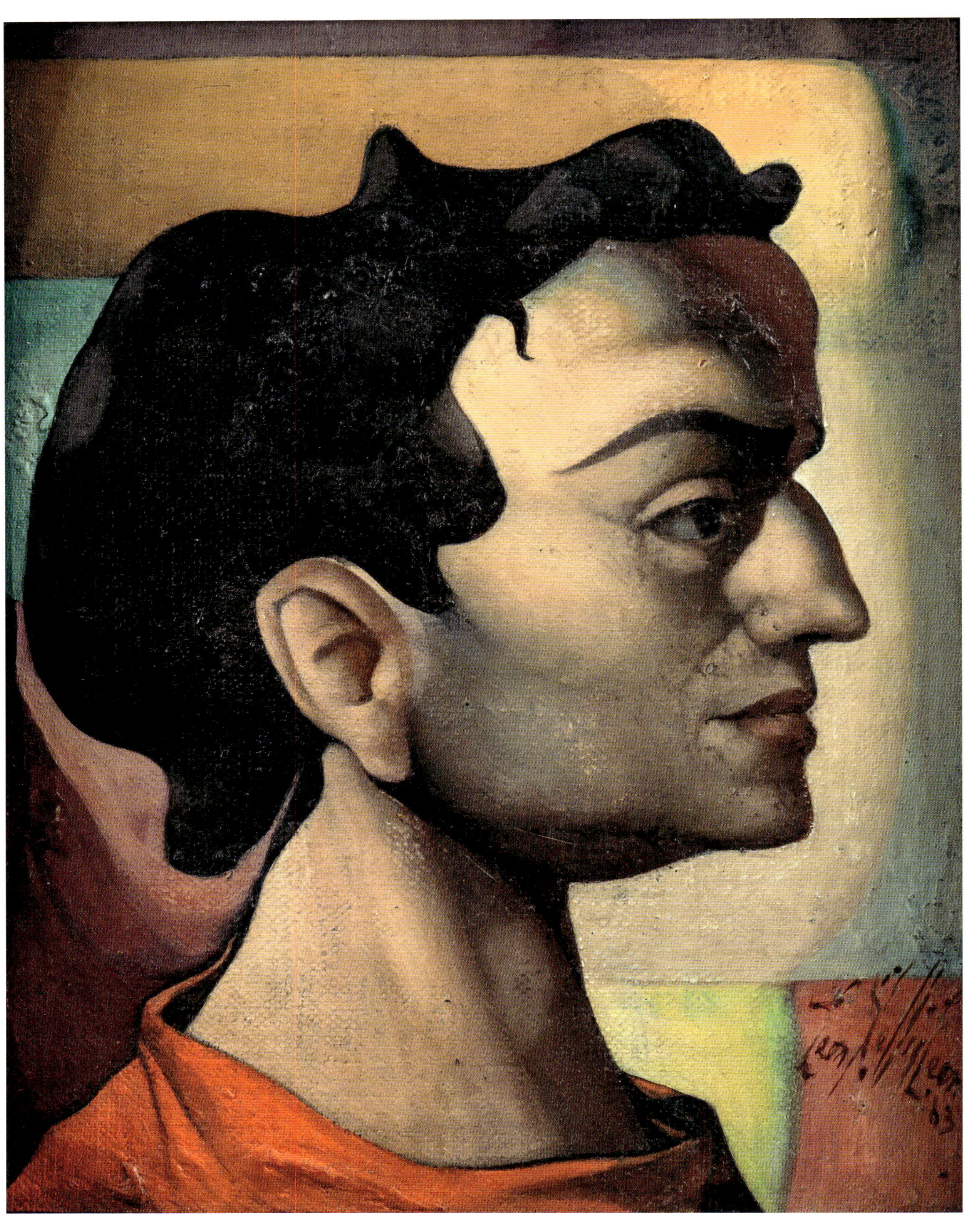

42
Imaginary Portrait, 1963
Oil on canvas, 23 × 18.5 cm

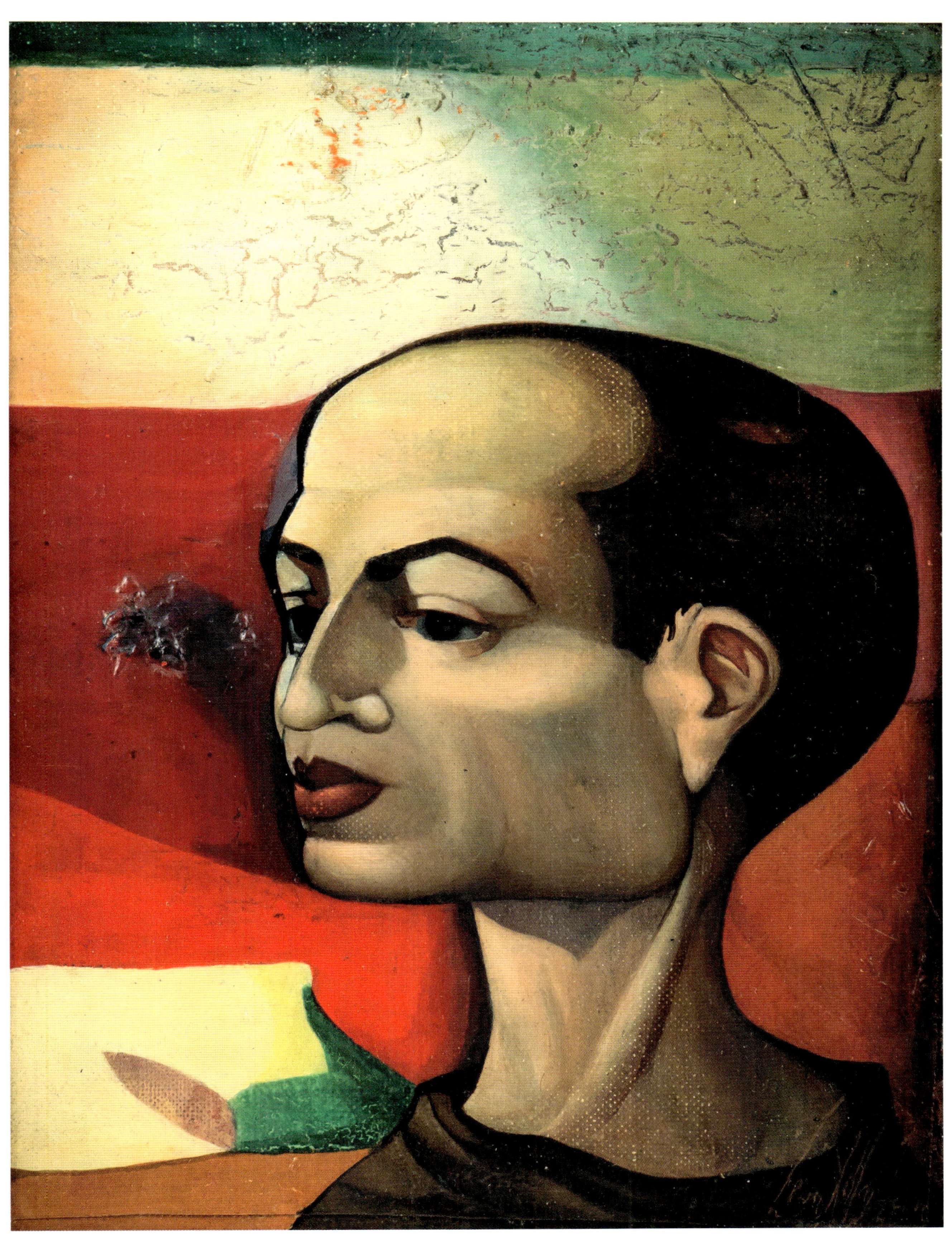

43
In Memory of Francisco Stamato, 1963
Oil on canvas, 25.5 × 20.5 cm

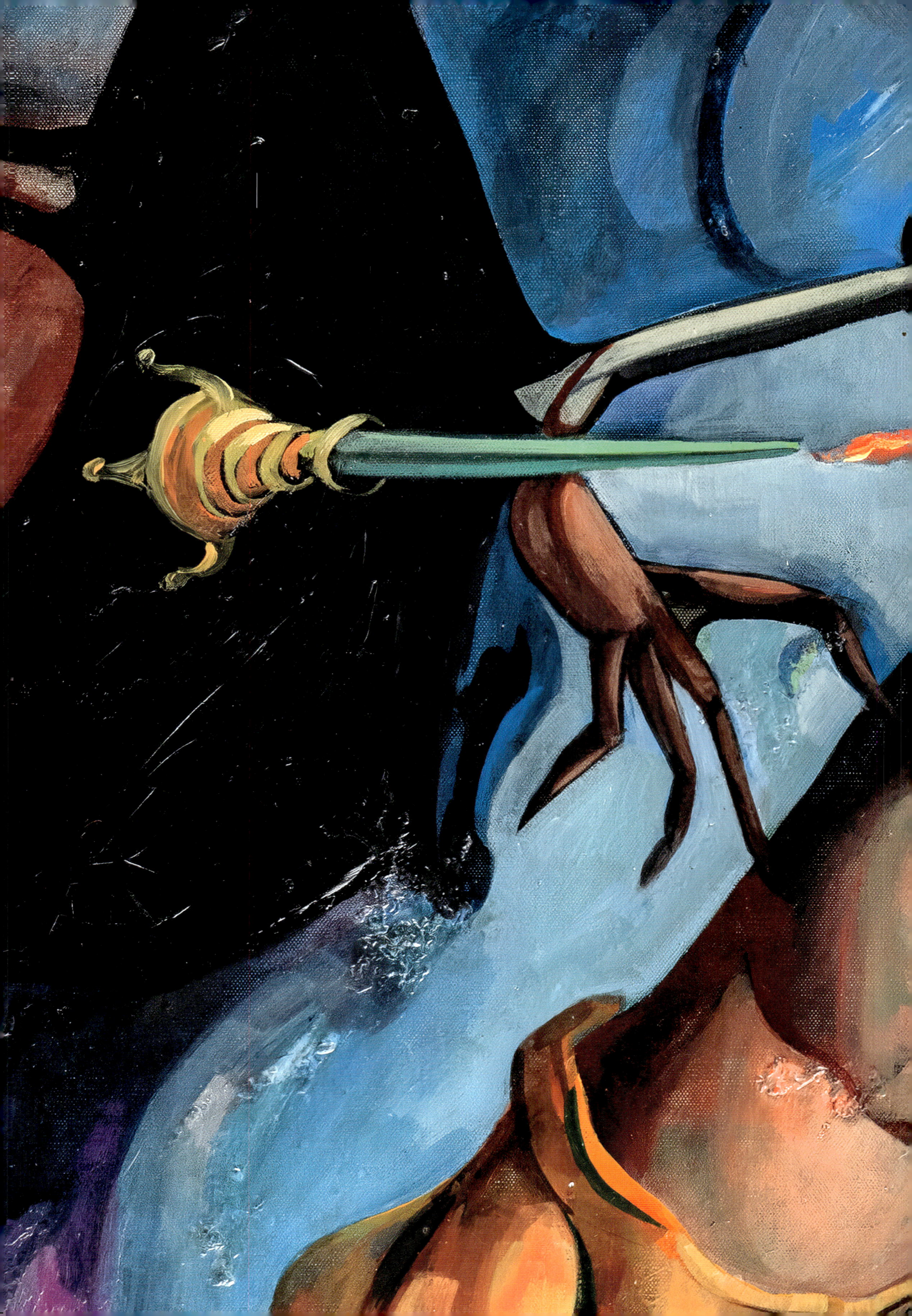

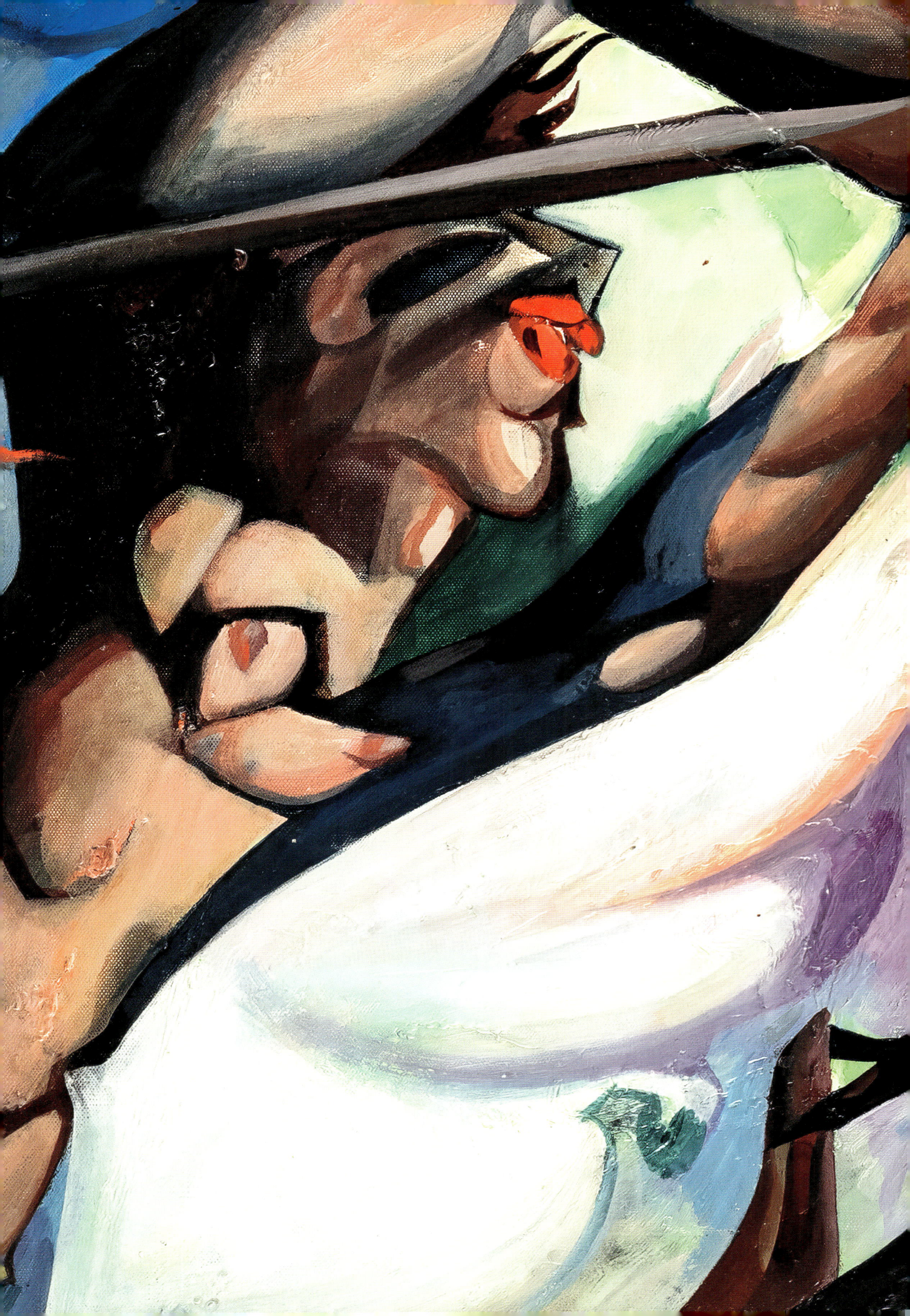

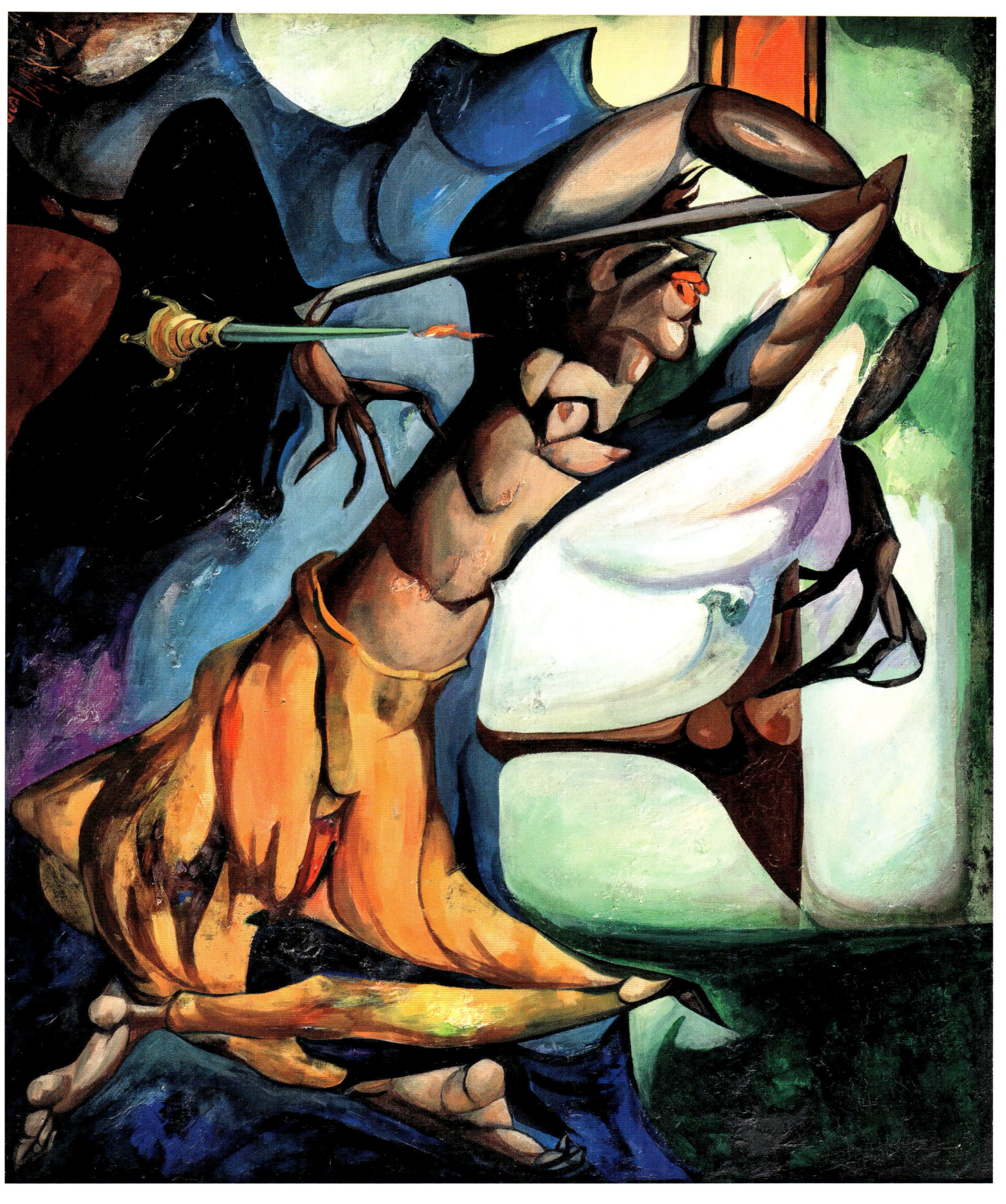

44
Sylvia in the Levantine Cocoon, 1964
Oil on canvas, 63 × 76 cm

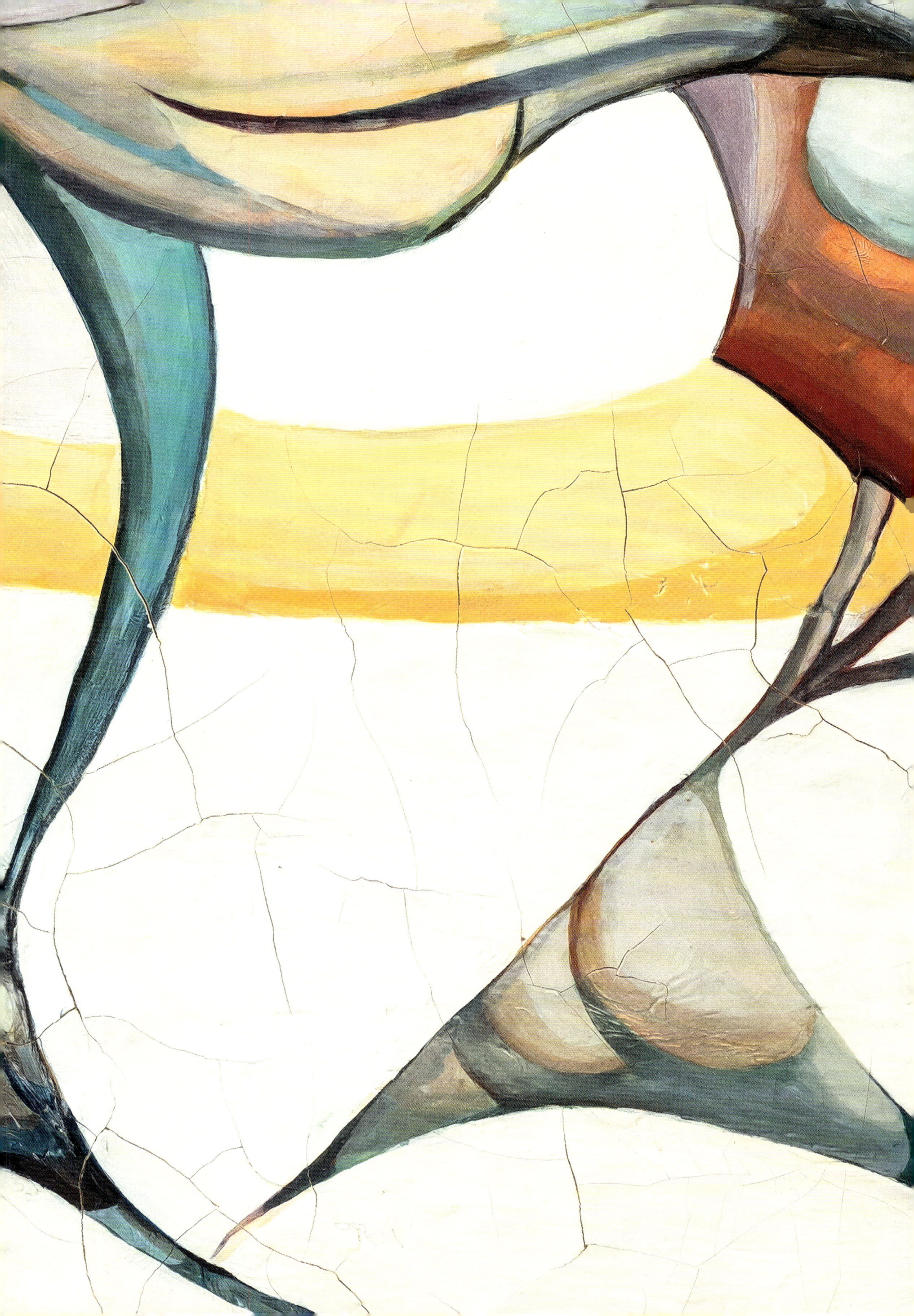

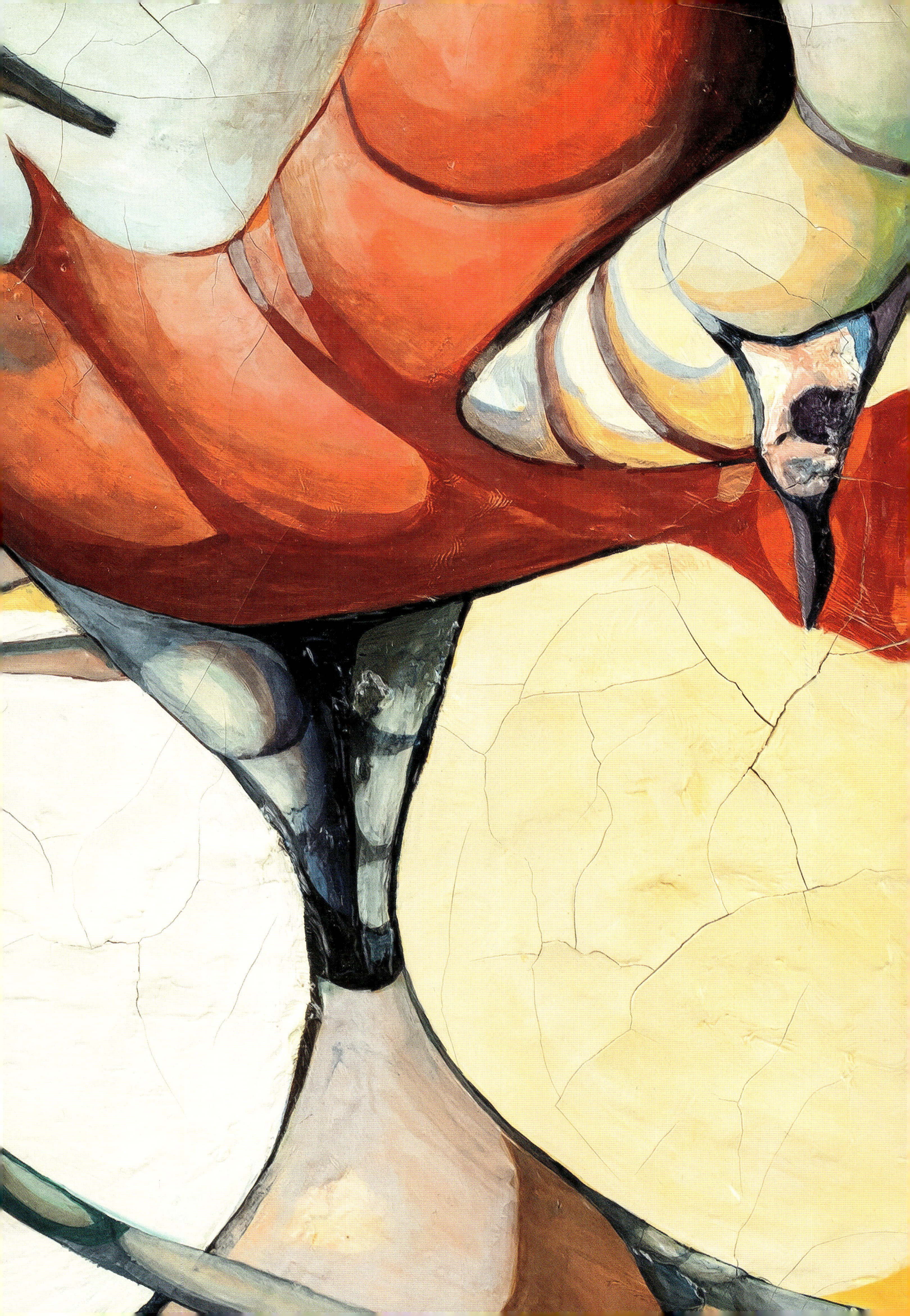

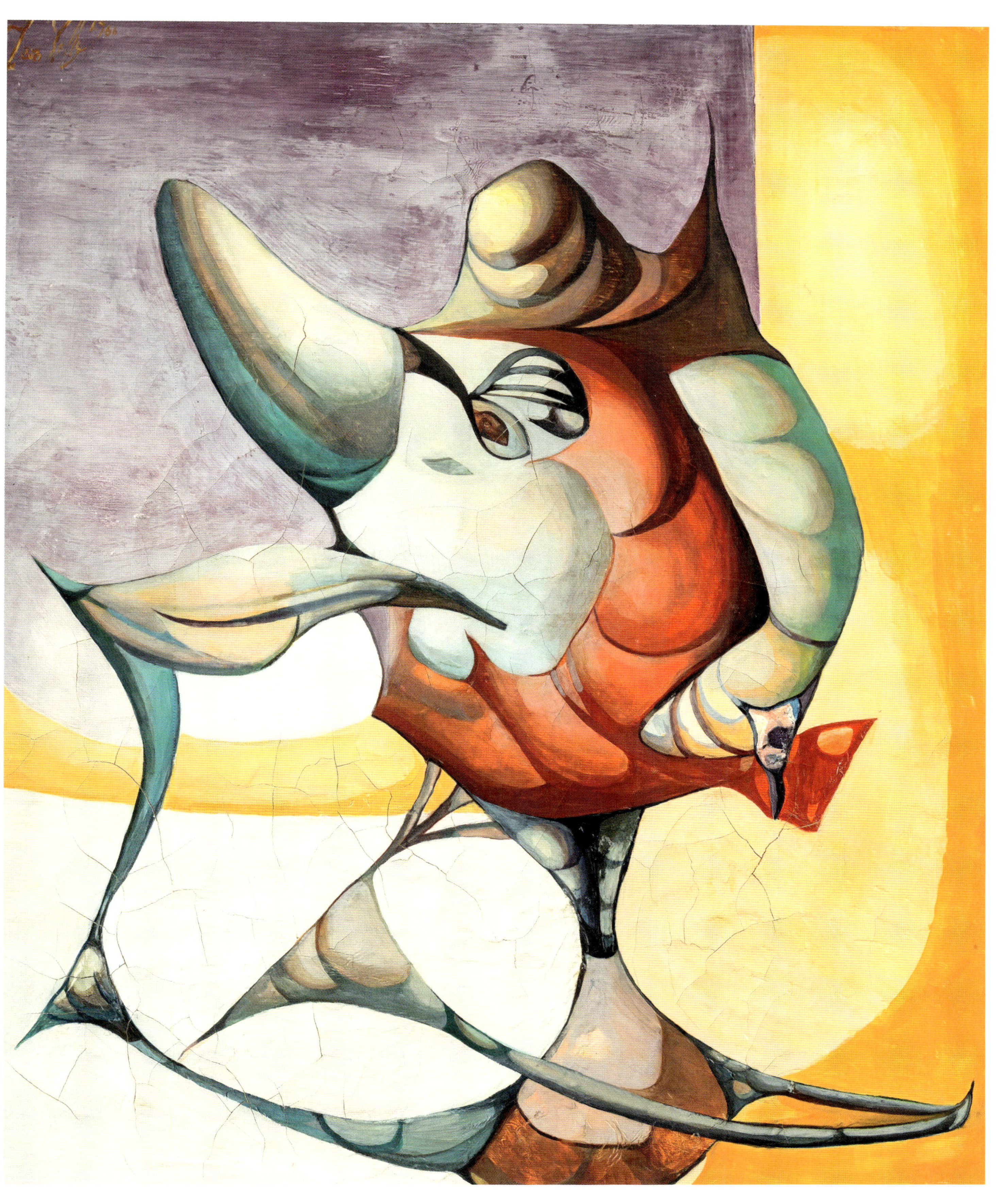

45
Sylvia as a Child, 1966
Oil on canvas, 55 × 46 cm

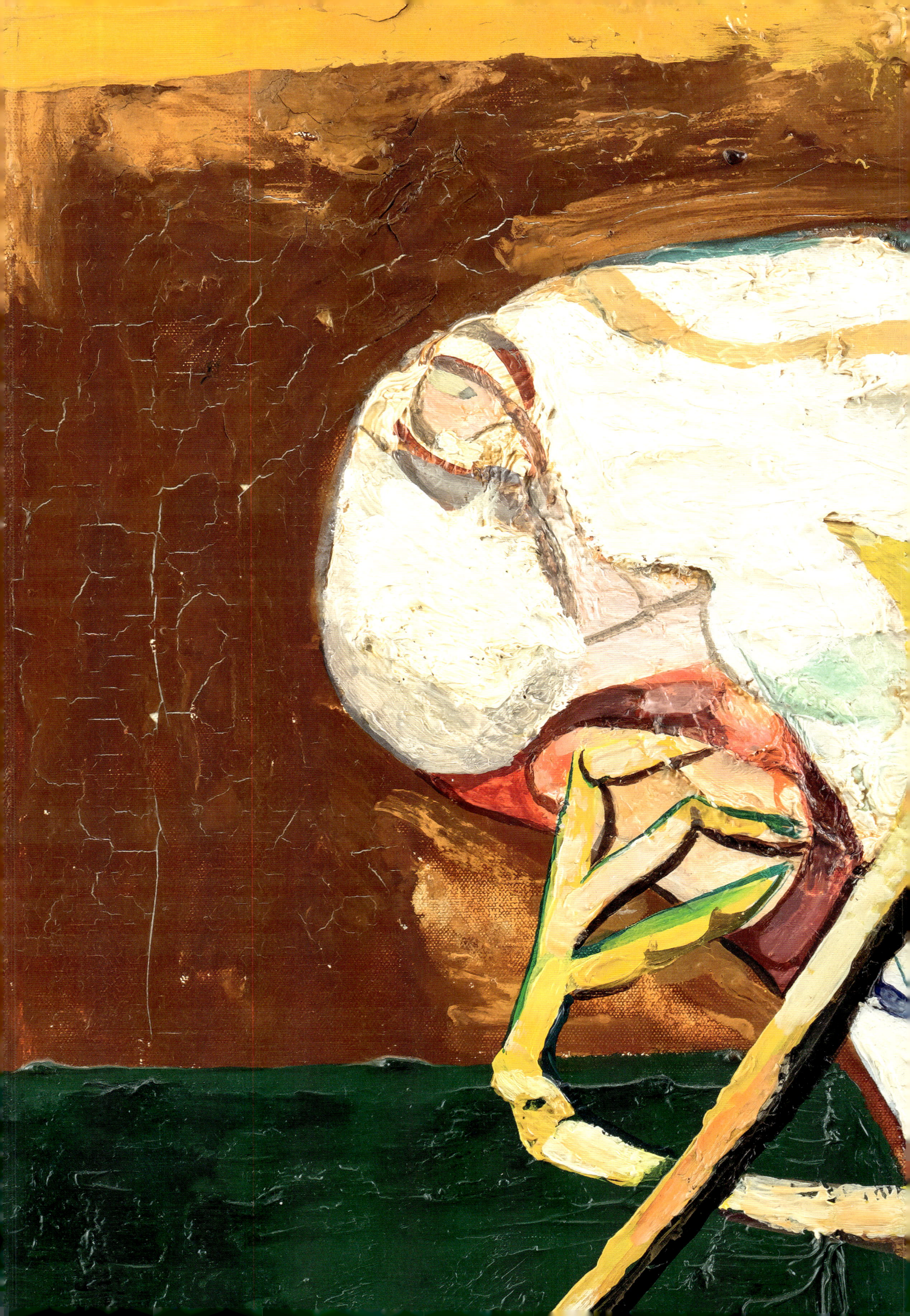

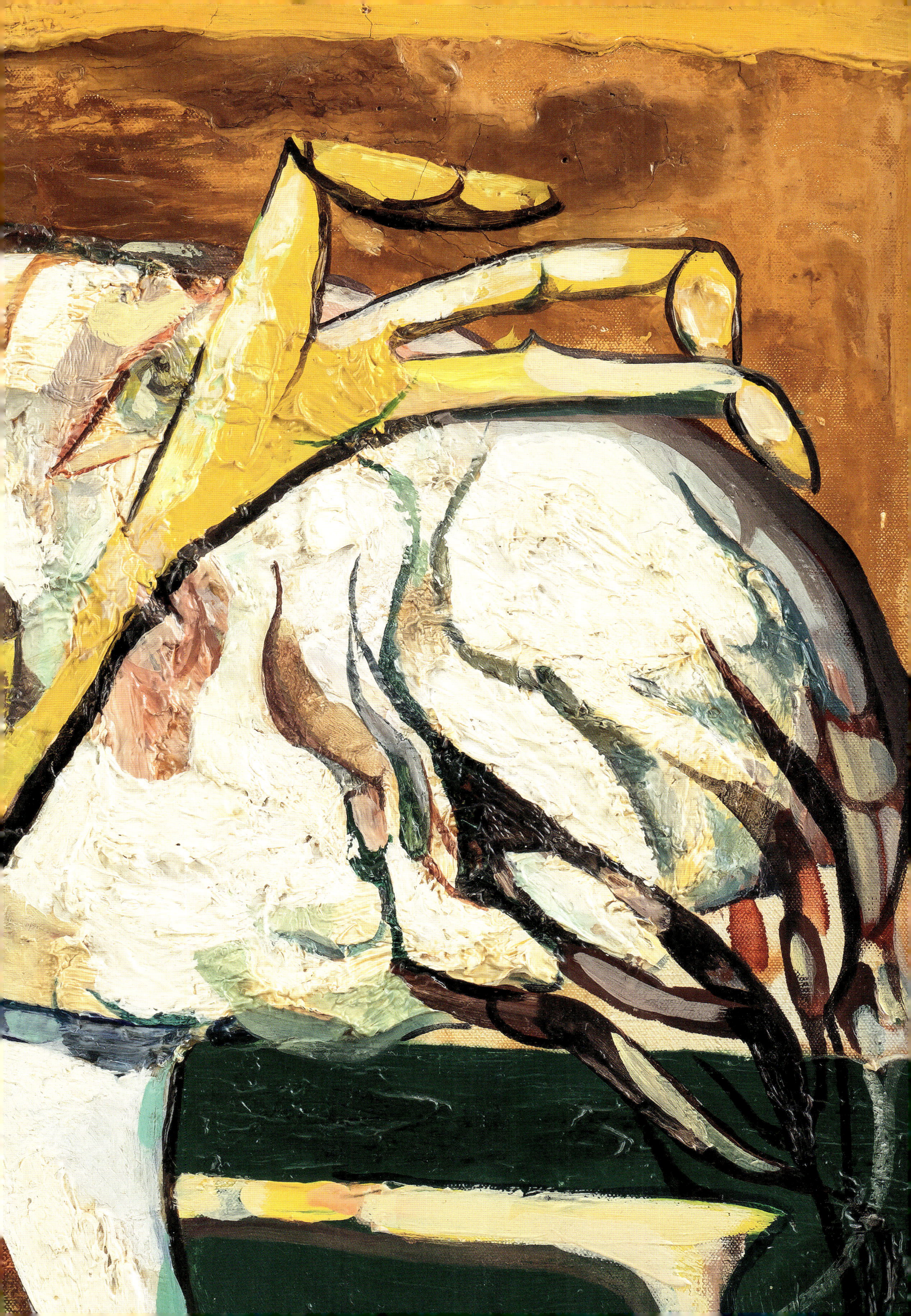

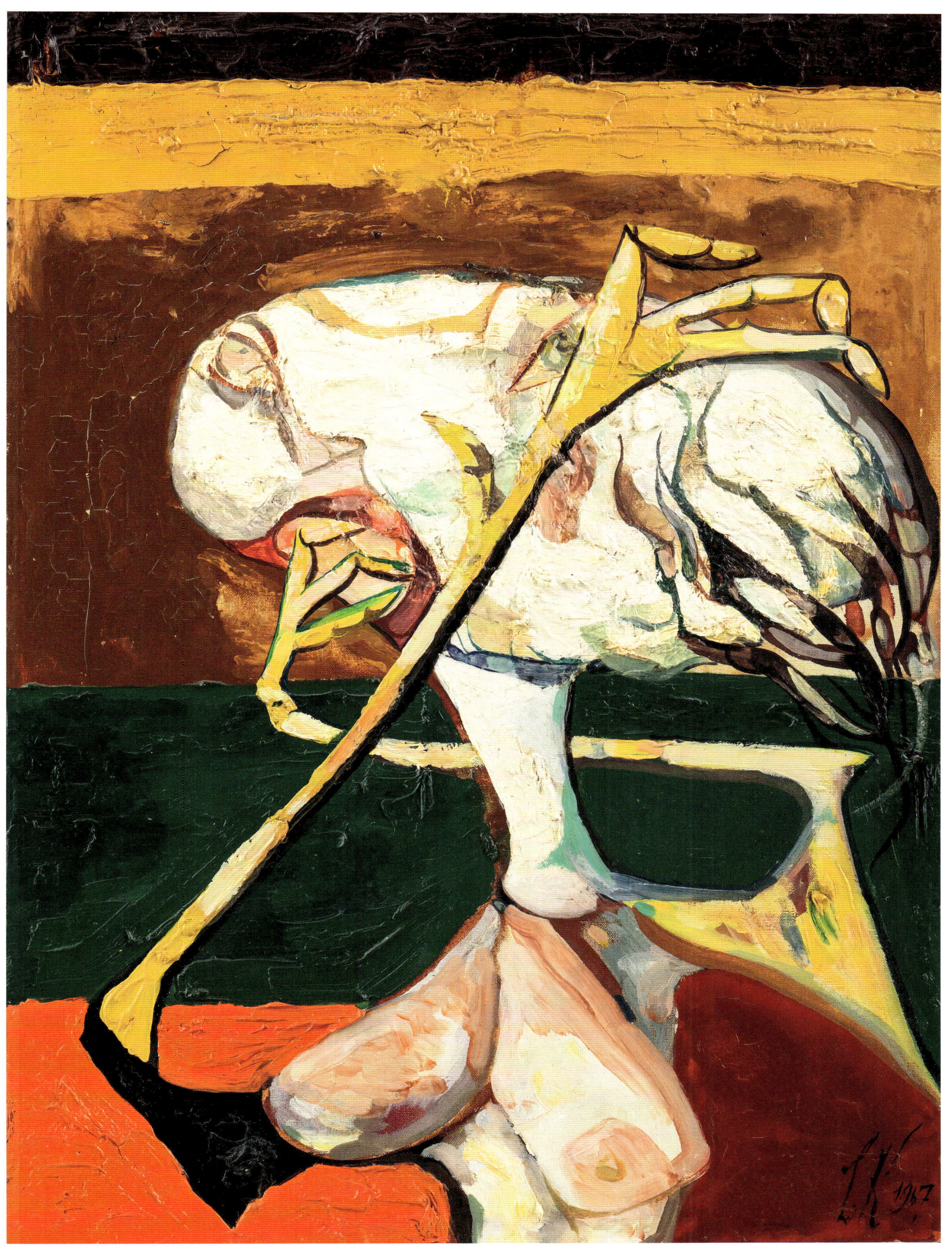

46
Frightened Child, 1967
Oil on canvas, 61 × 20.5 cm

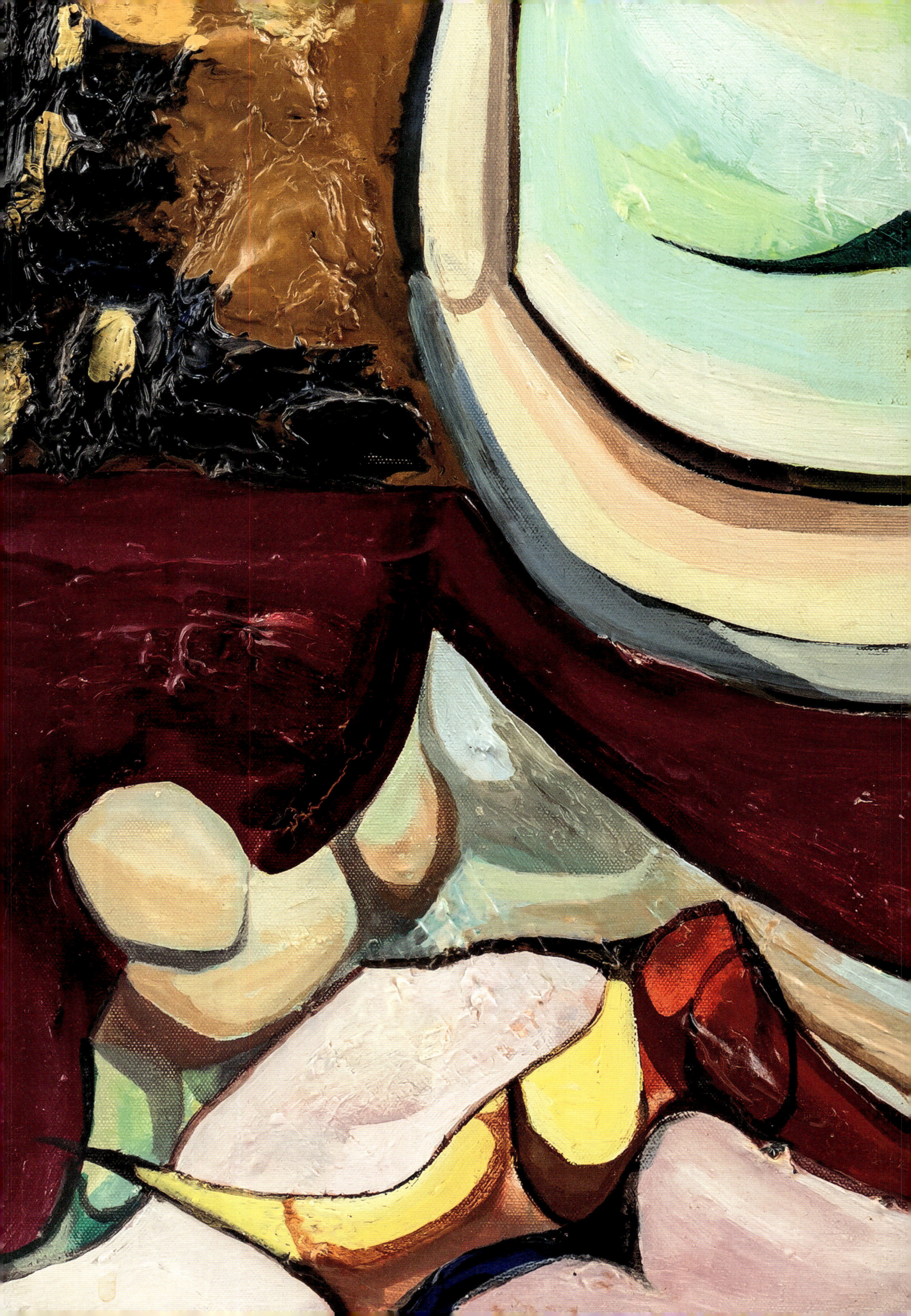

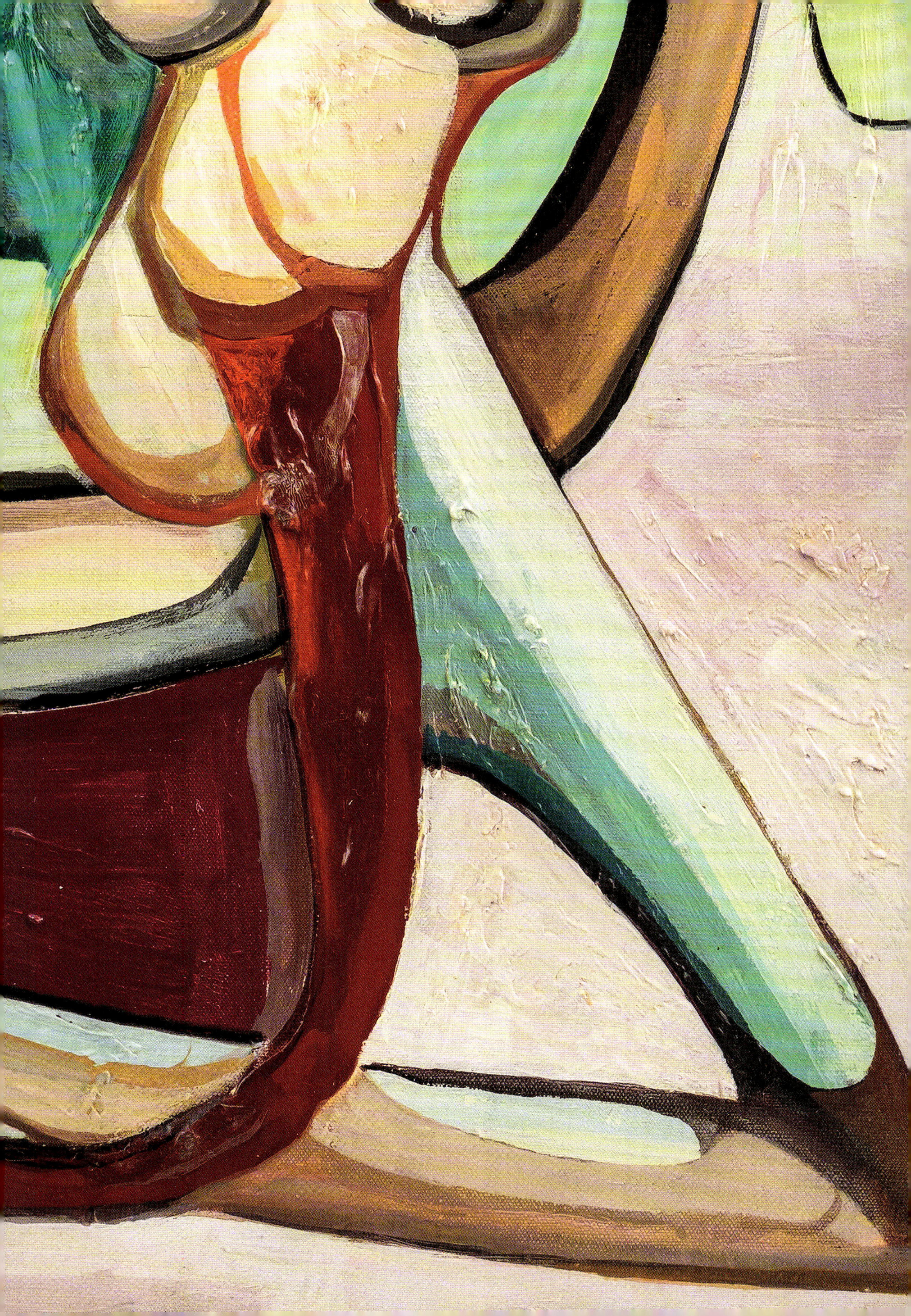

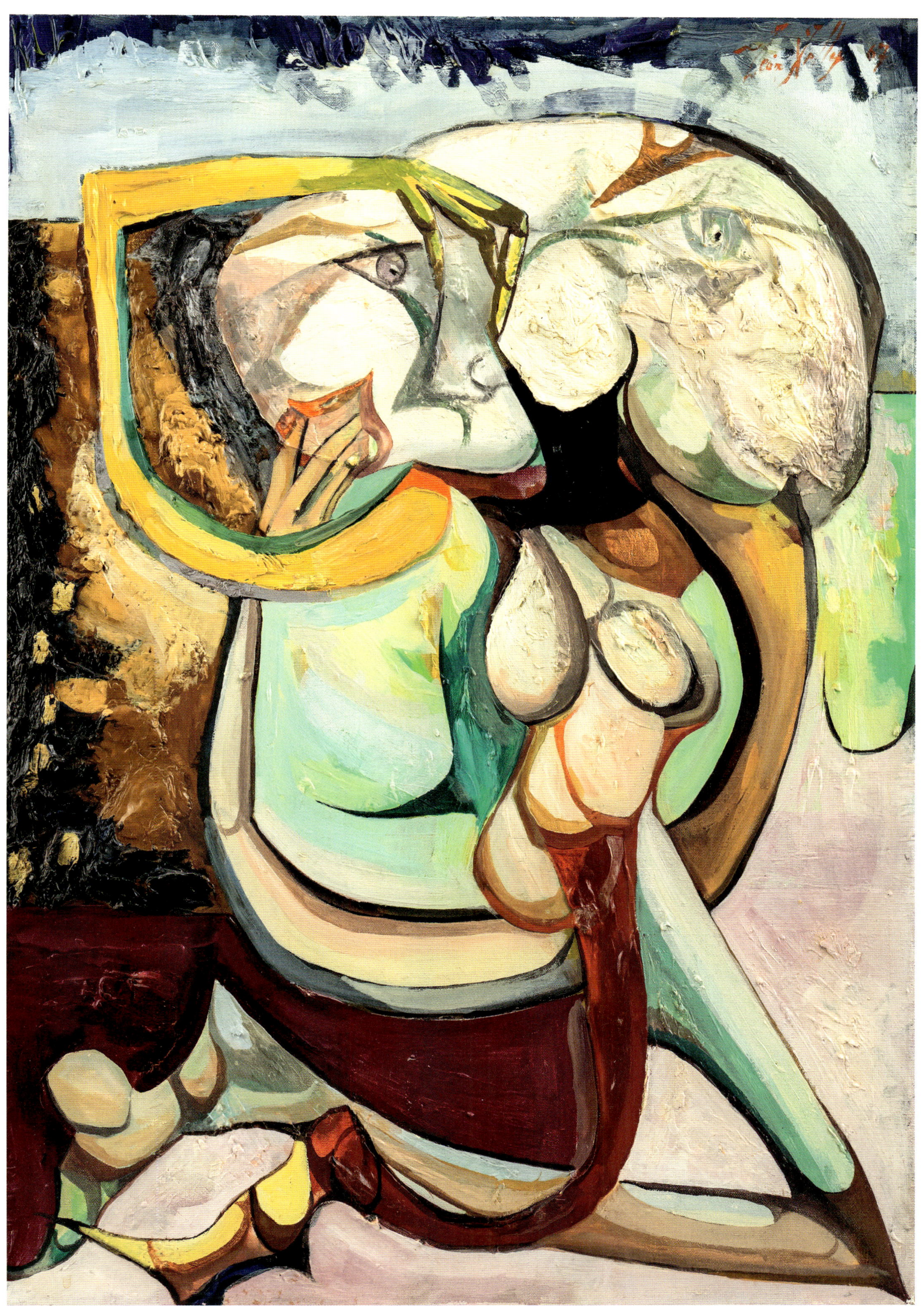

47
Kneeling Child, 1967
Oil on canvas, 61 × 46 cm

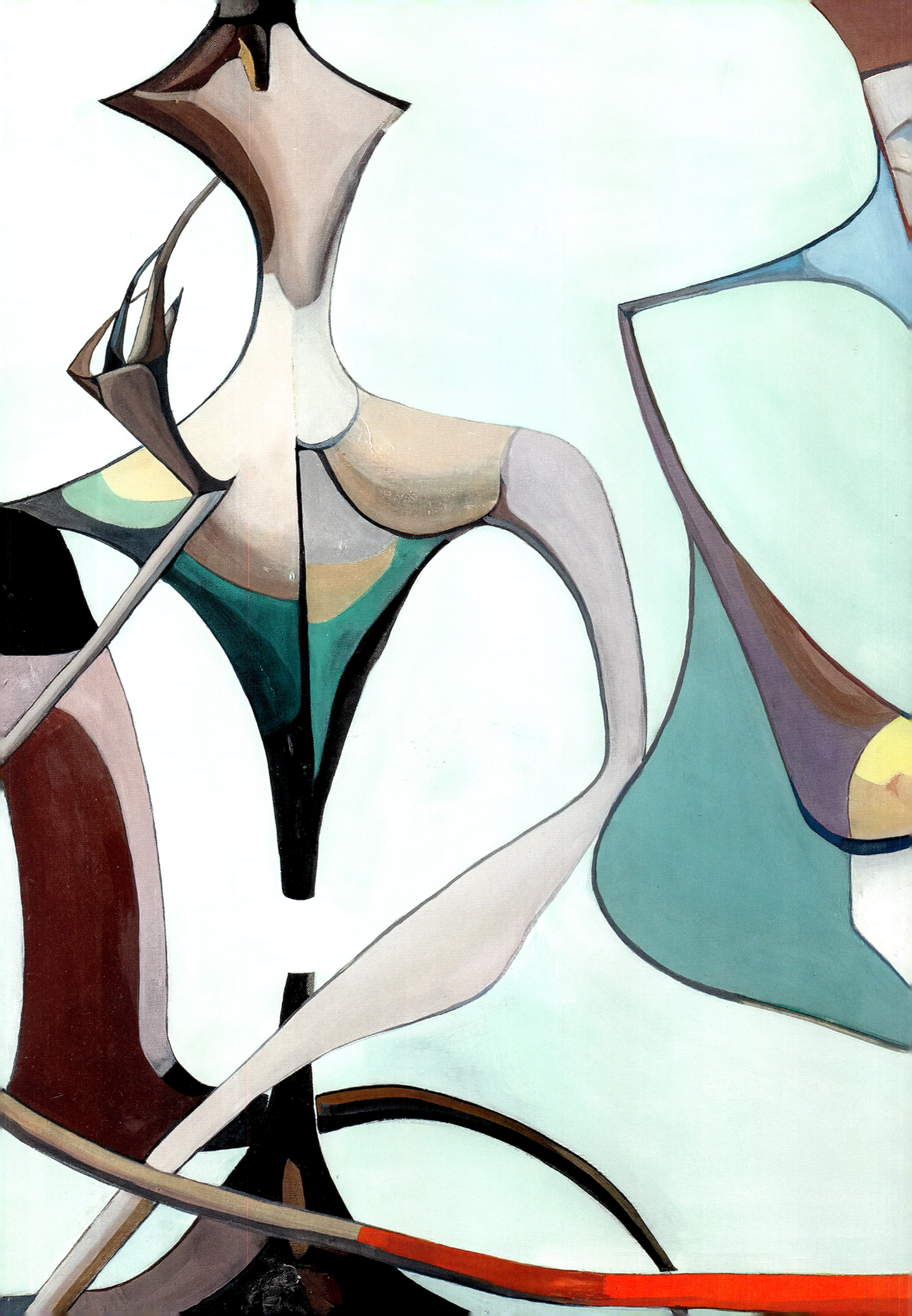

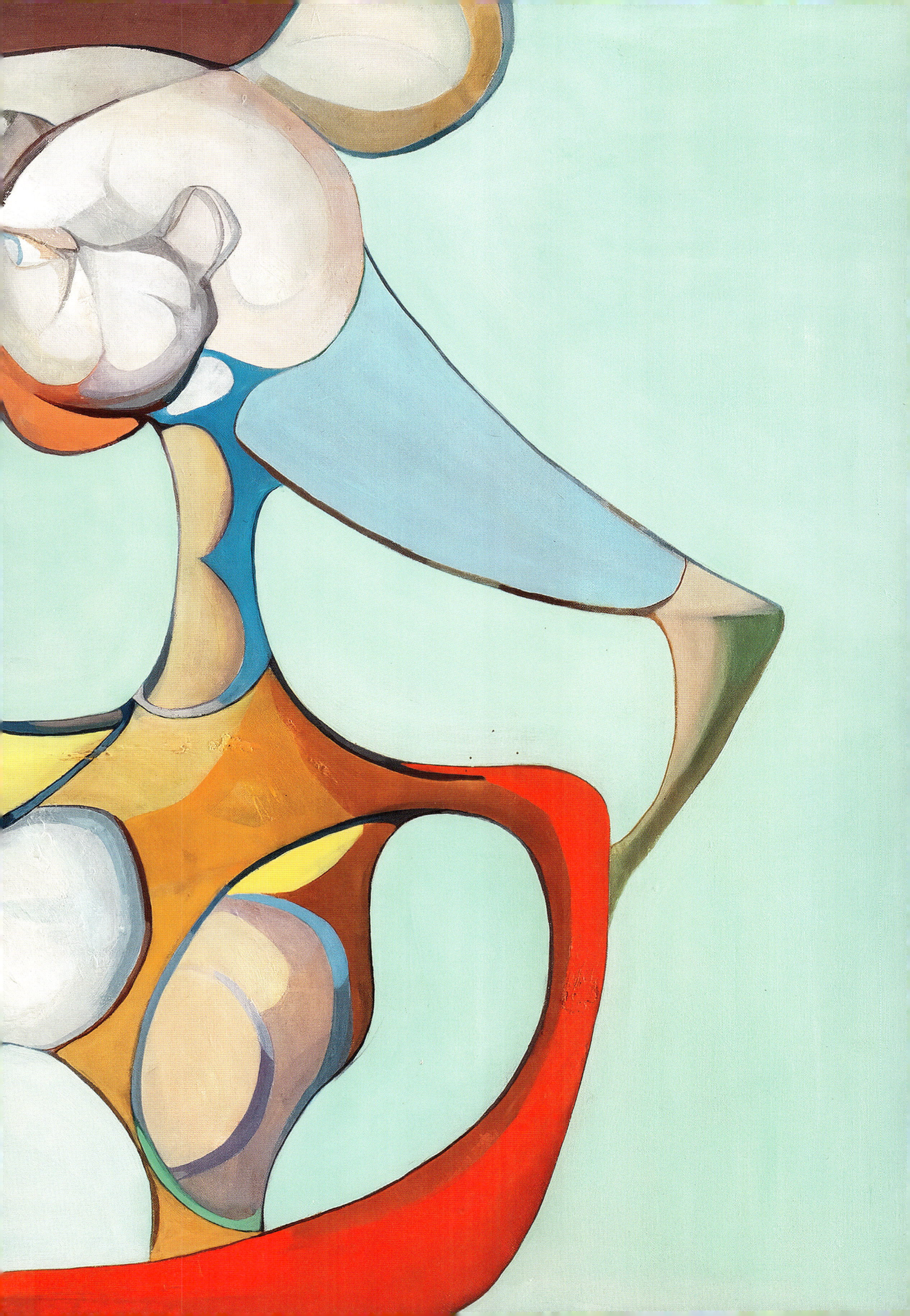

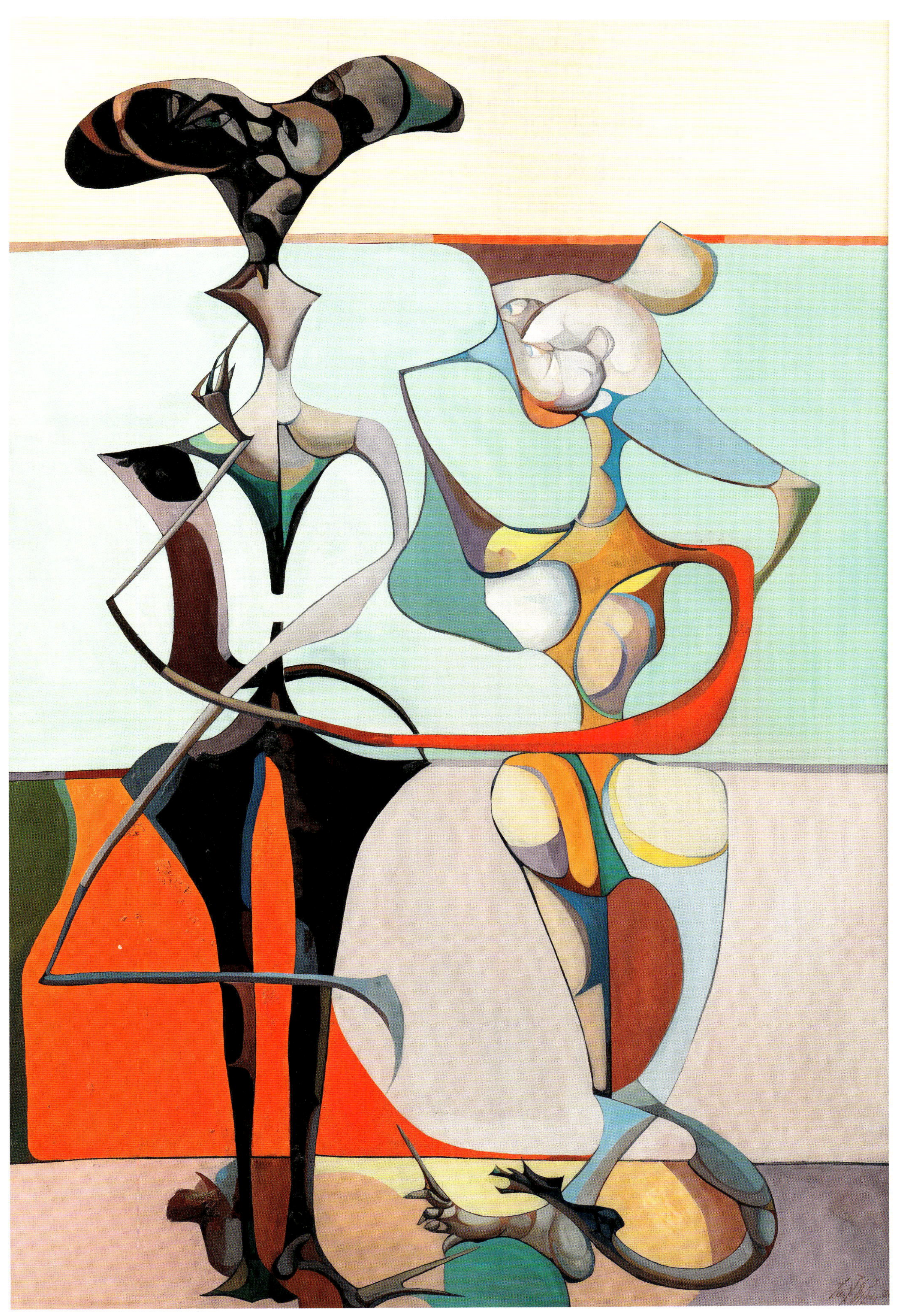

48
Moment of Harmony, 1937
Oil on canvas, 183 × 122 cm

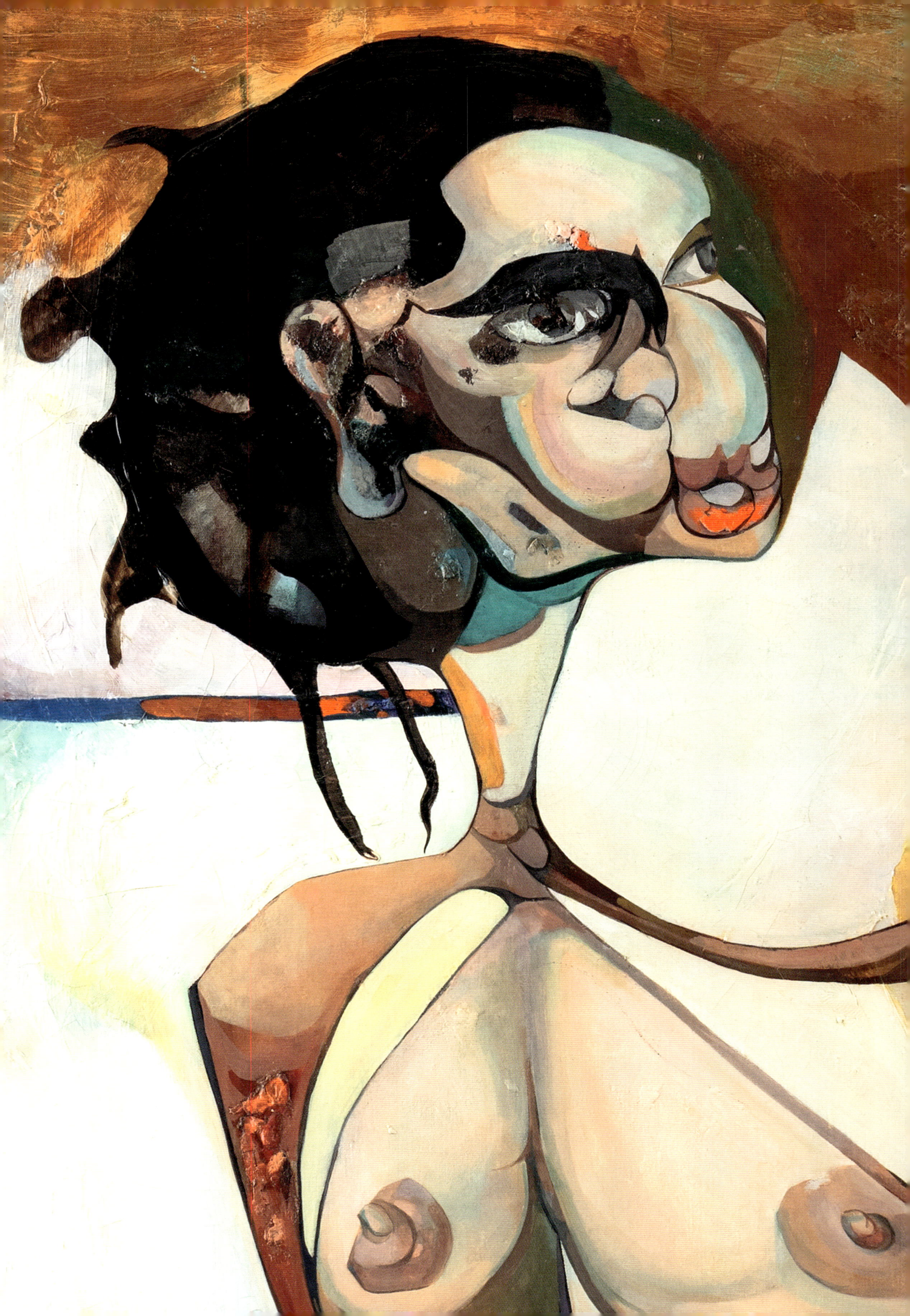

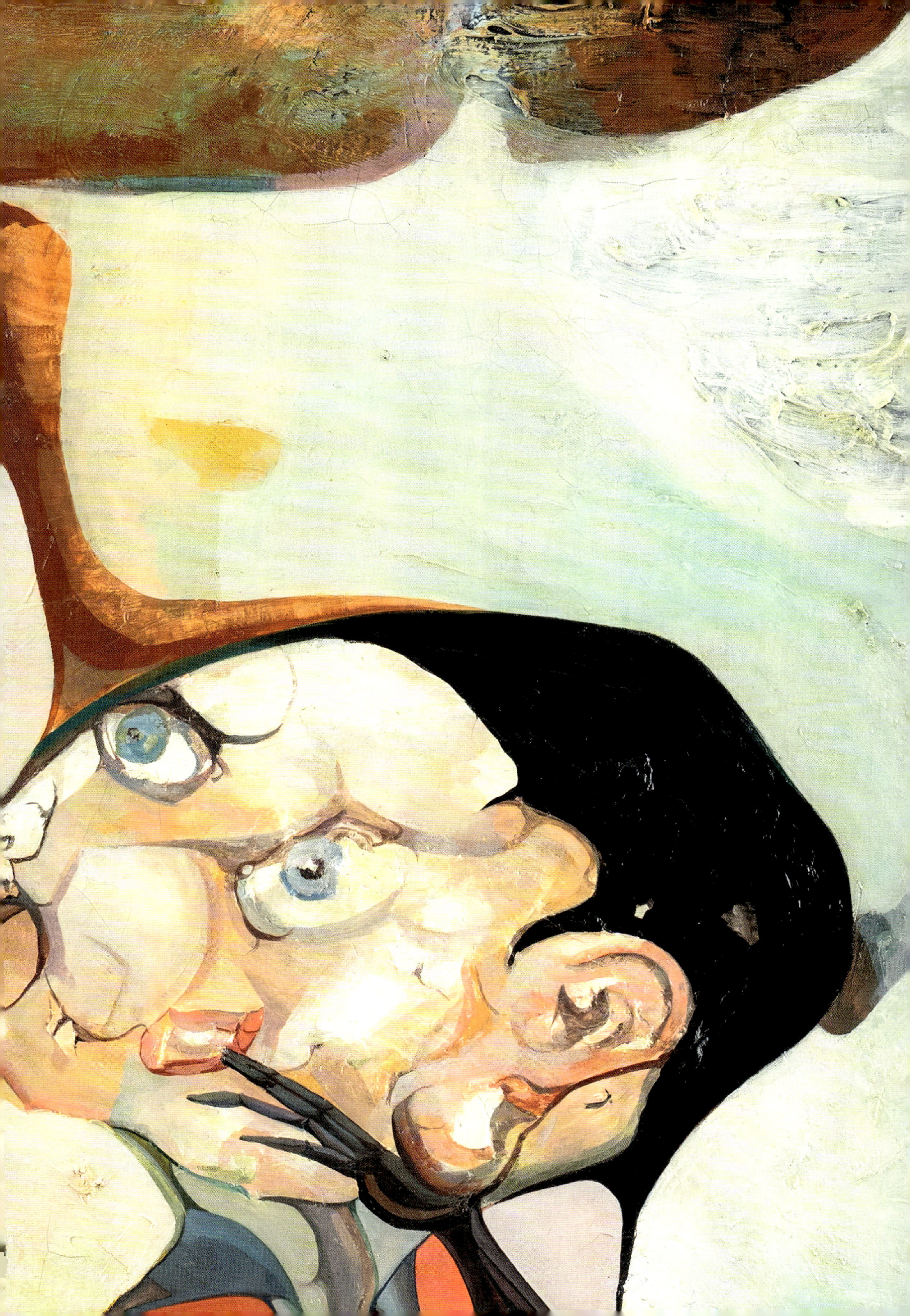

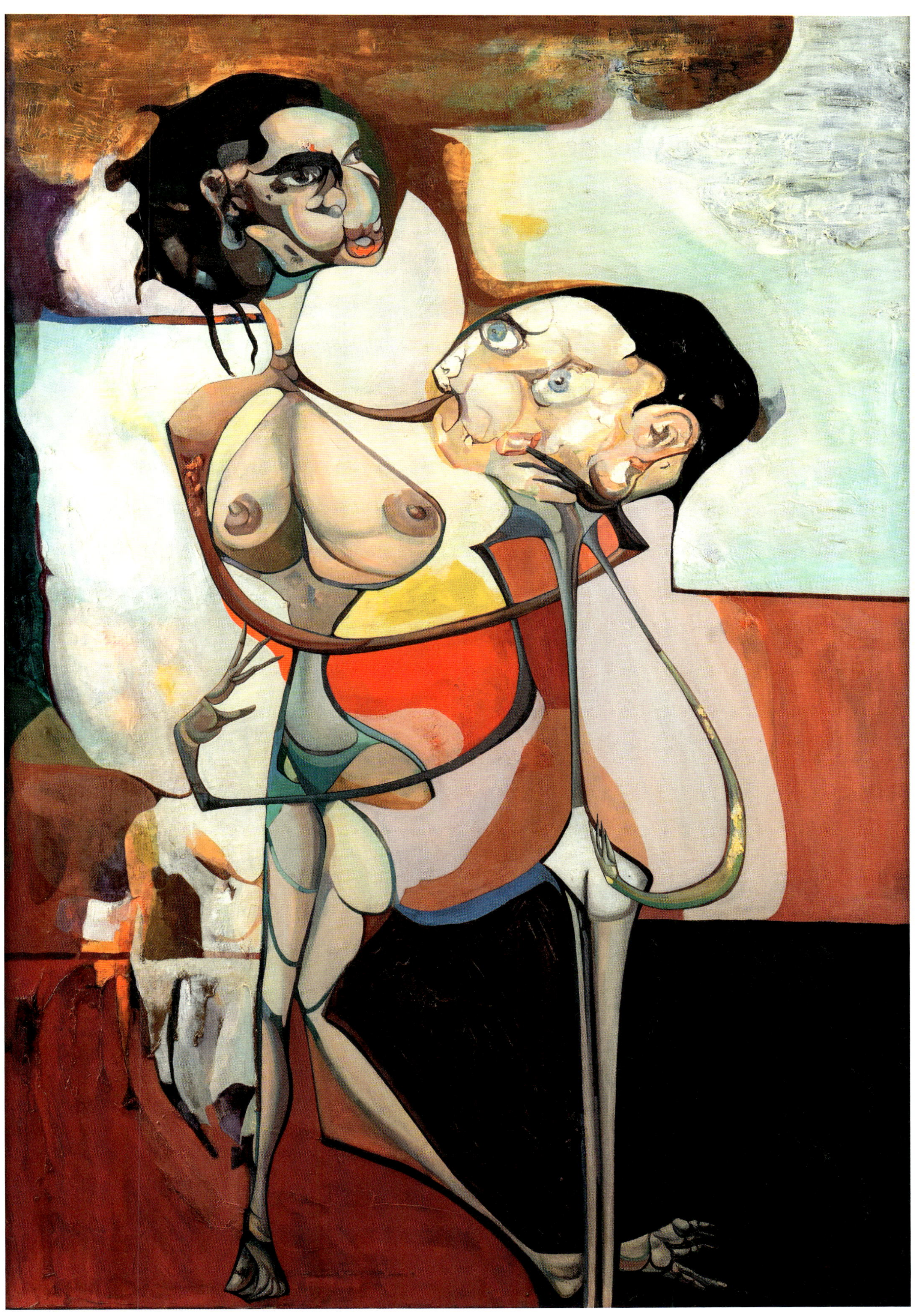

49
Encounter of the Adolescent Bather, 1968/69
Oil on canvas, 183 × 135 cm

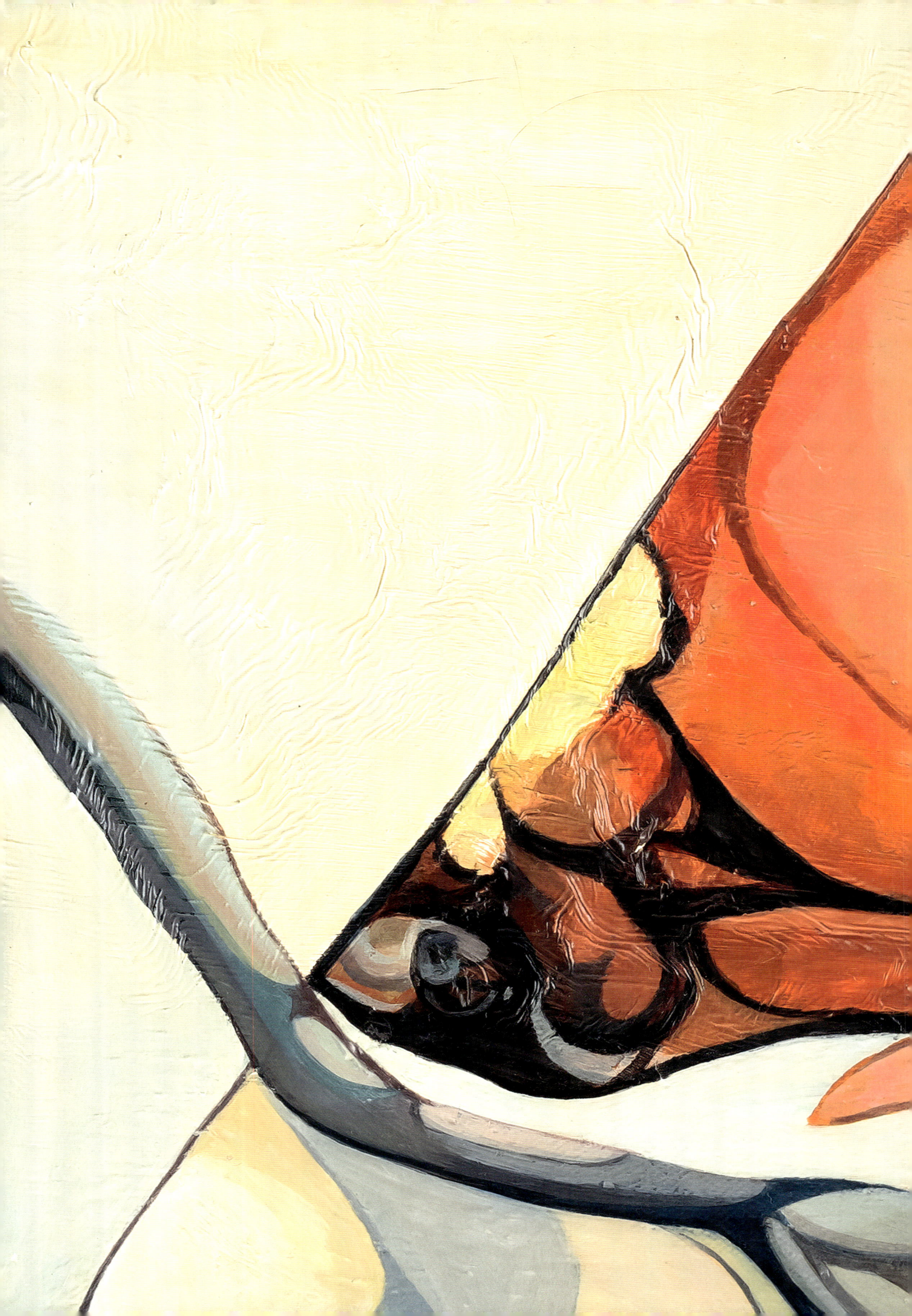

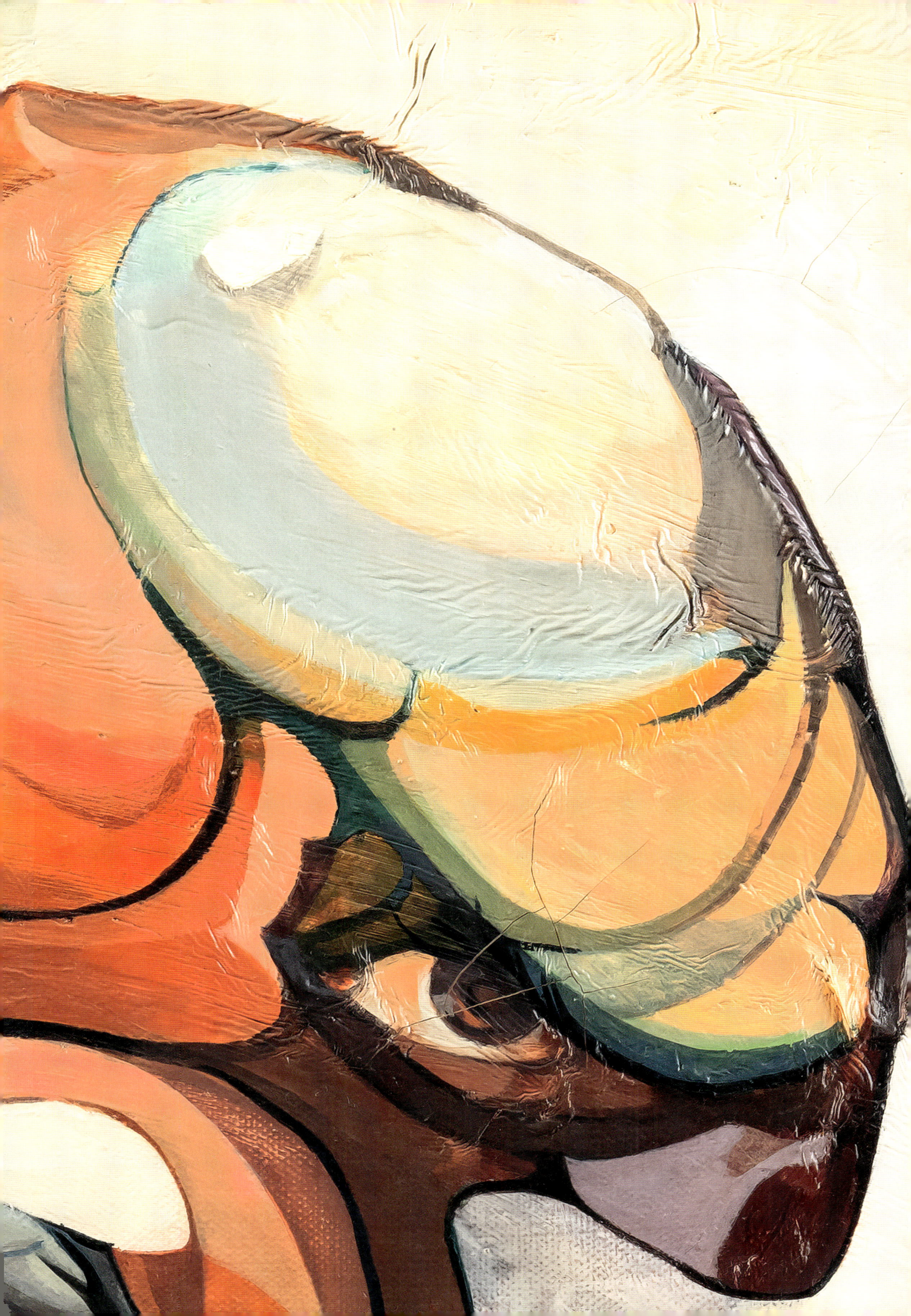

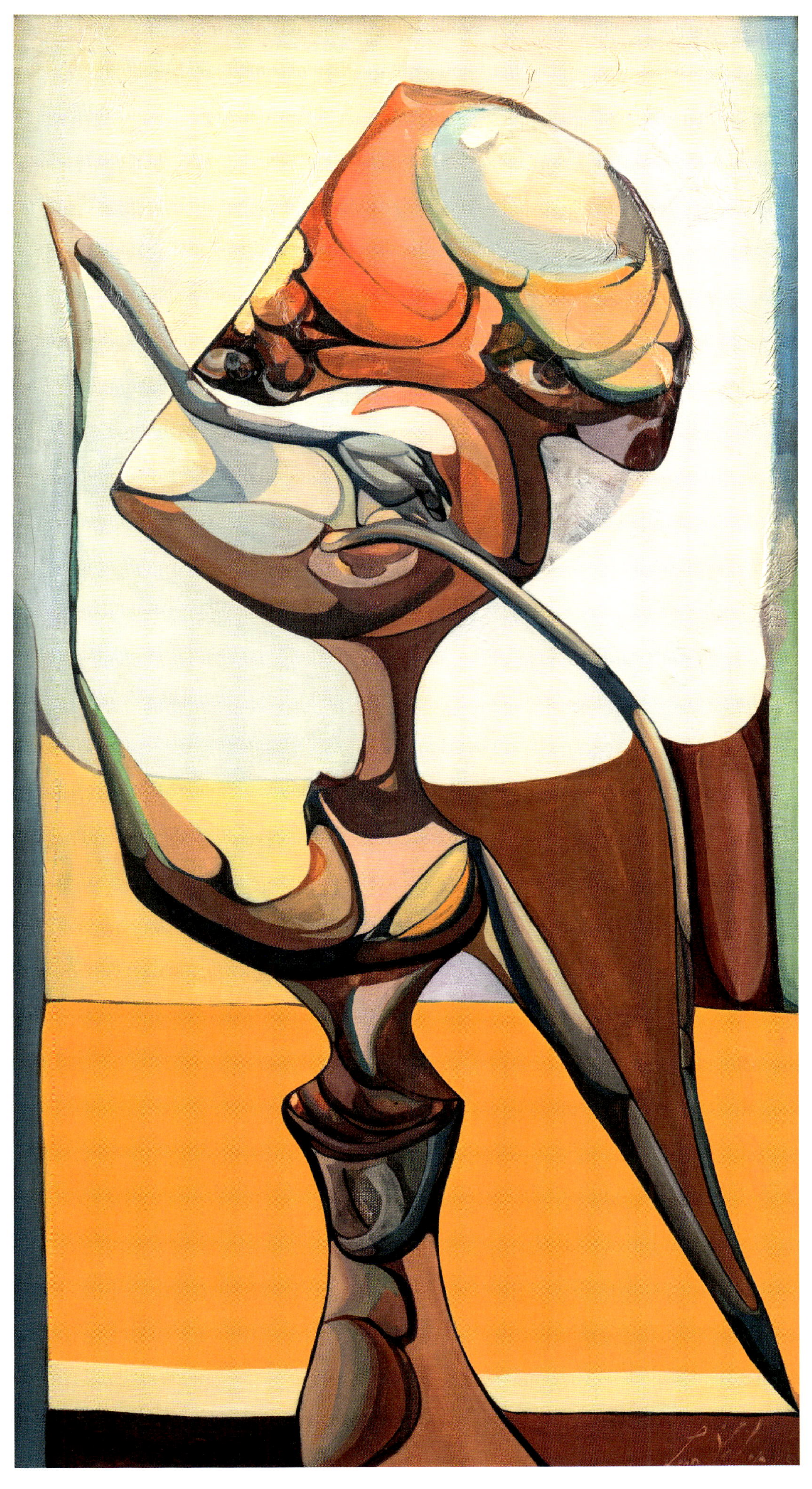

50
Woman Talking, 1969
Oil on canvas, 66 × 35.5 cm

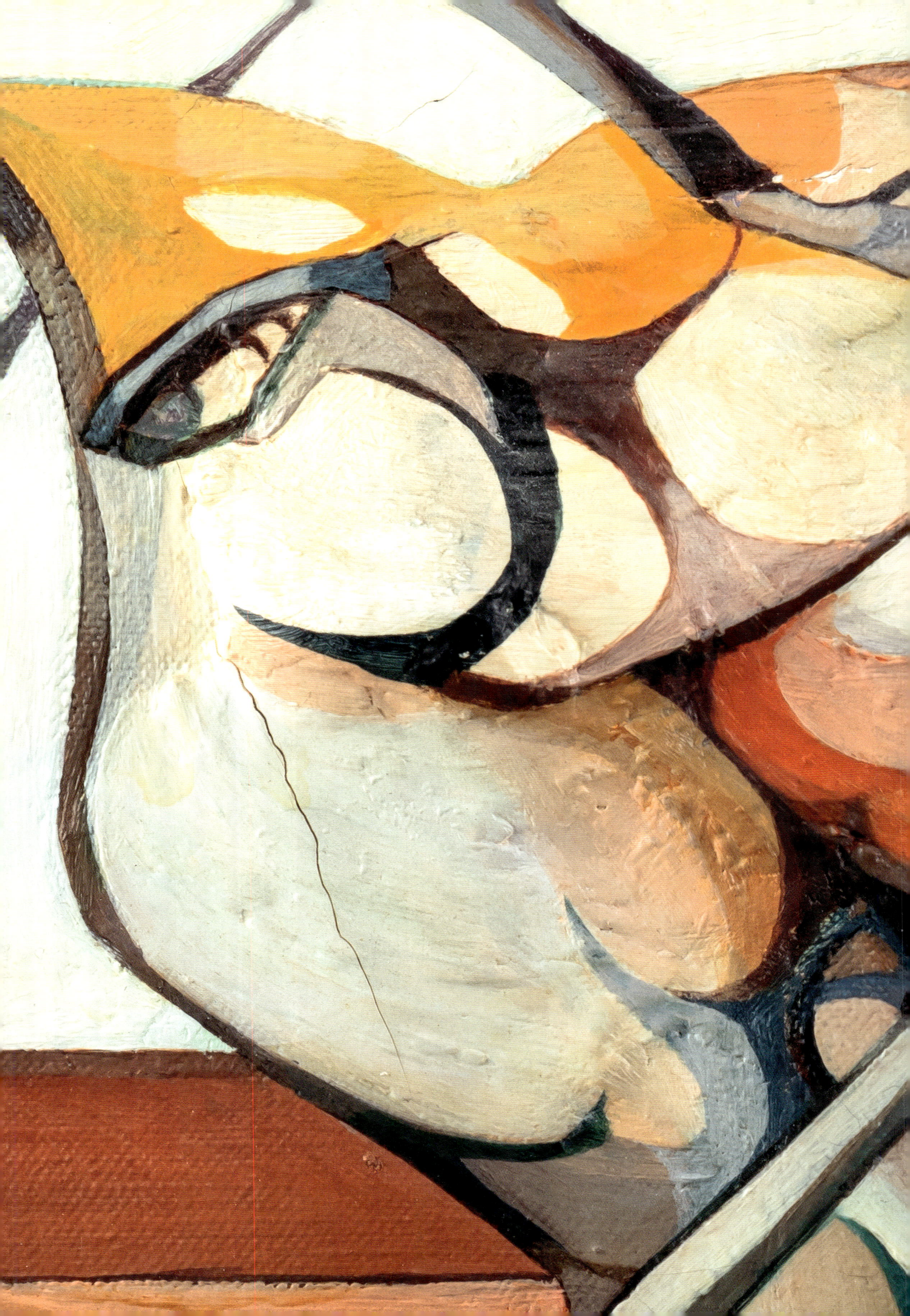

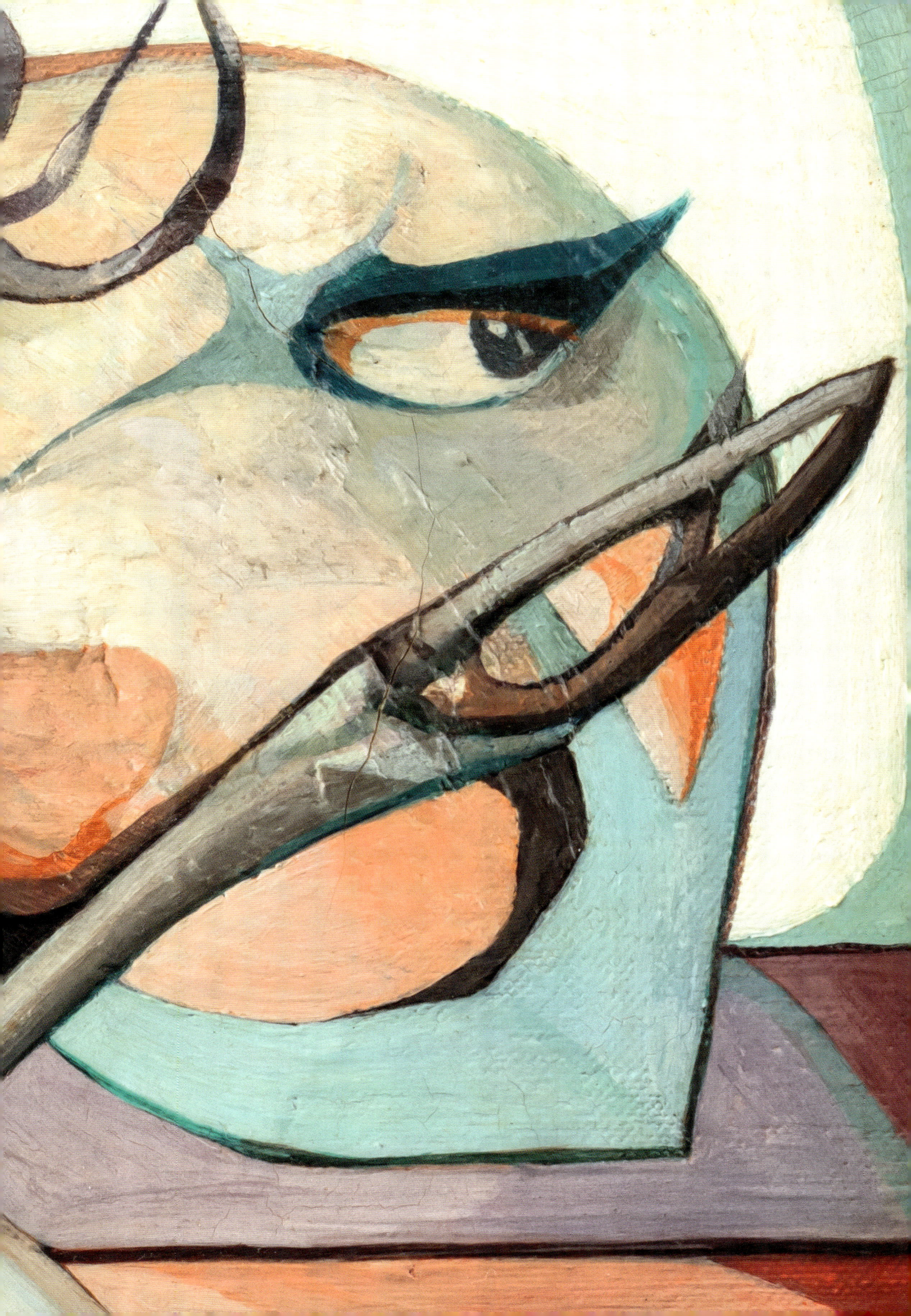

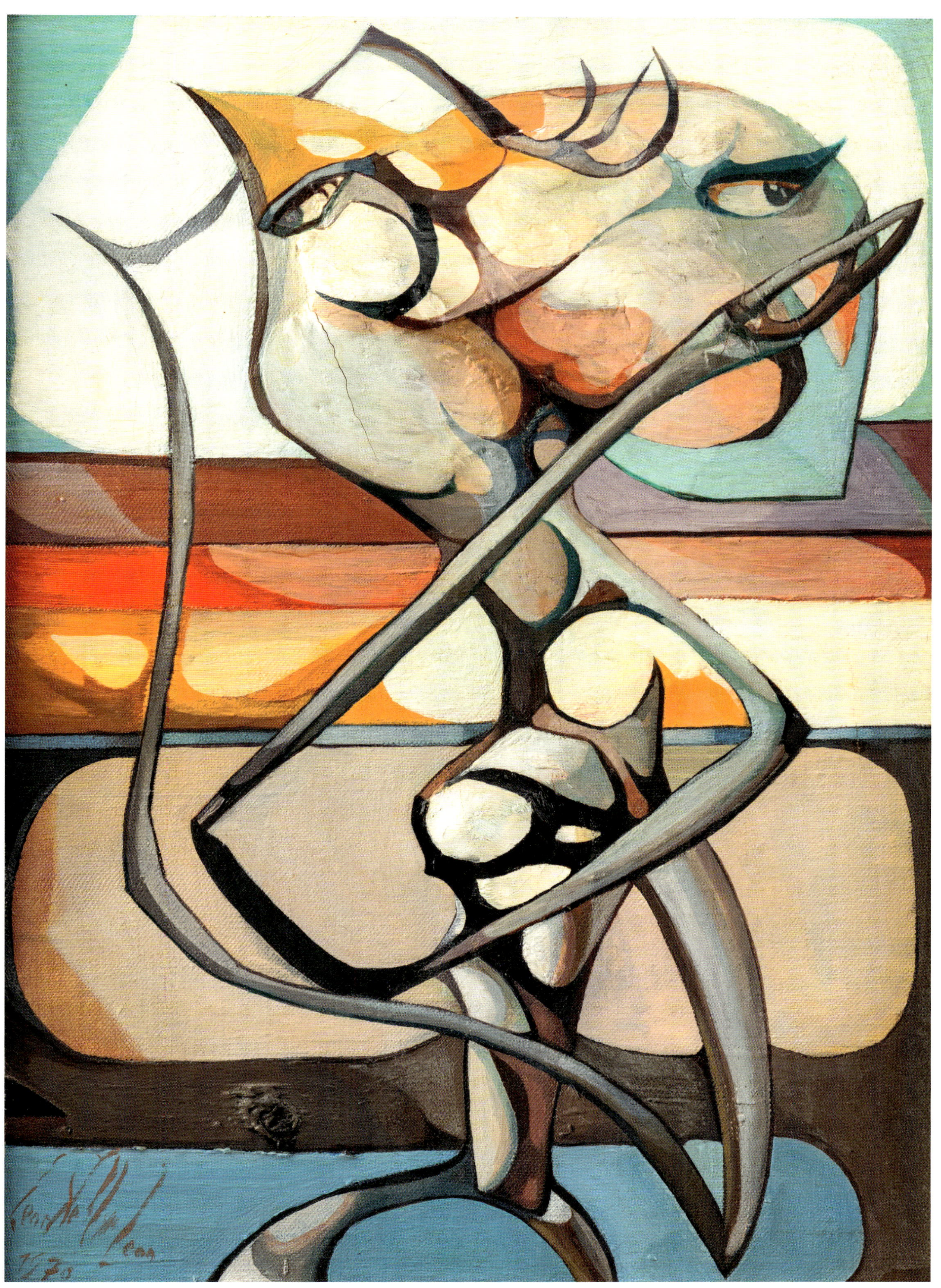

51
Child Bather at San Vincente Cove, 1970
Oil on canvas, 35.5 × 25.5 cm

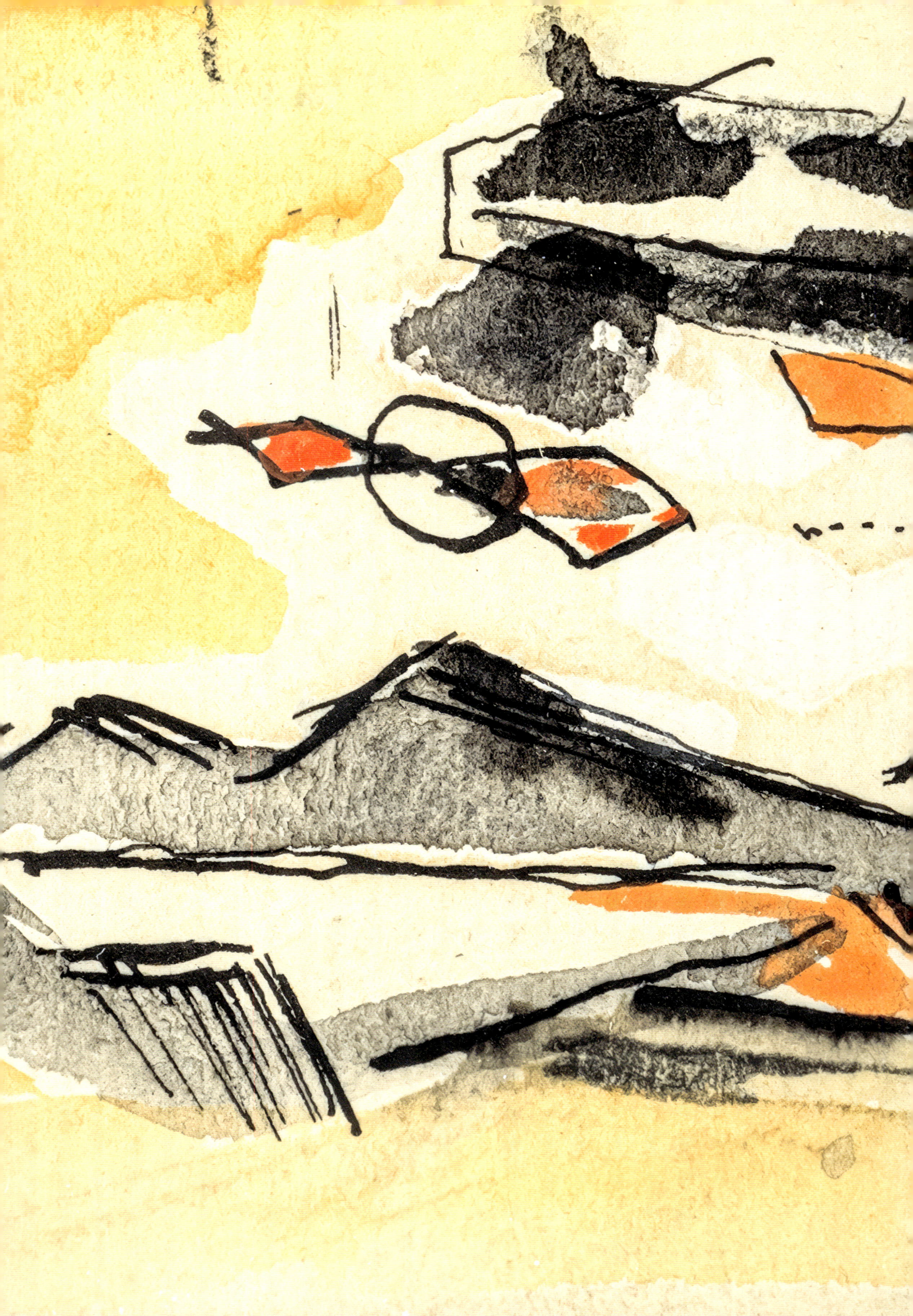

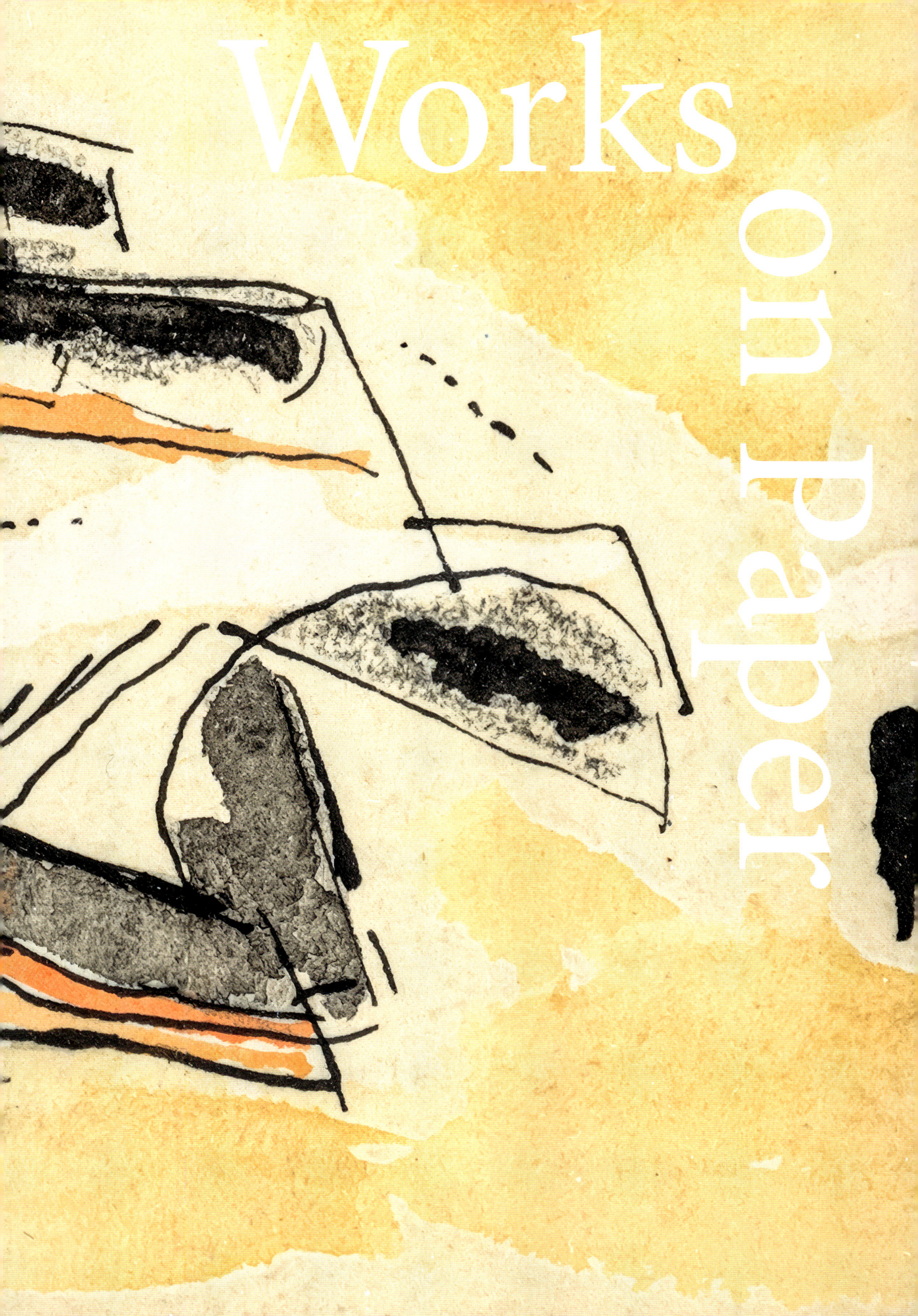
Works
on
Paper

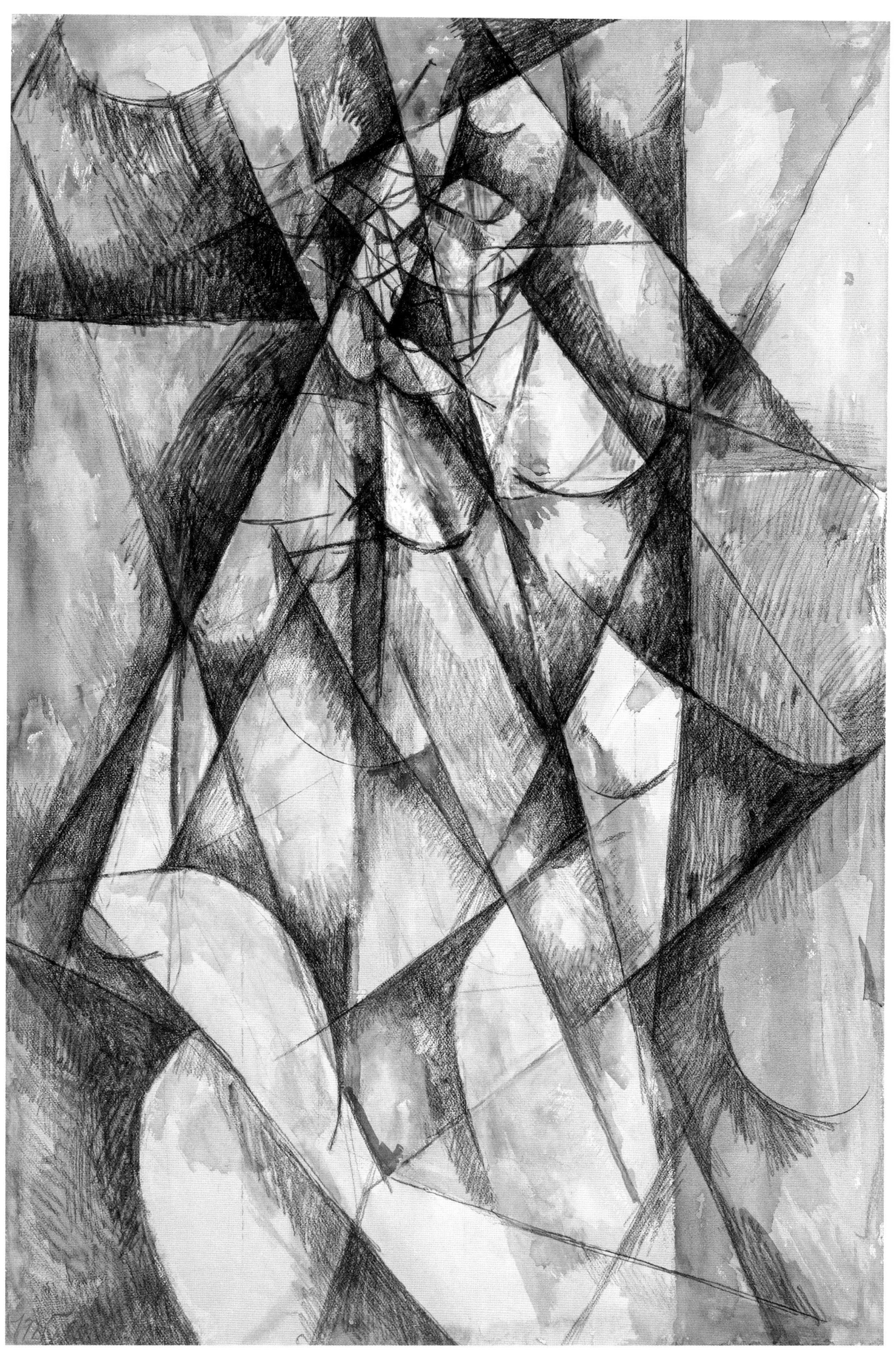

52
Untitled, ca. 1921
Charcoal and gouache, 96 × 64 cm

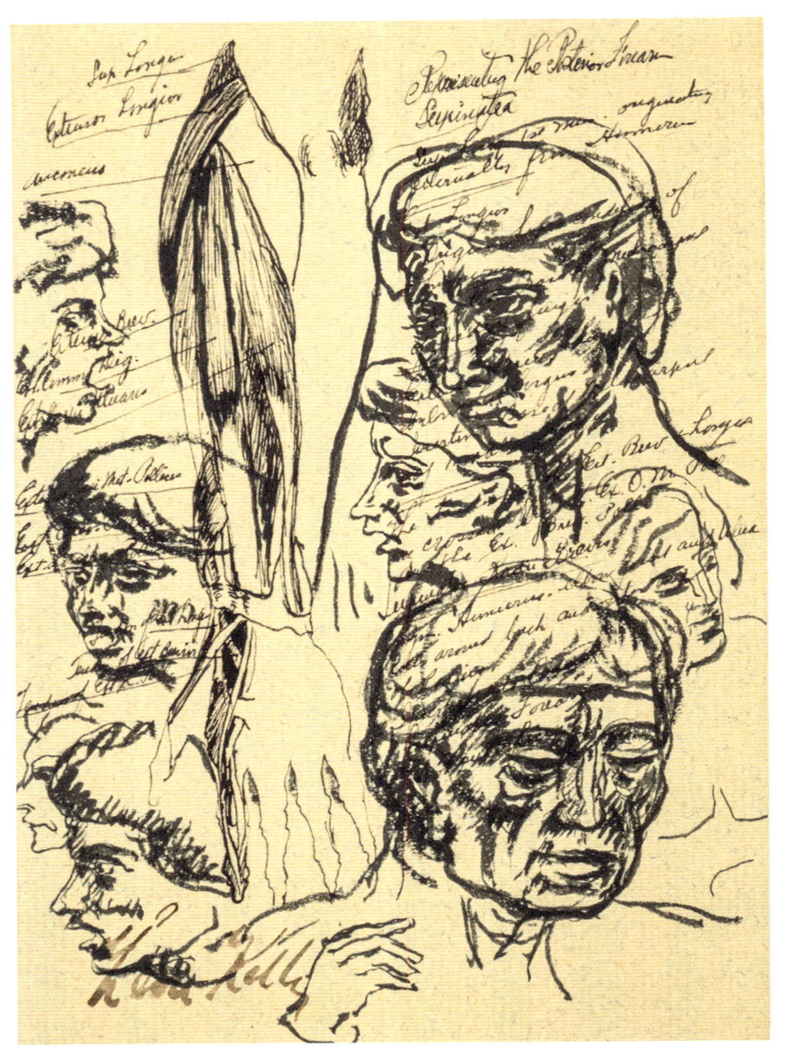

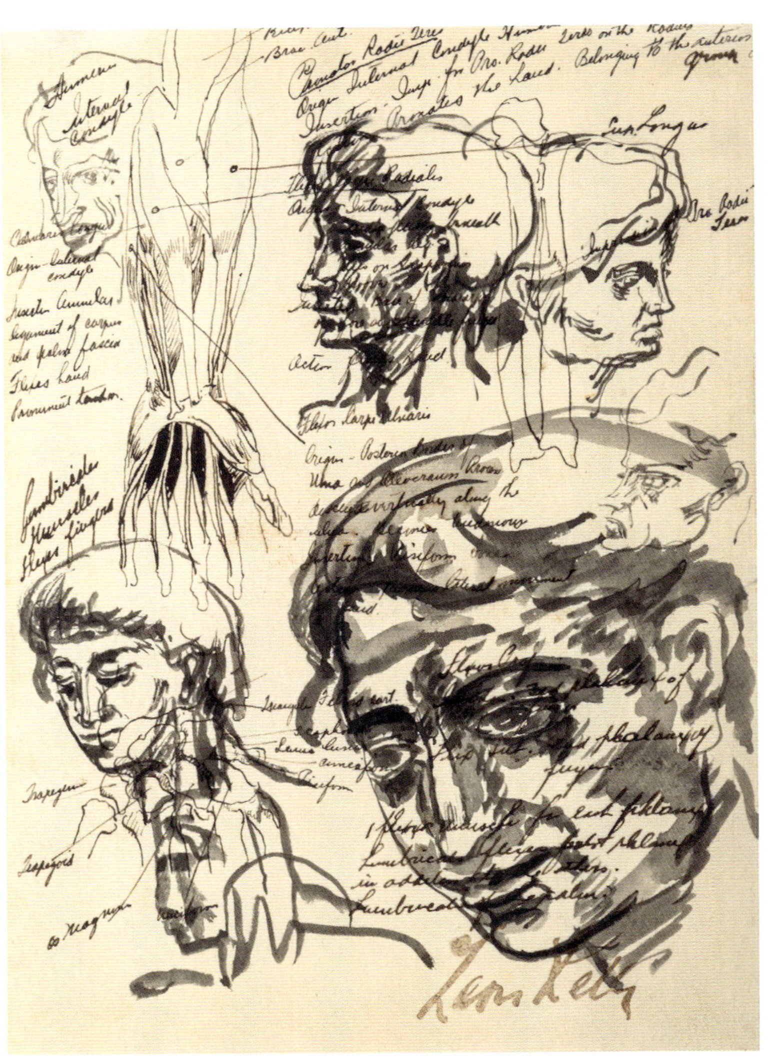

53
Untitled, ca. 1922
Ink, 18 × 12.5 cm

54
Untitled, ca. 1922
Ink, 18.5 × 13 cm

55
Untitled, ca. 1922
Ink, 24.5 × 24 cm

56
Untitled, ca.1922
Ink, 24 × 24.5 cm

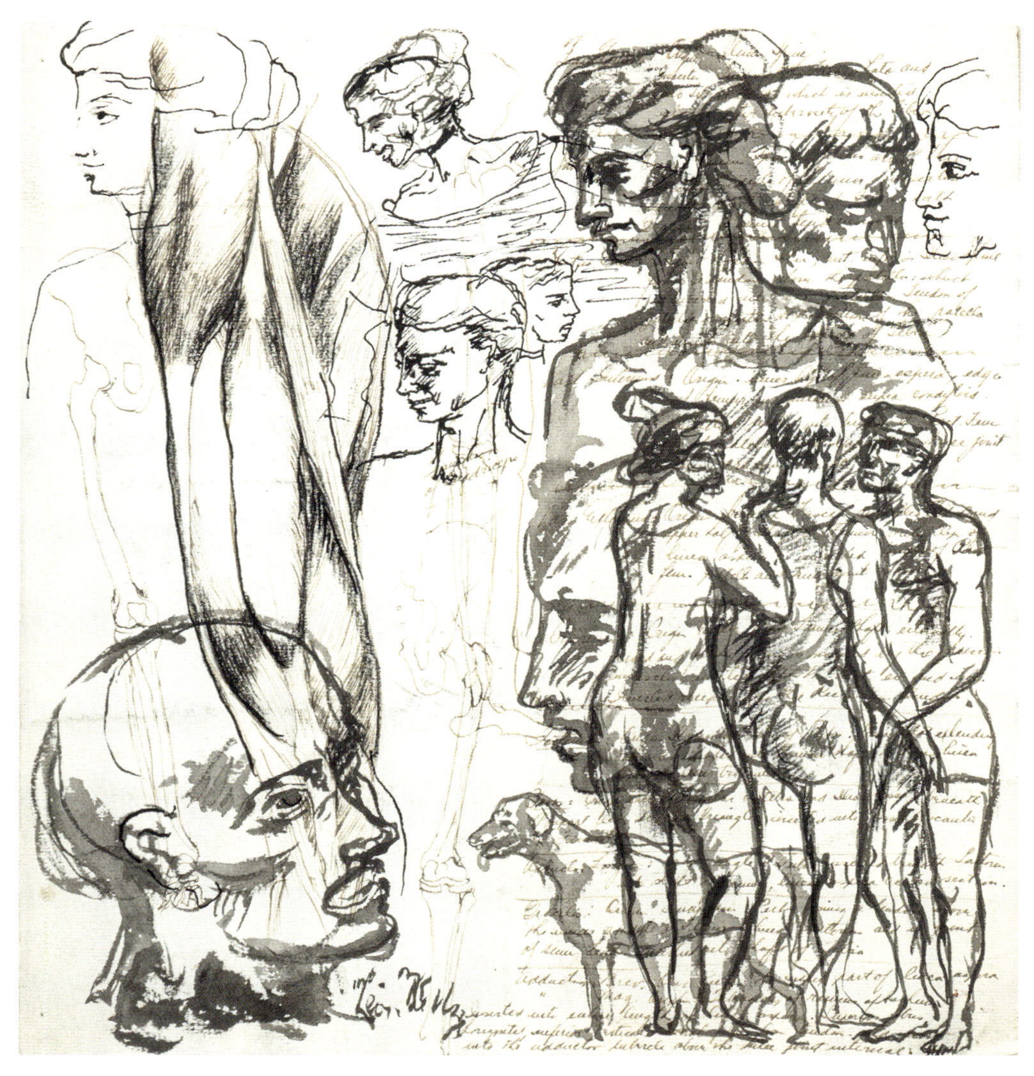

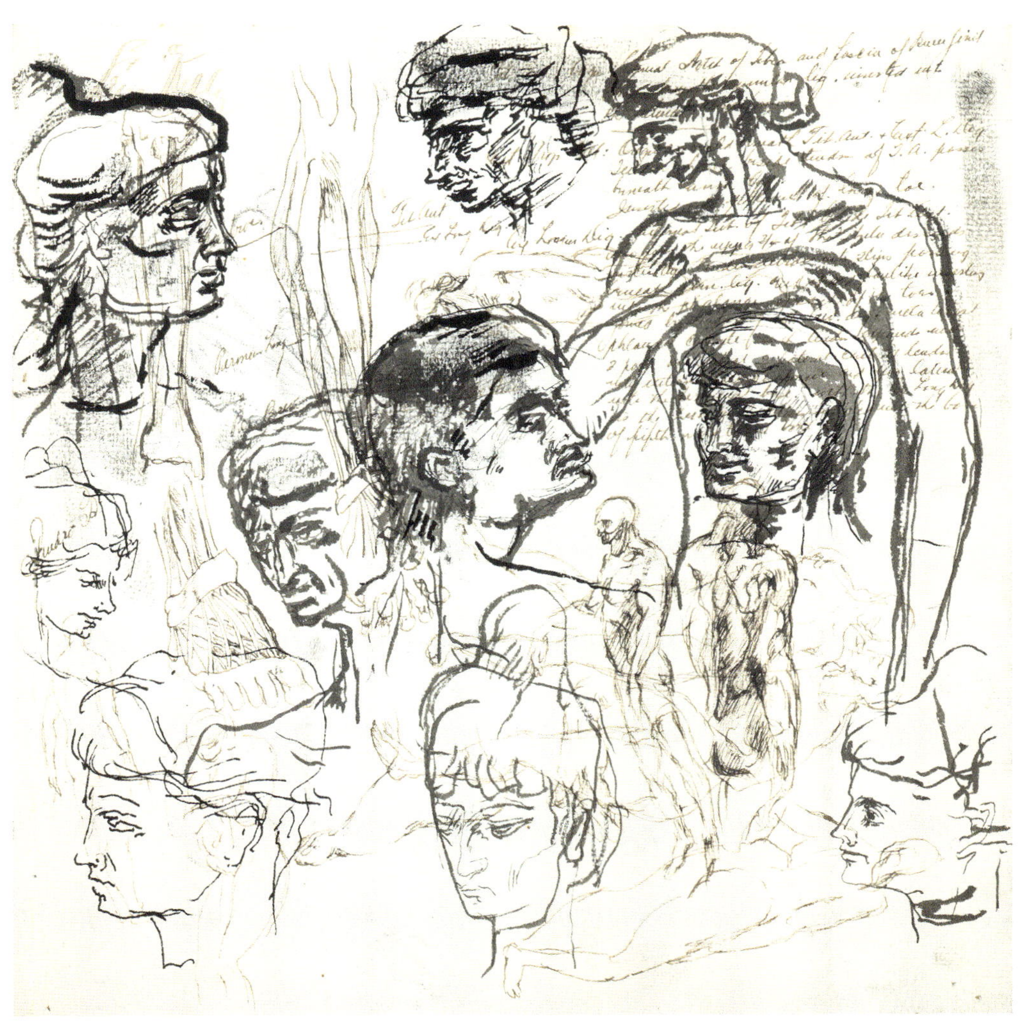

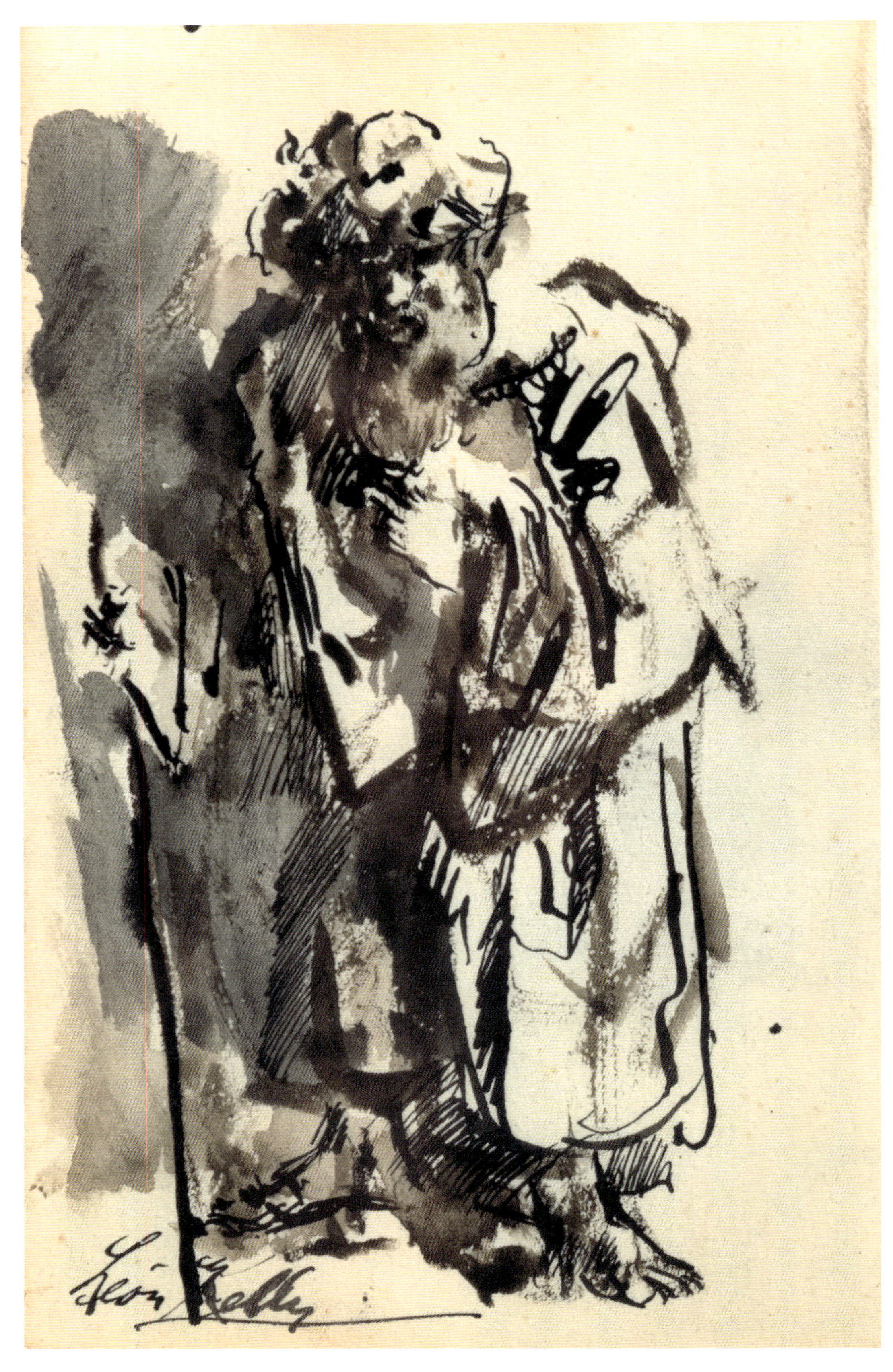

57
Untitled
Ink, 14 × 9 cm

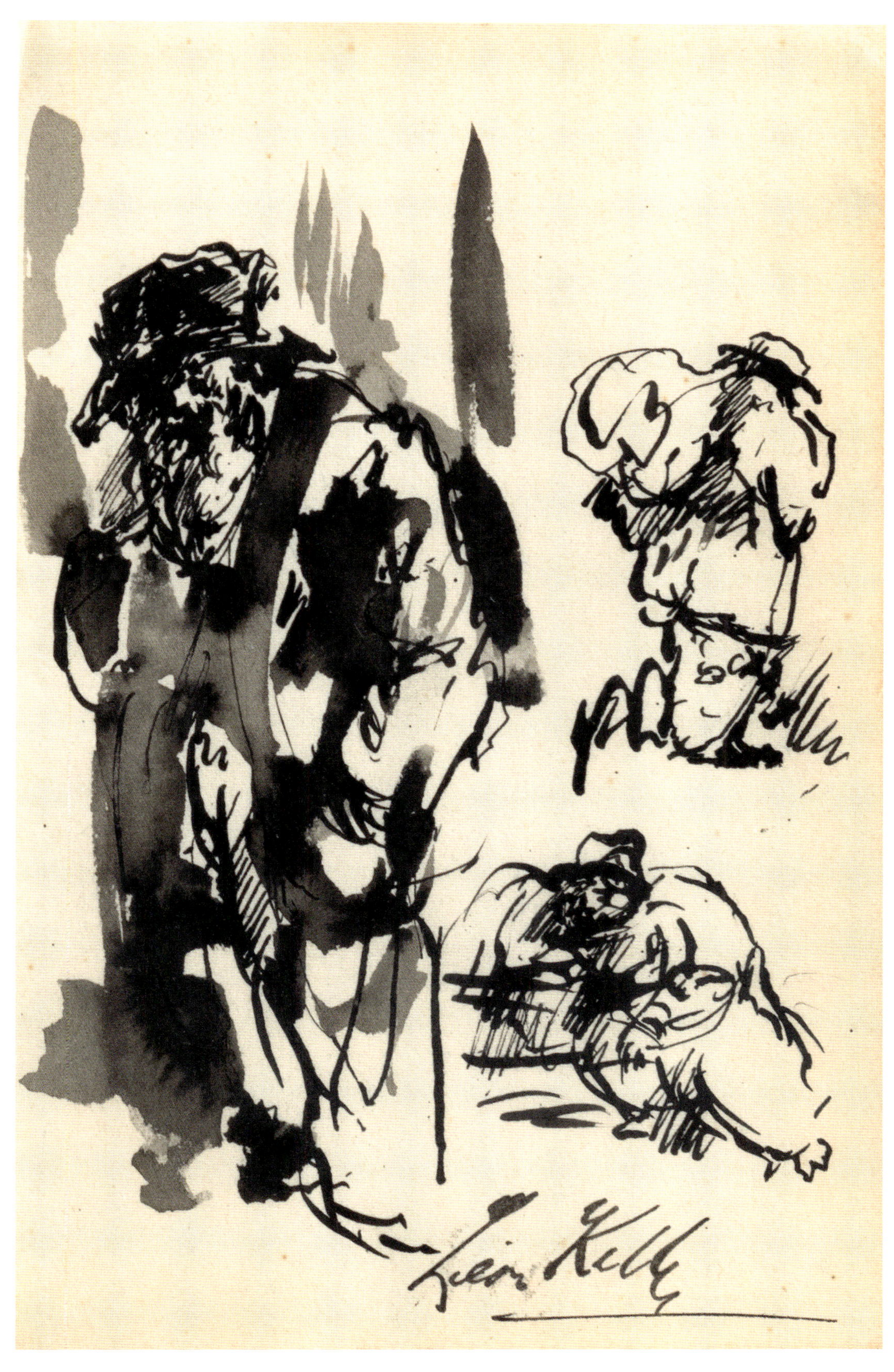

58
Untitled
Ink, 14 × 9 cm

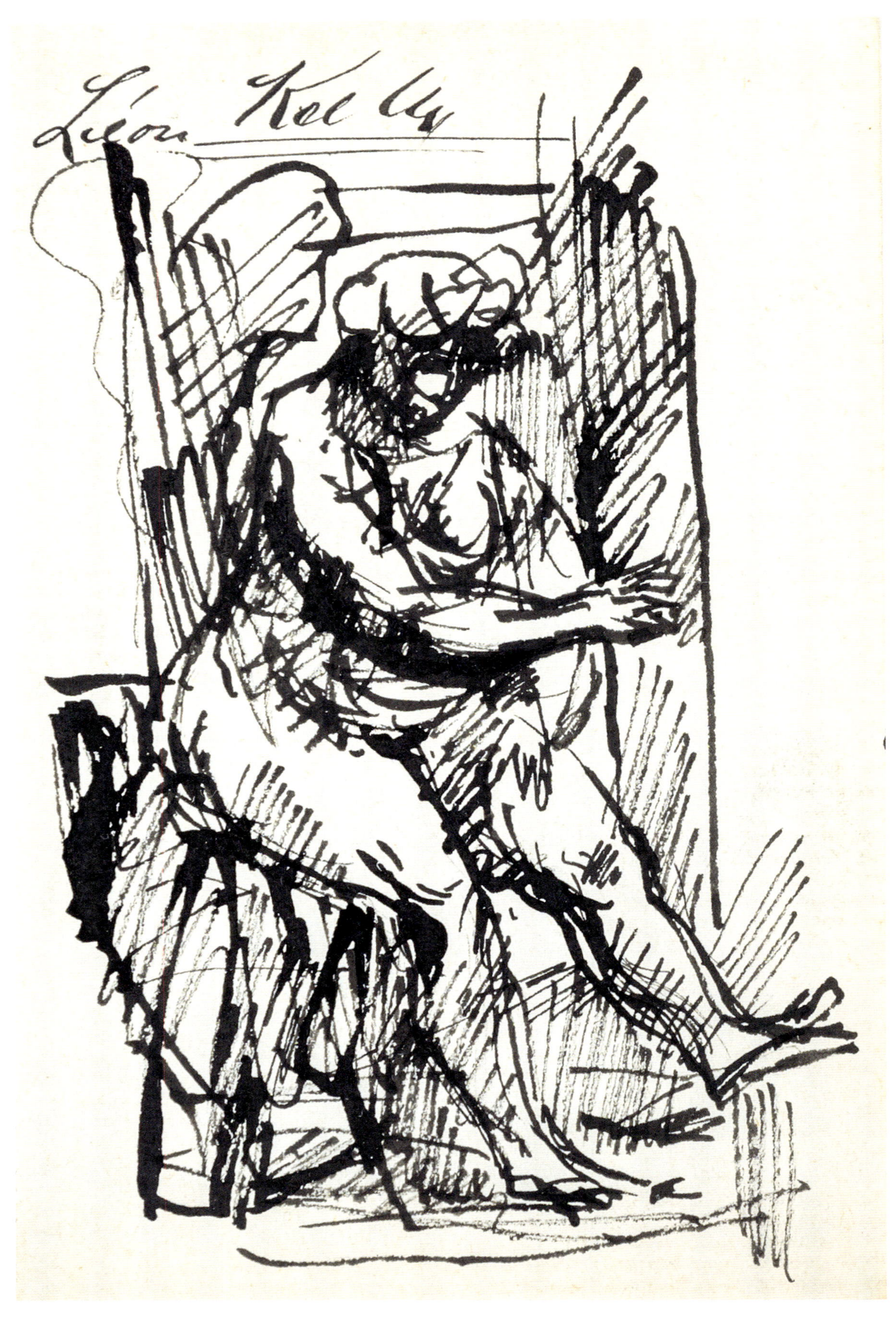

59
Untitled
Ink, 15 × 10 cm

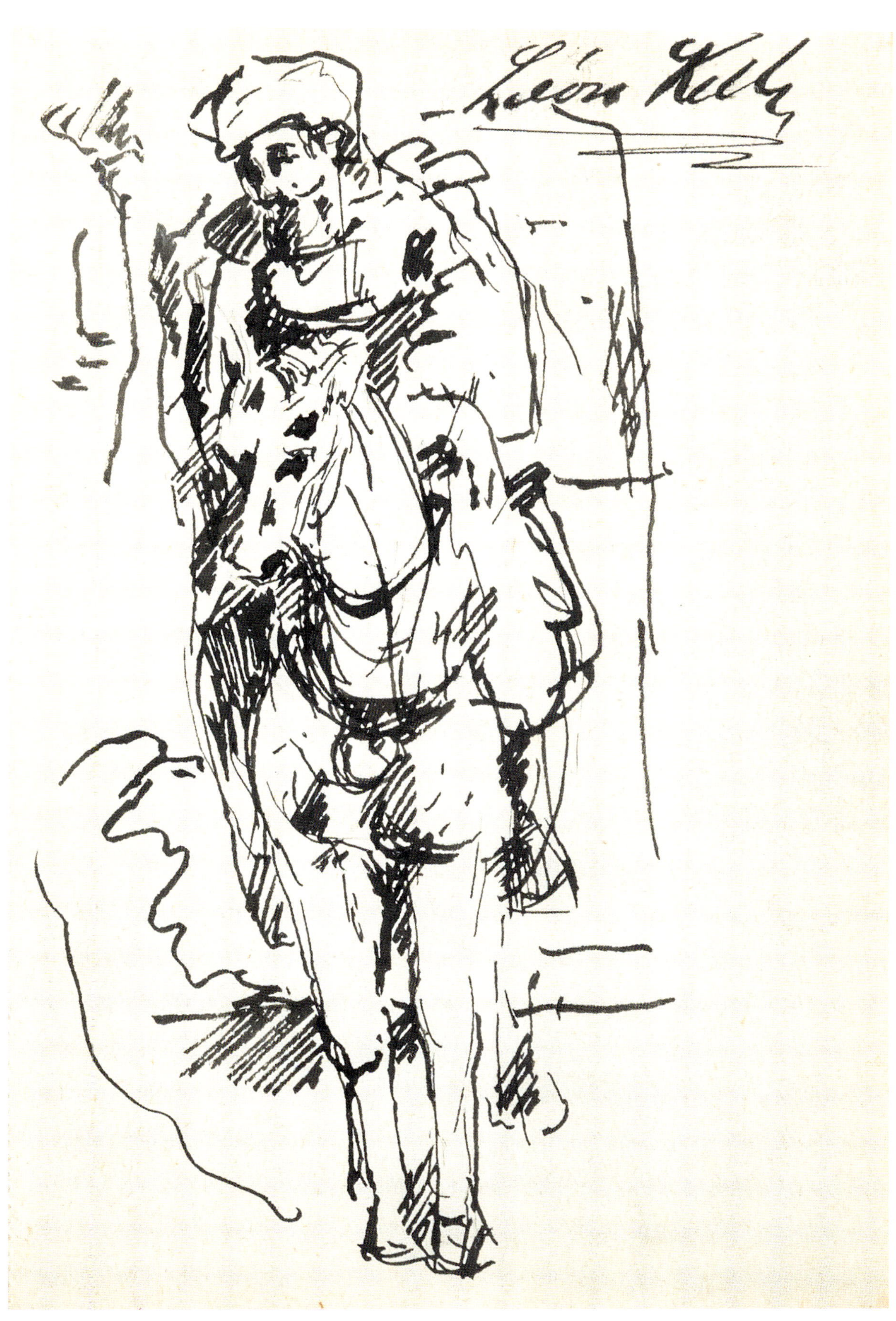

60
Untitled
Ink, 15 × 10 cm

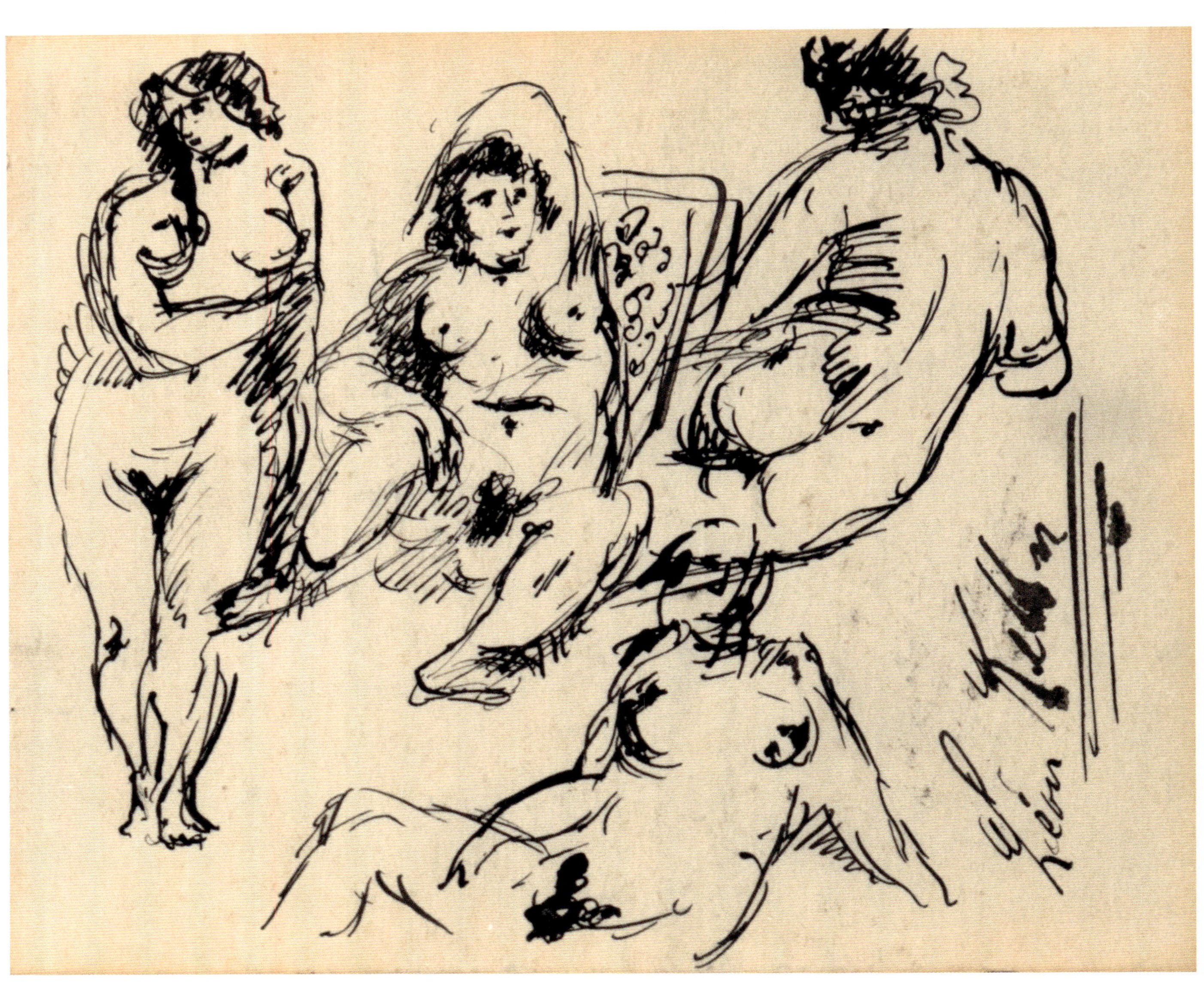

61
Untitled
Ink, 10 × 12.5 cm

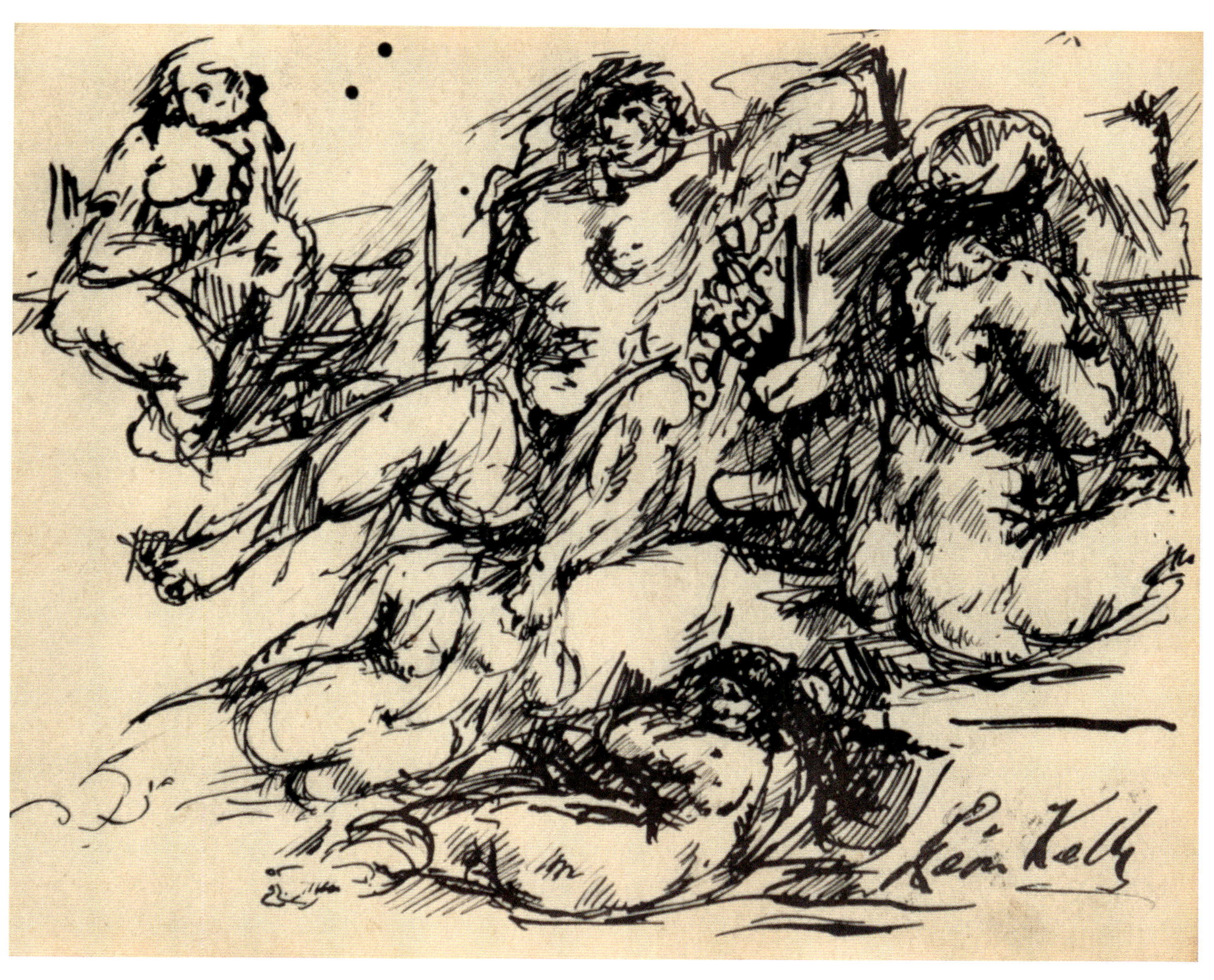

62
Untitled
Ink, 10 × 12.5 cm

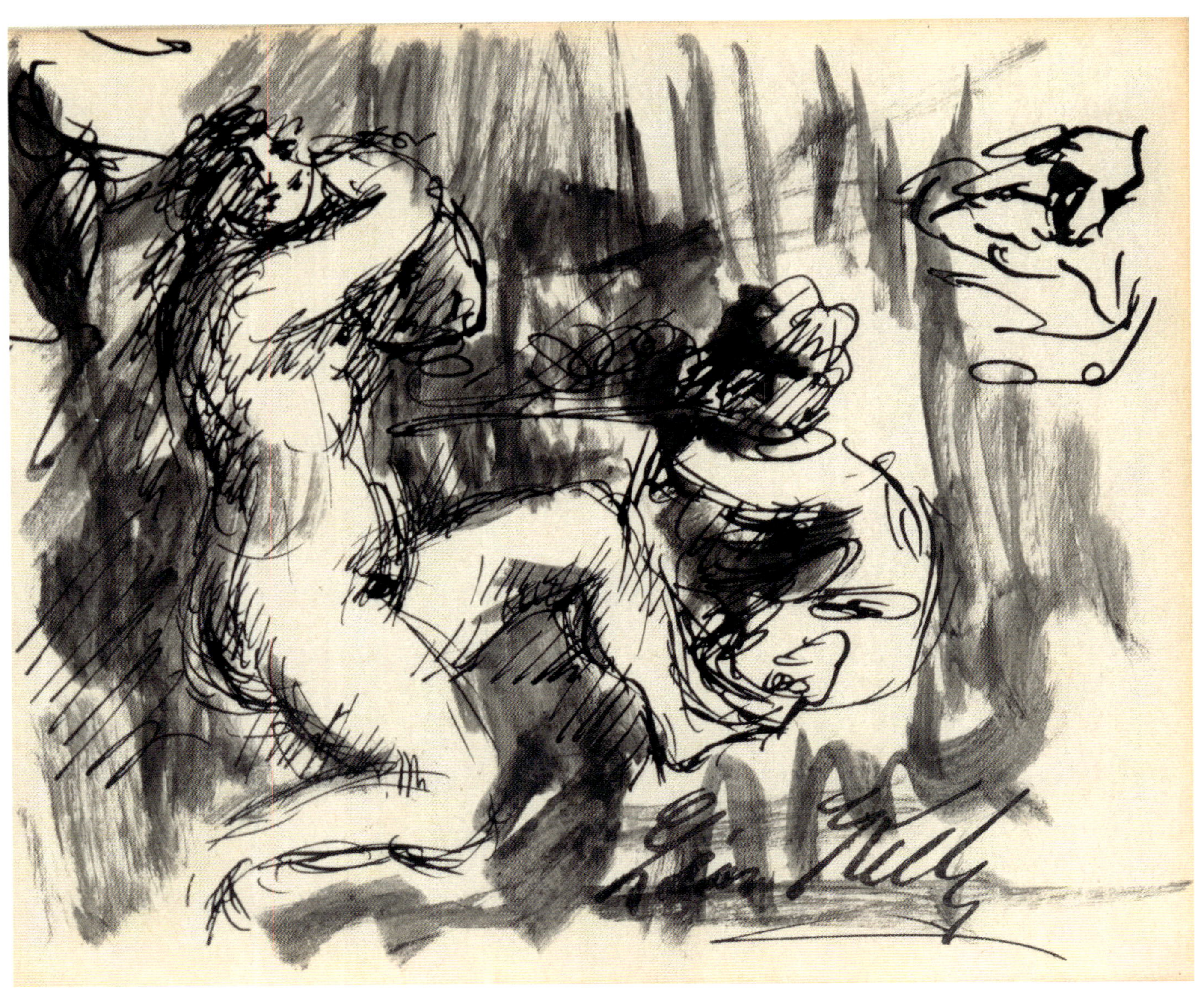

63
Untitled
Ink, 10 × 12.5 cm

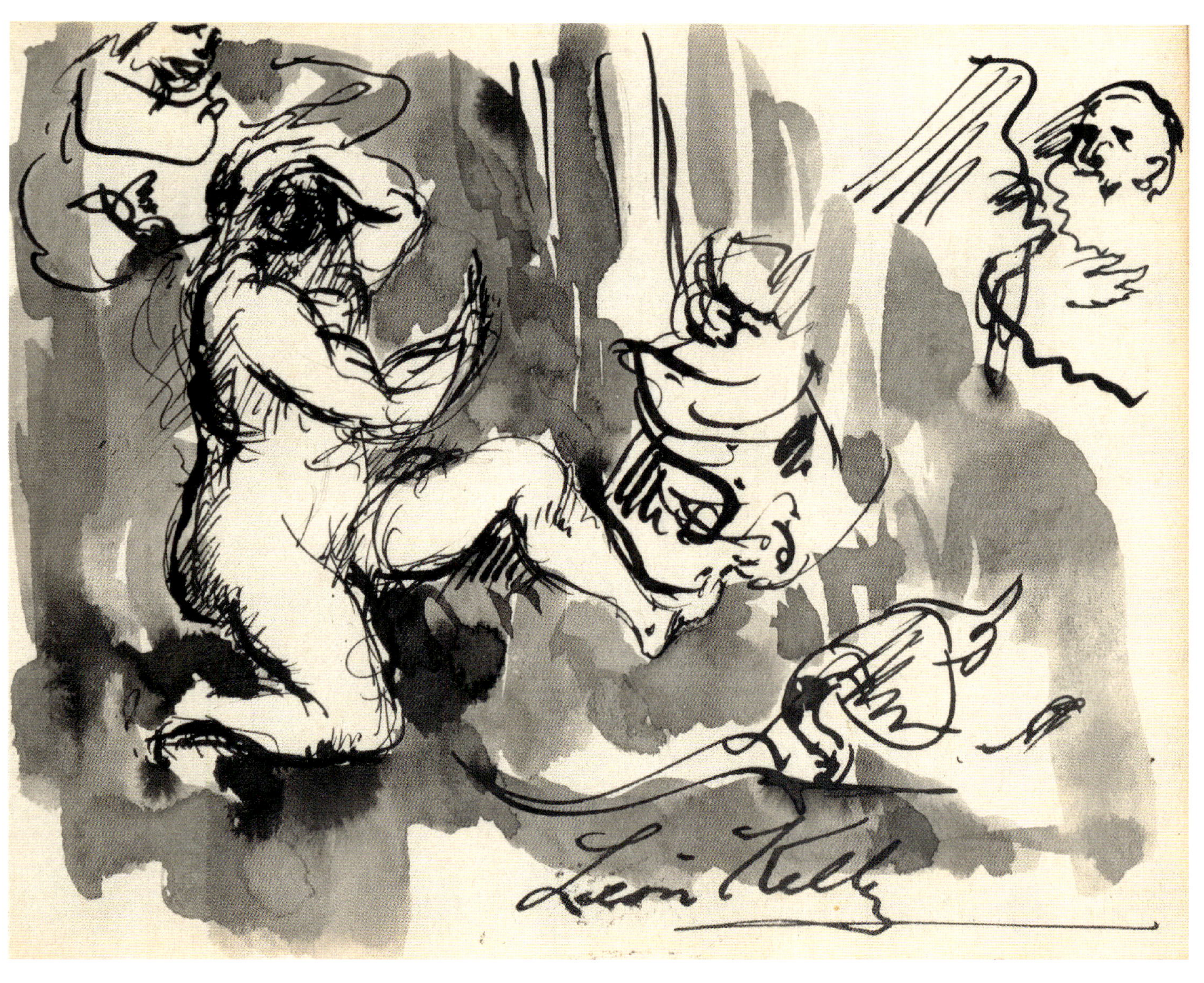

64
Untitled
Ink, 10 × 12.5 cm

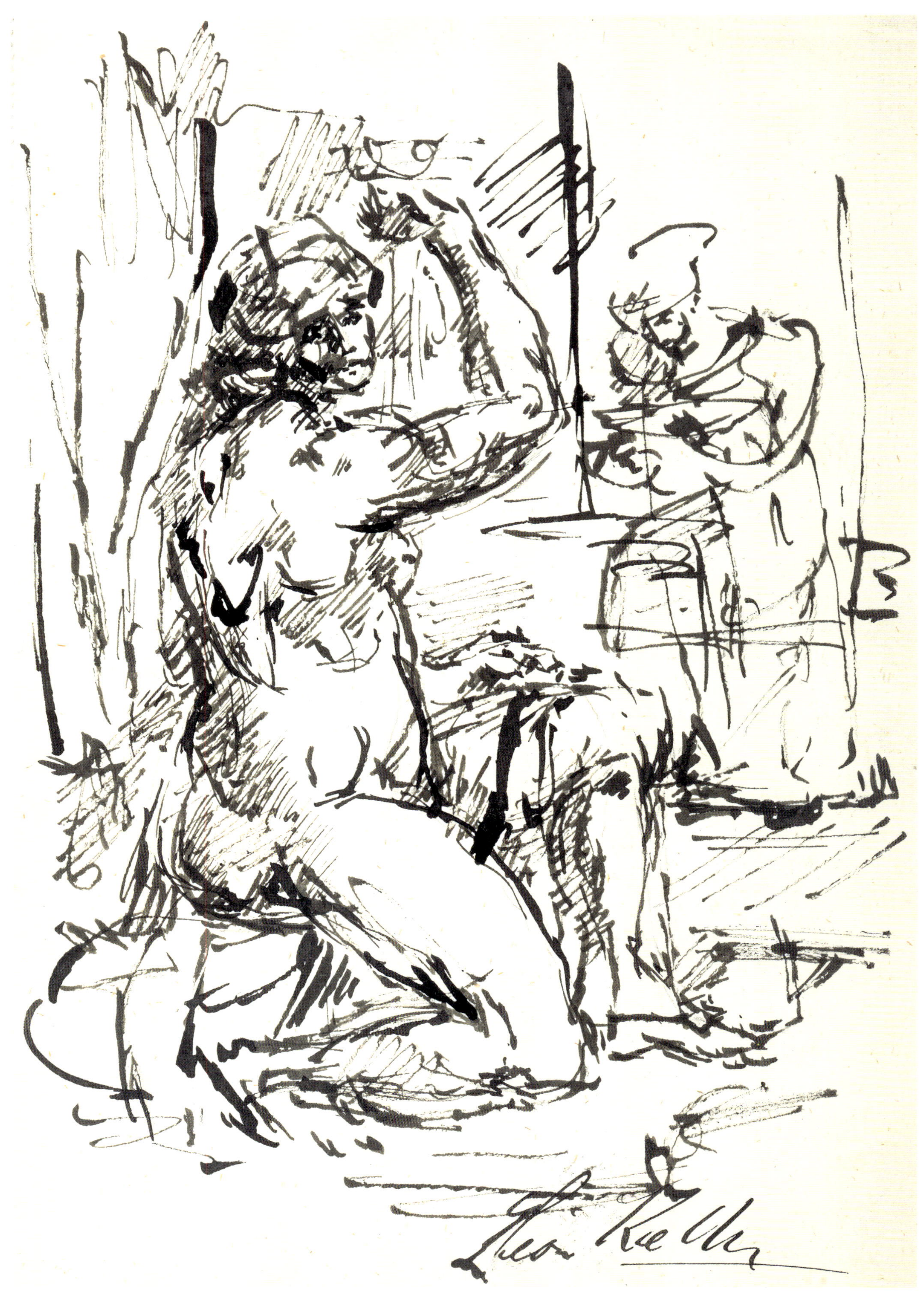

65
Untitled
Ink, 19 × 14 cm

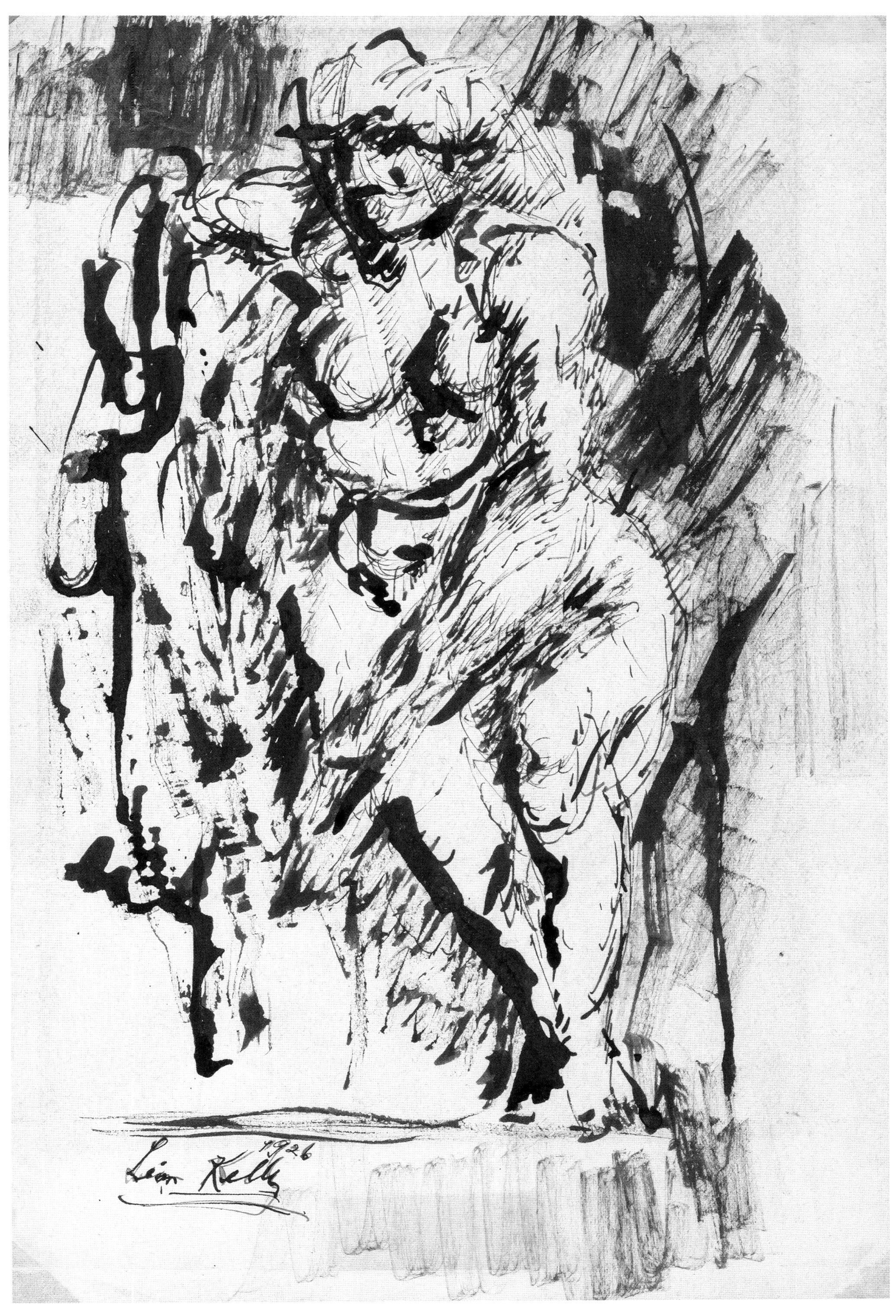

66
Seated Model, 1926
Ink, 27.5 × 18 cm

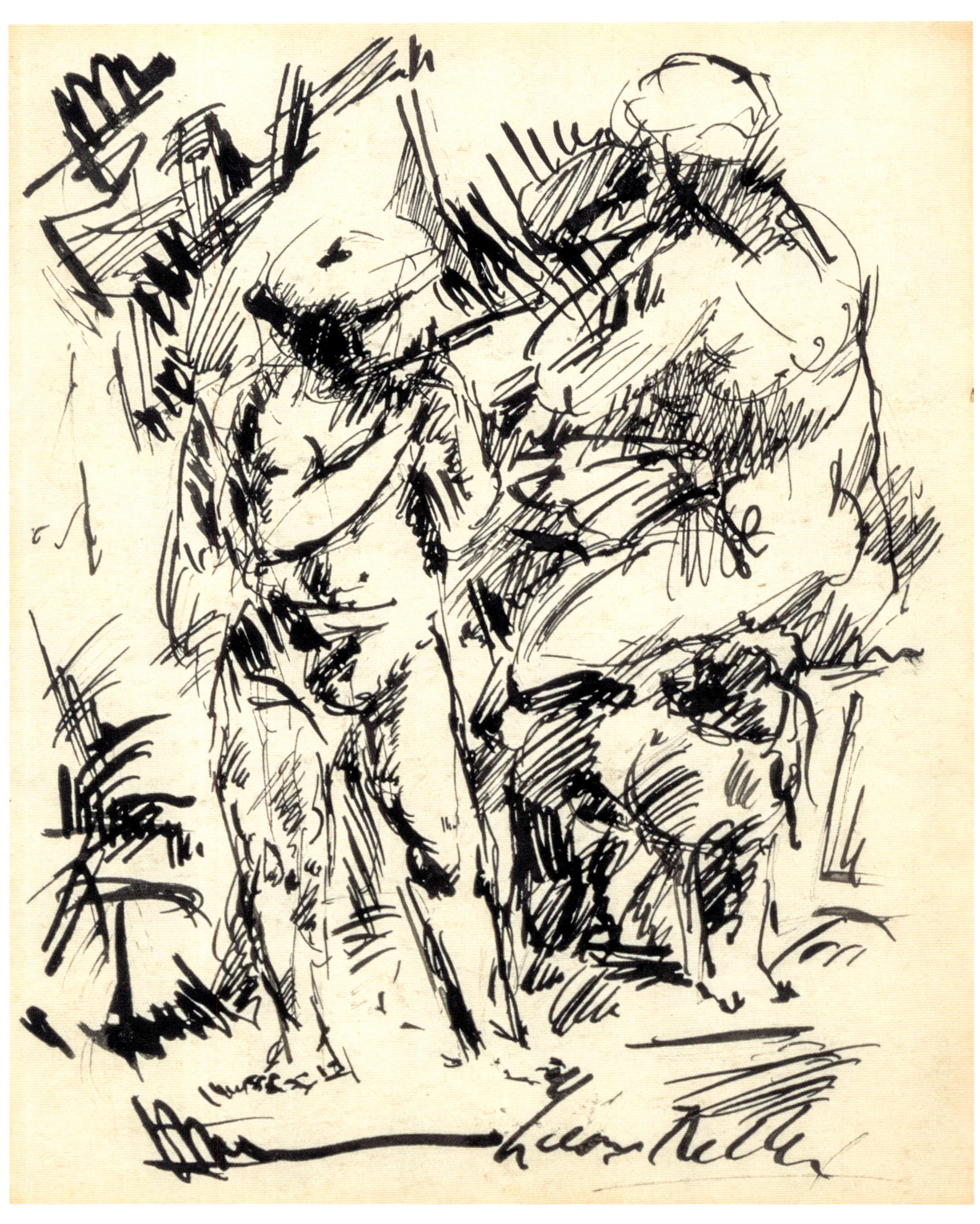

67
Untitled
Ink, 14 × 9 cm

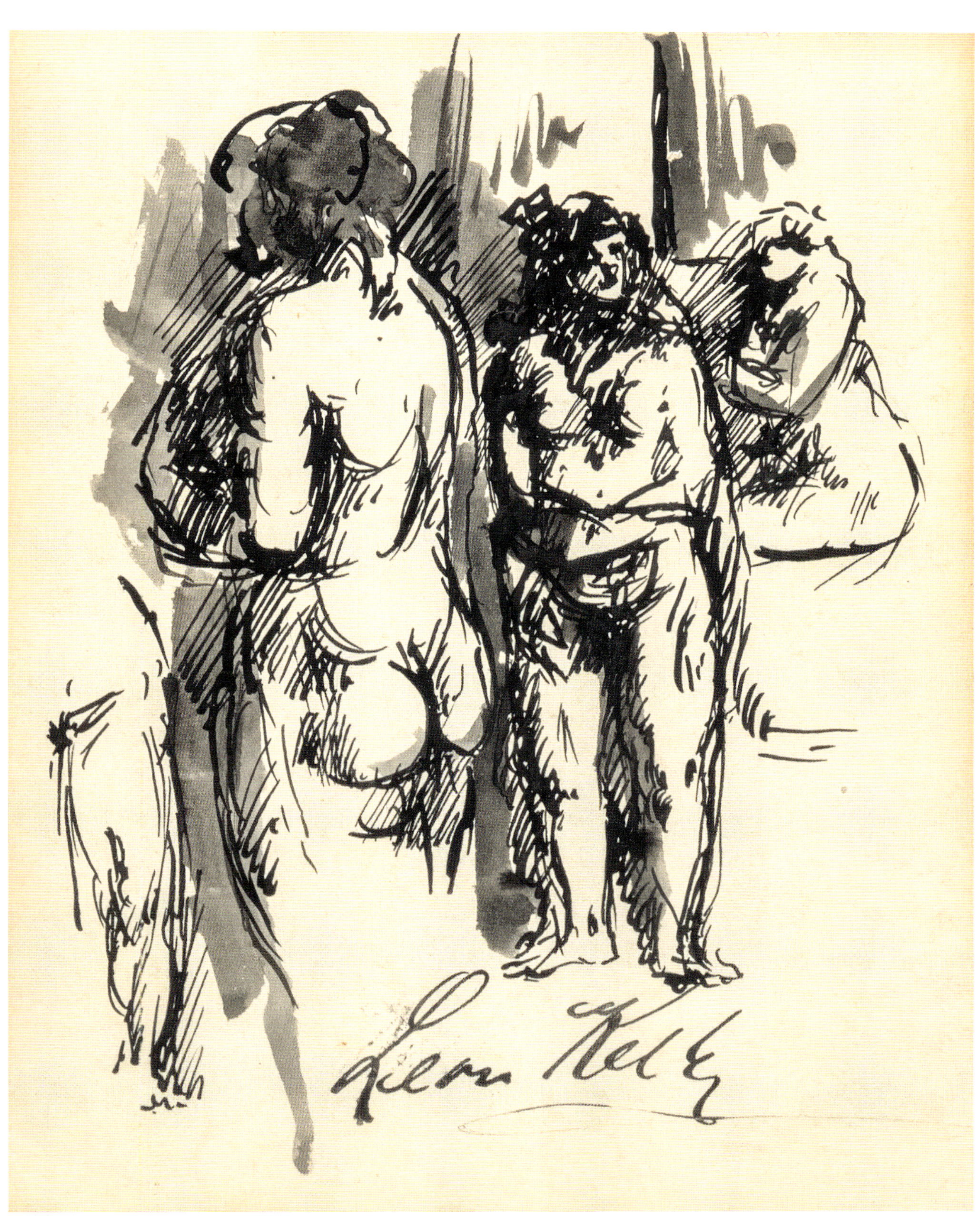

68
Untitled
Ink, 14 × 9 cm

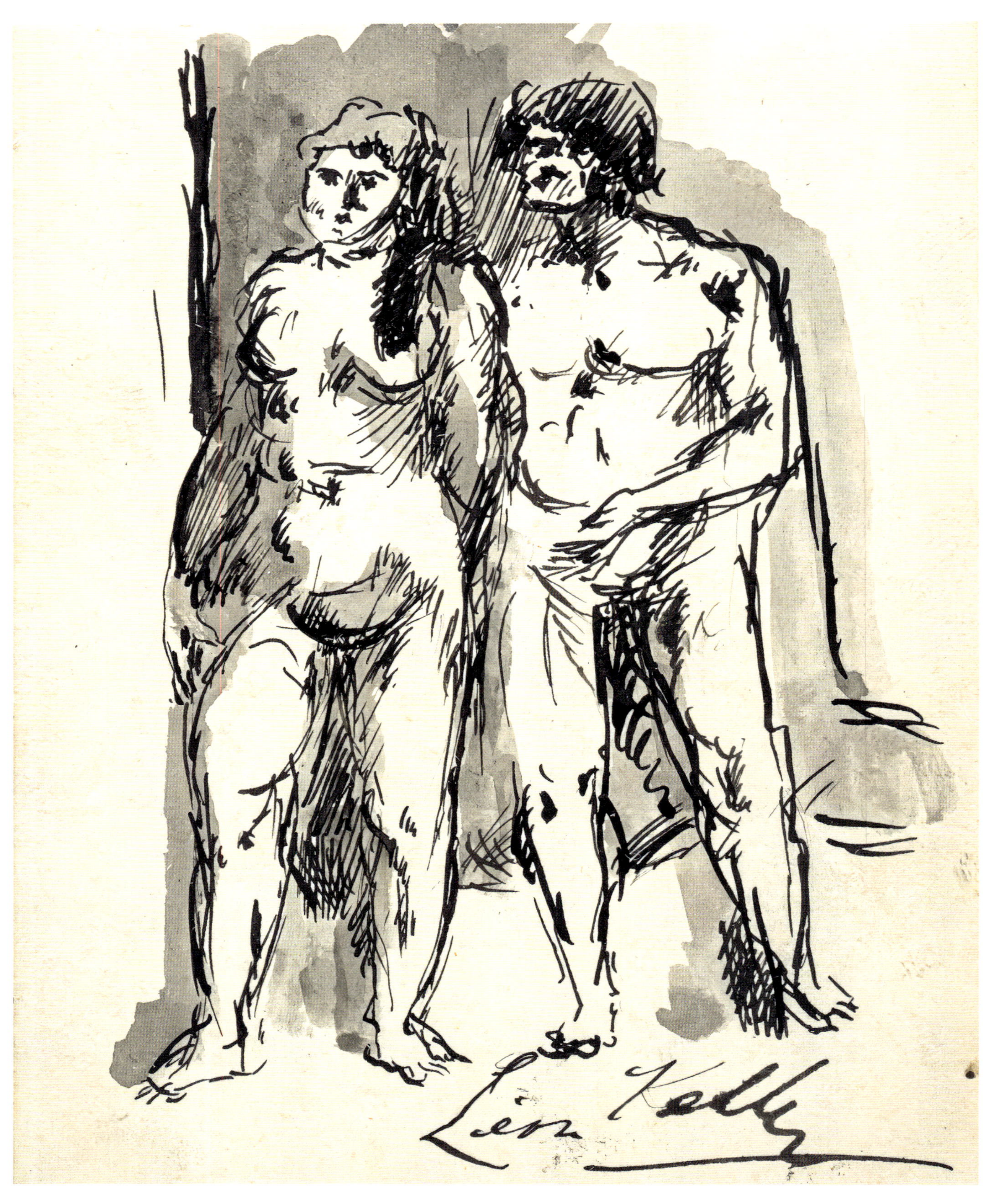

69
Untitled
Ink, 12 × 10 cm

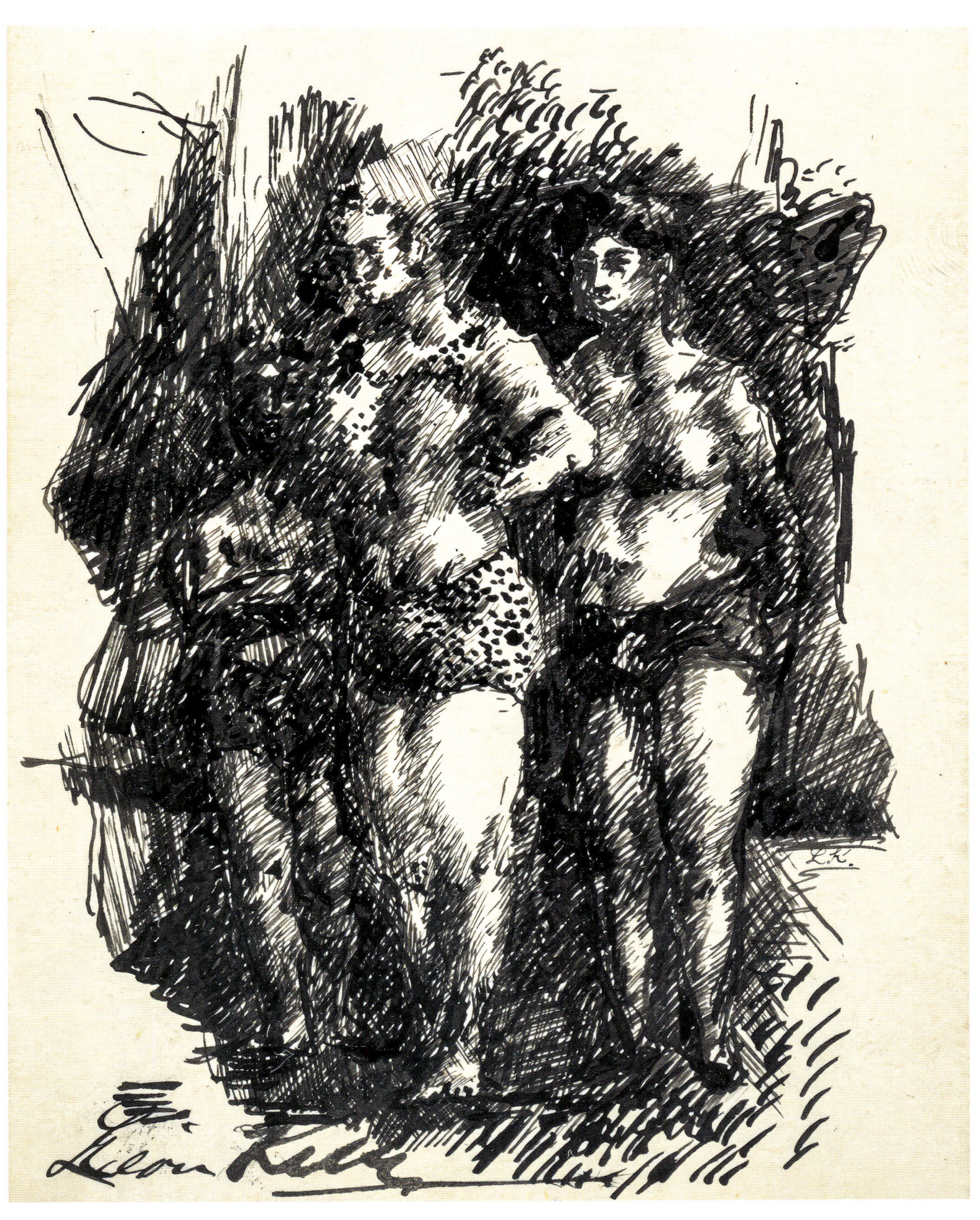

70
Untitled
Ink, 12 × 10 cm

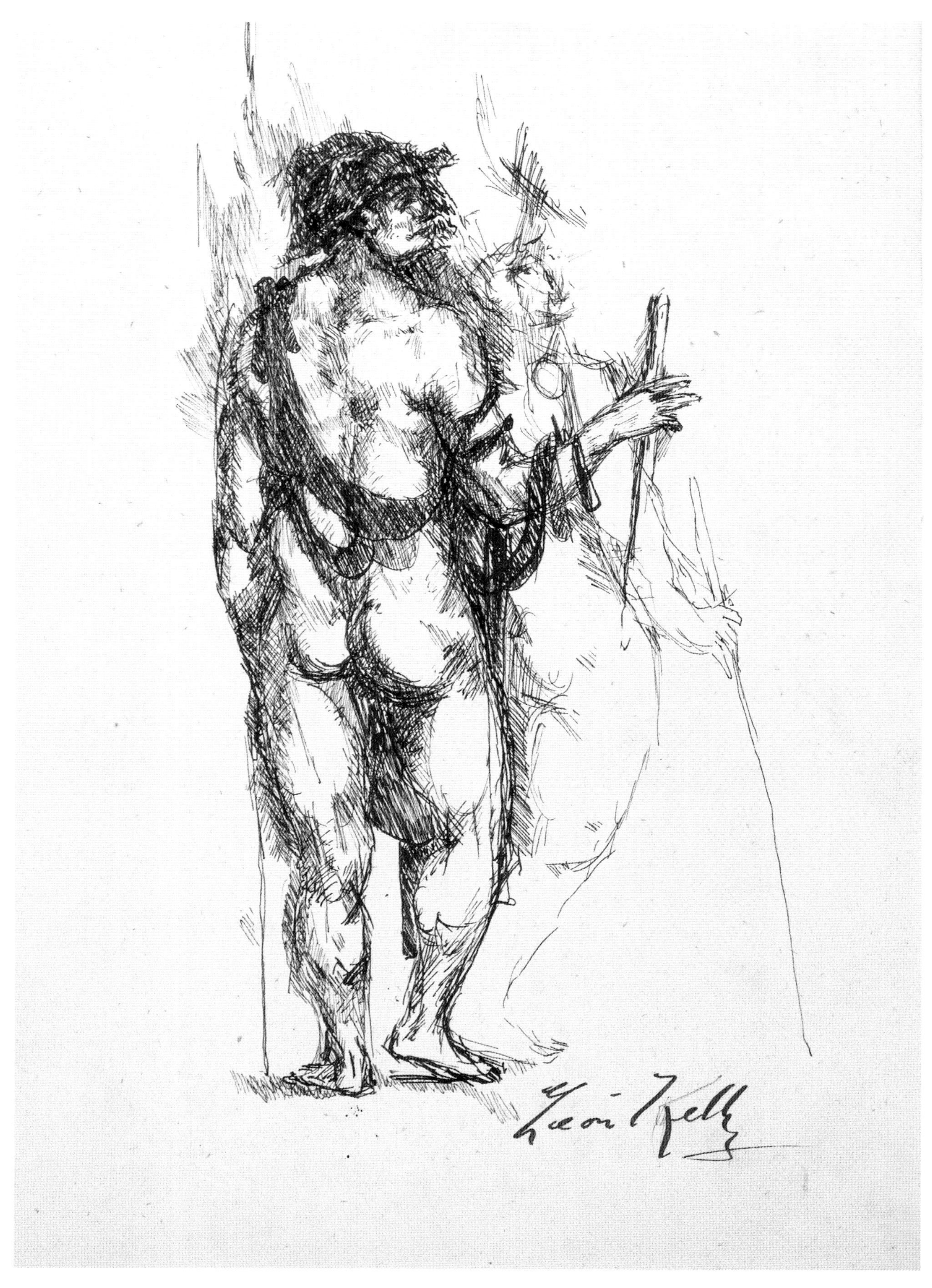

71
Untitled
Ink, 19 × 14 cm

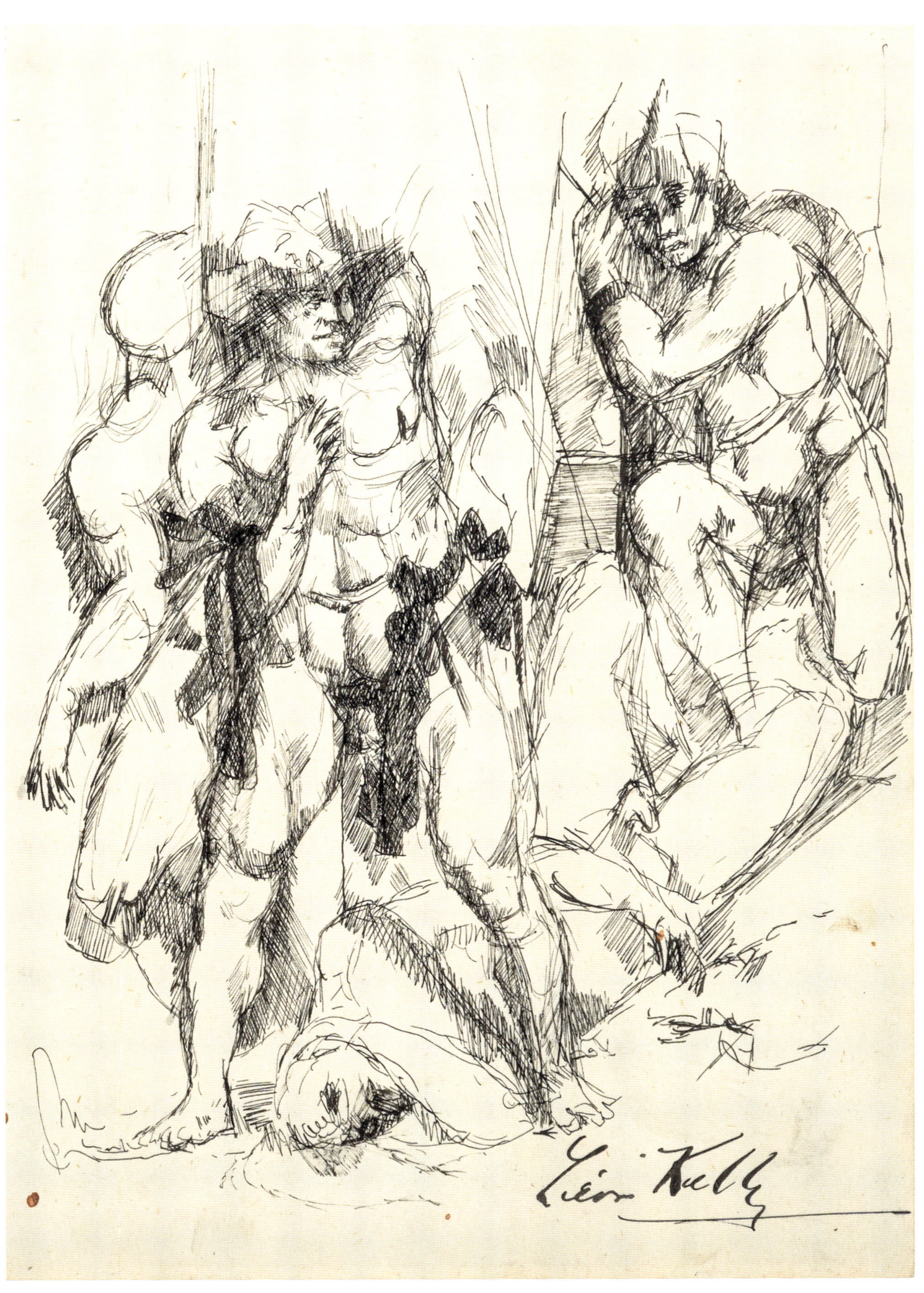

72
Untitled
Ink, 19 × 14 cm

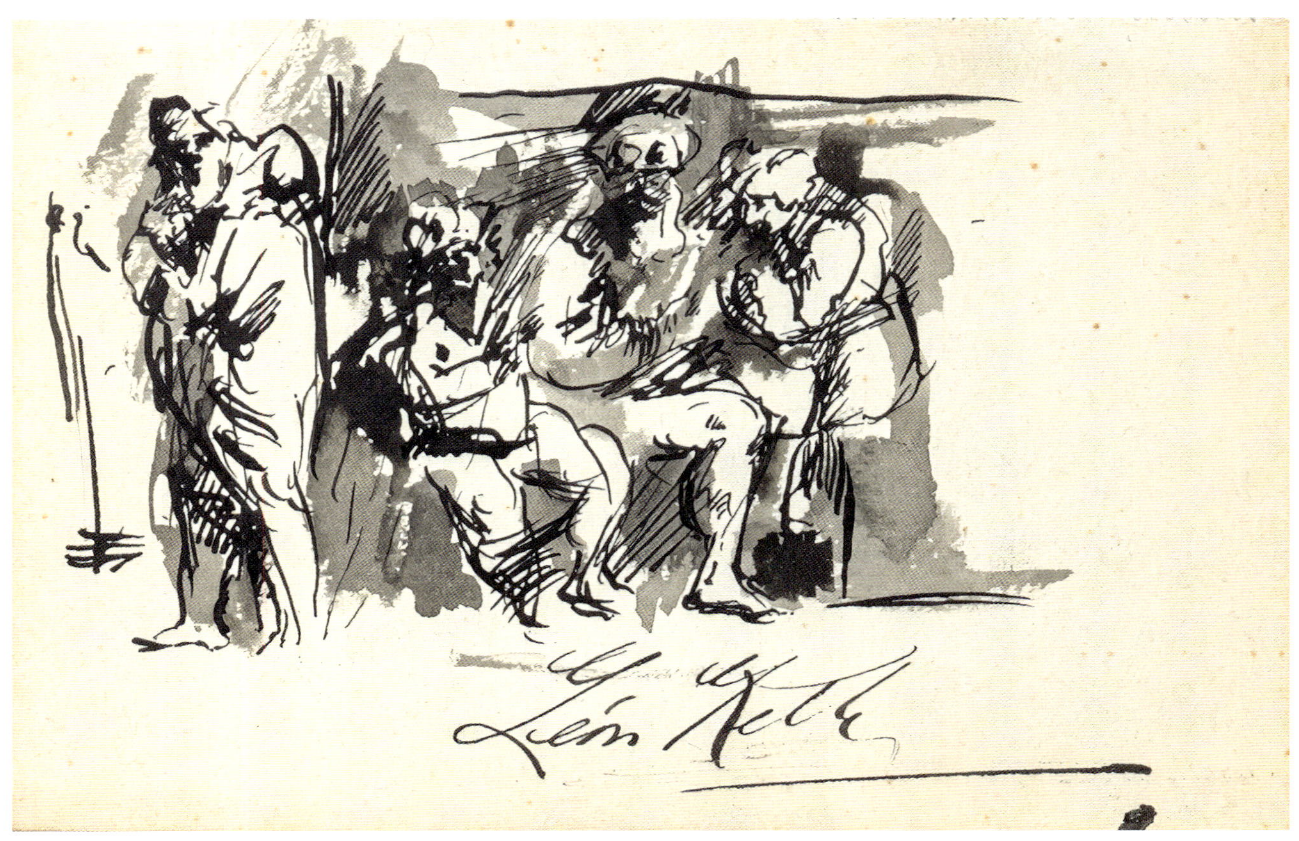

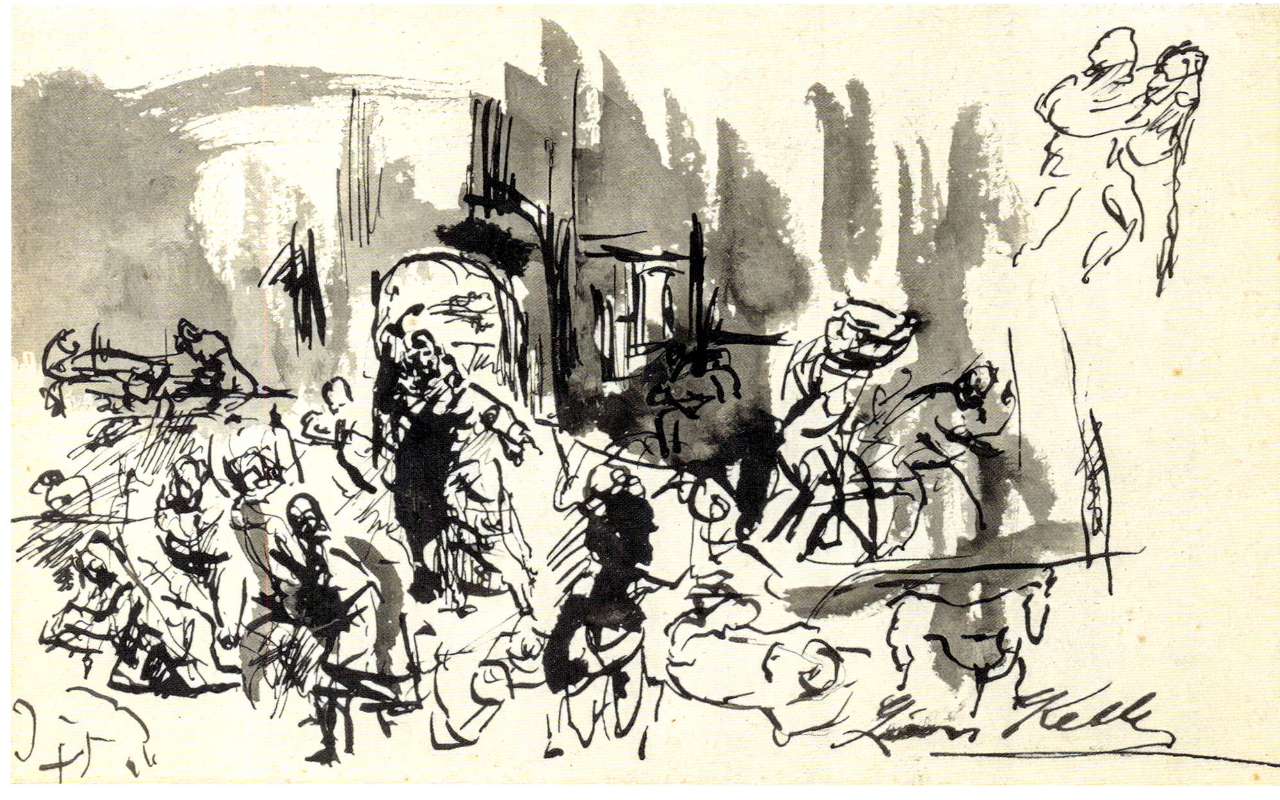

73
Untitled
Ink, 9 × 14 cm

74
Untitled
Ink, 9 × 14 cm

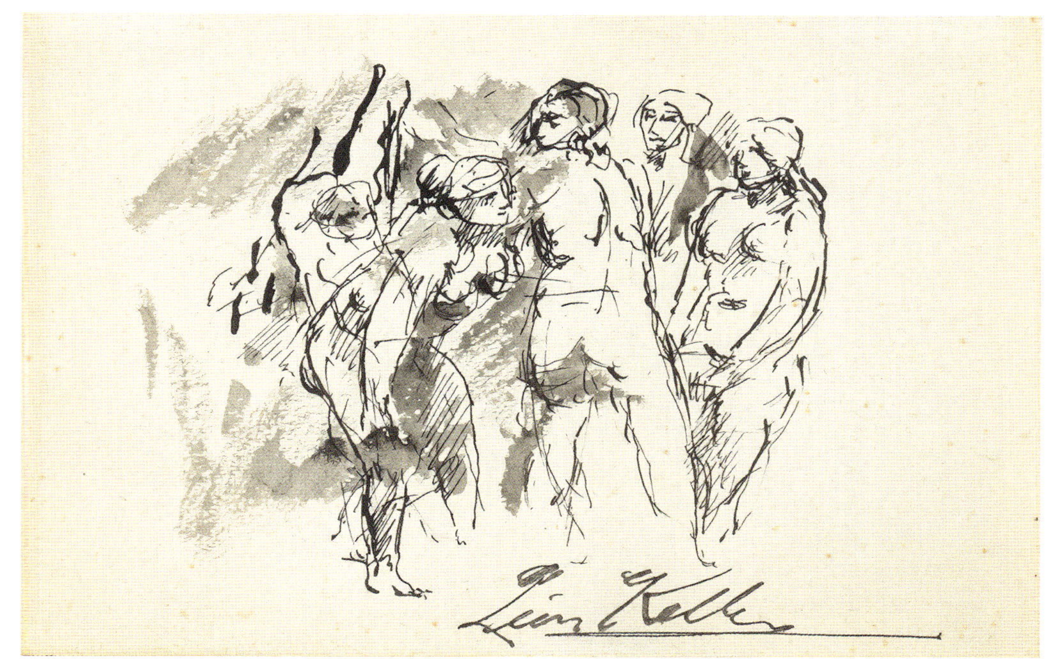

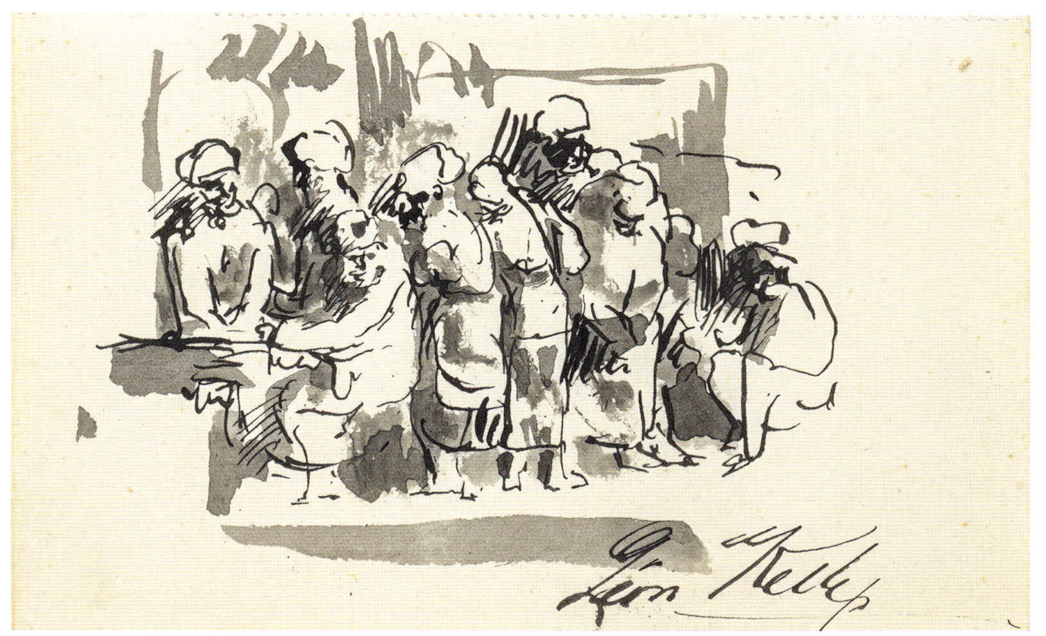

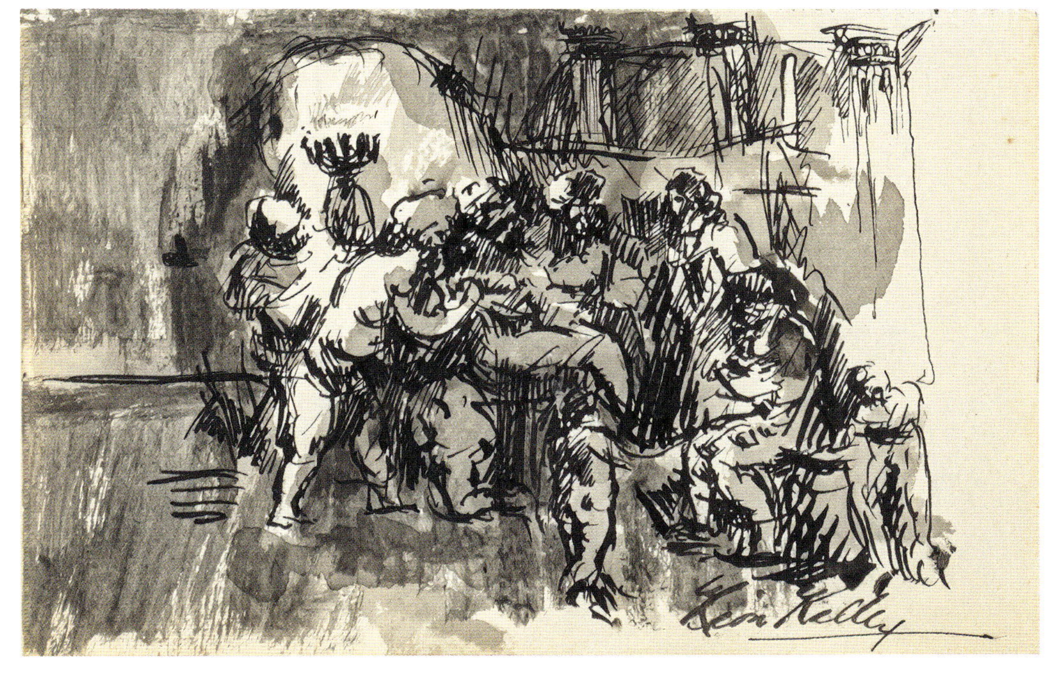

75
Untitled
Ink, 9 × 14 cm

76
Untitled
Ink, 9 × 14 cm

77
Untitled
Ink, 19 × 14 cm

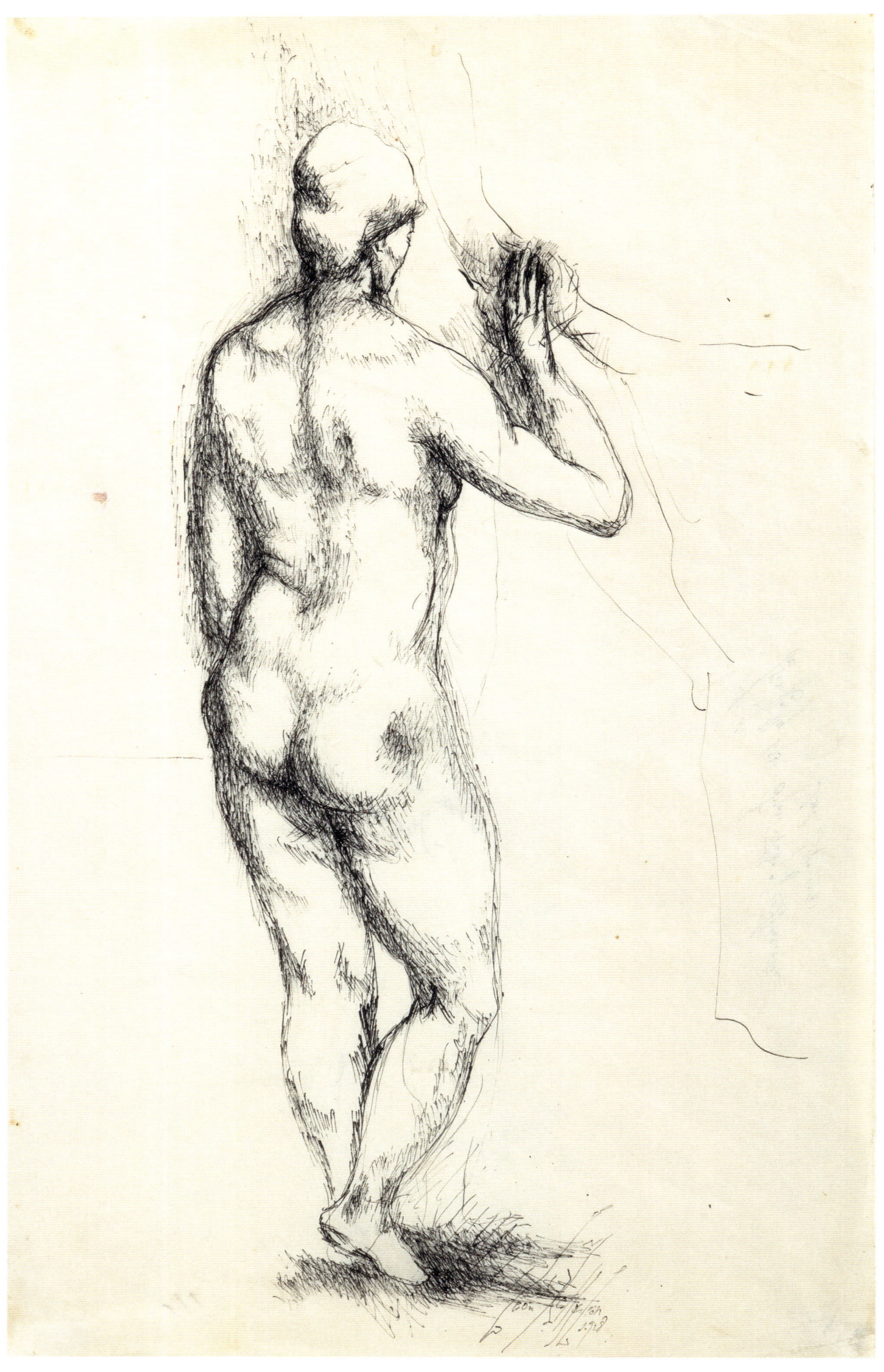

78
Untitled, 1928
Ink, 43 × 30 cm

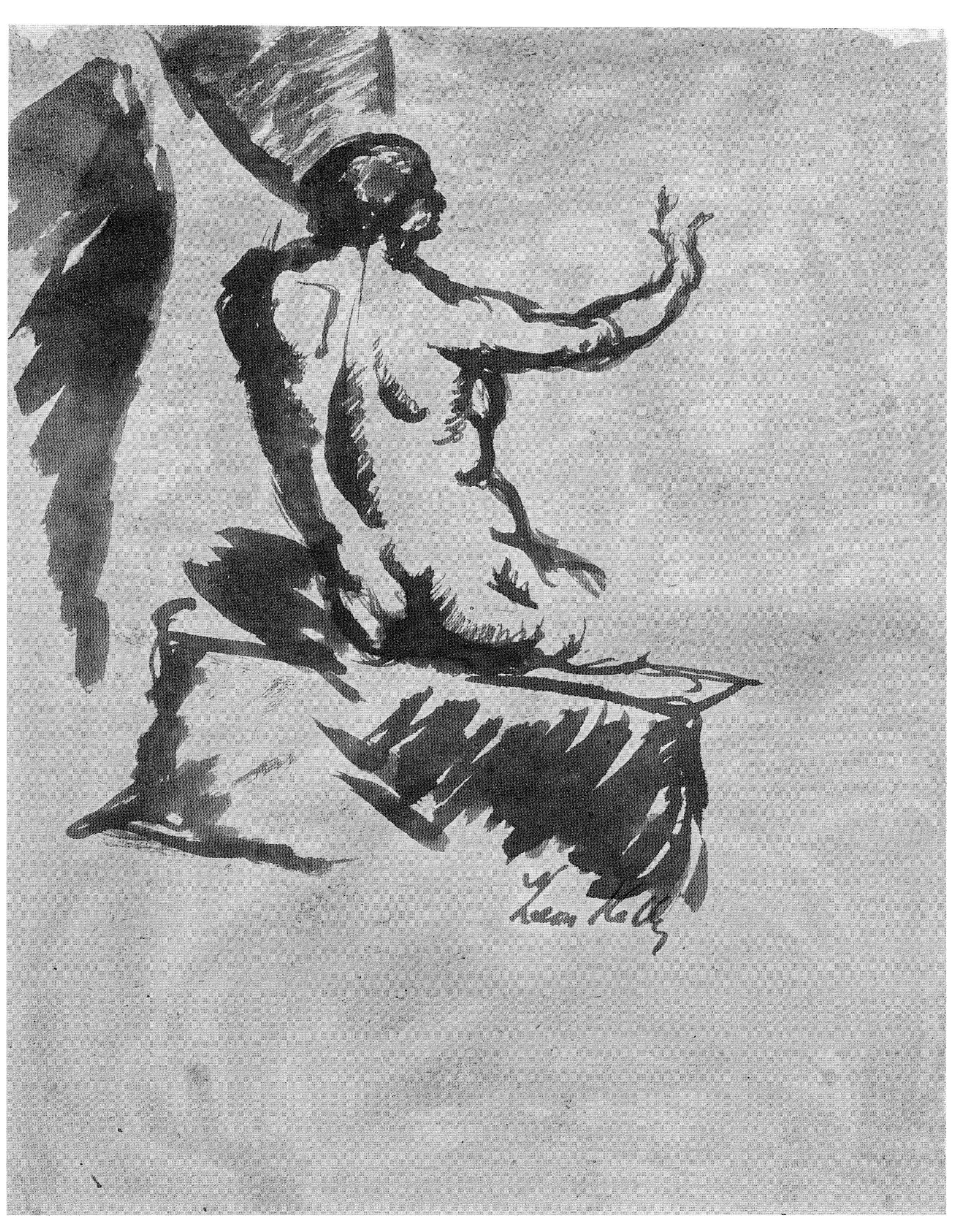

79
Untitled
Ink, 30 × 23 cm

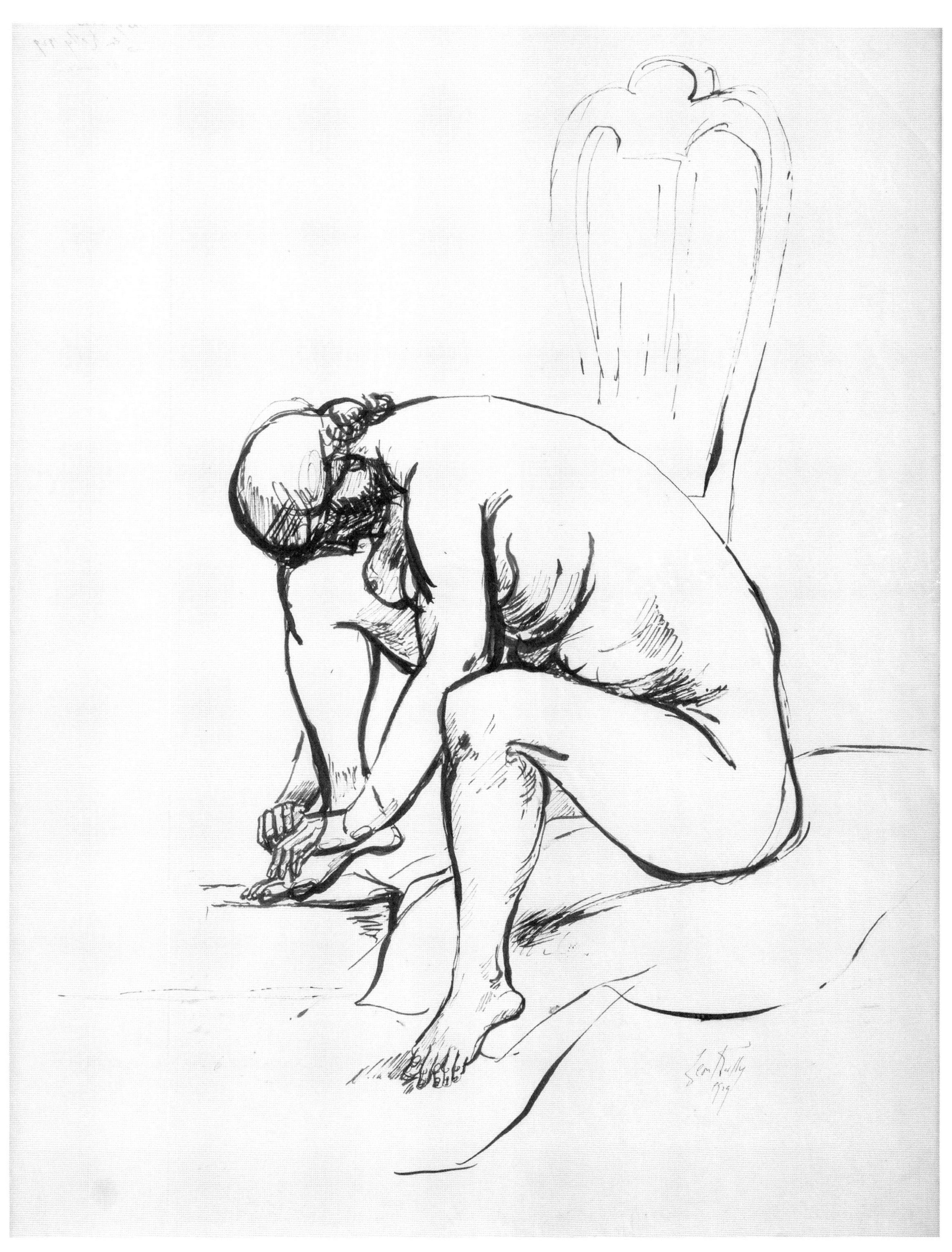

80
Untitled, 1929
Ink, 54.5 × 41 cm

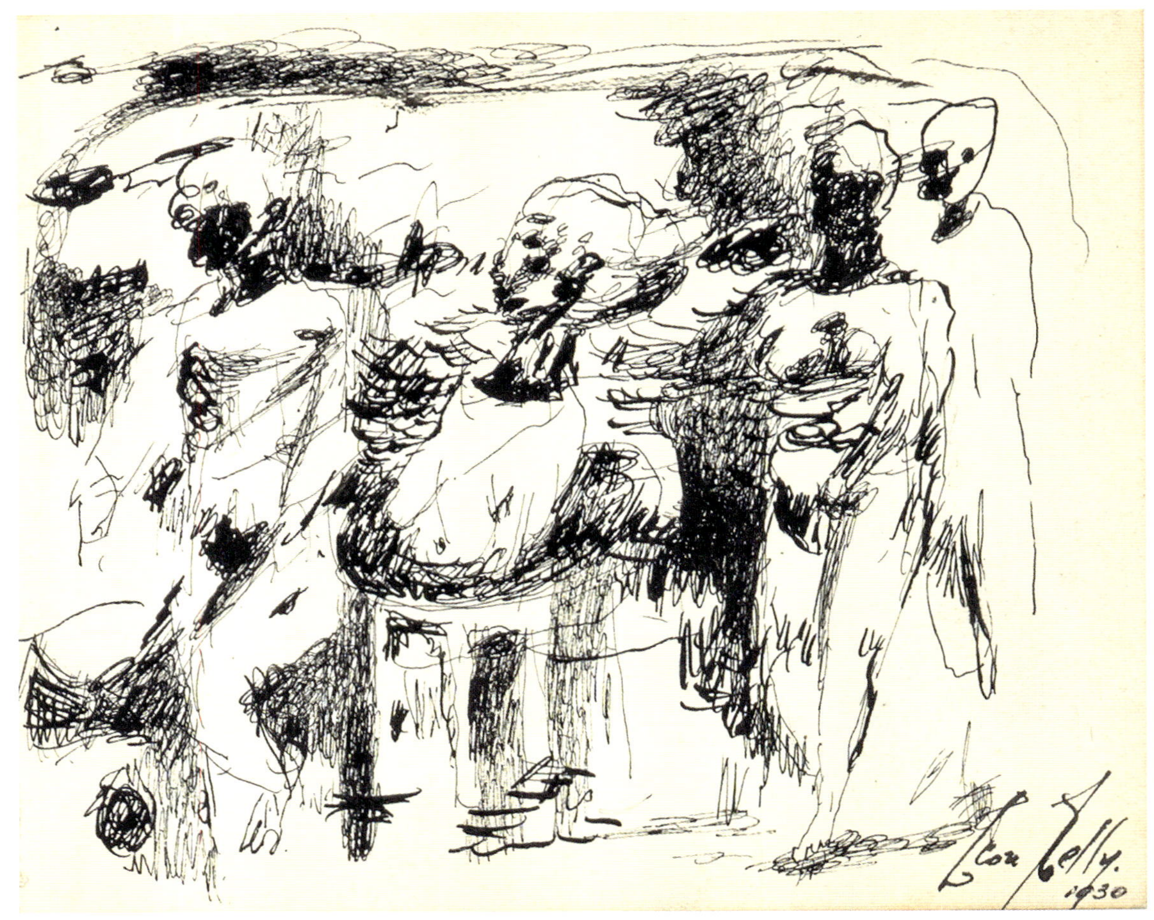

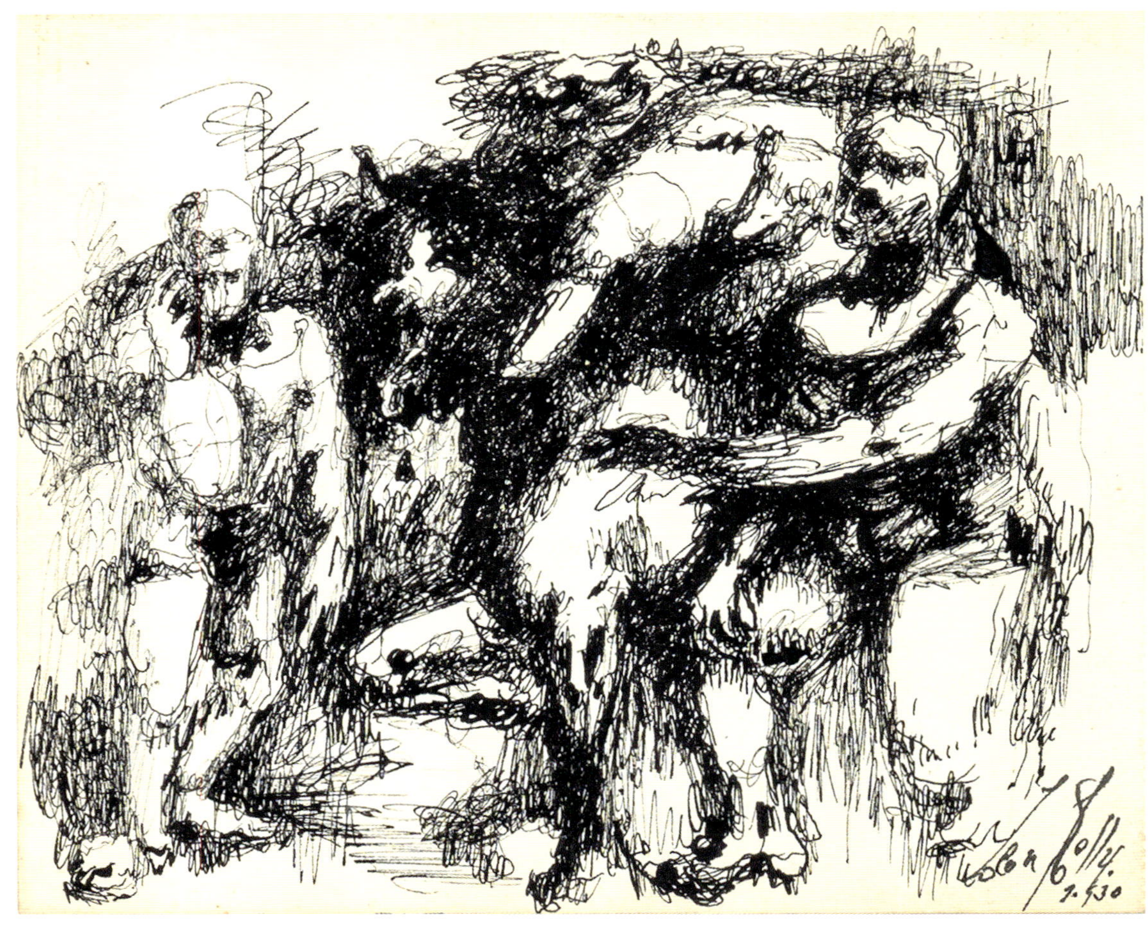

80
Untitled, 1930
Ink, 12 × 14.5 cm

81
Untitled, 1930
Ink, 12 × 14.5 cm

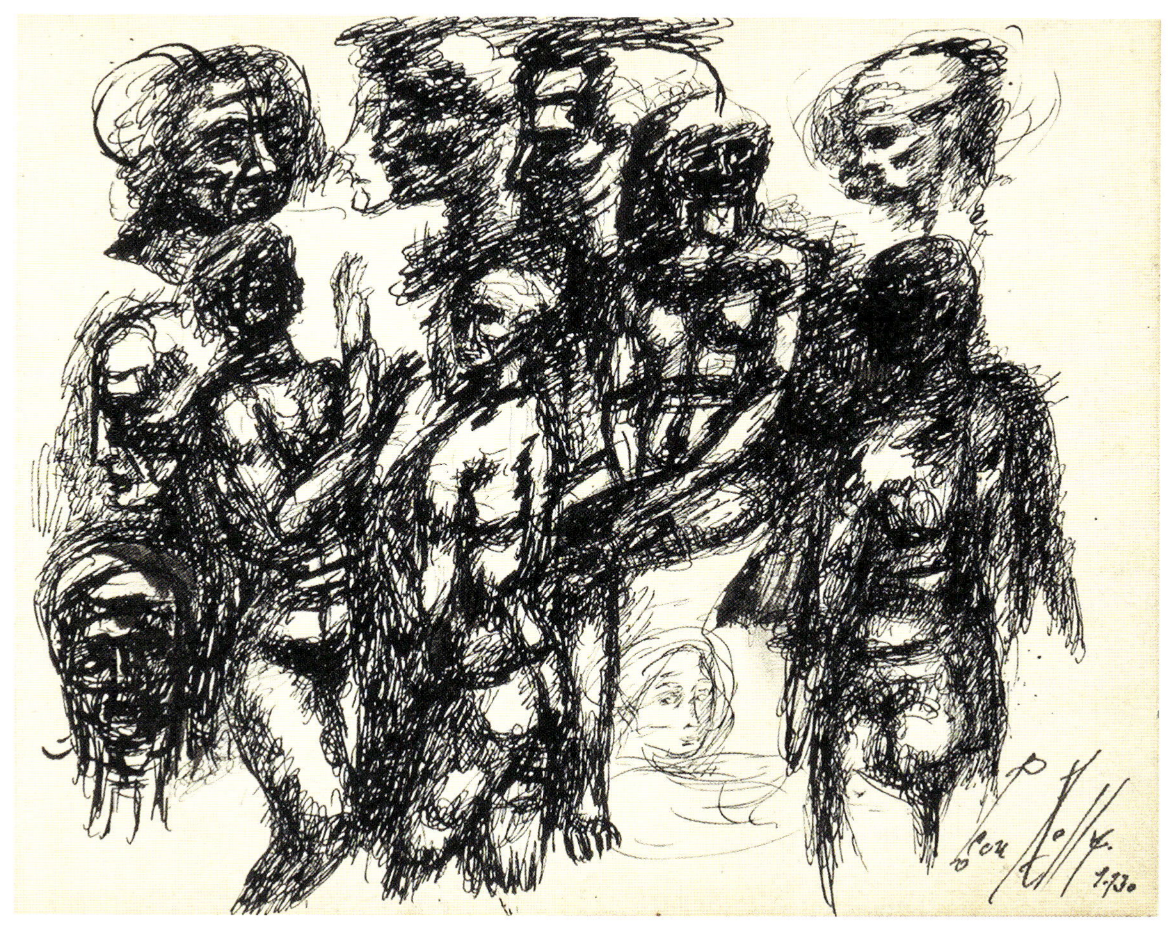

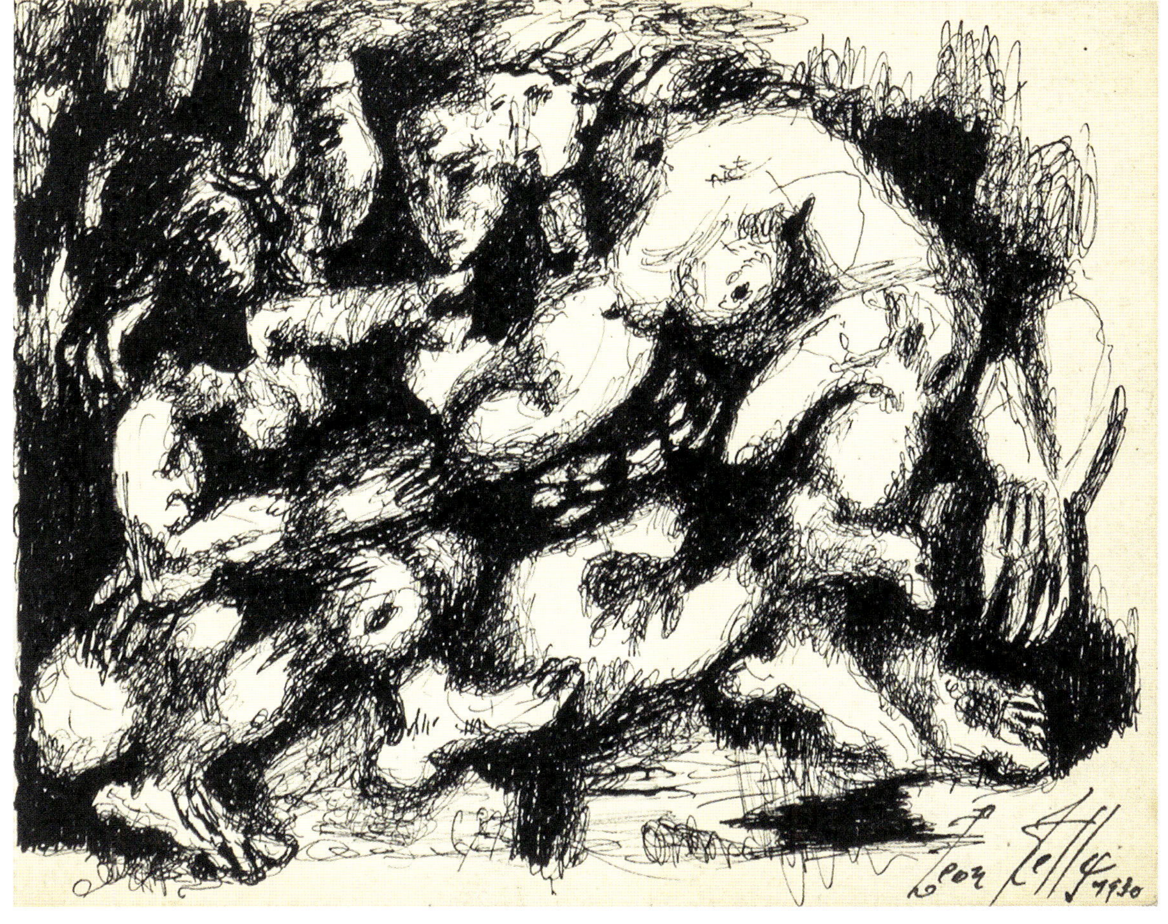

83
Untitled, 1930
Ink, 12 × 14.5 cm

84
Untitled, 1930
Ink, 12 × 14.5 cm

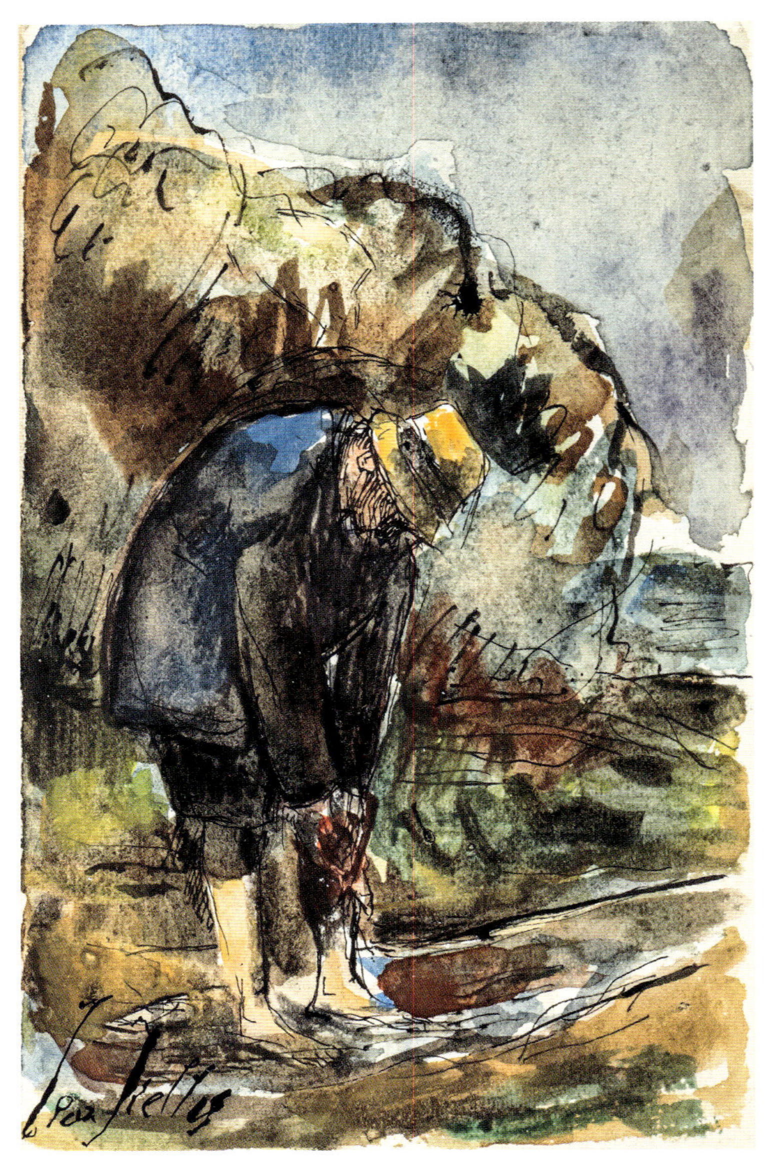

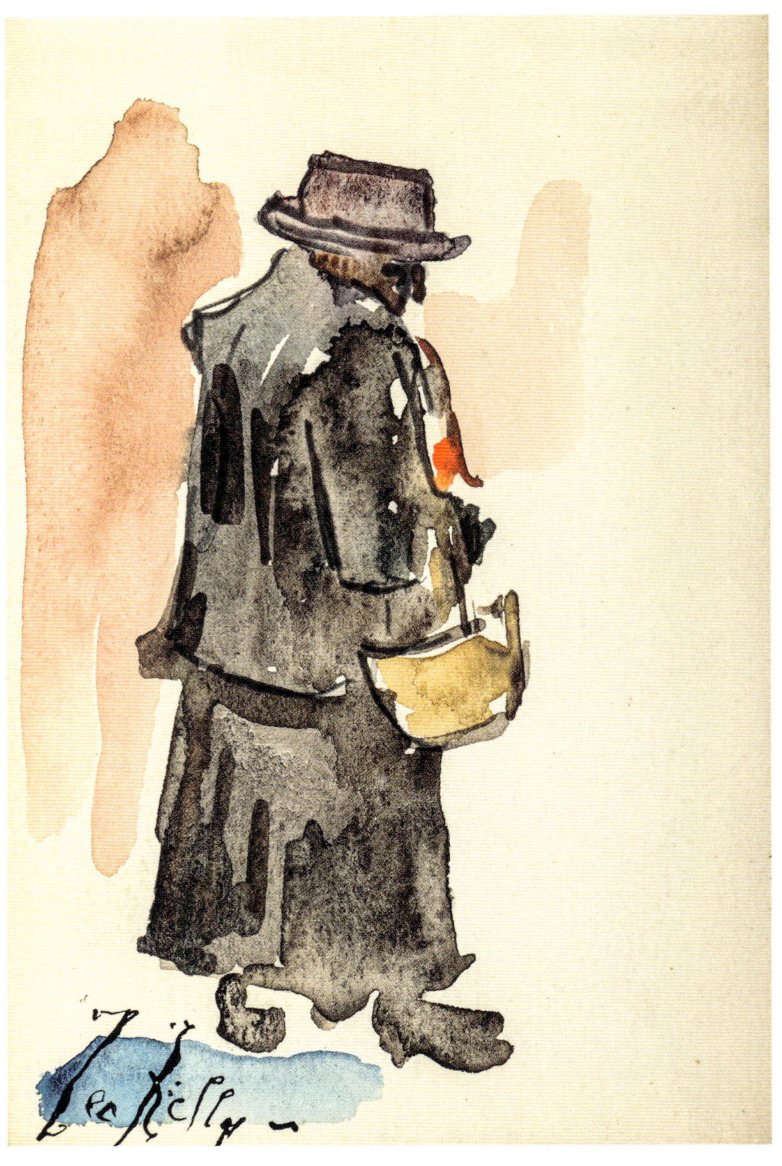

85
Untitled
Ink and watercolors, 15 × 9.5 cm

86
Untitled, 1930
Watercolors, 17 × 12 cm

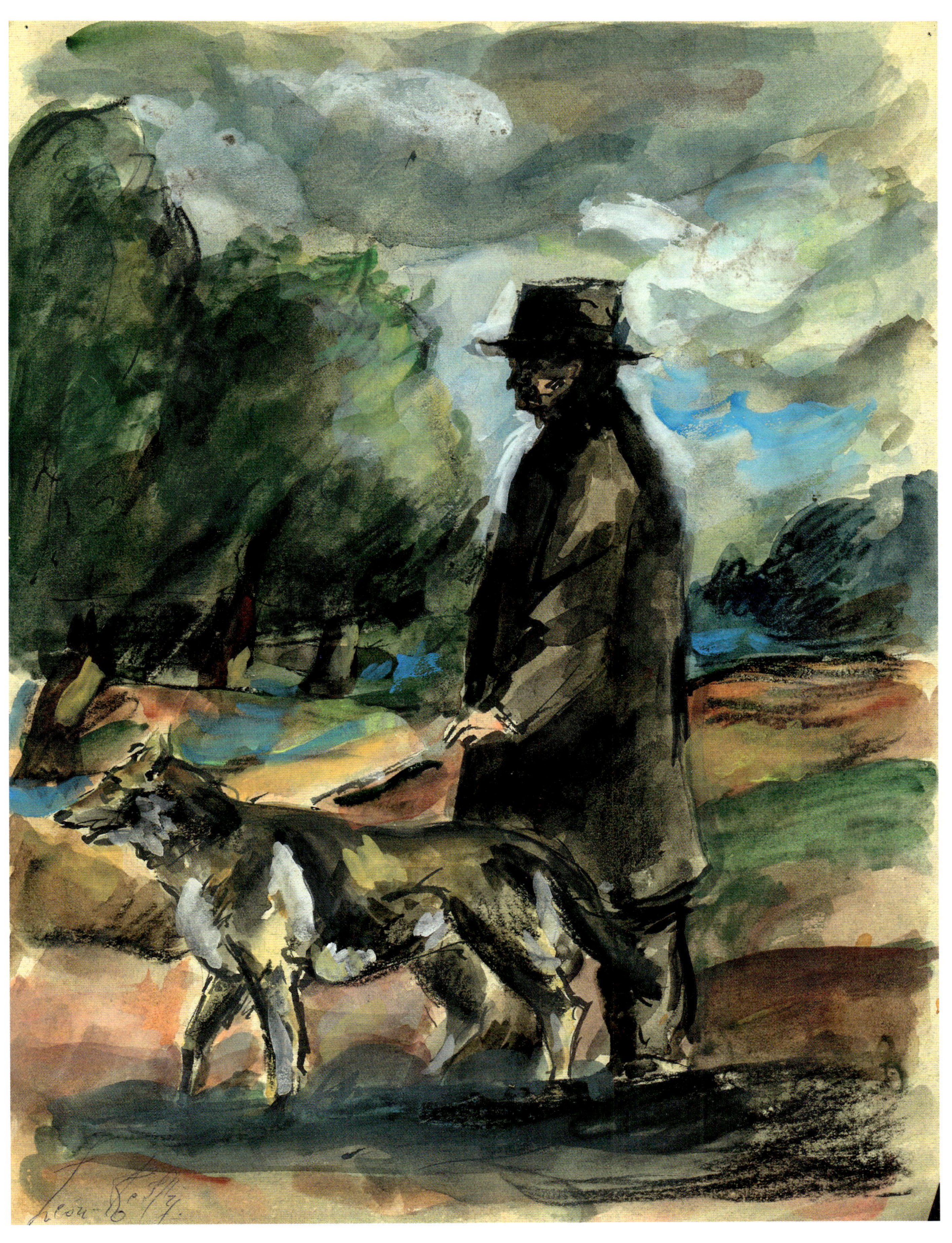

87
Untitled, ca. 1930
Watercolors, 30 × 22.5 cmm

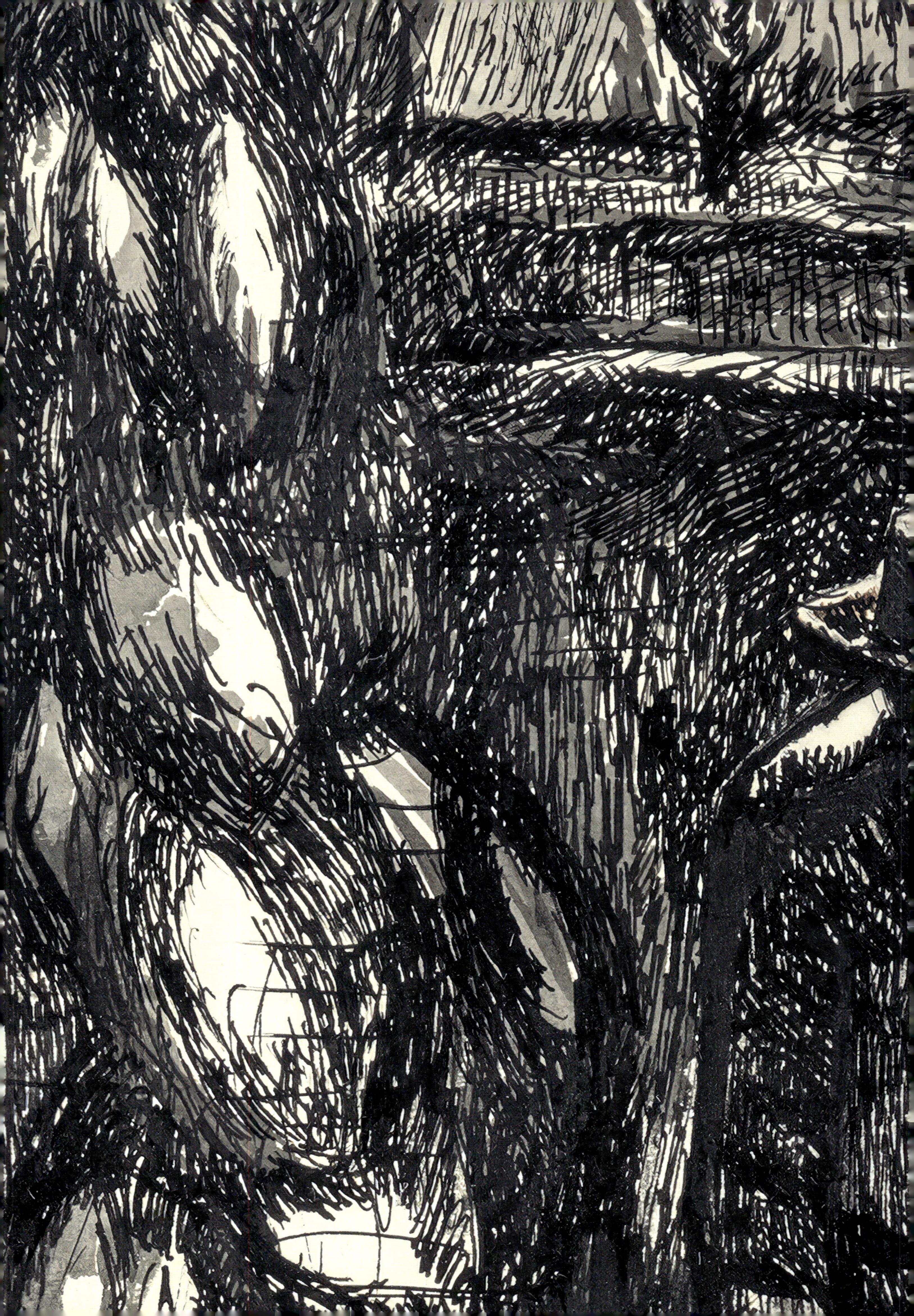

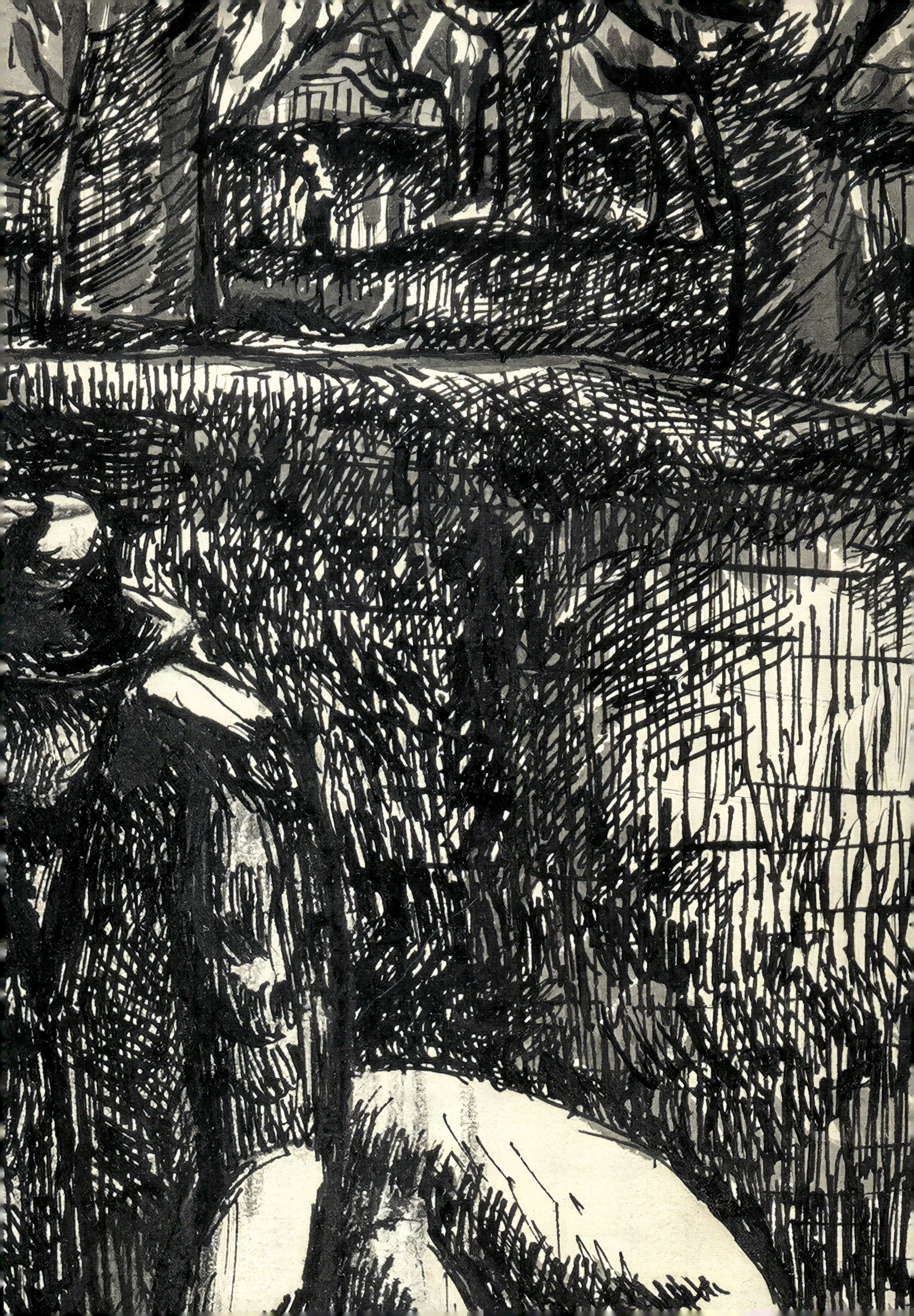

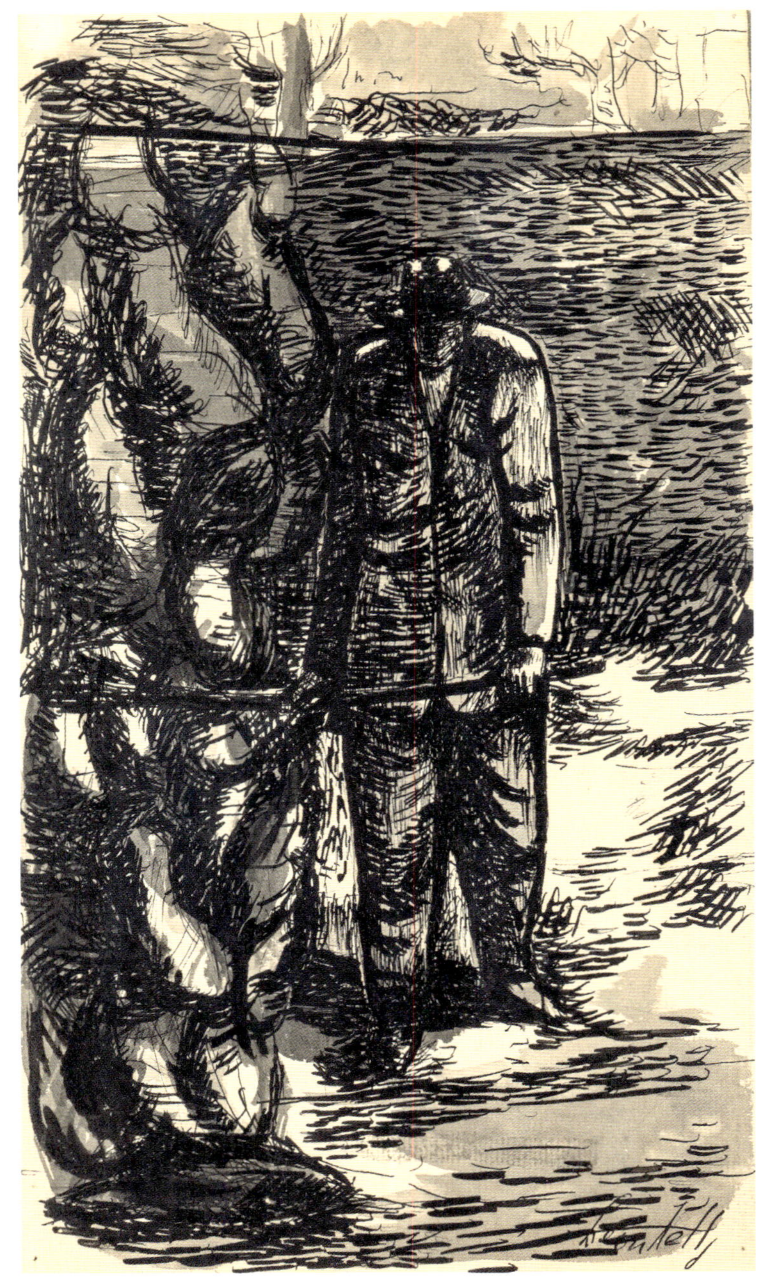

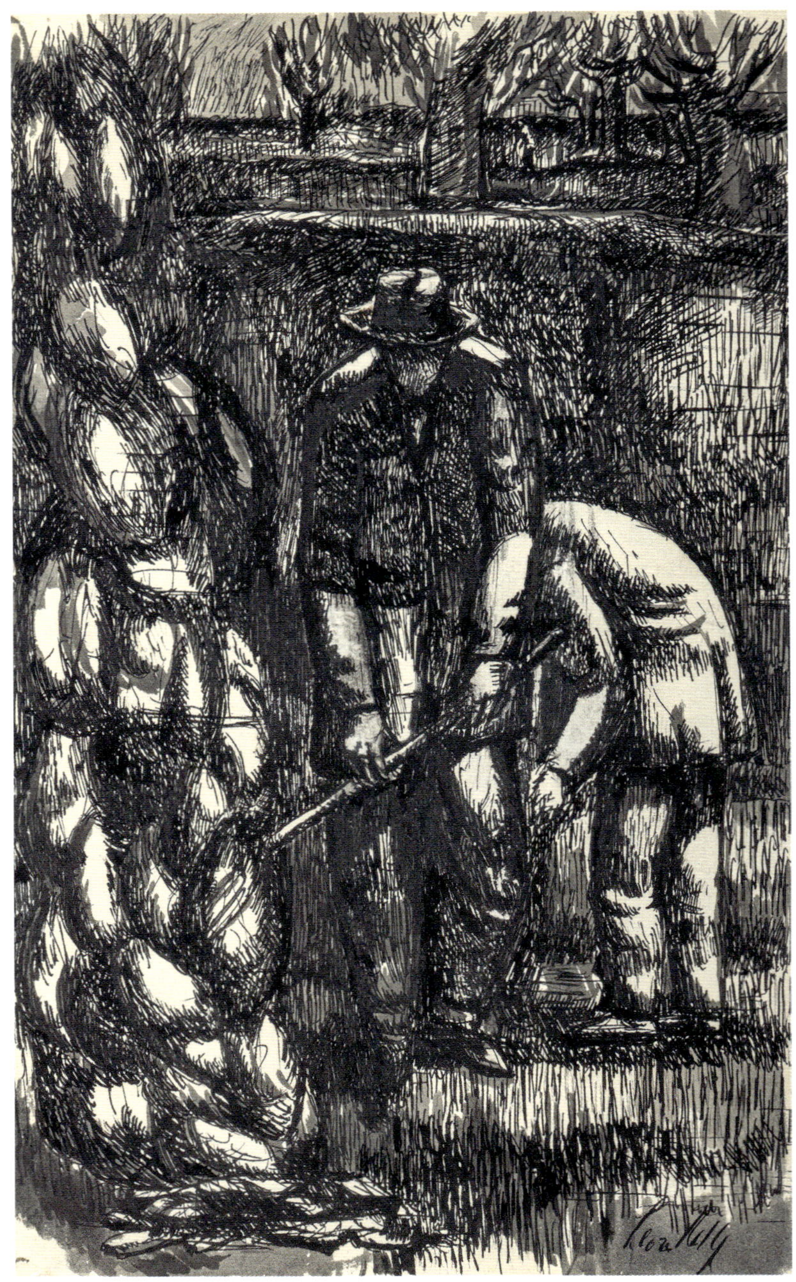

88
Untitled, ca. 1930
Ink, 29 × 17 cm

89
Untitled
Ink, 29 × 17.5 cm

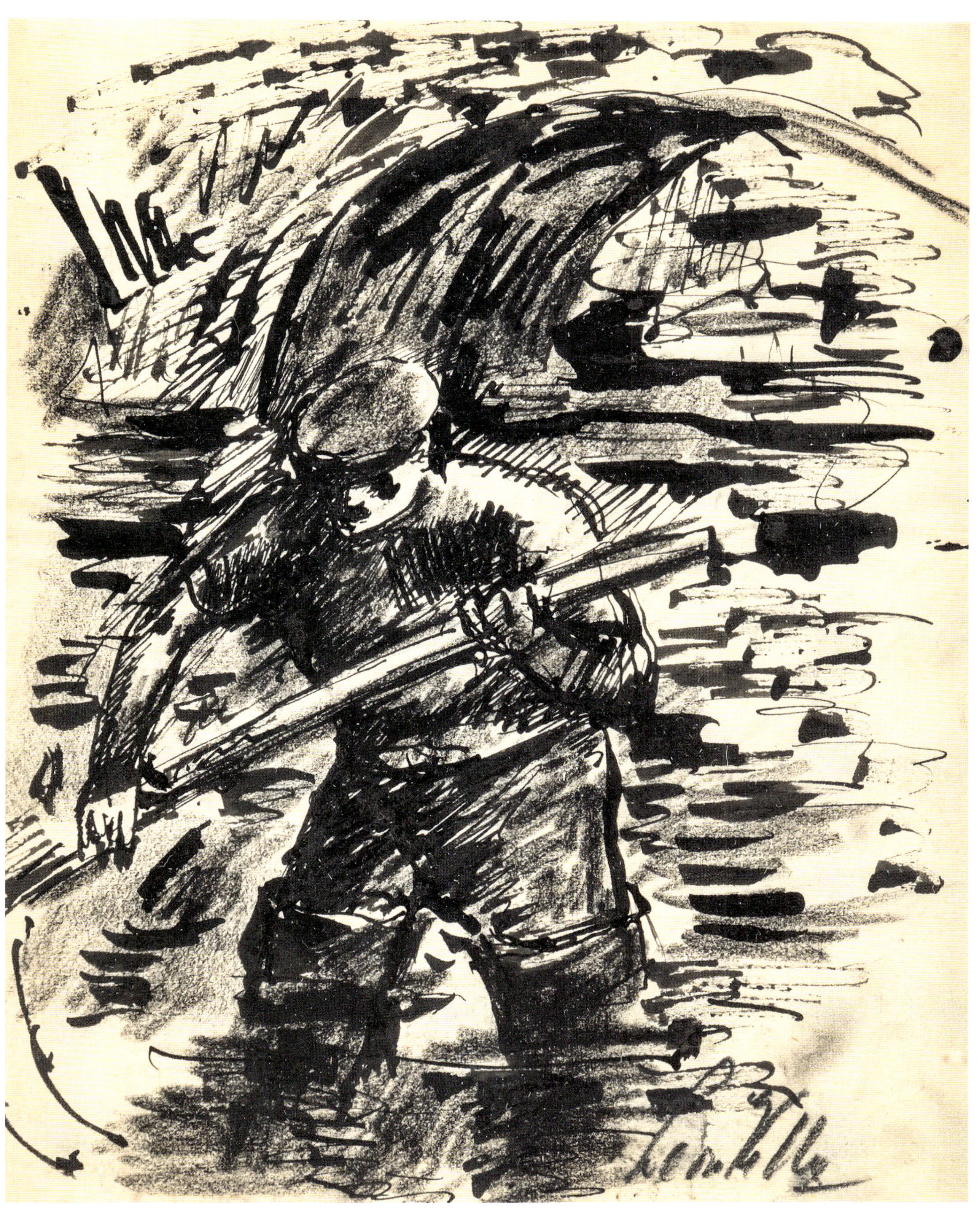

90
Untitled
Ink, 17 × 13.5 cm

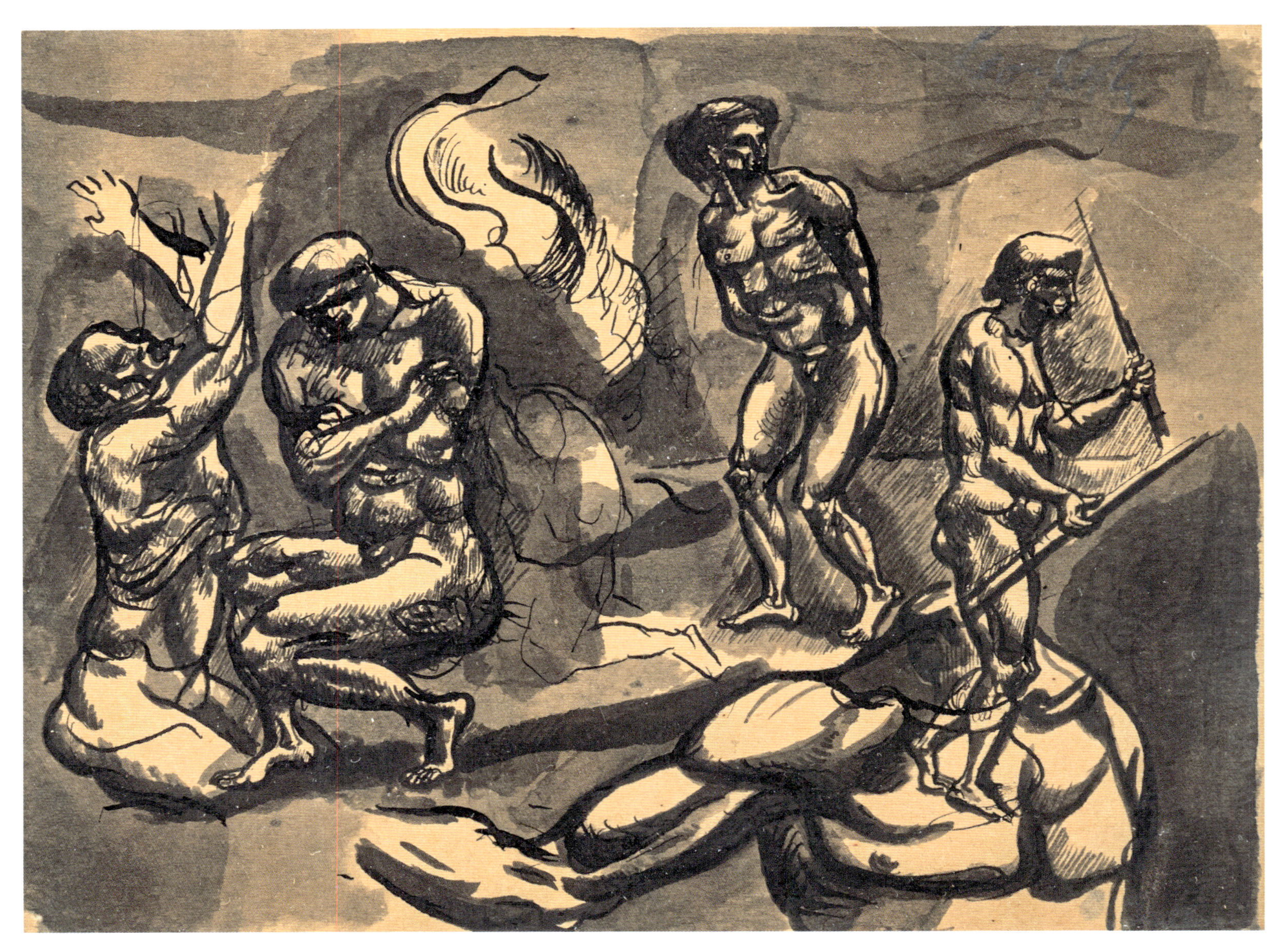

91
Untitled
Ink, 13 × 17 cm

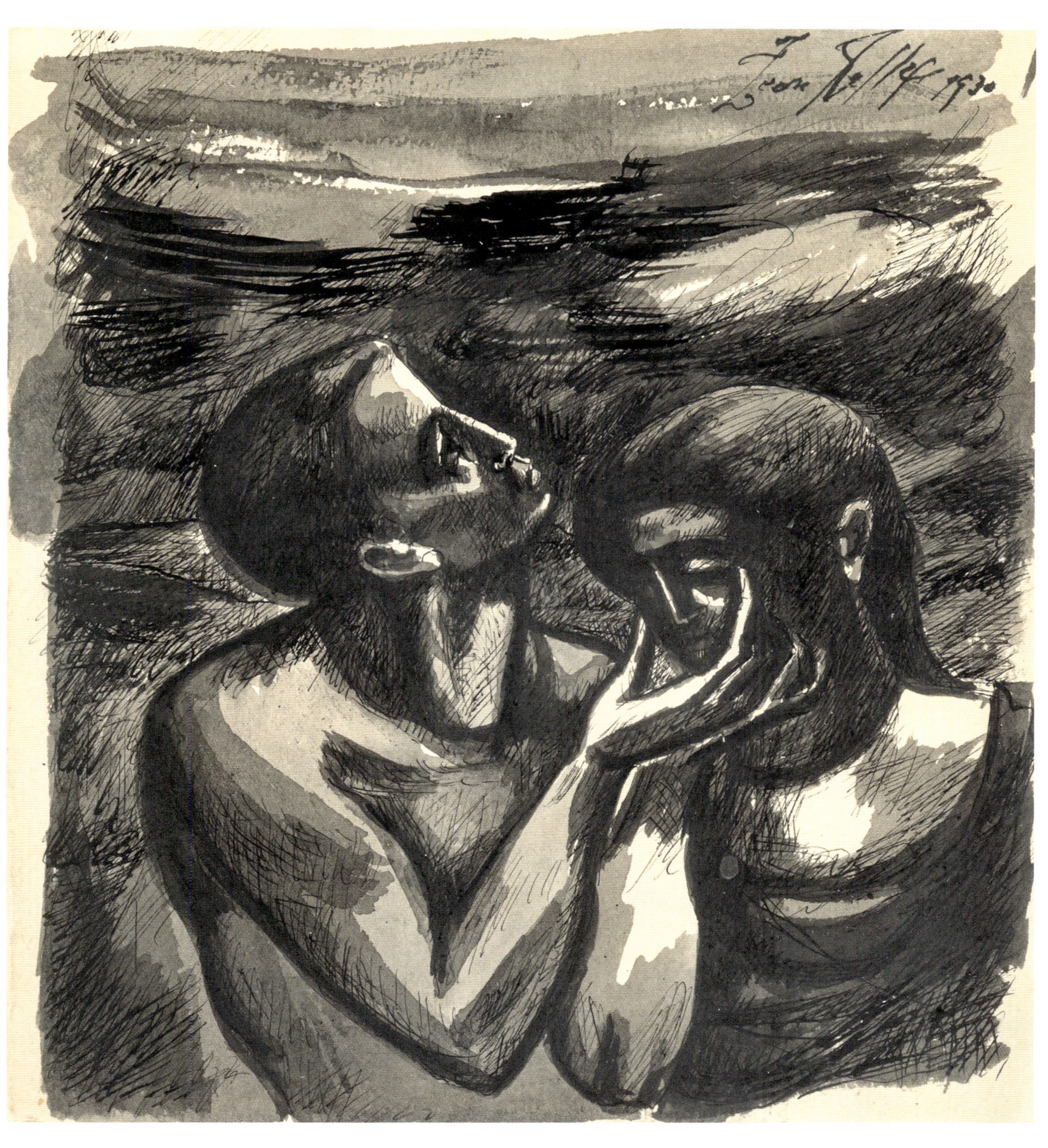

92
Untitled, 1930
Ink, 17 × 16 cm

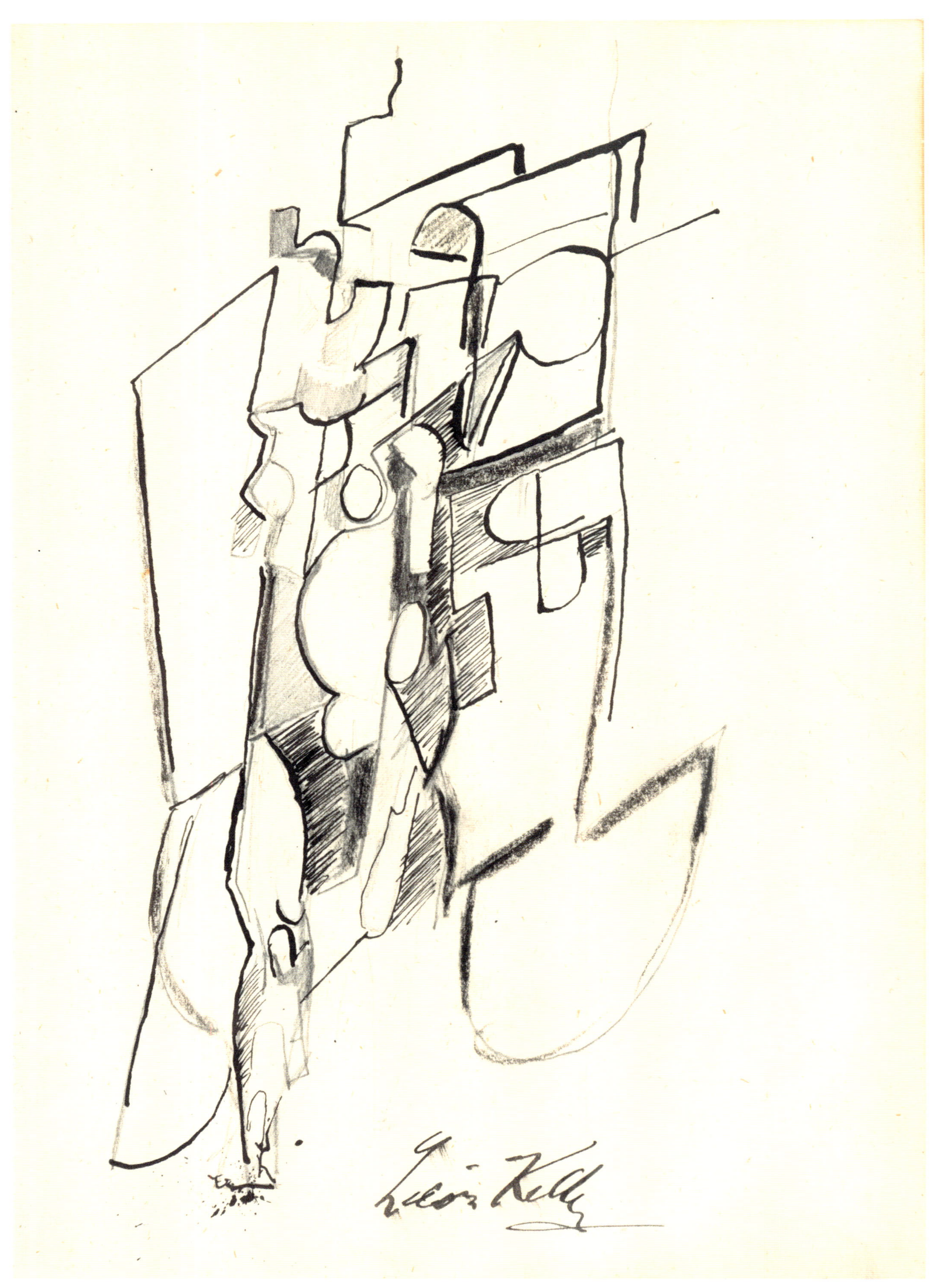

93
Untitled, ca. 1930
Ink, 18.5 × 13.5 cm

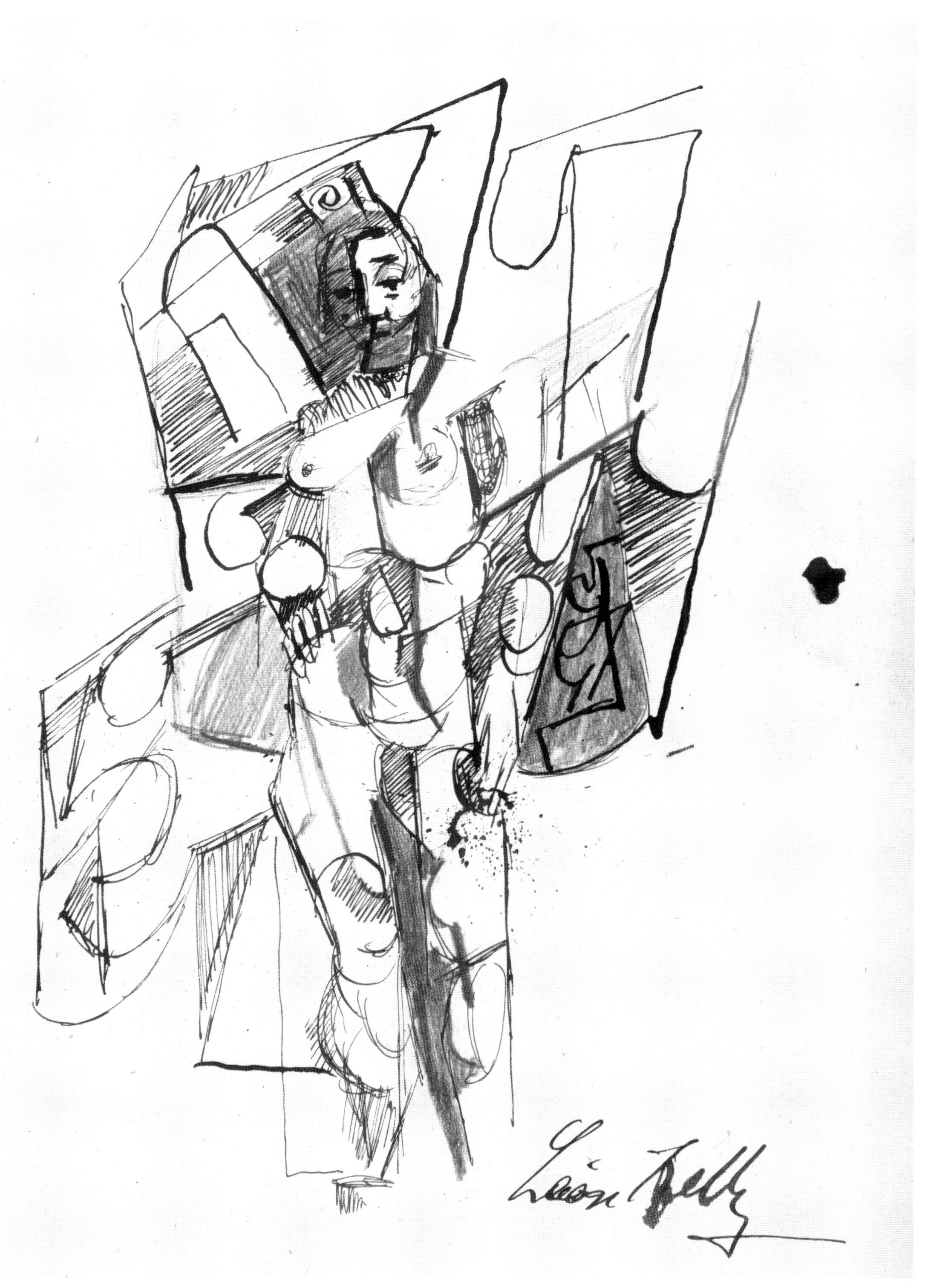

94
Untitled, ca. 1931
Ink, 18.5 × 13.5 cm

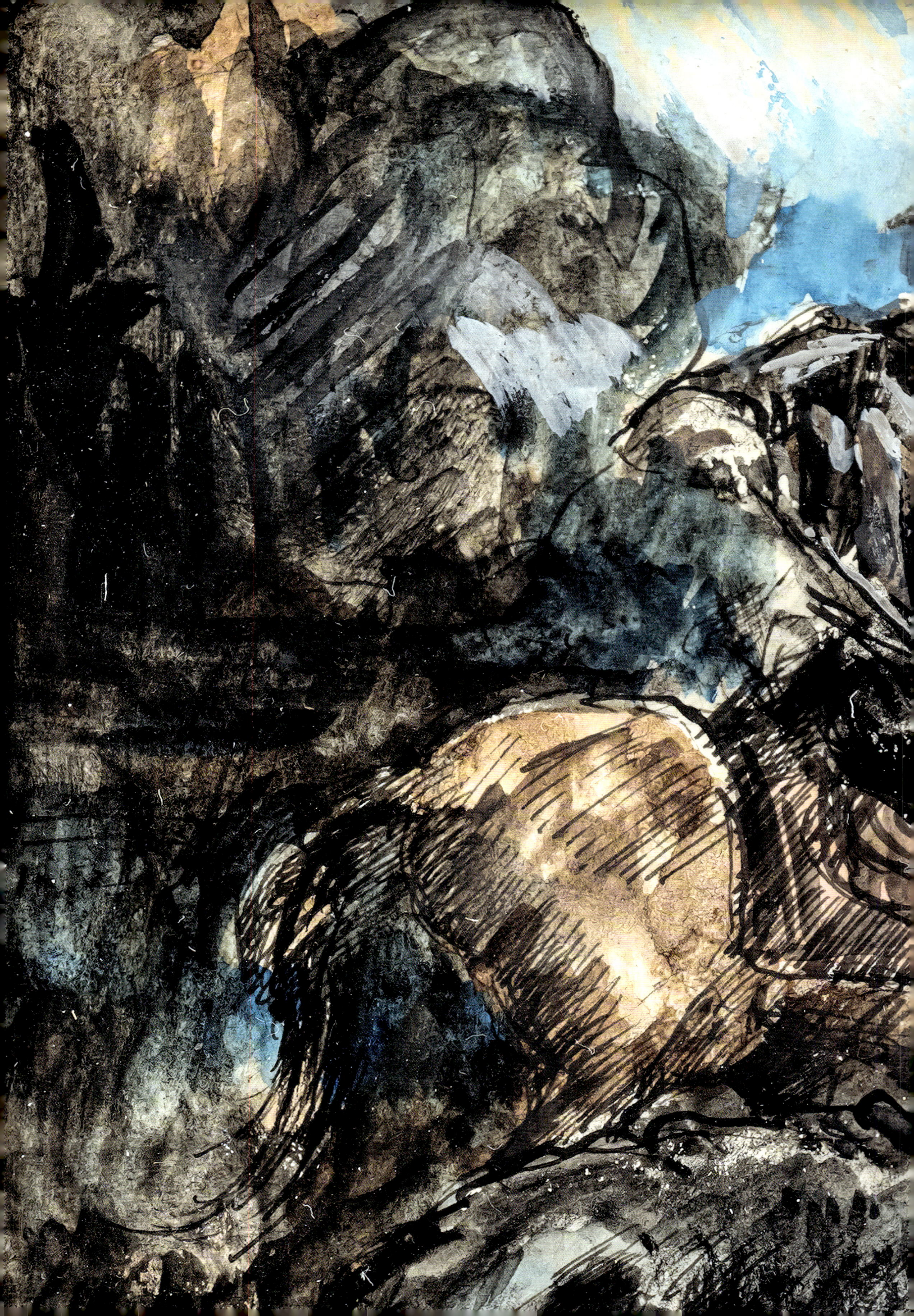

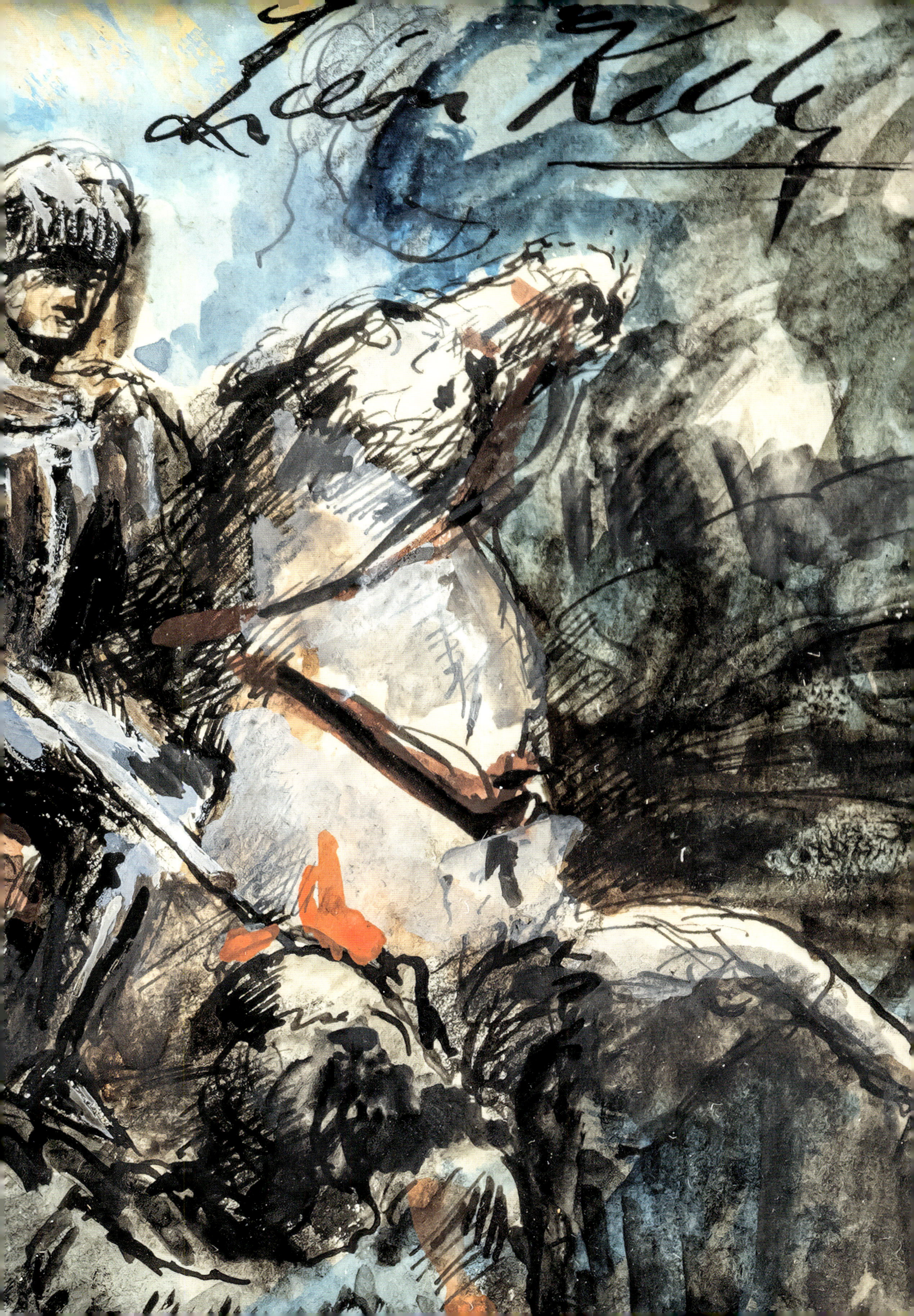

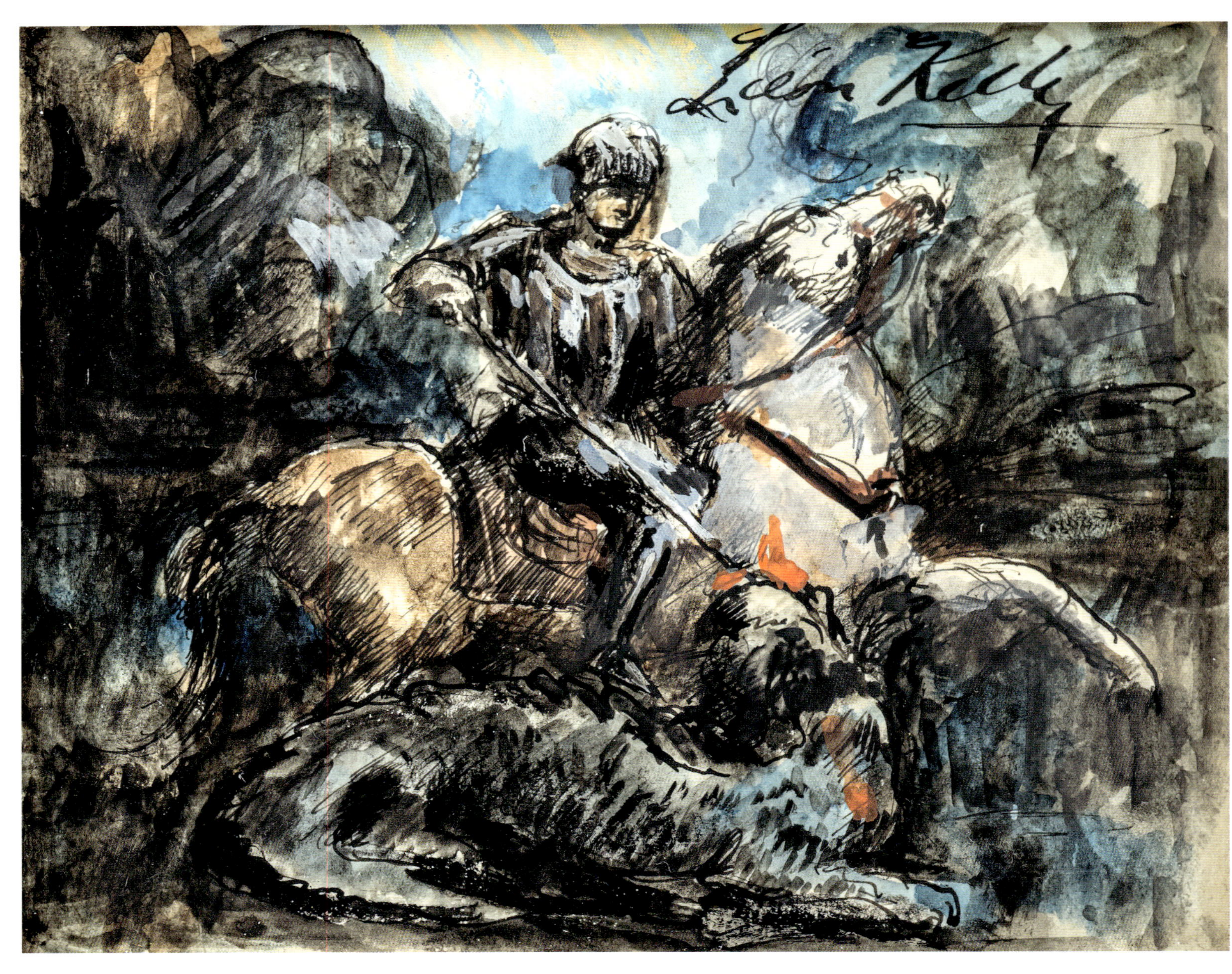

95
Untitled
Ink and watercolors, 10.5 × 12.5 cm

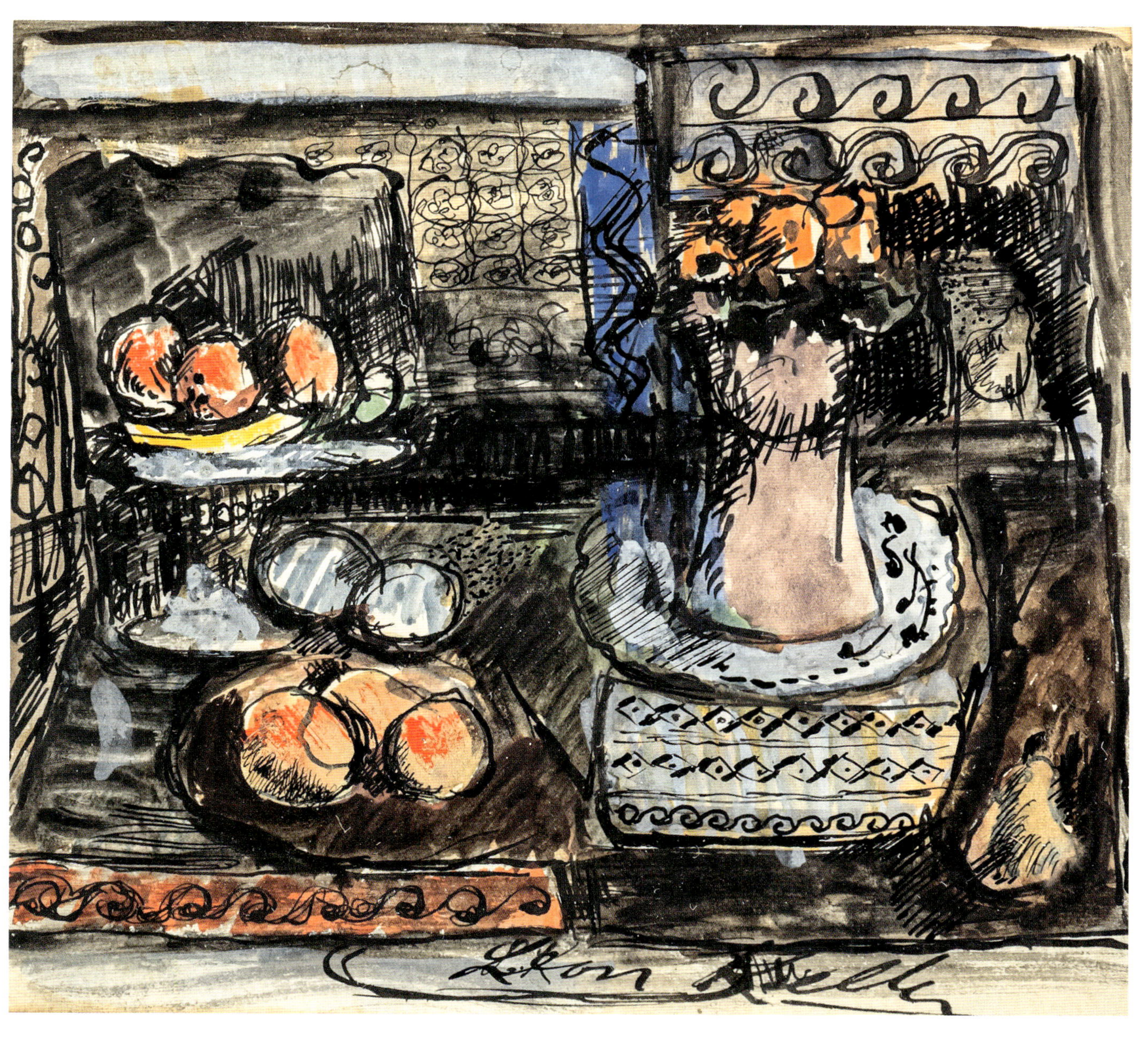

96
Untitled
Ink and watercolors, 10 × 11 cm

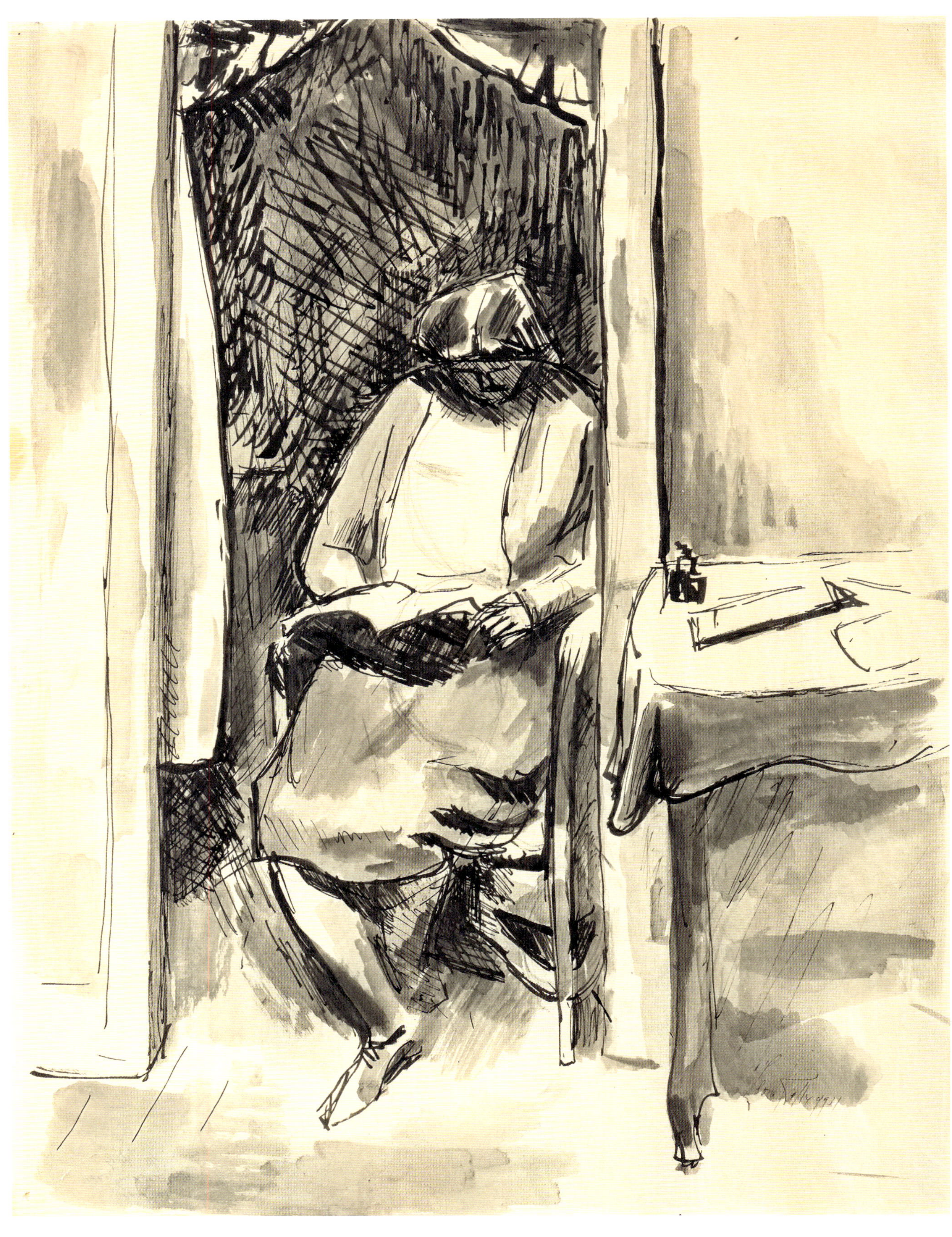

97
Untitled, 1931
Ink, 55.5 × 42.5 cm

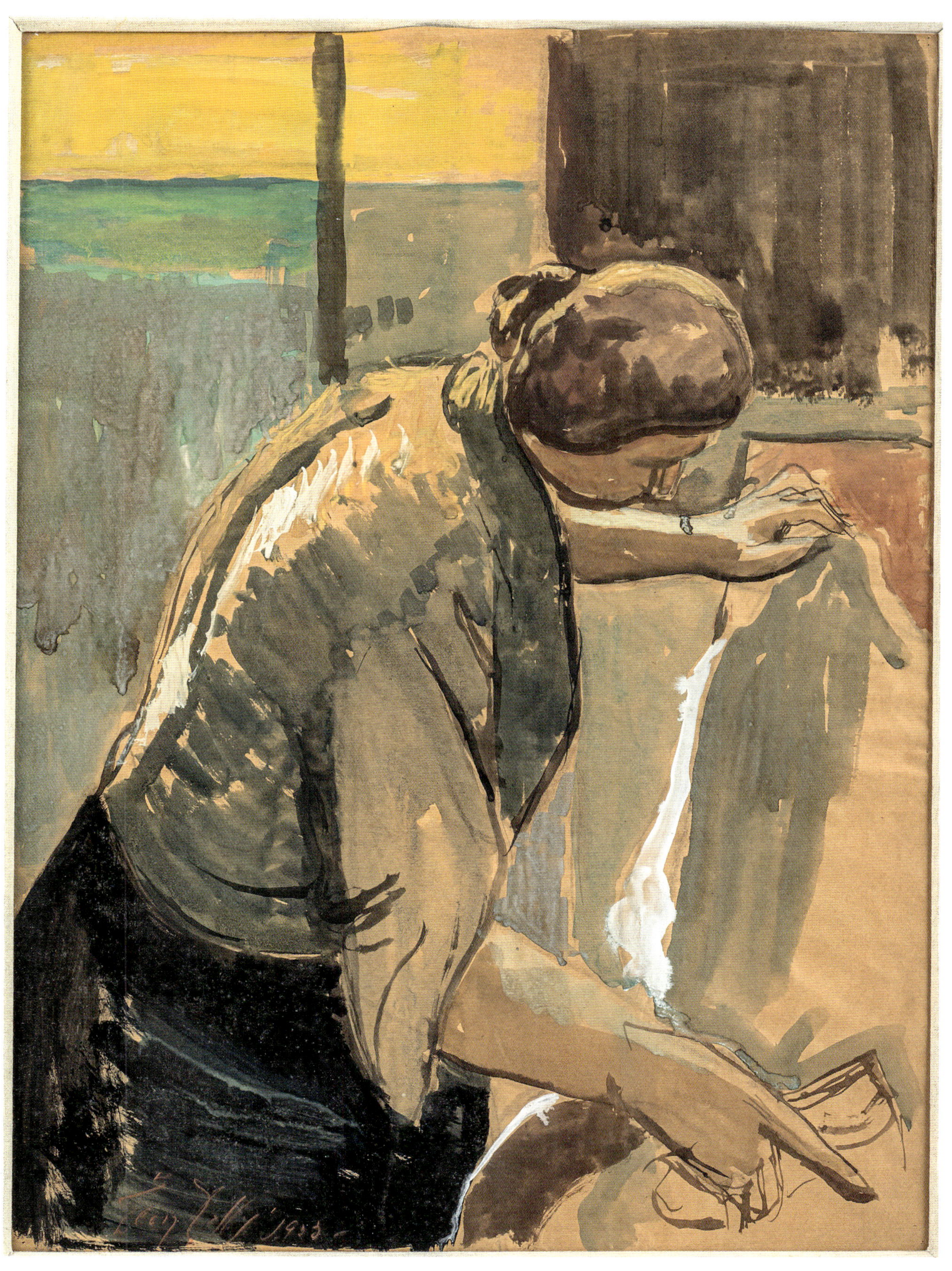

98
Untitled, 1933
Gouache, 60 × 45 cm (compare no. 22, p. 57)

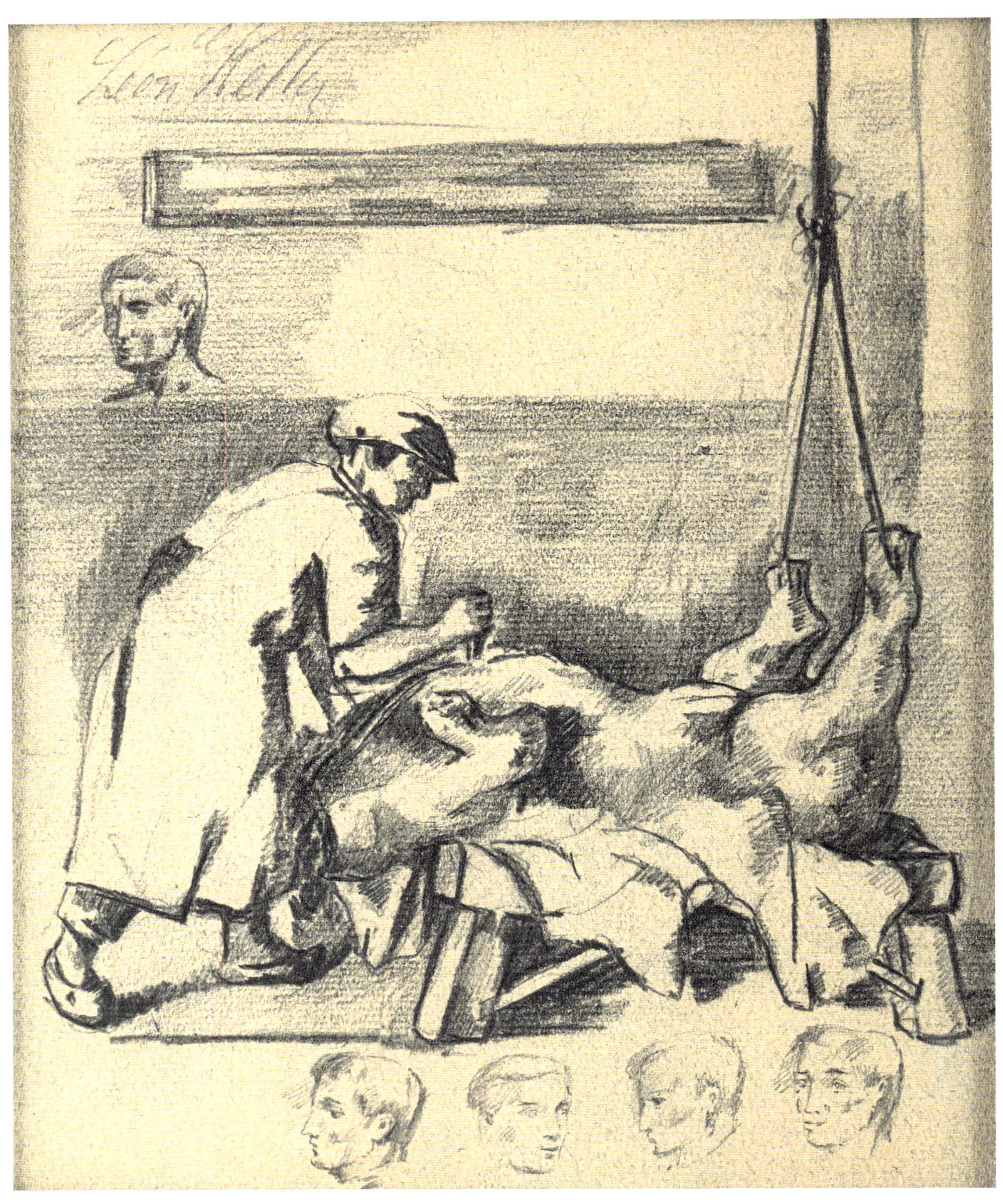

99
Untitled
Charcoal, 22.5 × 18.5 cm

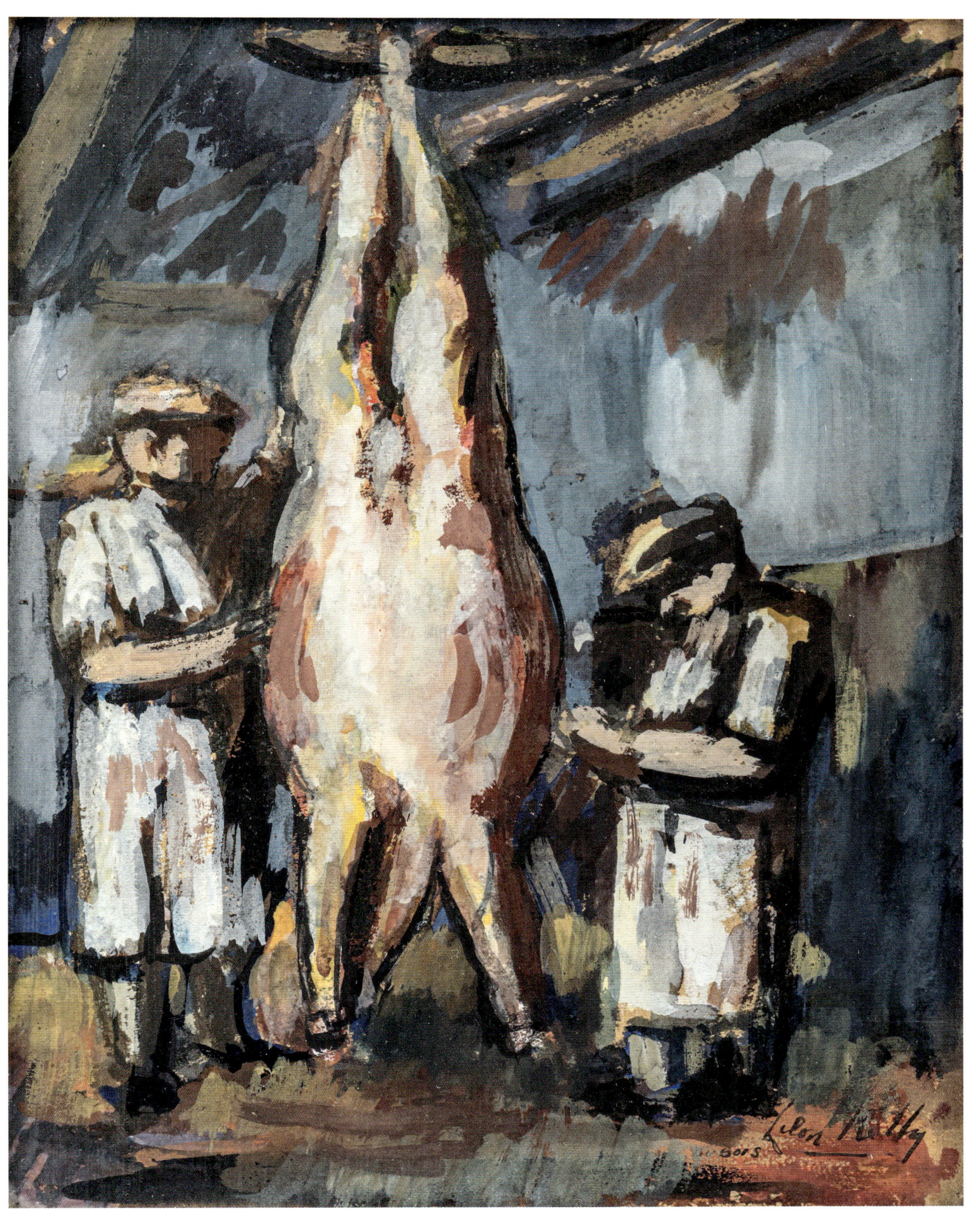

100
Untitled
Gouache, 23.5 × 18.5 cm

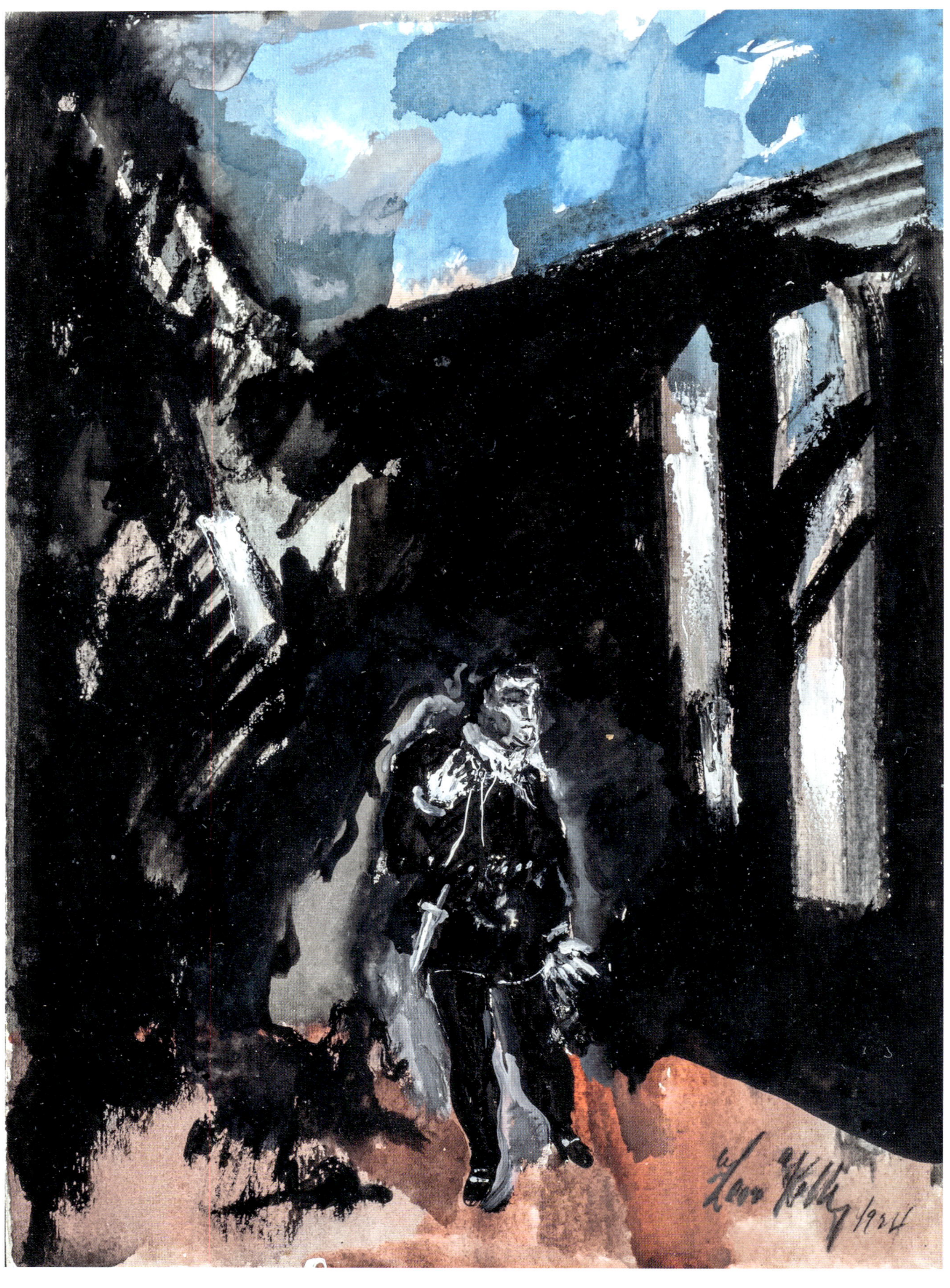

101
Untitled
Ink and gouache, 28 × 21 cm

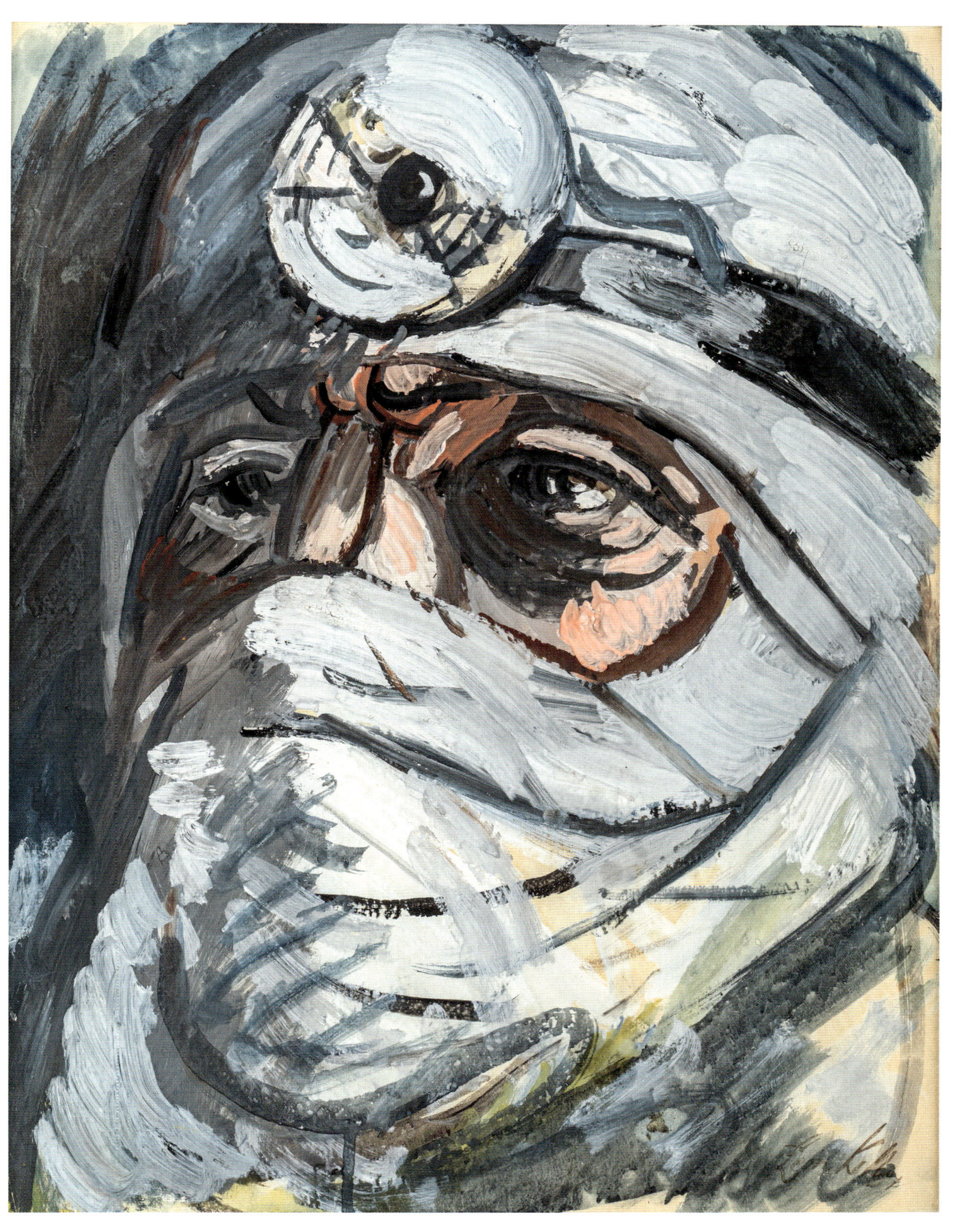

102
Untitled
Gouache, 54.5 × 41.5 cm

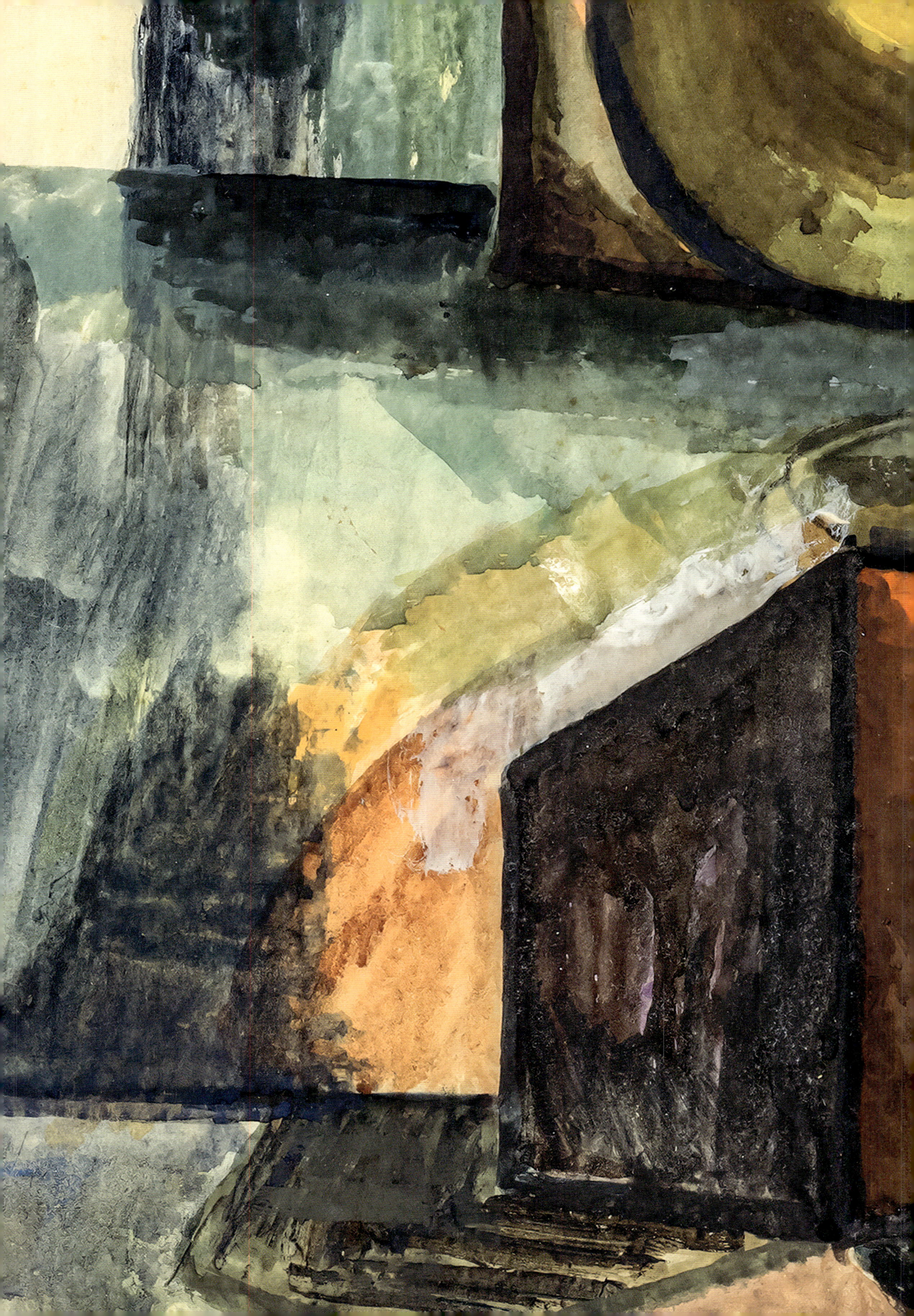

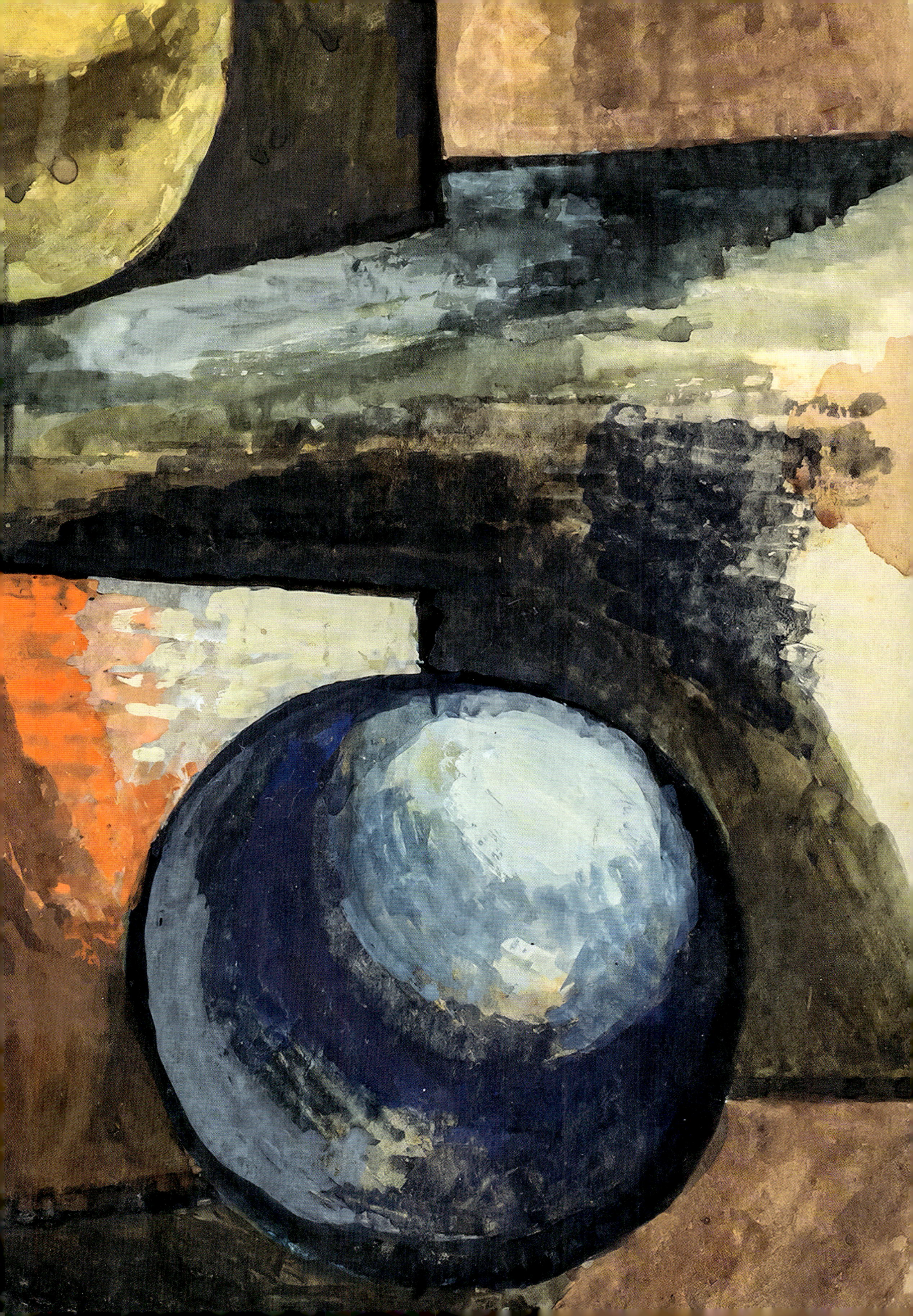

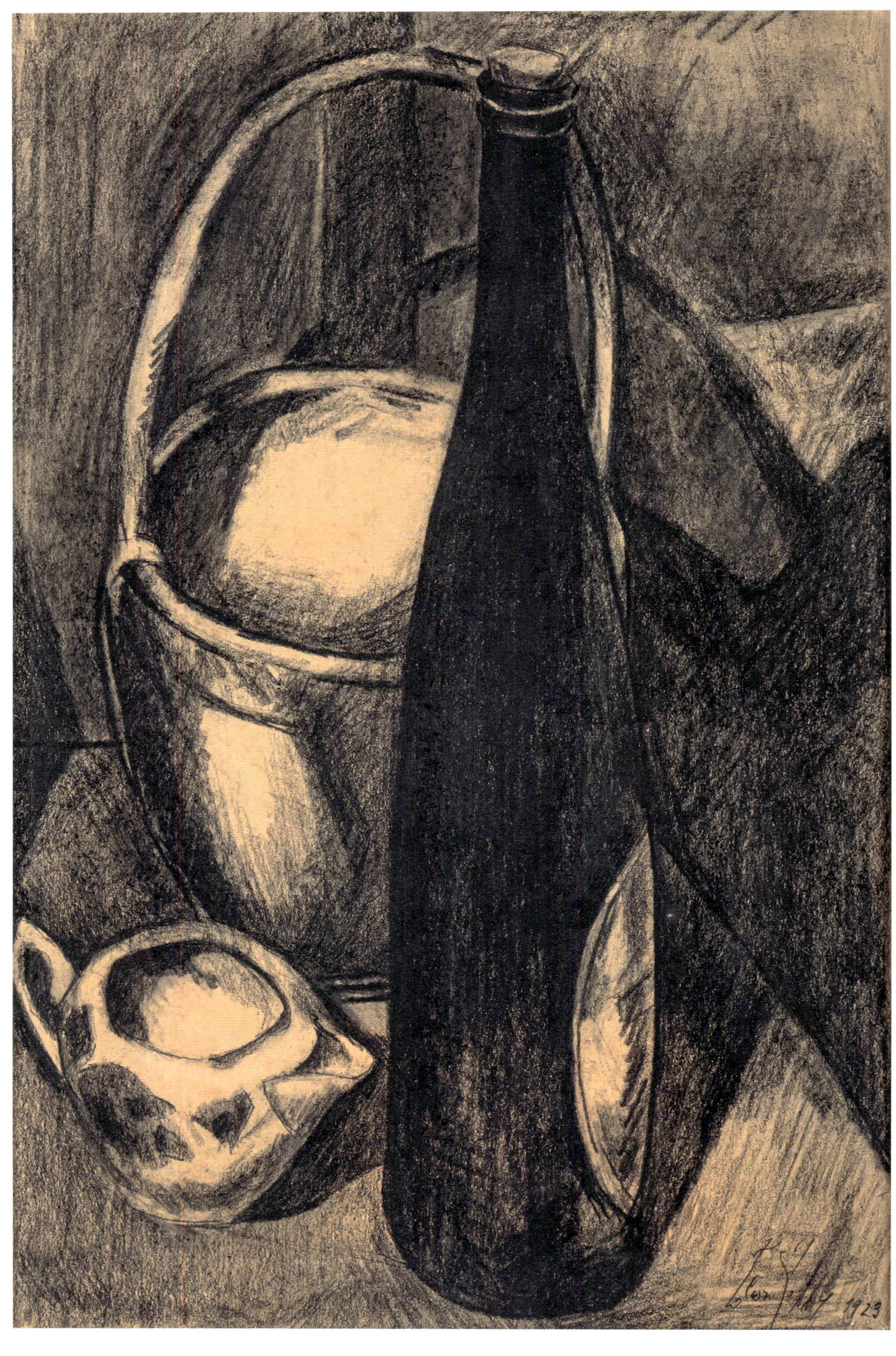

103
The Rhine Wine Bottle, 1923
Charcoal, 45 × 30 cm

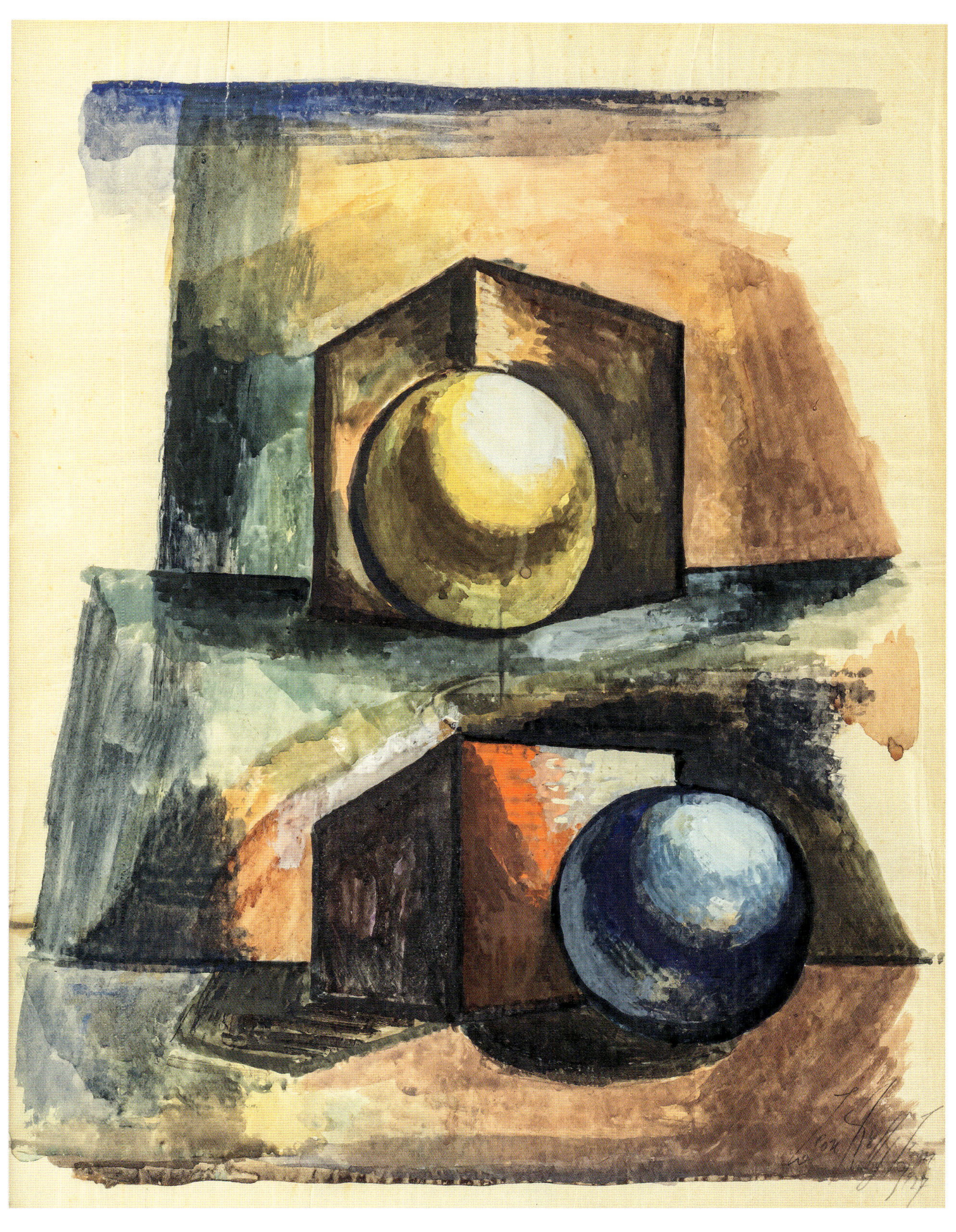

104
Untitled, 1933
Gouache, 54.5 × 42 cm

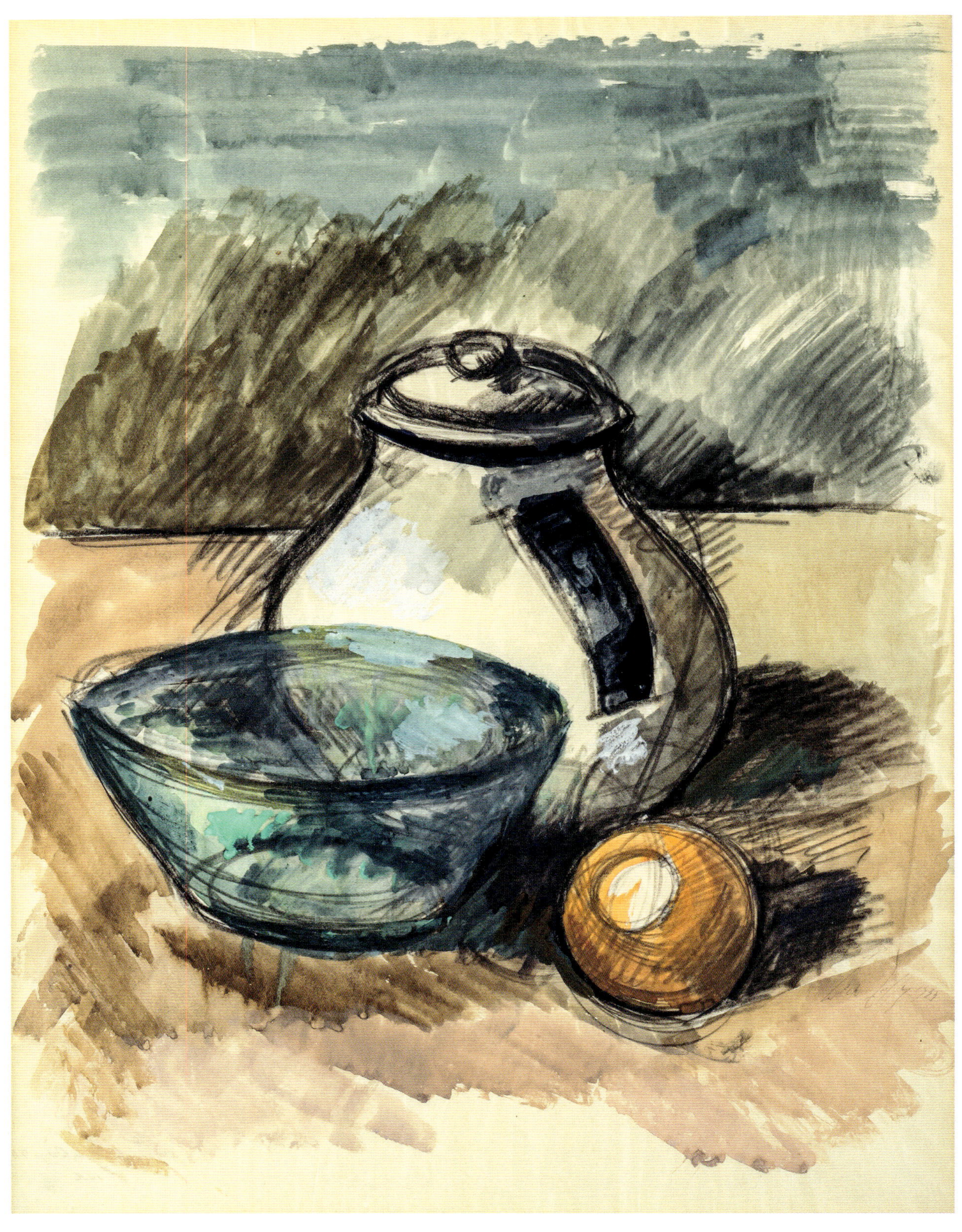

105
Untitled
Gouache, 54.5 × 42 cm

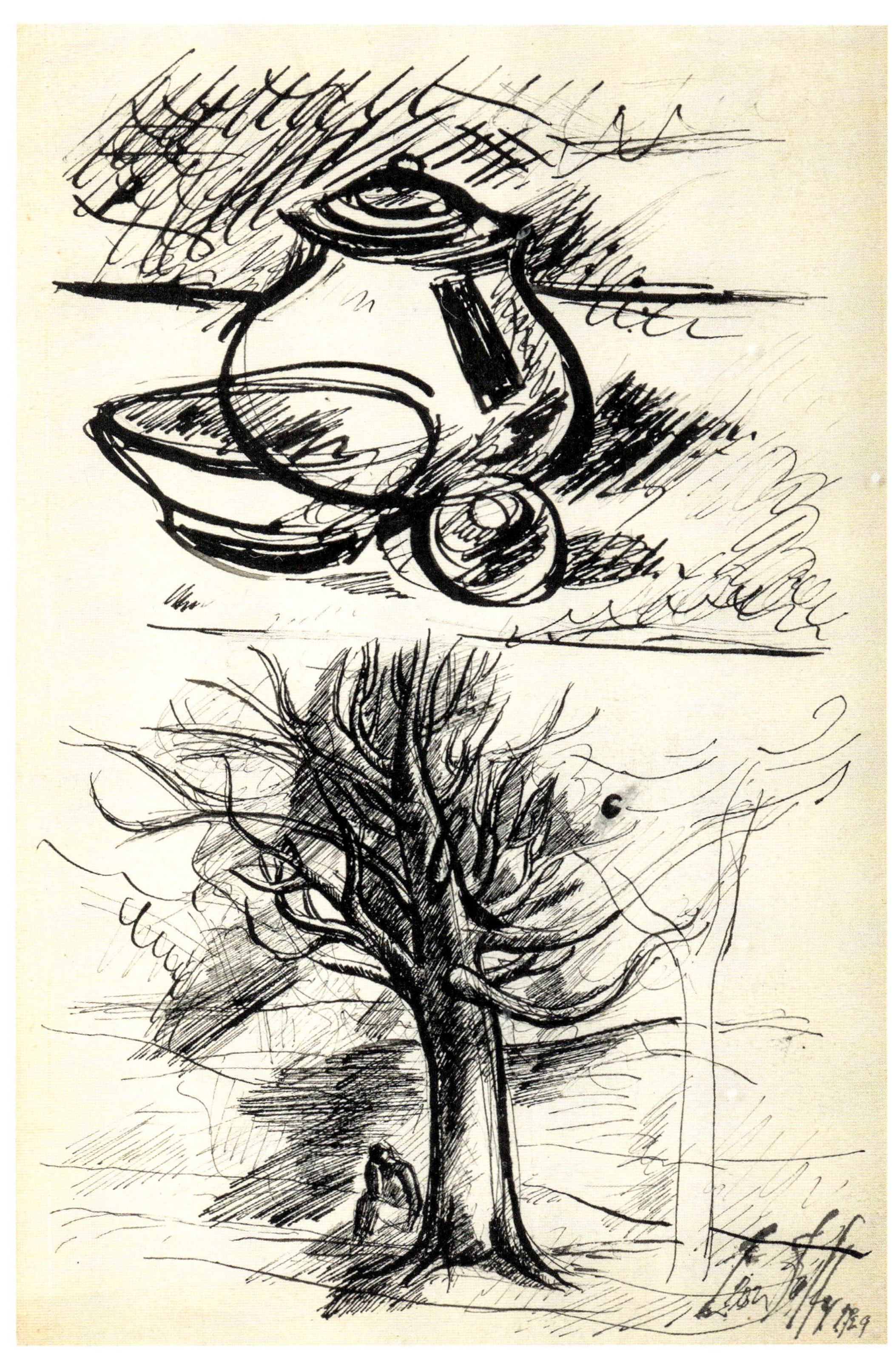

106
Untitled
Ink, 21 × 13 cm

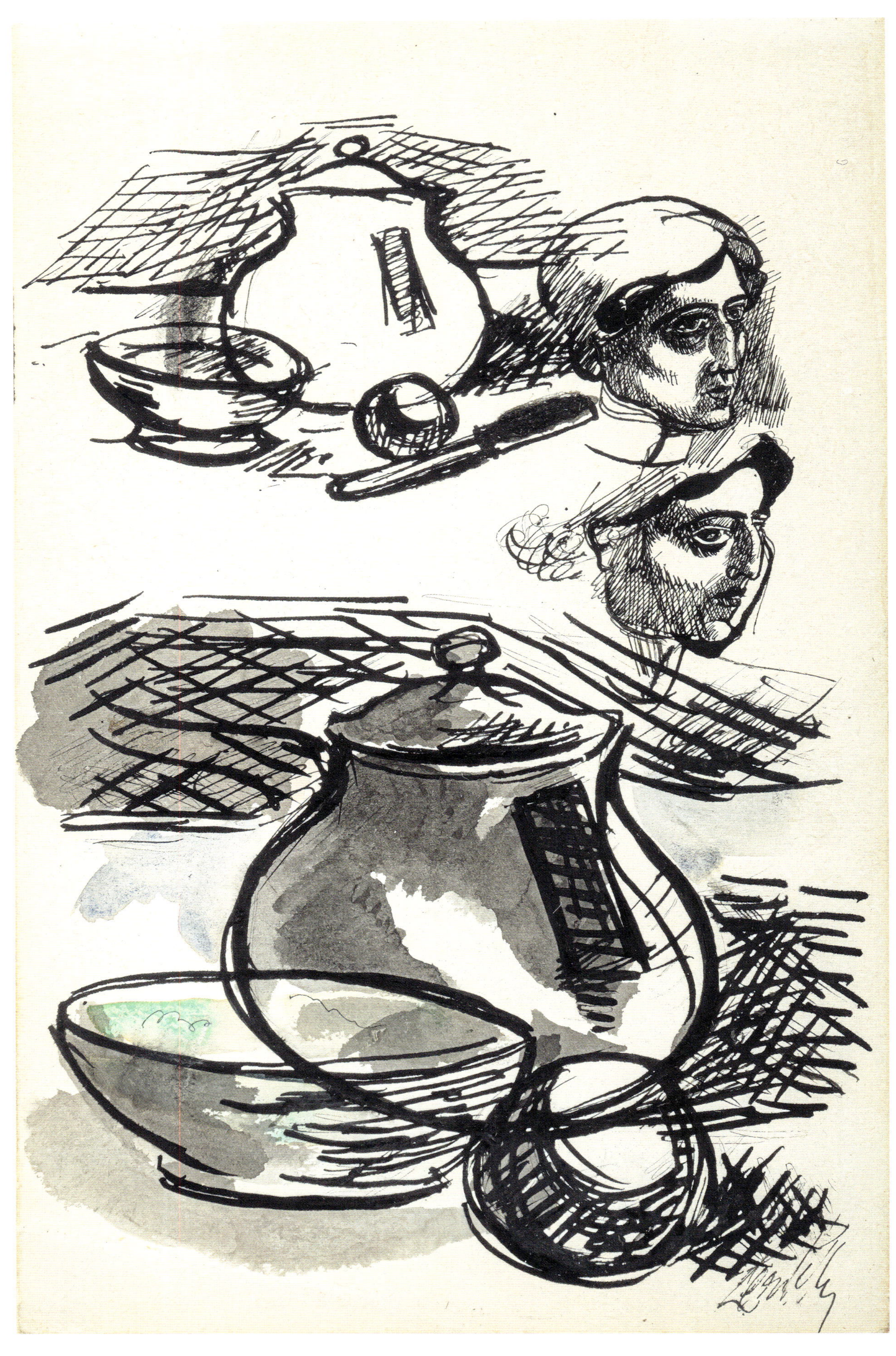

107
Untitled
Watercolor, 22 × 13 cm

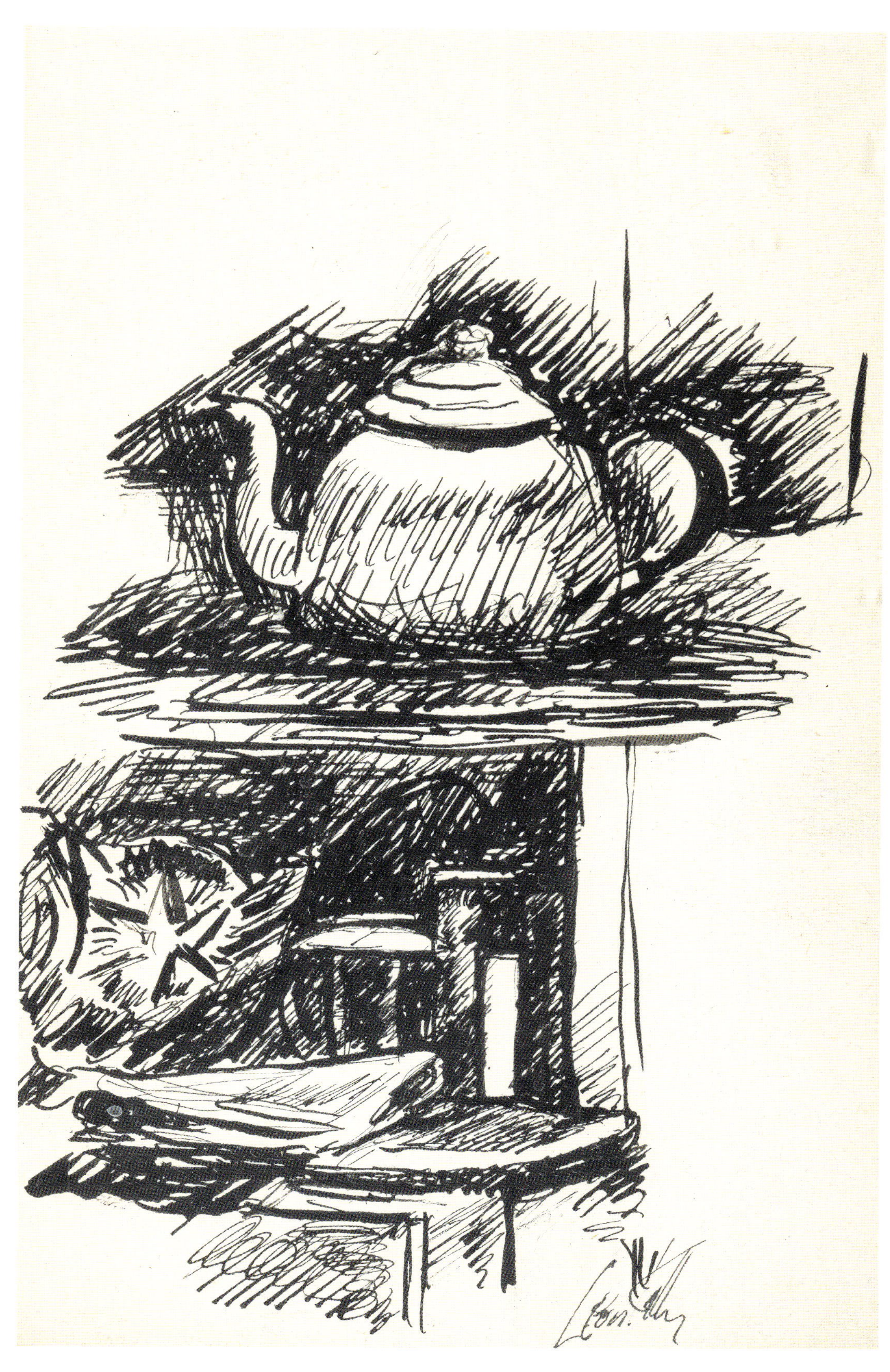

108
Untitled
Ink and watercolors, 12 × 13.5 cm

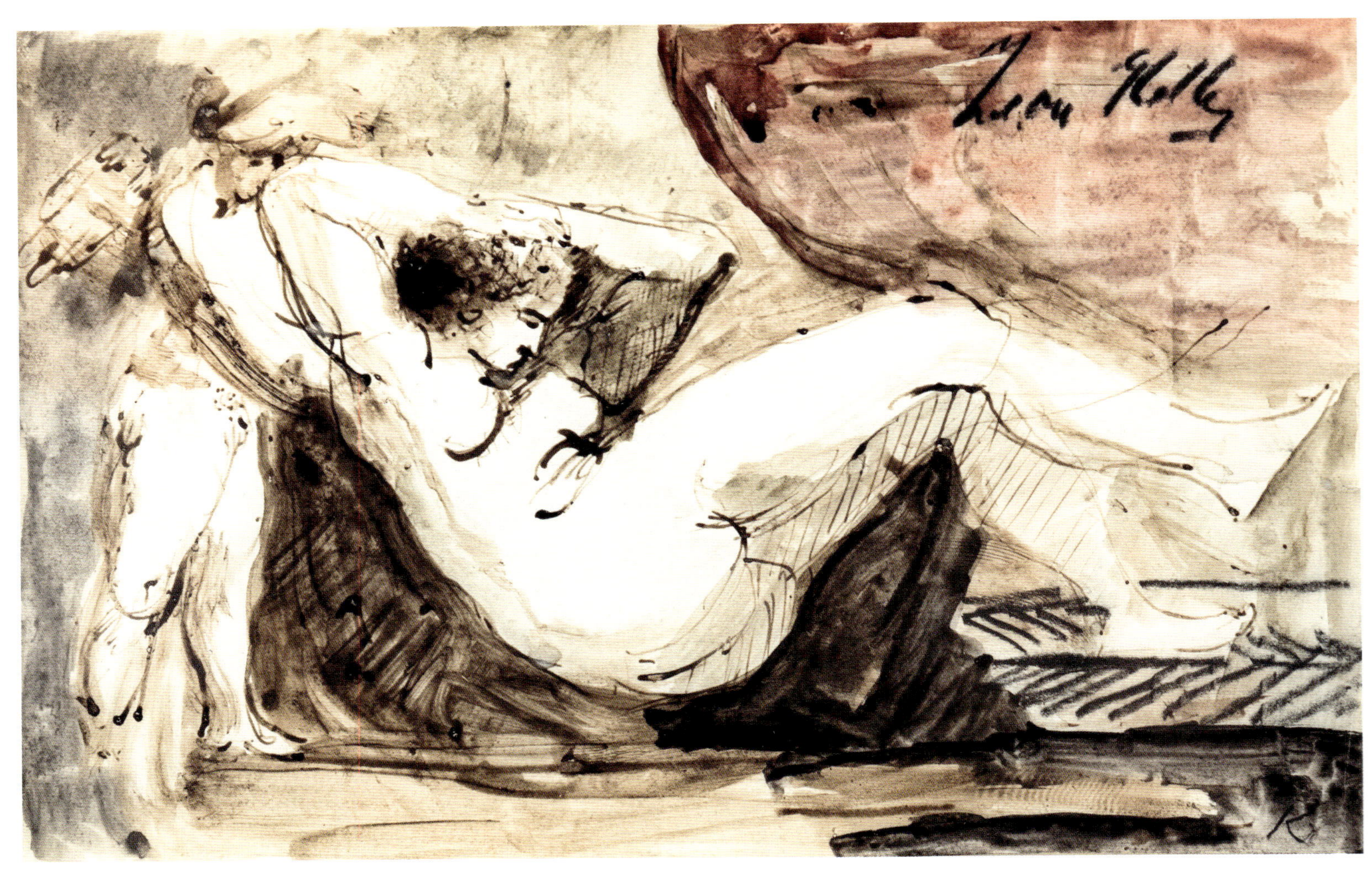

109
Untitled
Watercolors, 11 × 18 cm

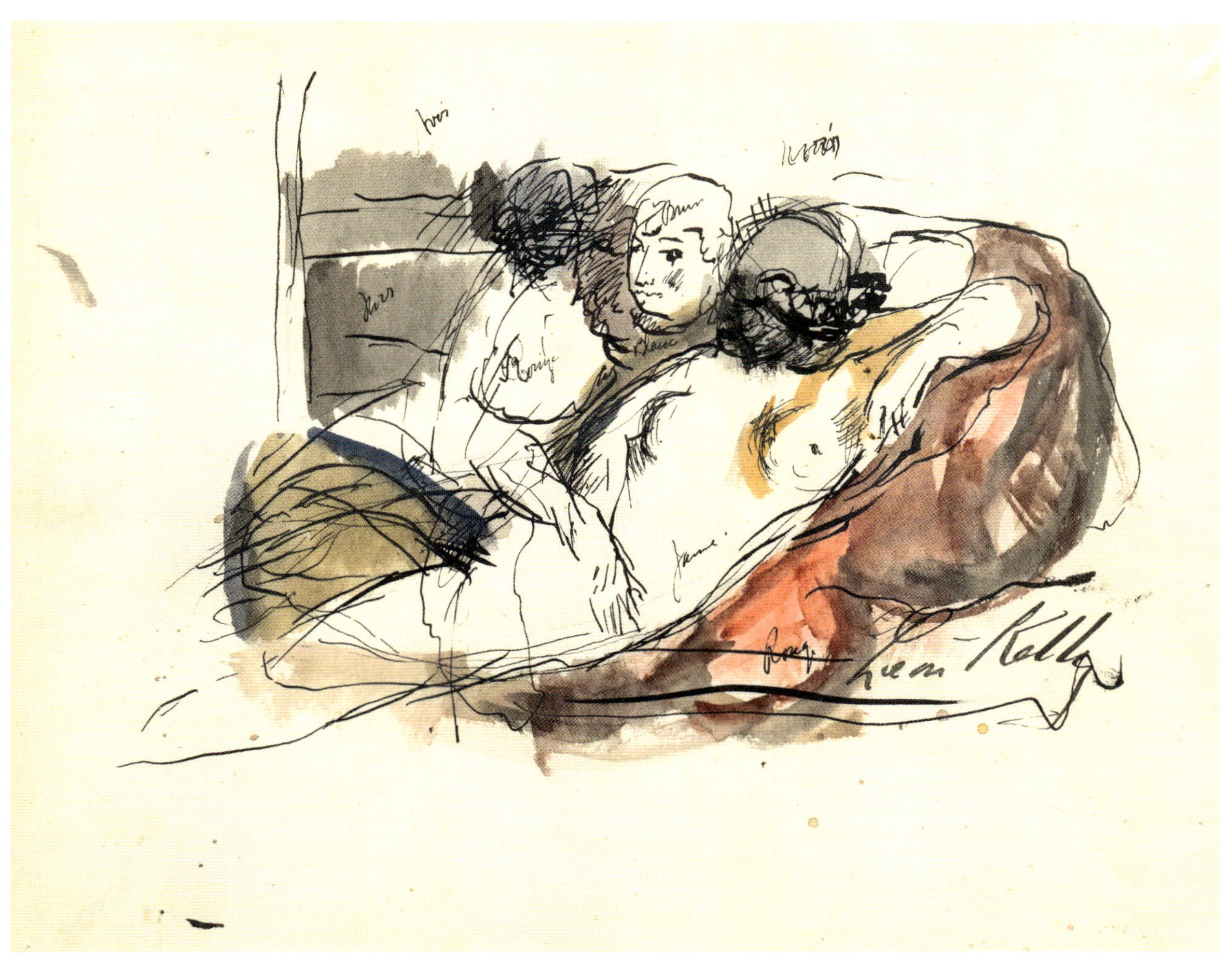

110
Untitled
Ink and watercolors, 18.5 × 24 cm

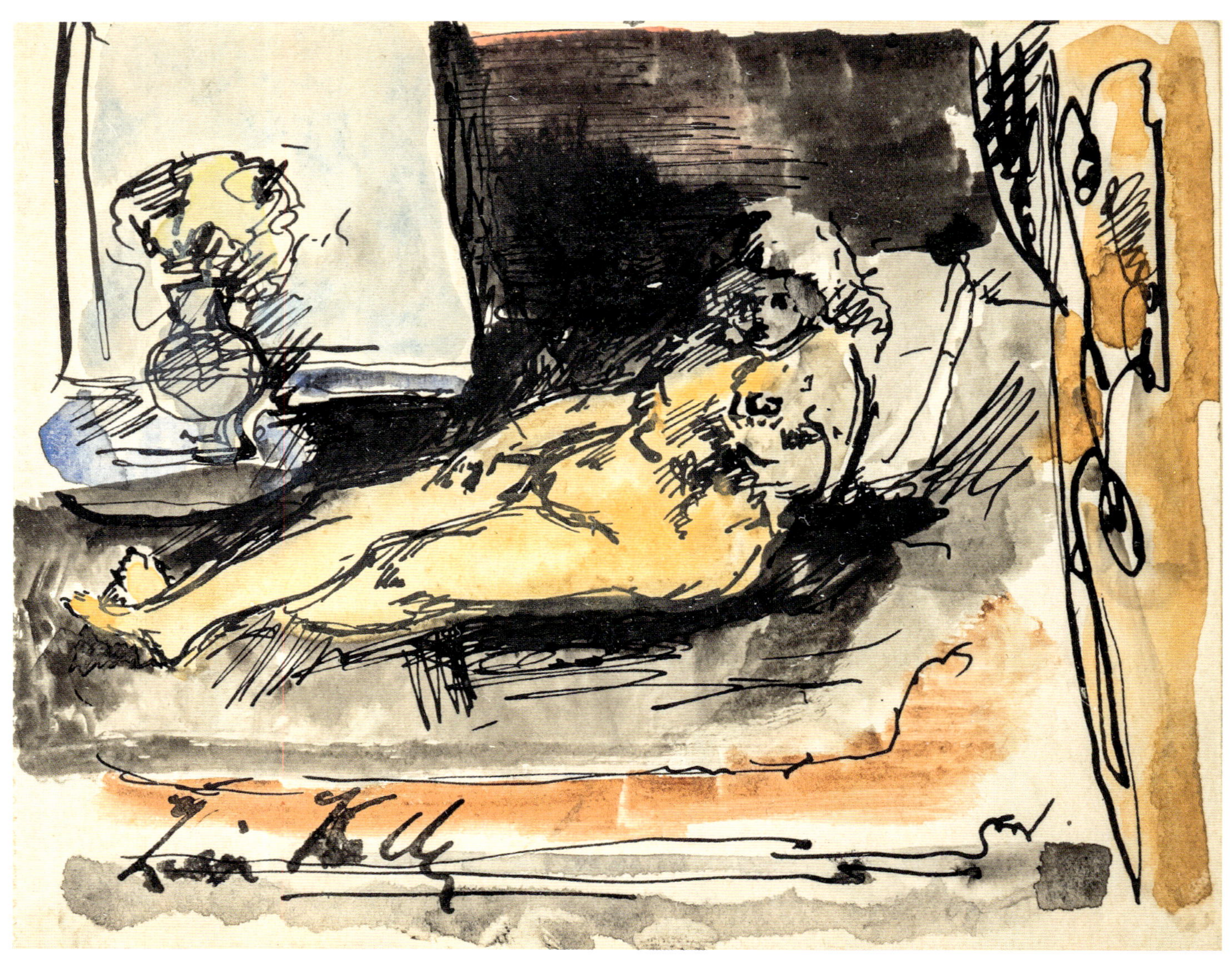

111
Untitled
Ink and watercolors, 10 × 12 cm

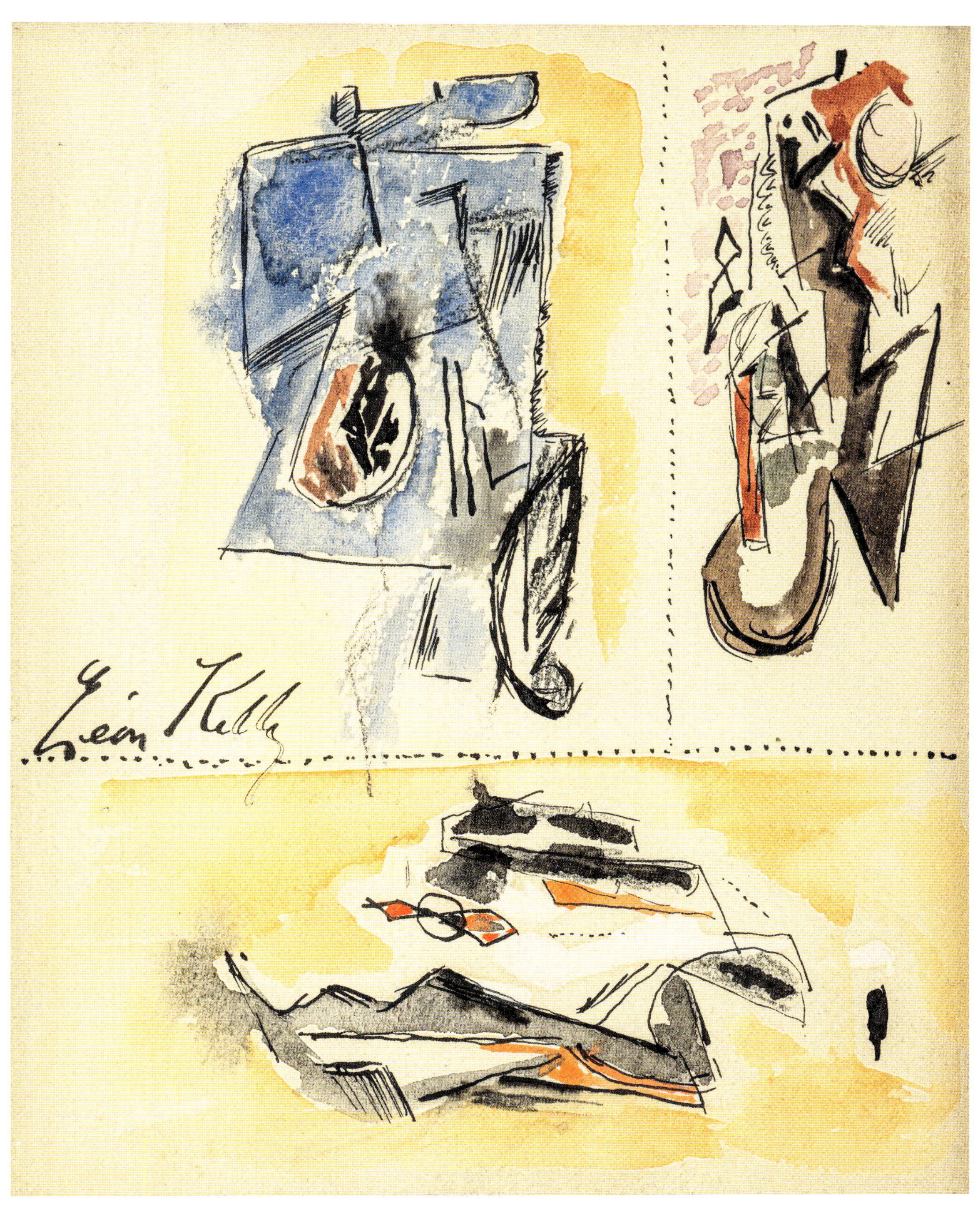

112
Untitled
Ink and watercolors, 14.5 × 11.5 cm

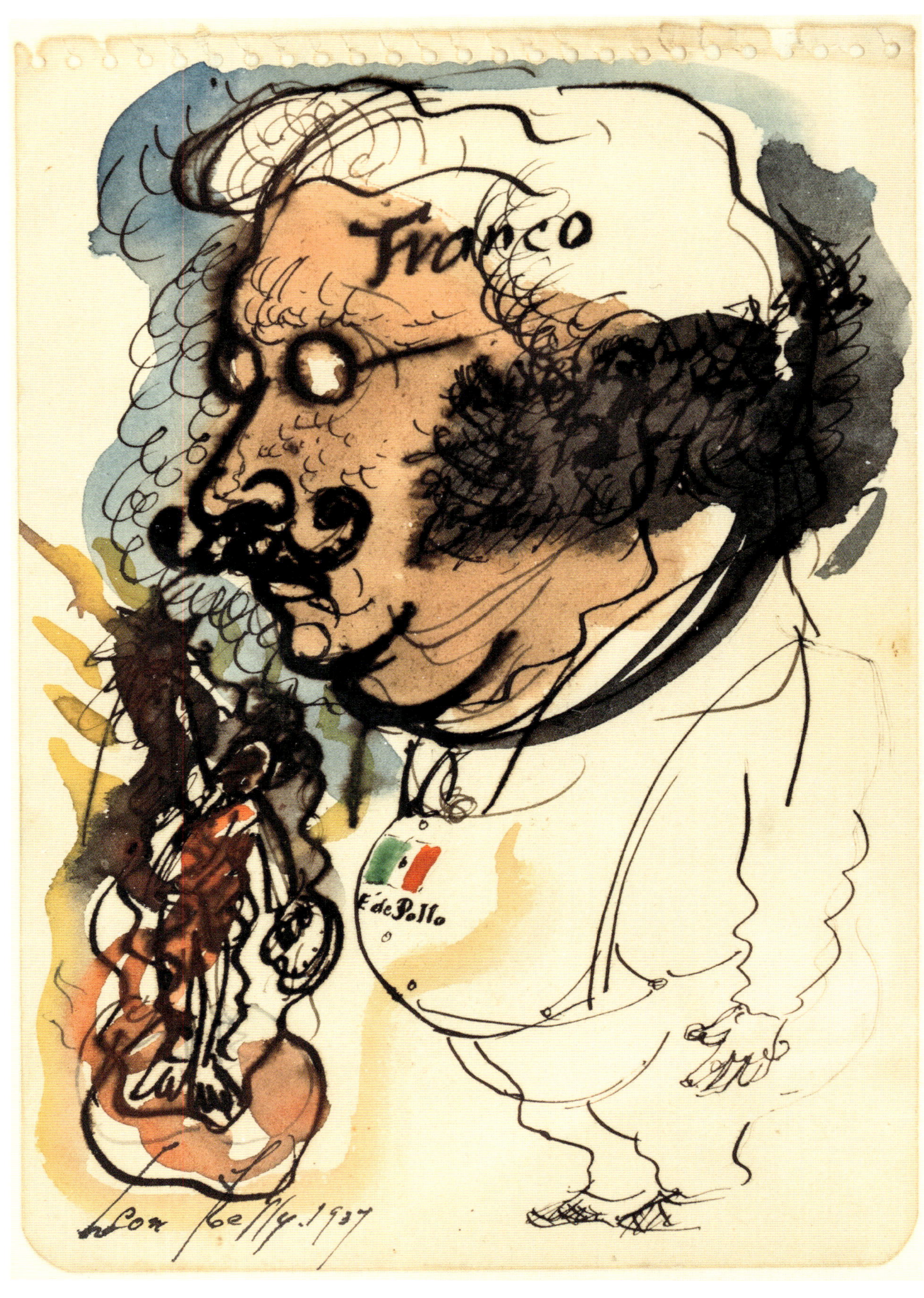

113
Franco, 1937
Ink and watercolors, 20 × 15 cm

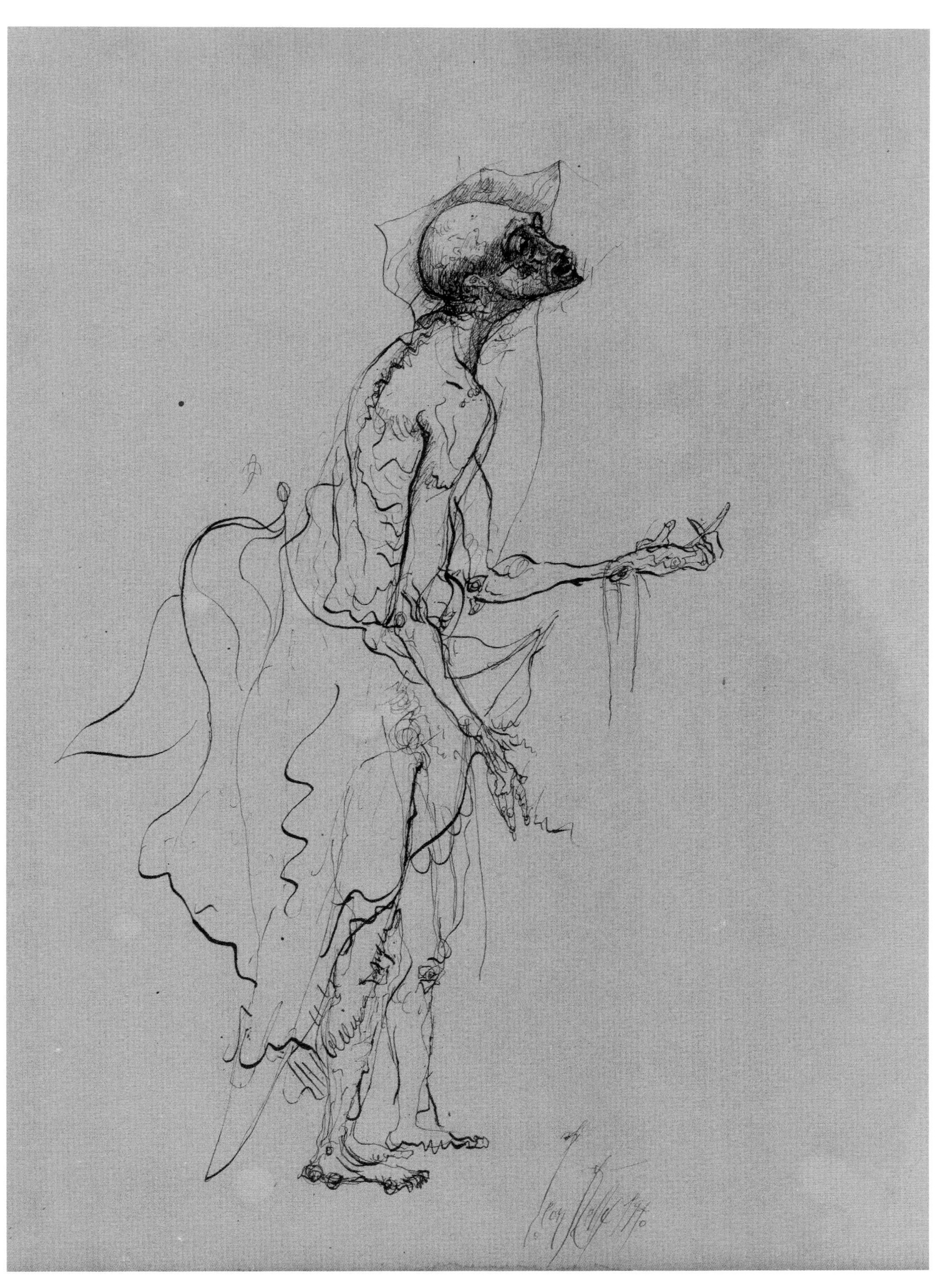

114
Untitled, 1940
Ink, 32 × 24 cm

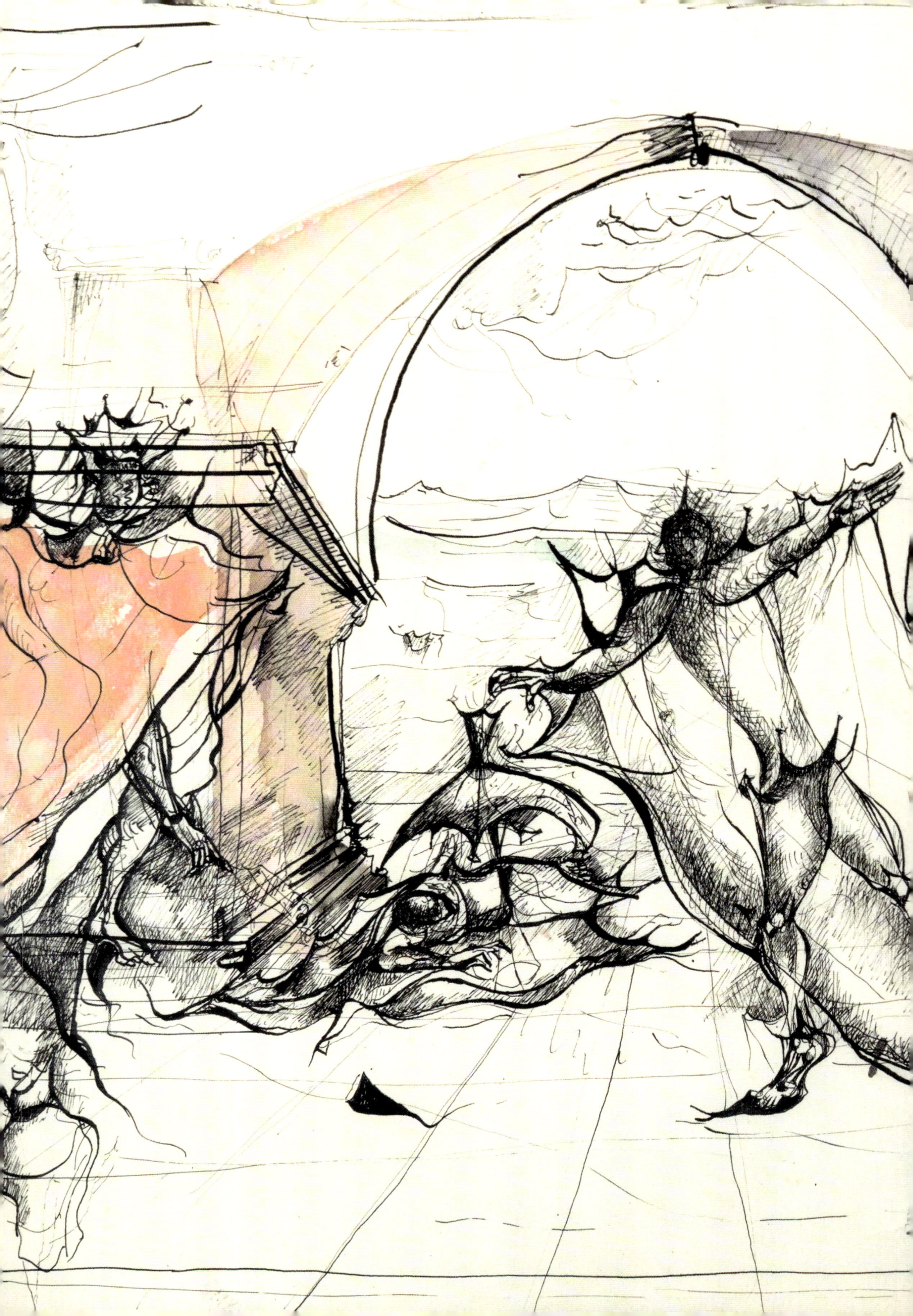

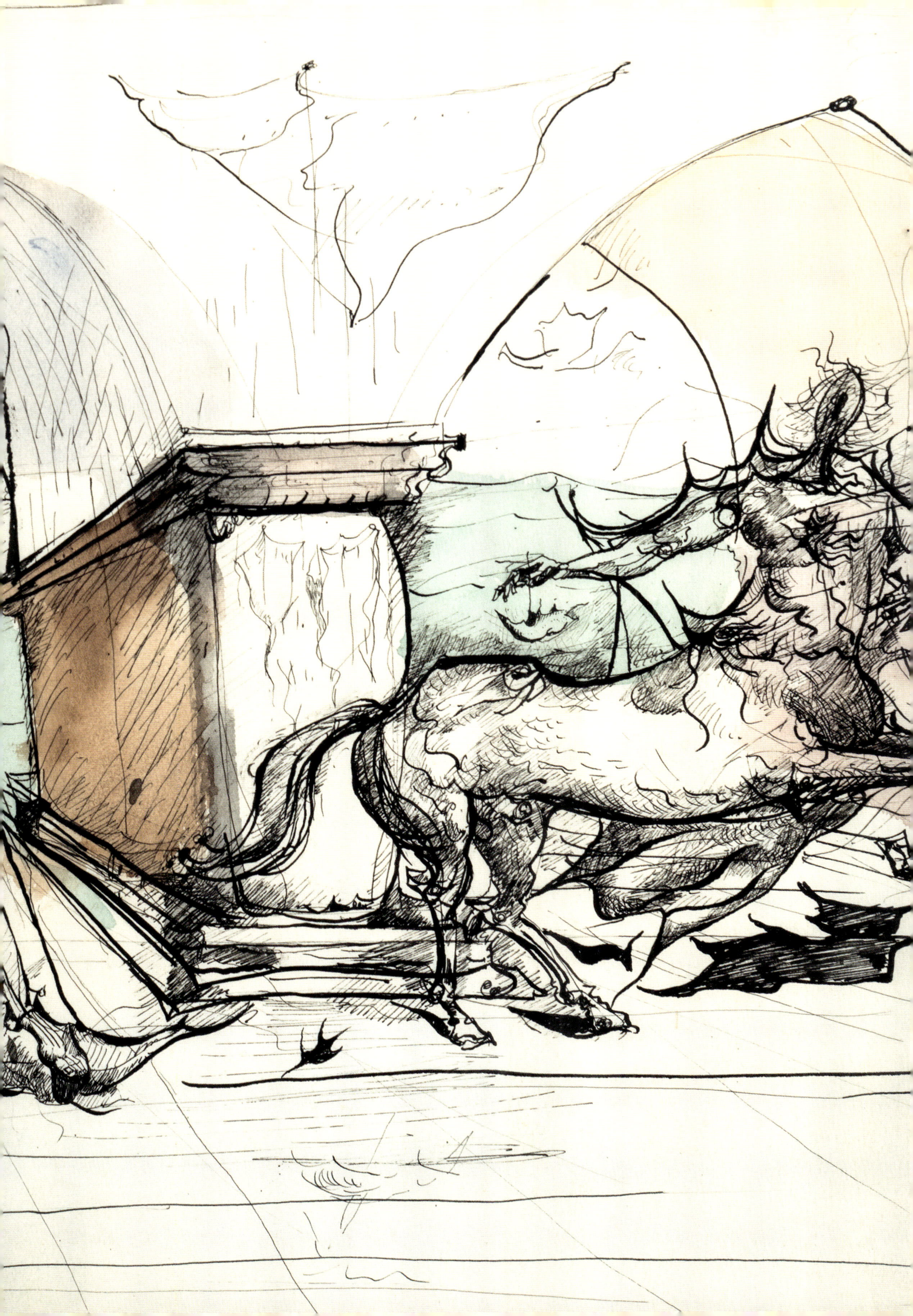

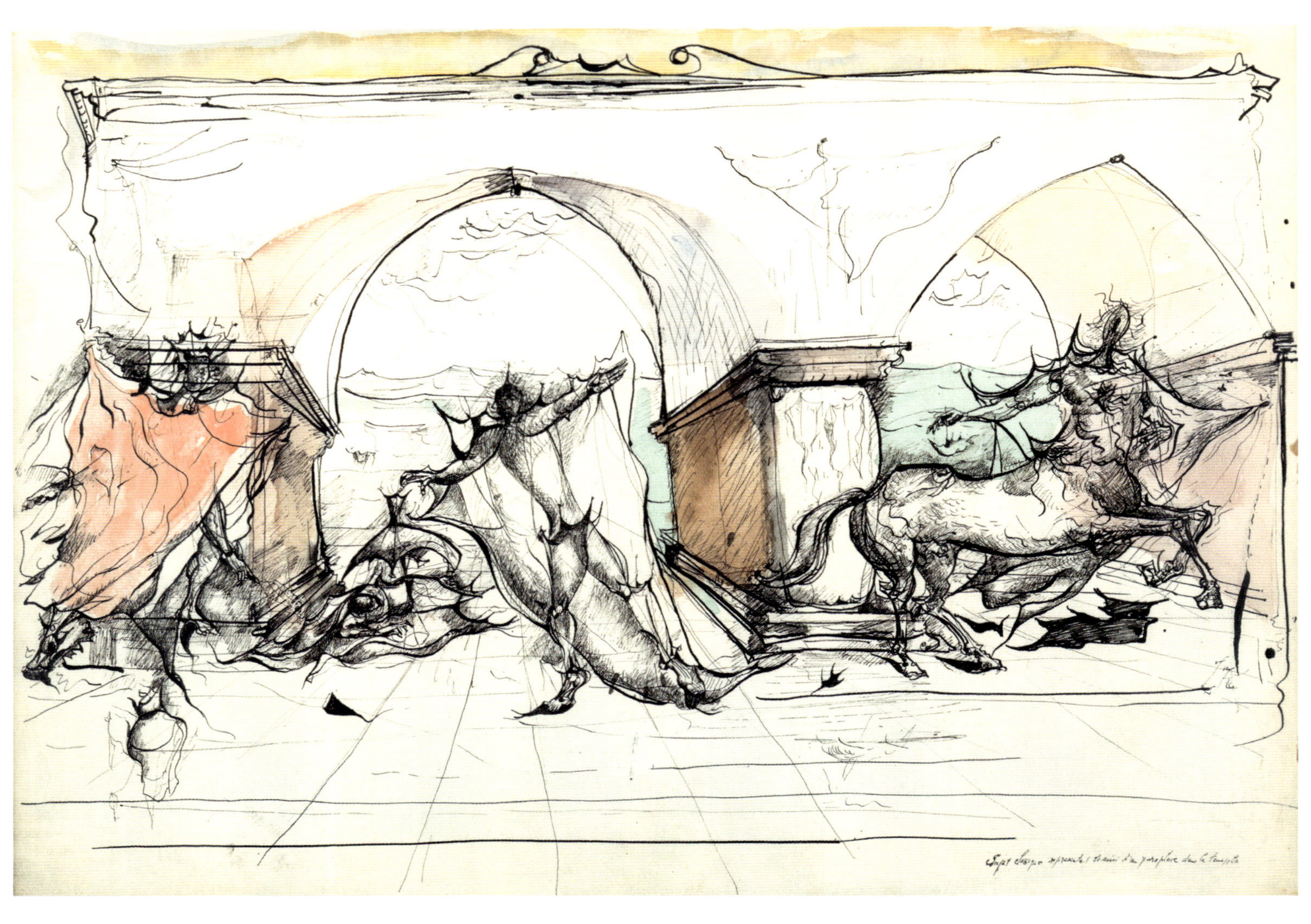

115
Sujet classique représentant le souci d'un parapluie dans le temple
Ink and watercolor, 35.5 × 51 cm

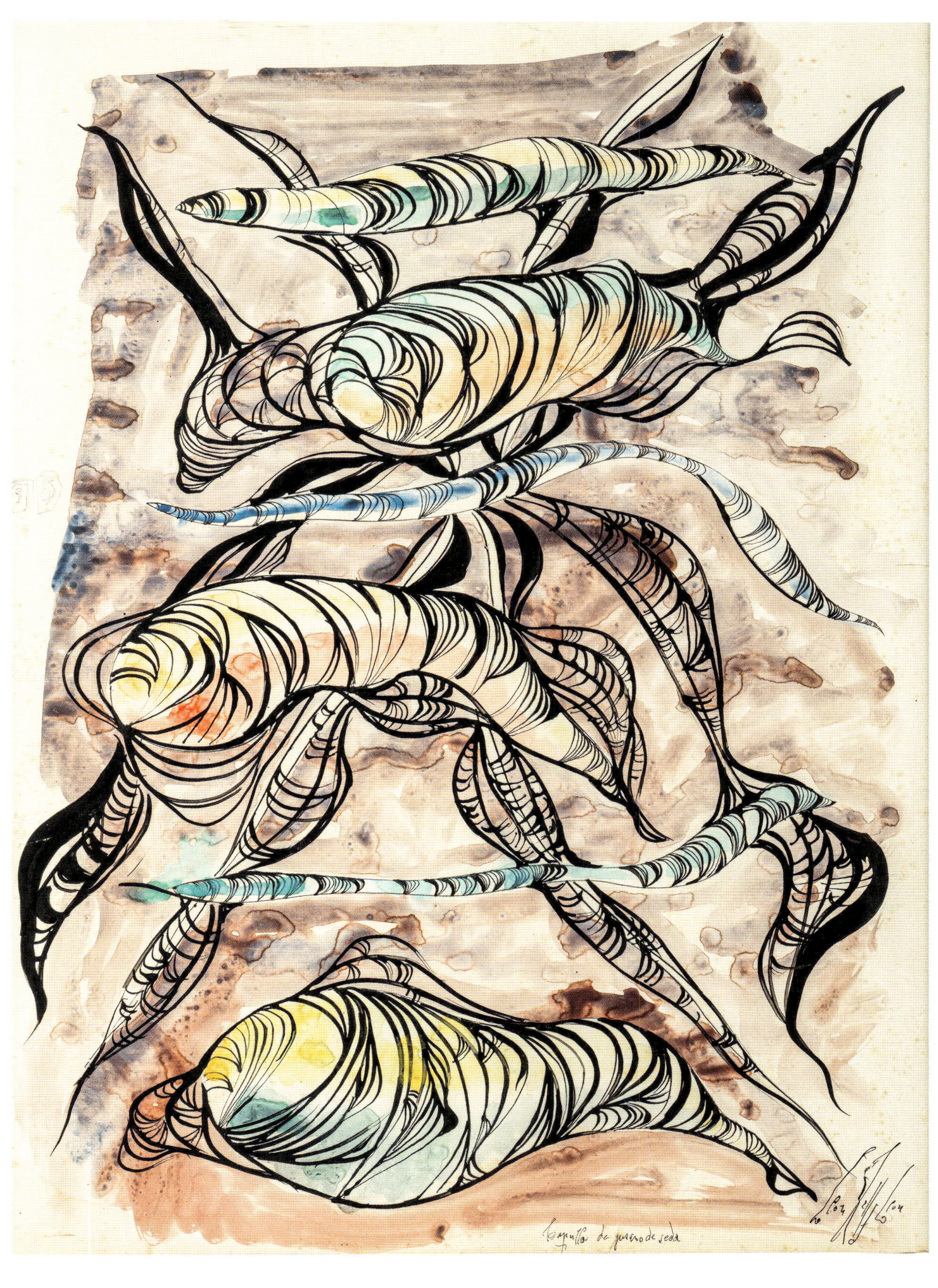

116
Capullo de gusano de seda
Ink and watercolors, 62 × 46.5 cm

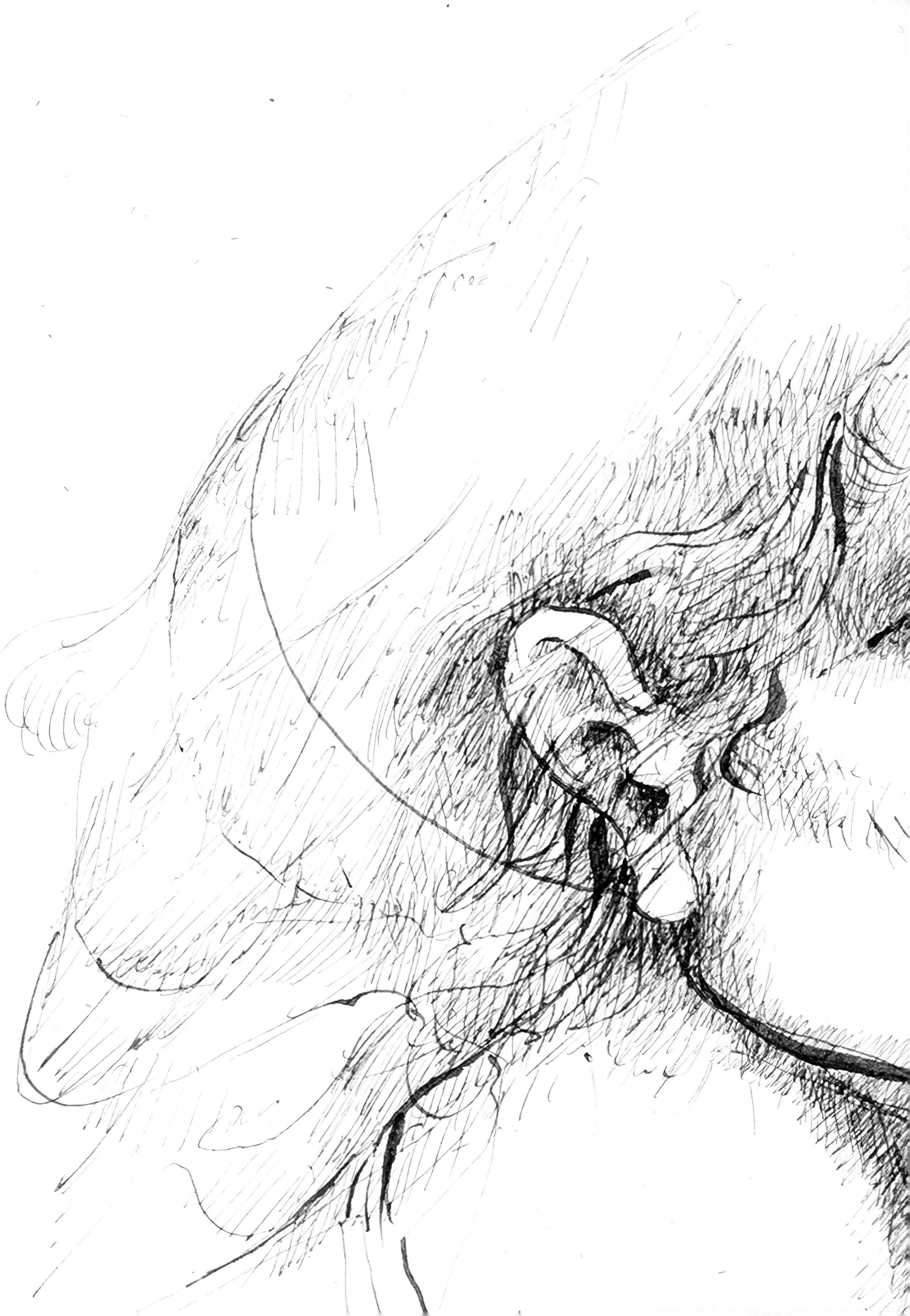

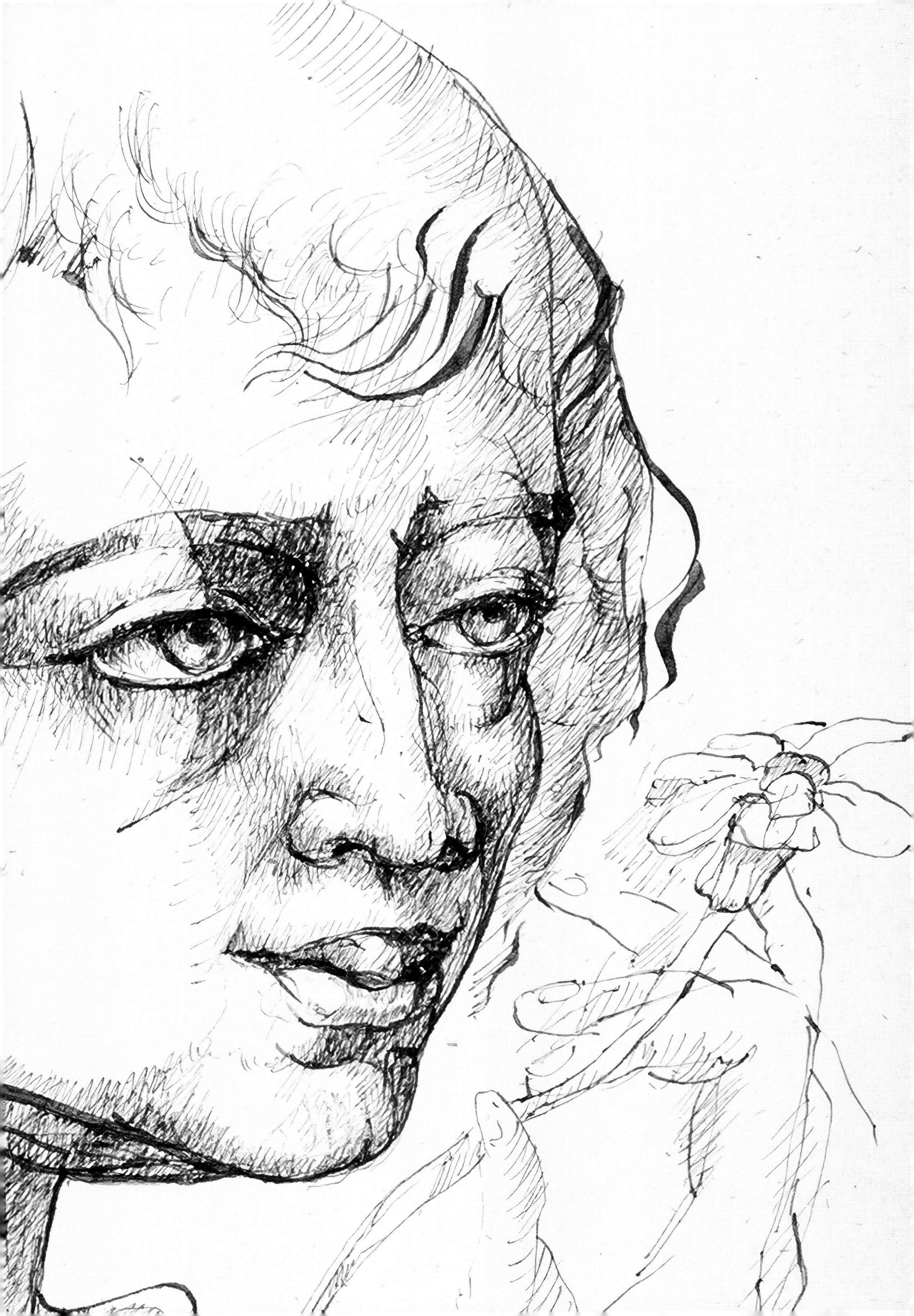

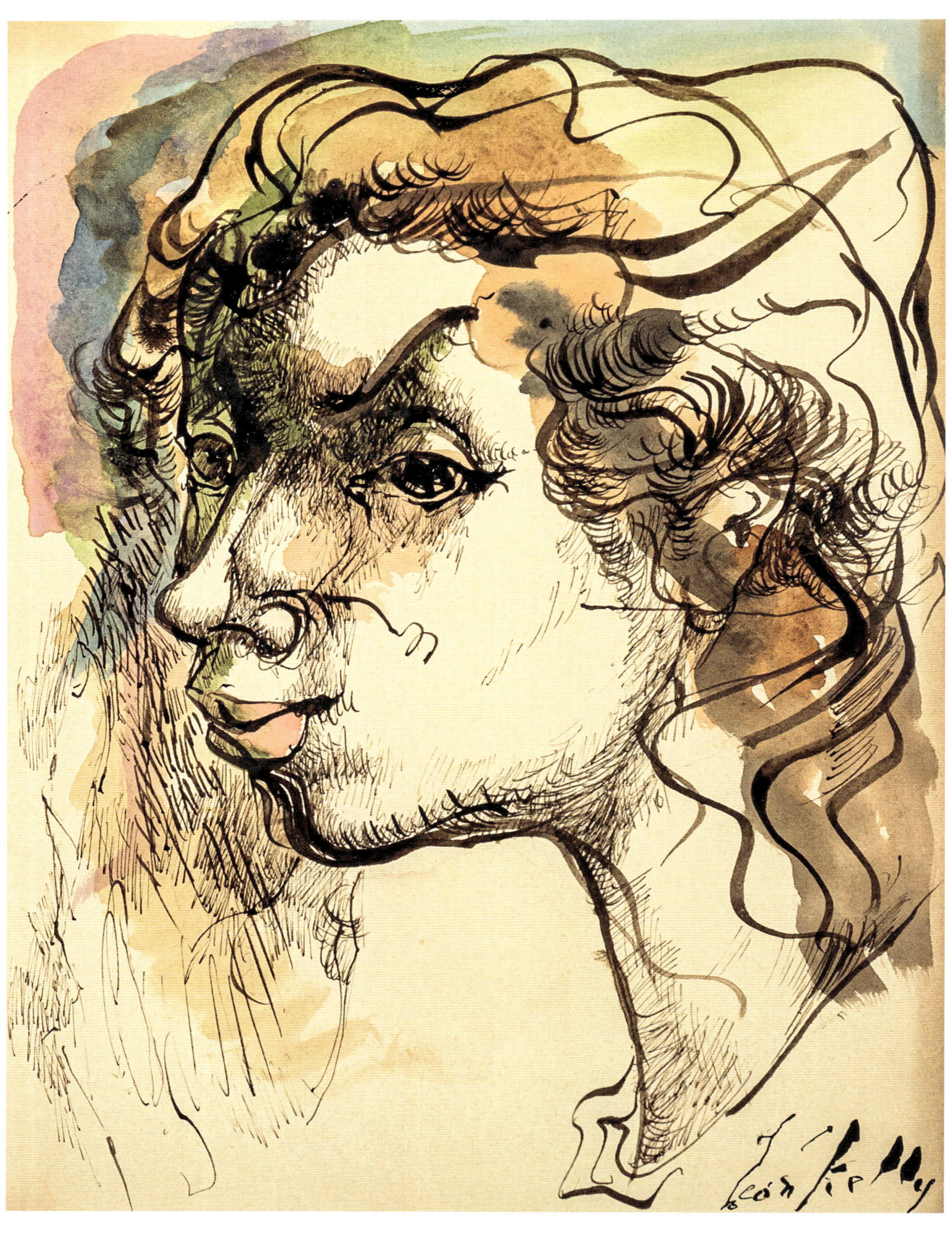

117
Untitled, ca. 1930
Ink and watercolors, 27 × 20.5 cm

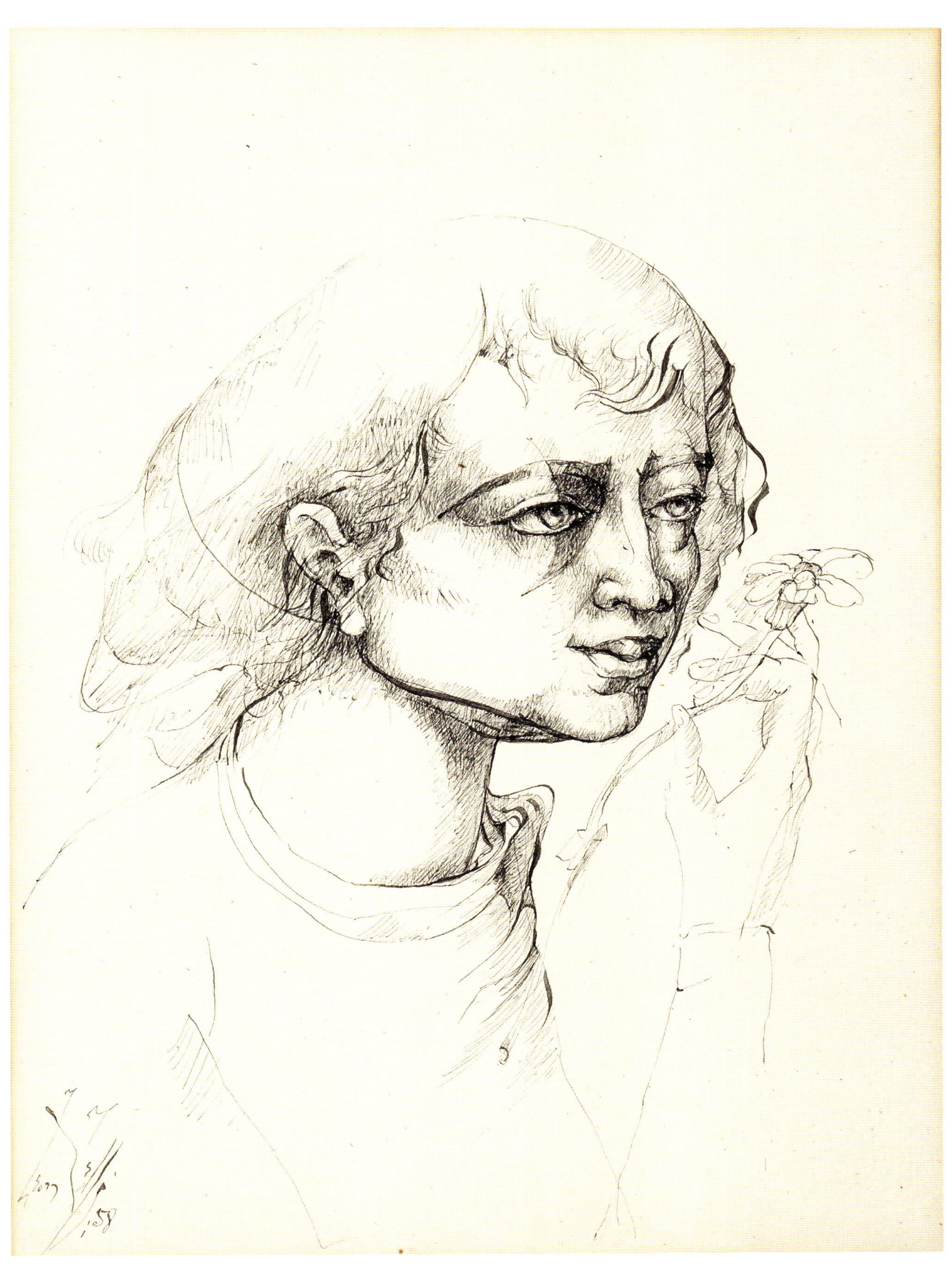

118
Untitled, 1958
Ink, 27 × 20.5 cm

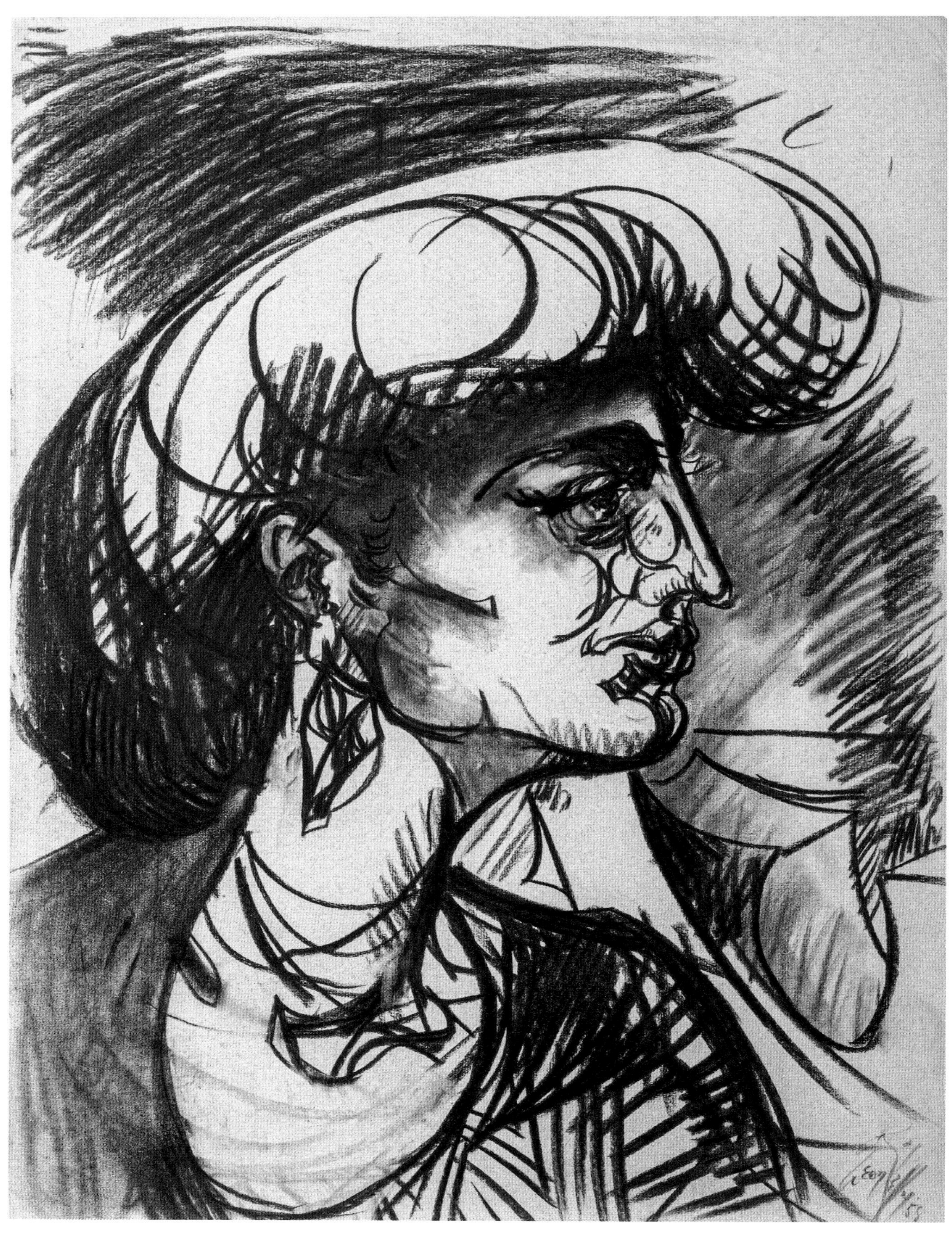

119
Untitled, 1955
Charcoal, 63.5 × 48 cm

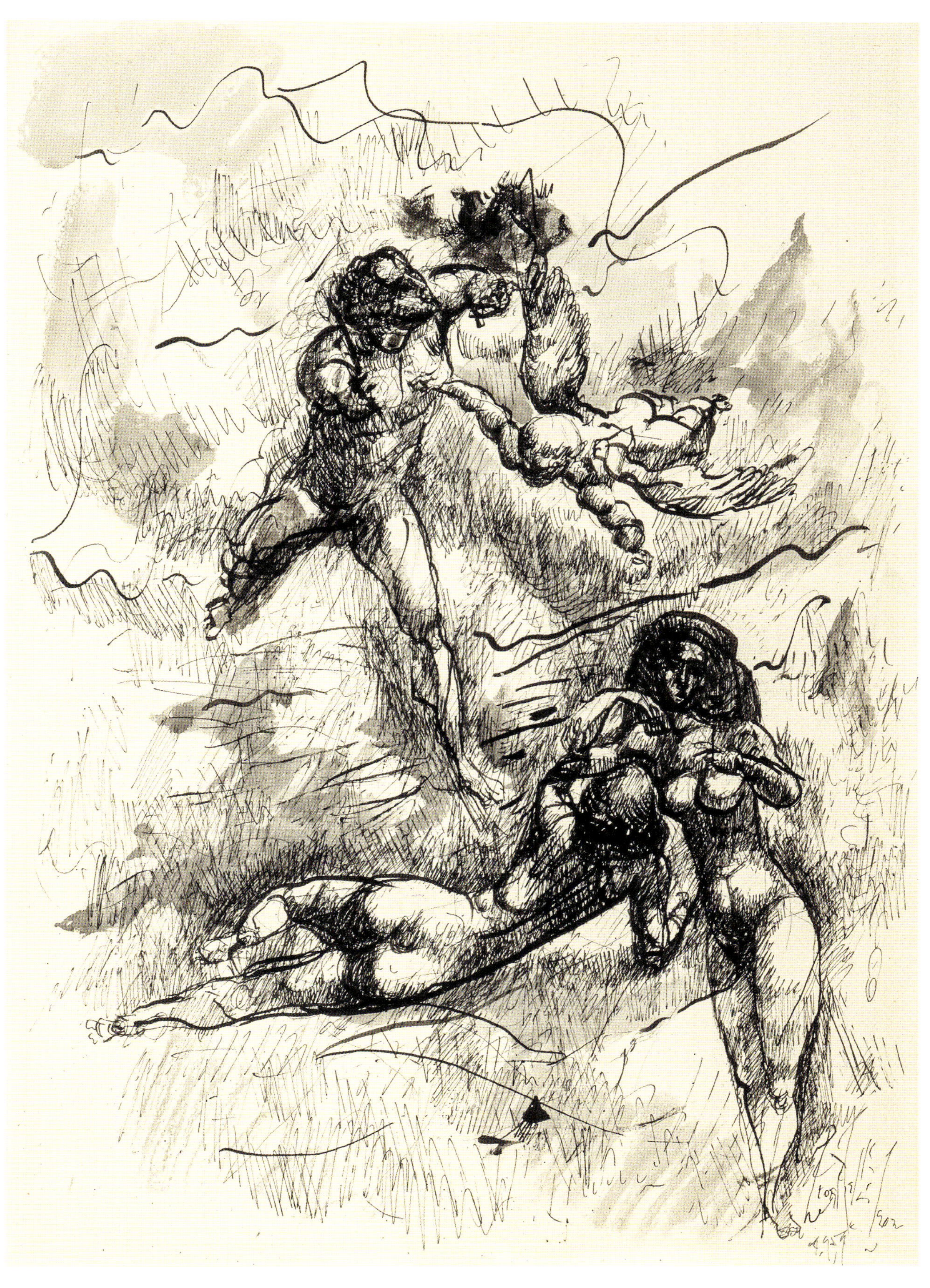

120
Untitled, 195(?)
Ink, 39 × 28 cm

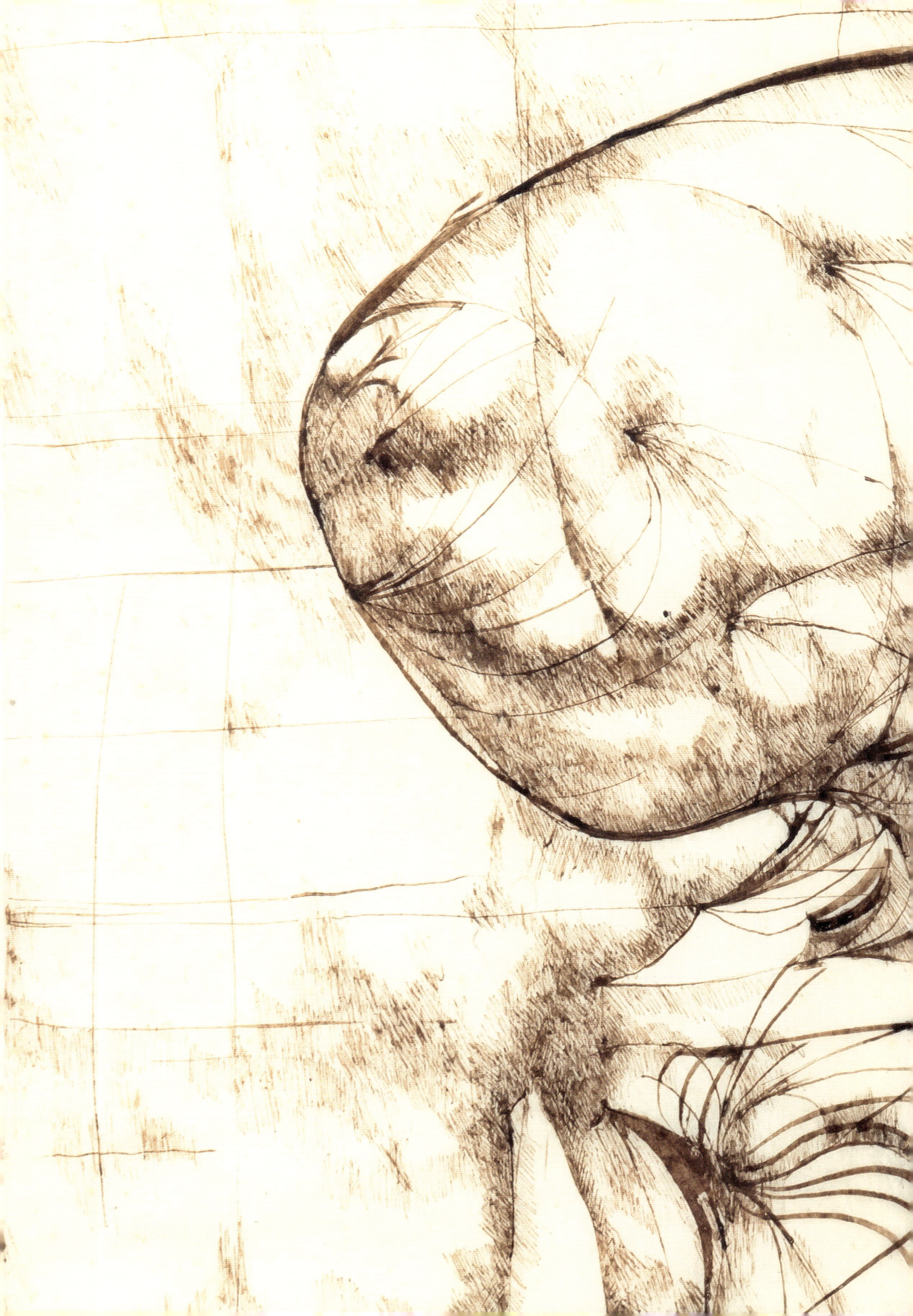

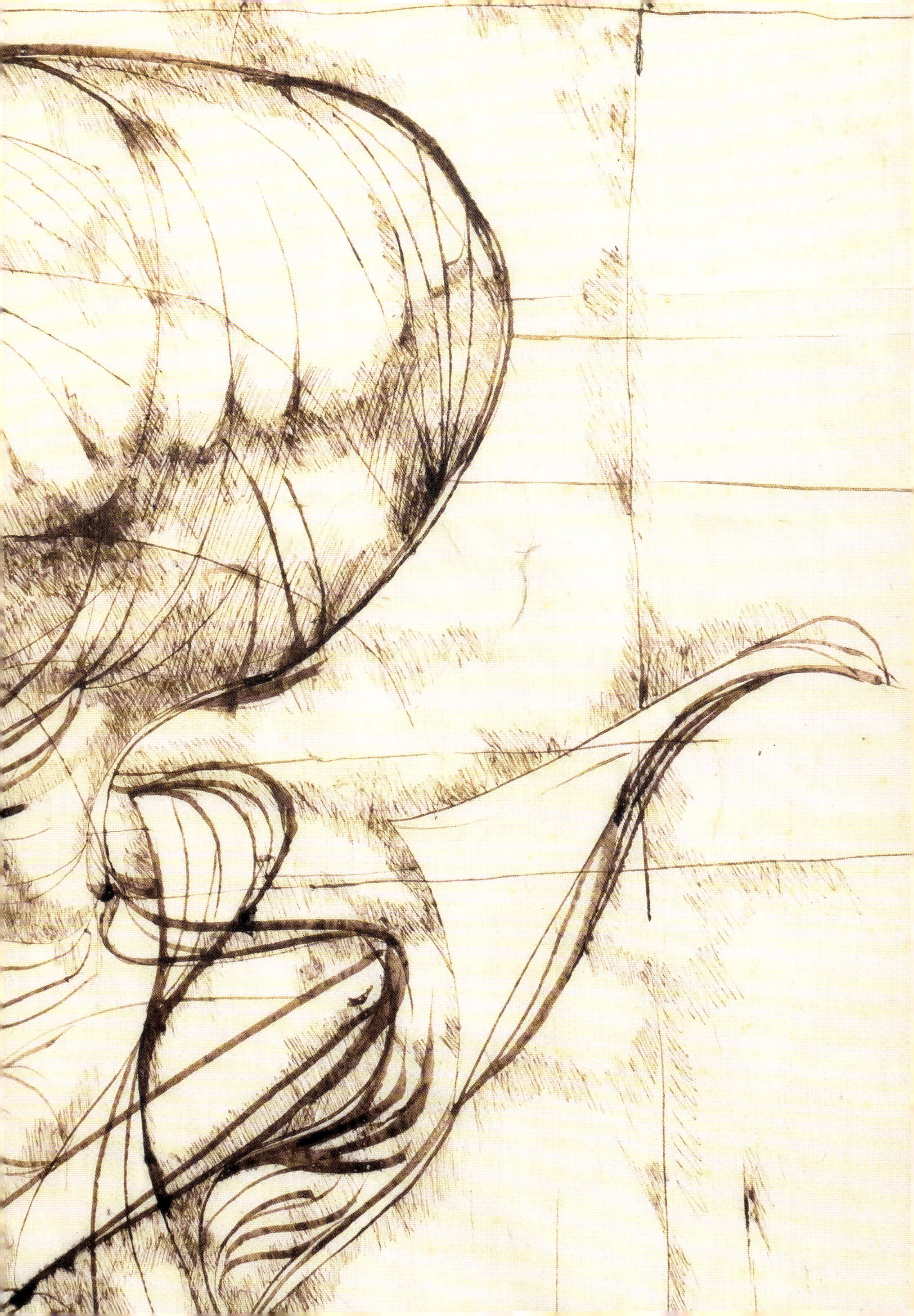

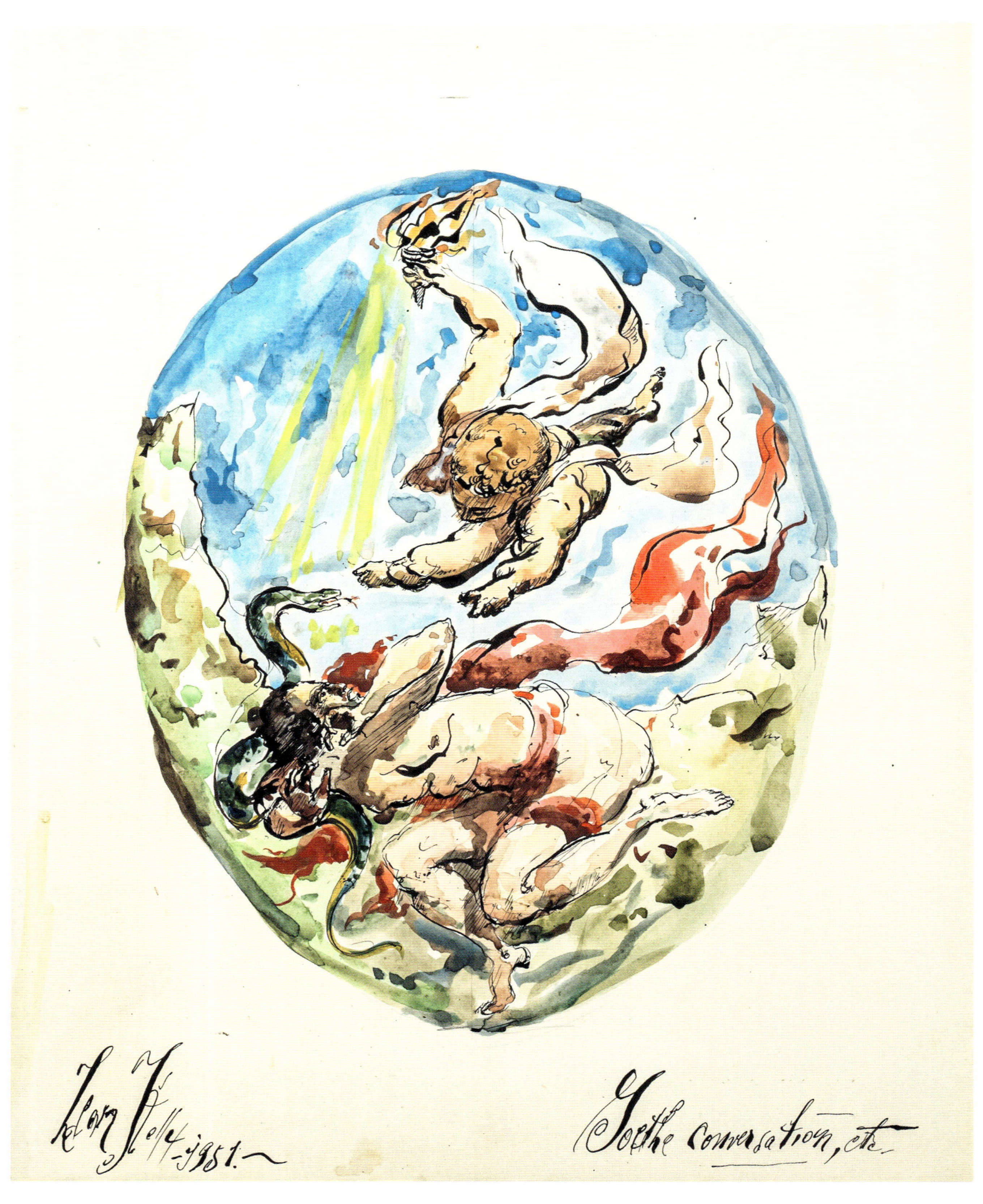

121
Goethe Conversation, etc, 1951
Ink and watercolors, 38 × 31.5 cm

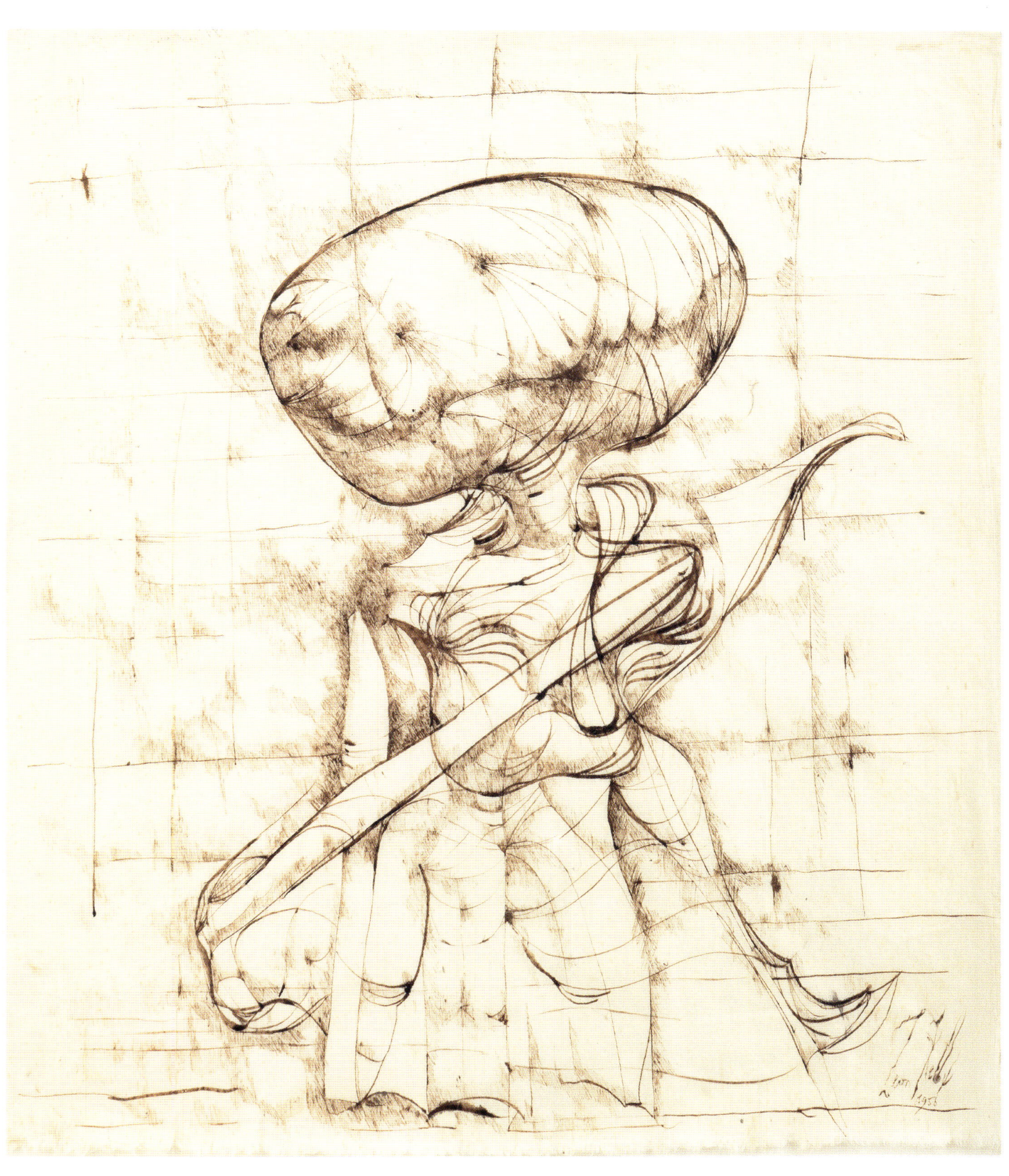

122
Moon Man, 1956
Pencil, 56 × 48 cm

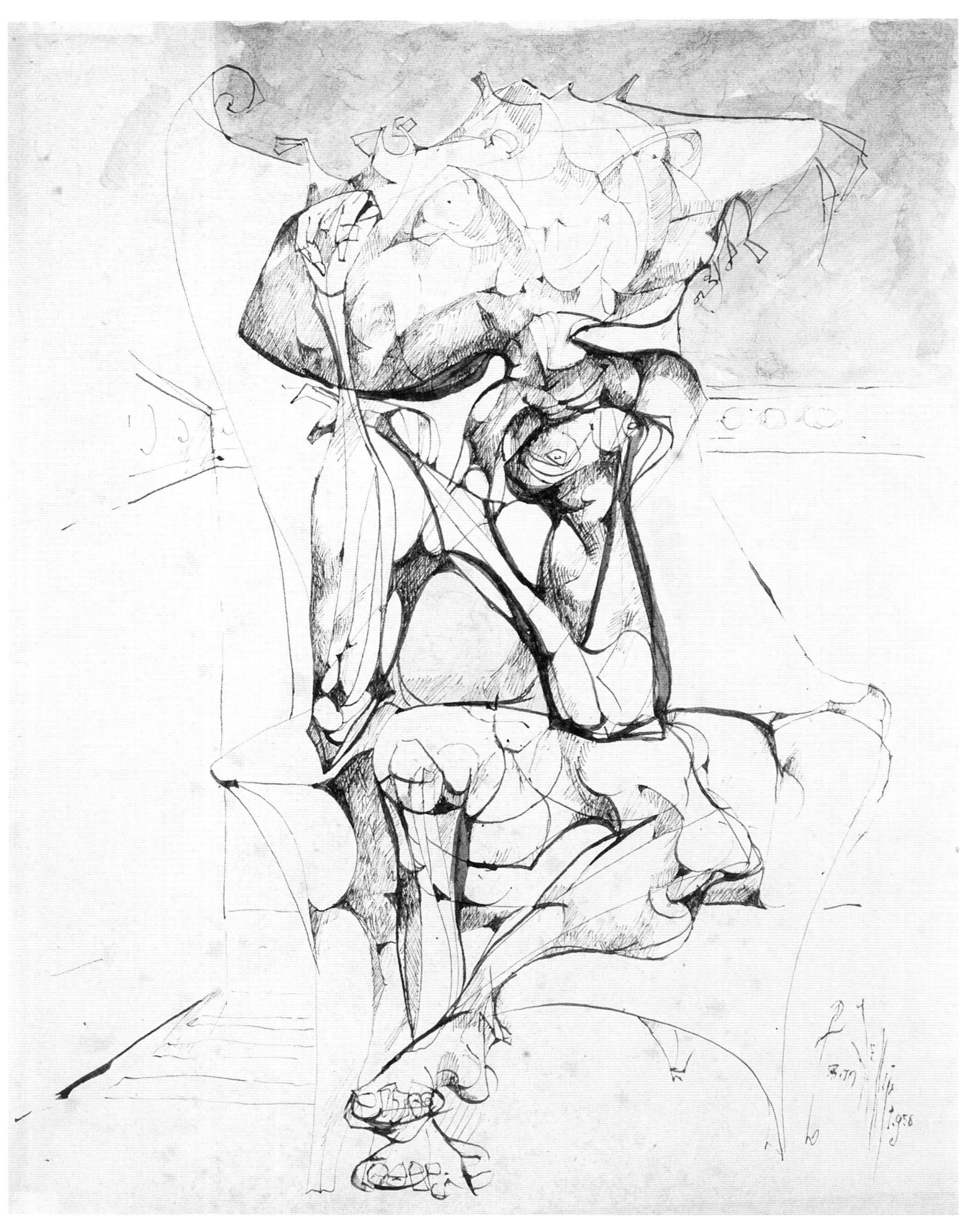

123
Untitled, 1956
Ink, 29 × 22.5 cm

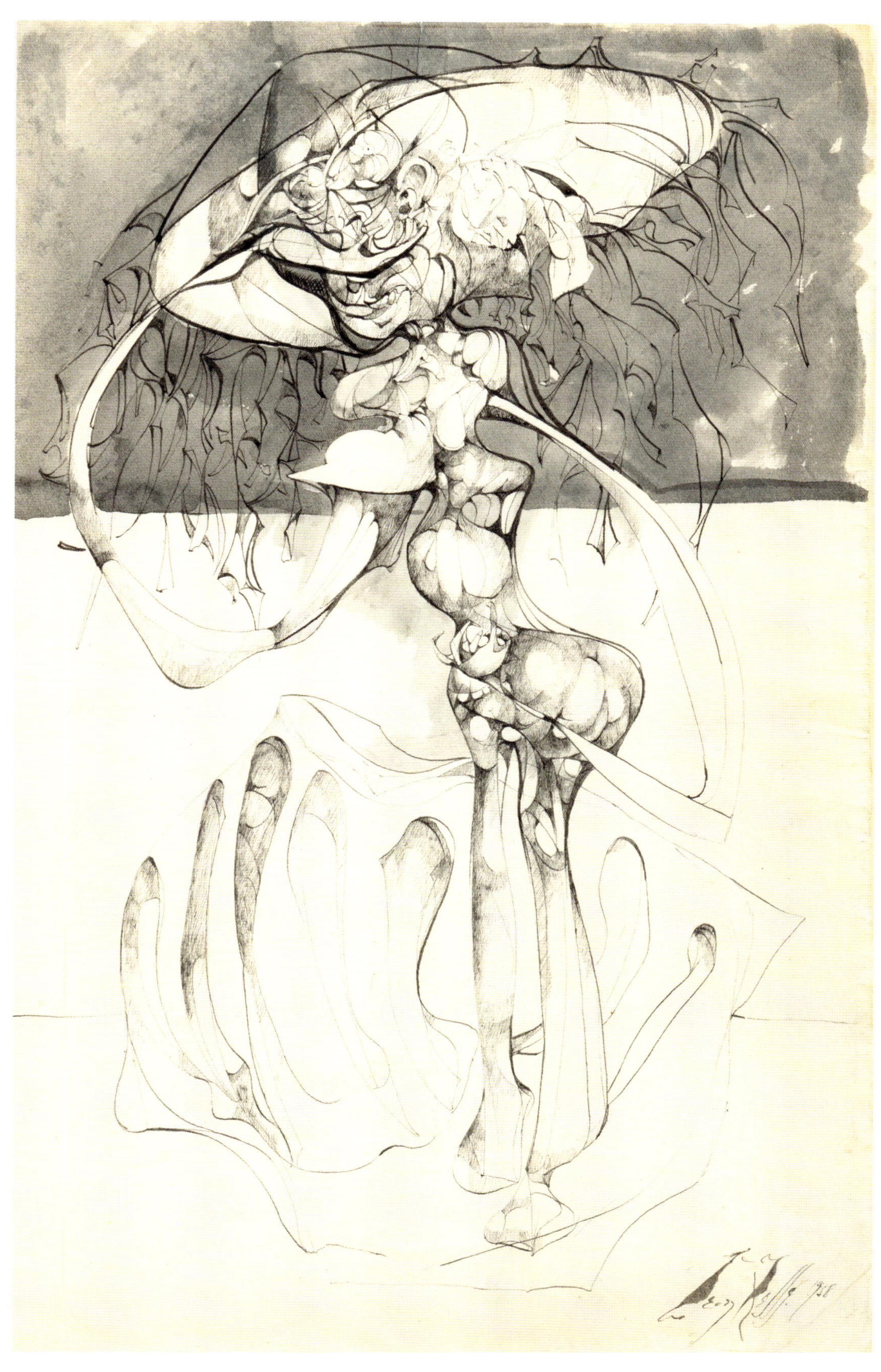

124
Untitled, 1958
Pencil, 48 × 31 cm

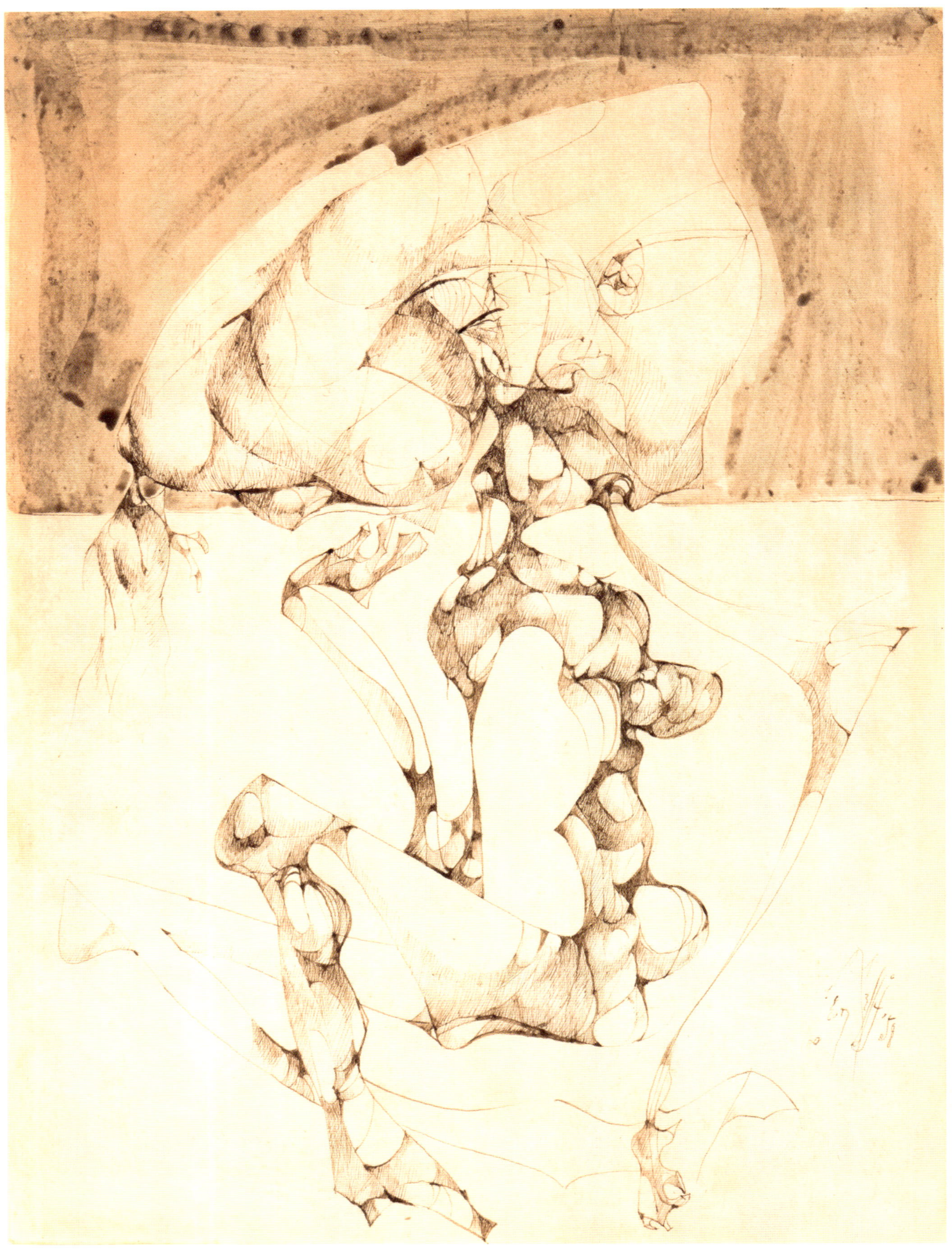

125
Untitled, 1958
Ink, 34 × 25.5 cm

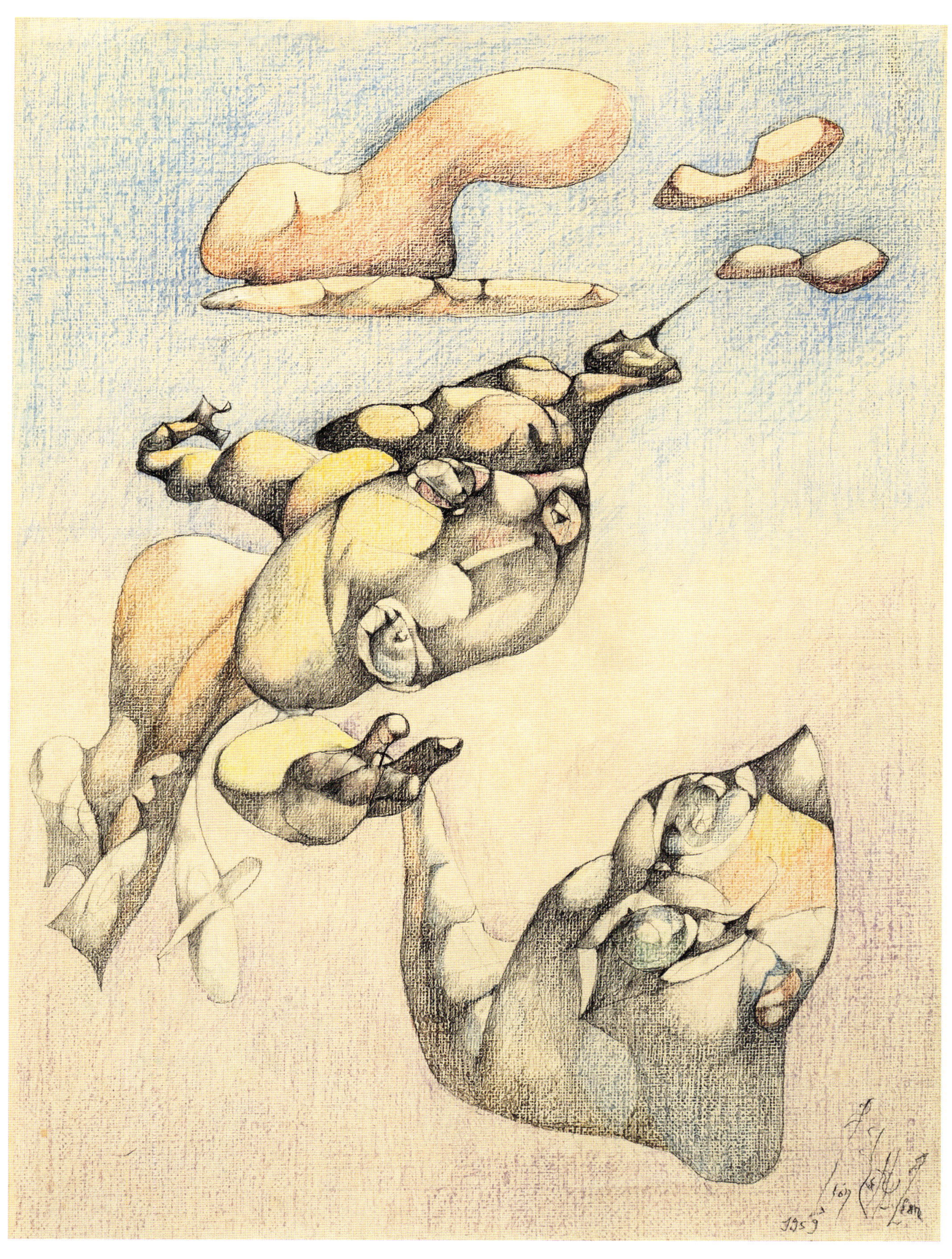

126
Untitled, ca. 1959
Ink and color pencil, 30.5 × 23 cm

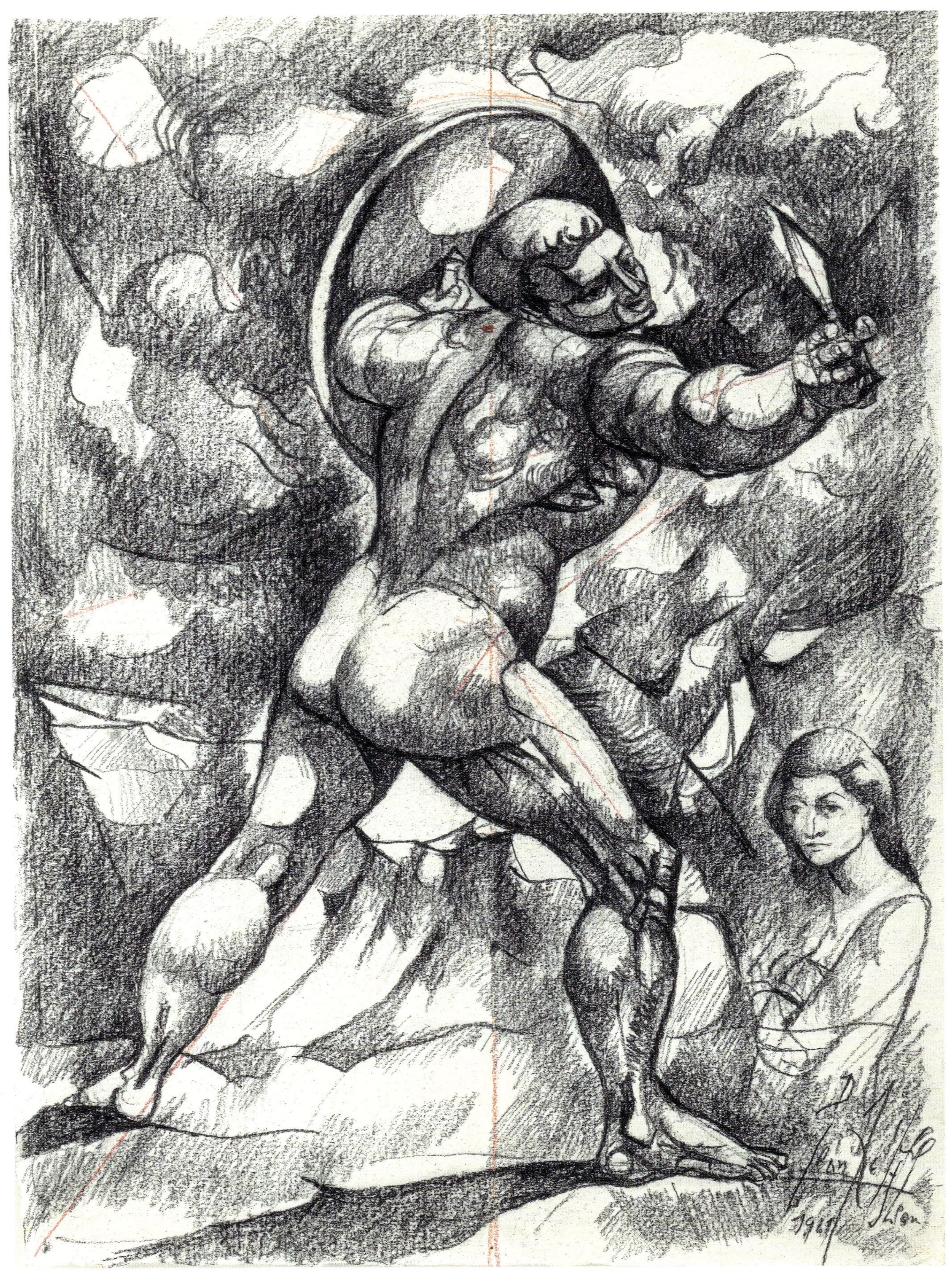

127
The Insane Mars, 1961
Graphite, 32 × 23.5 cm

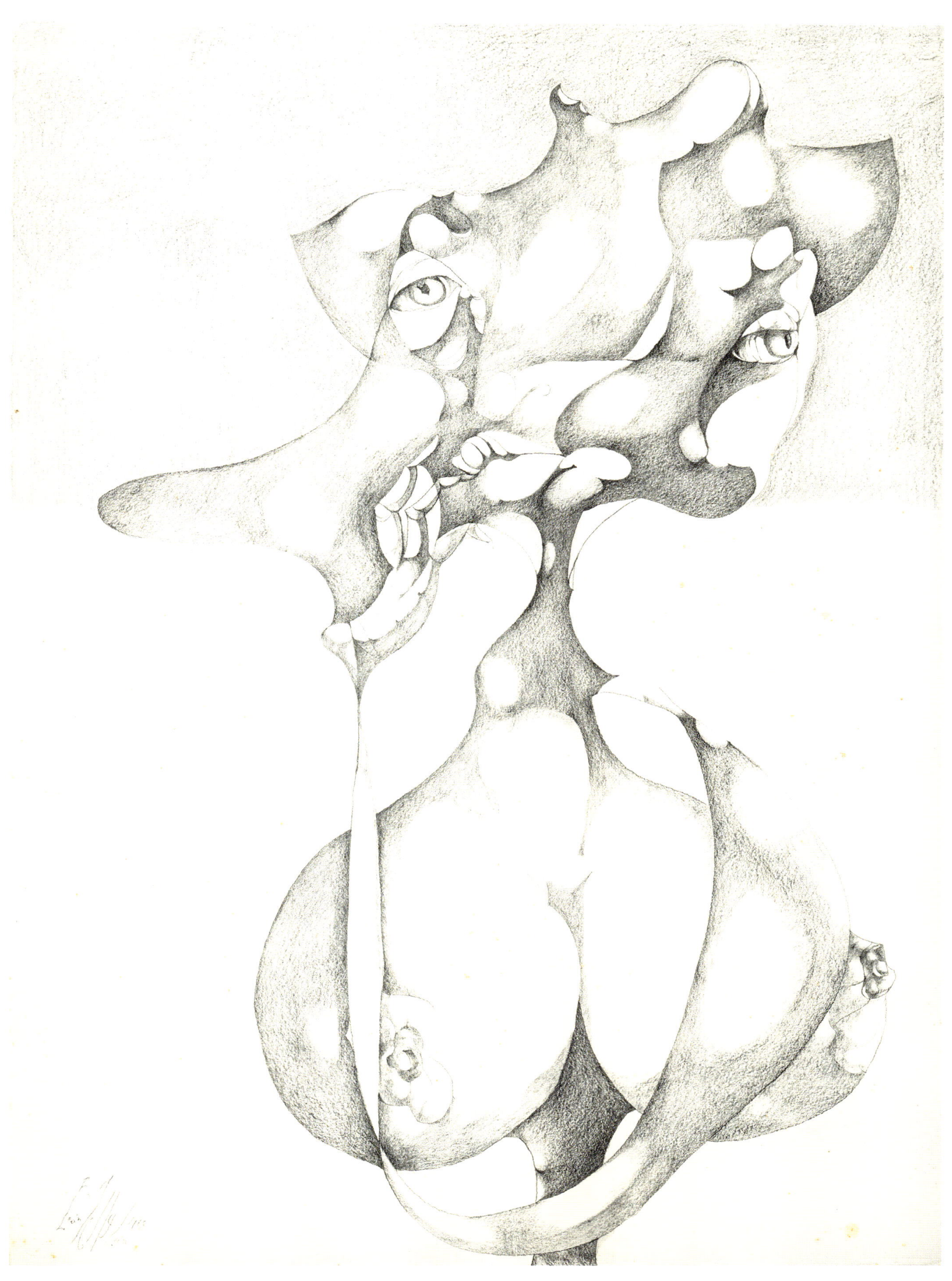

128
Untitled, 1968
Charcoal, 77.5 × 57.5 cm

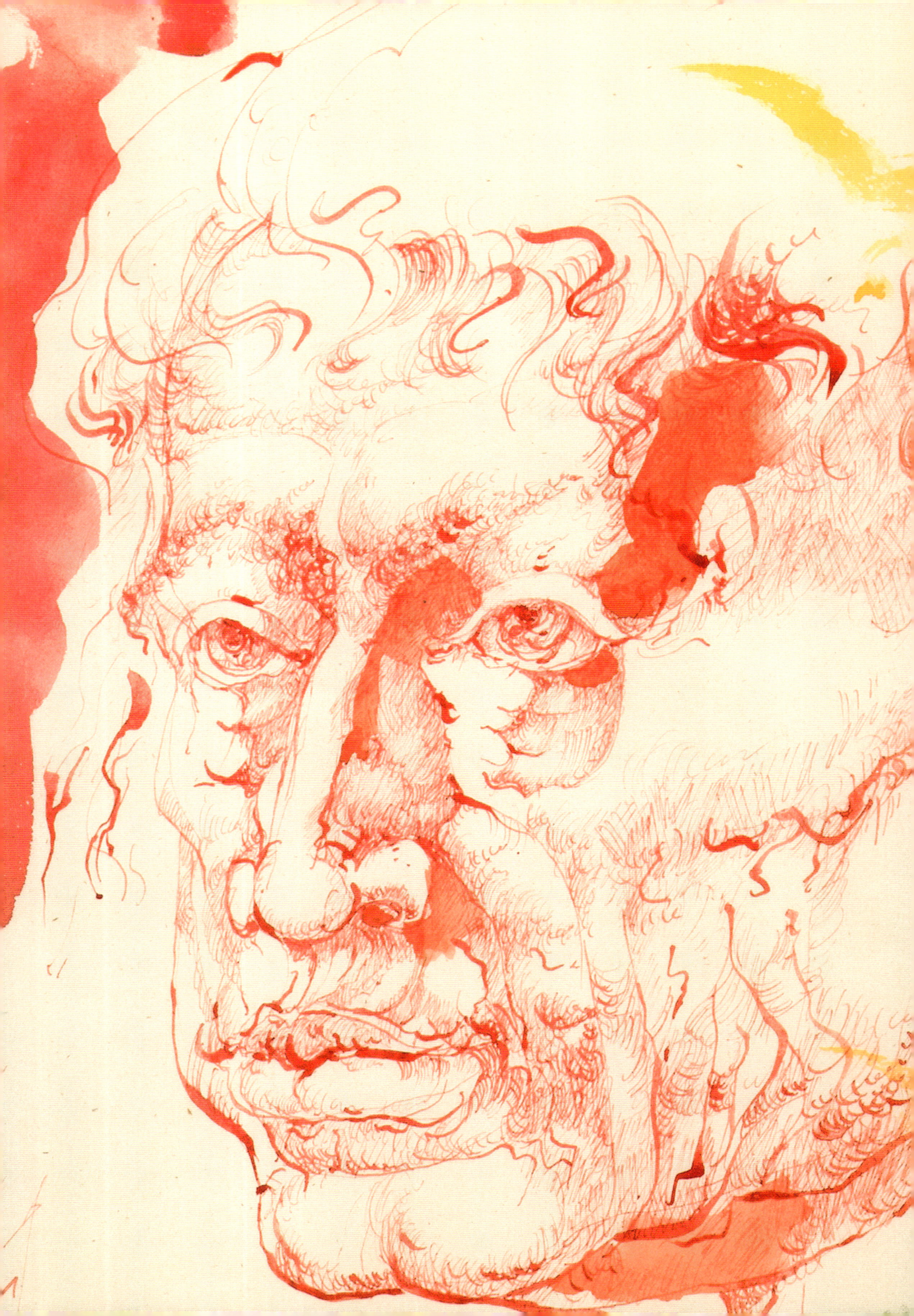

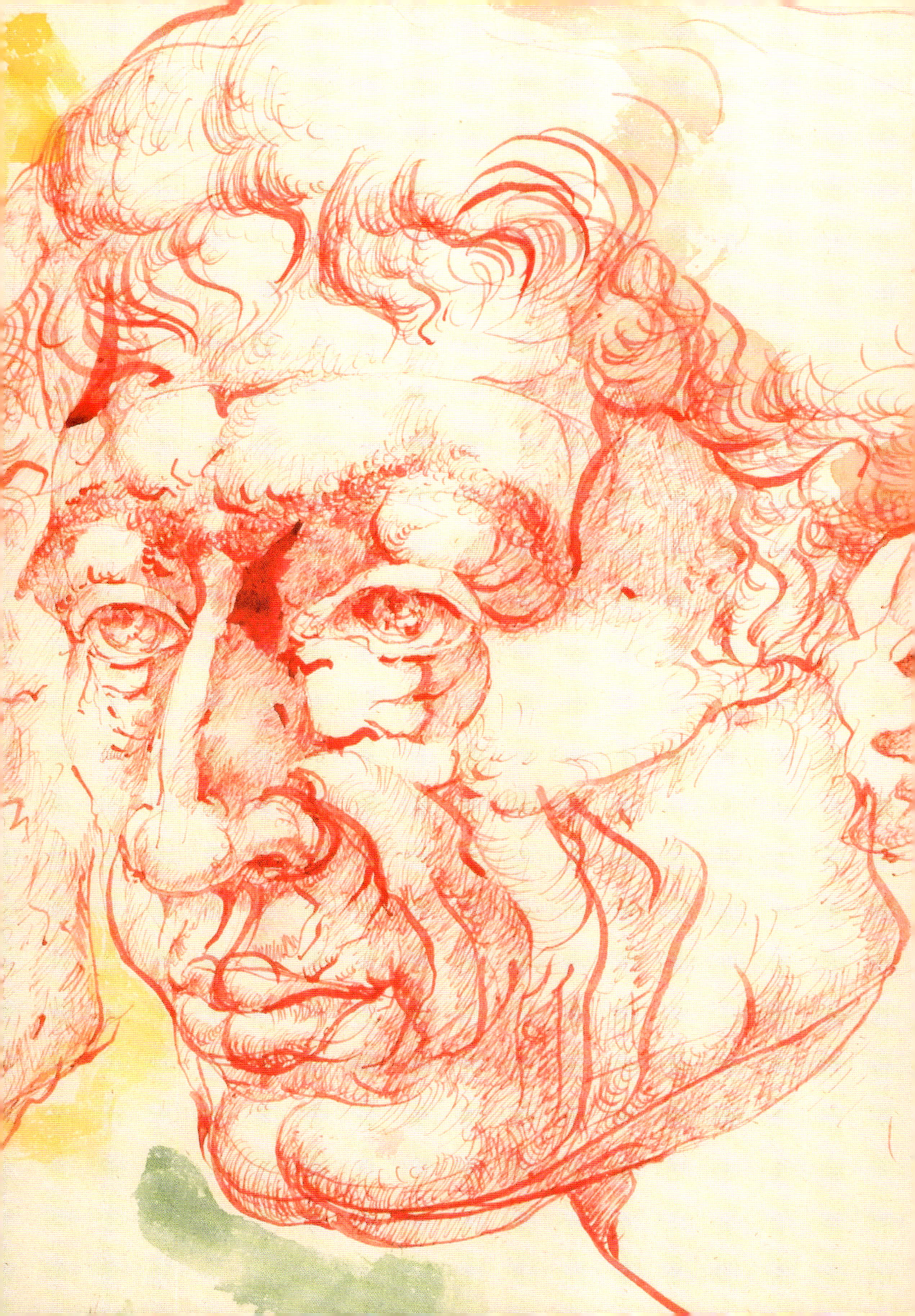

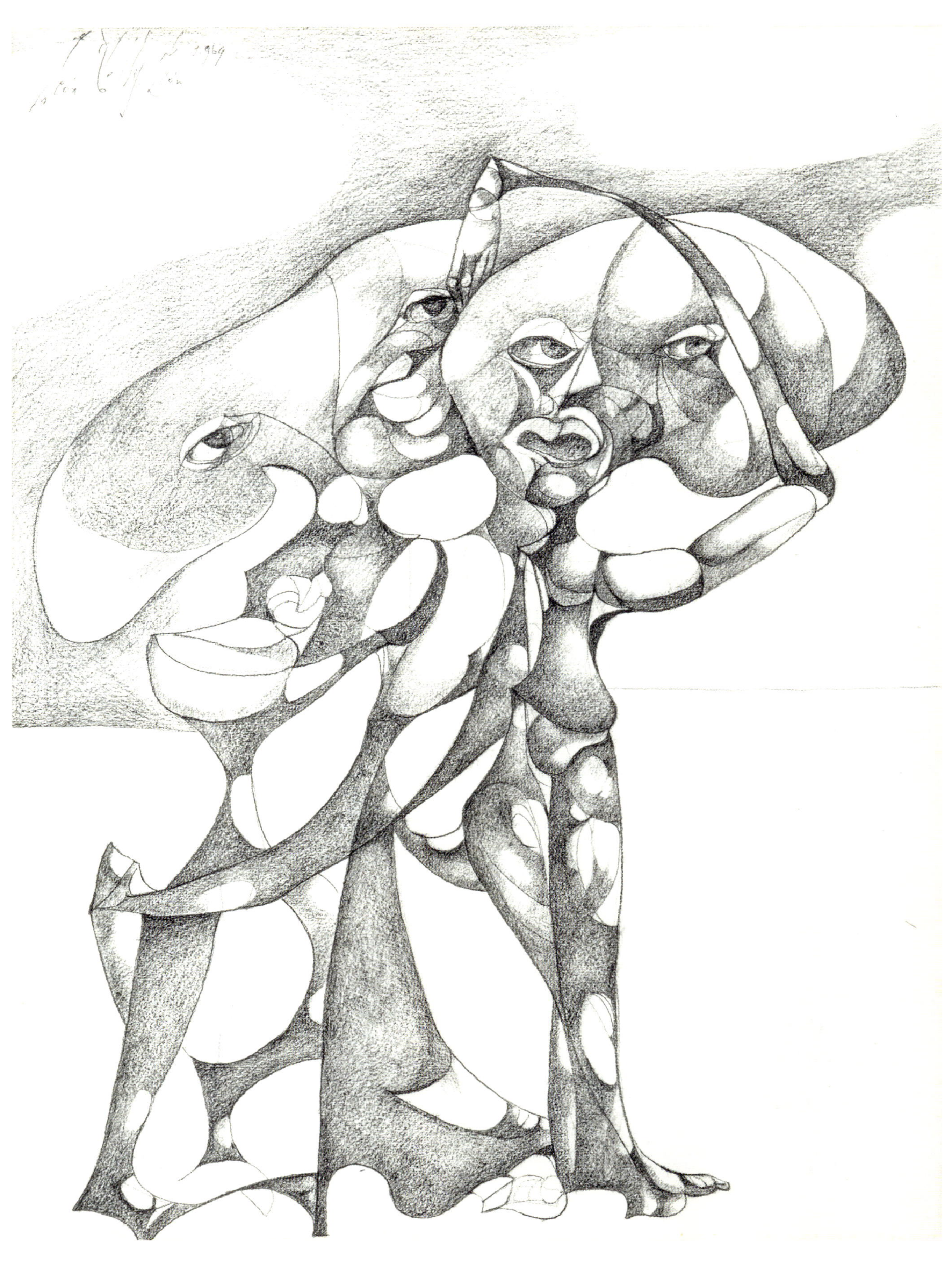

129
Mexican Indian Women Looking, 1969
Charcoal, 35 × 27 cm

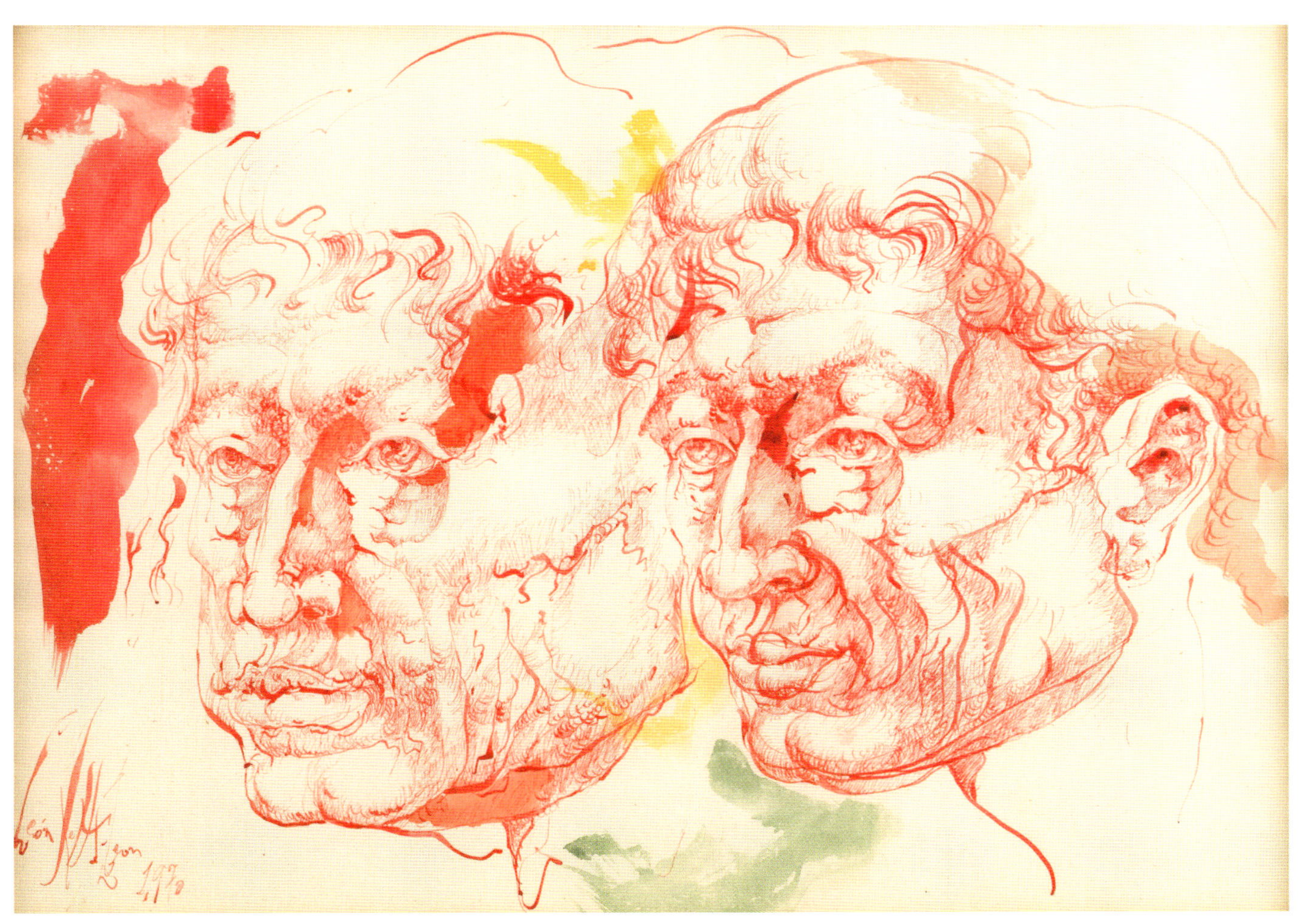

130
Untitled, 1970
Watercolors, 29 × 40 cm

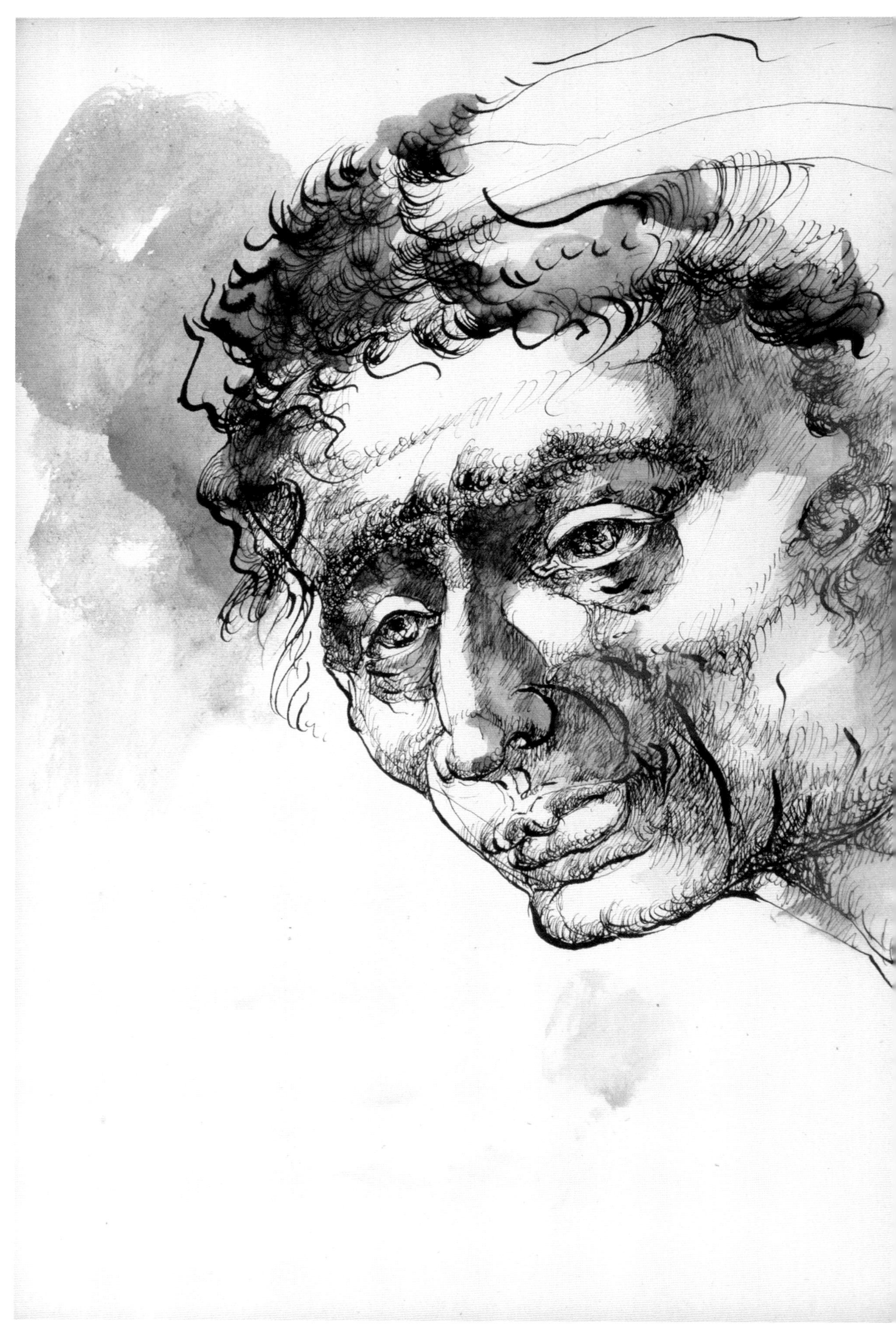

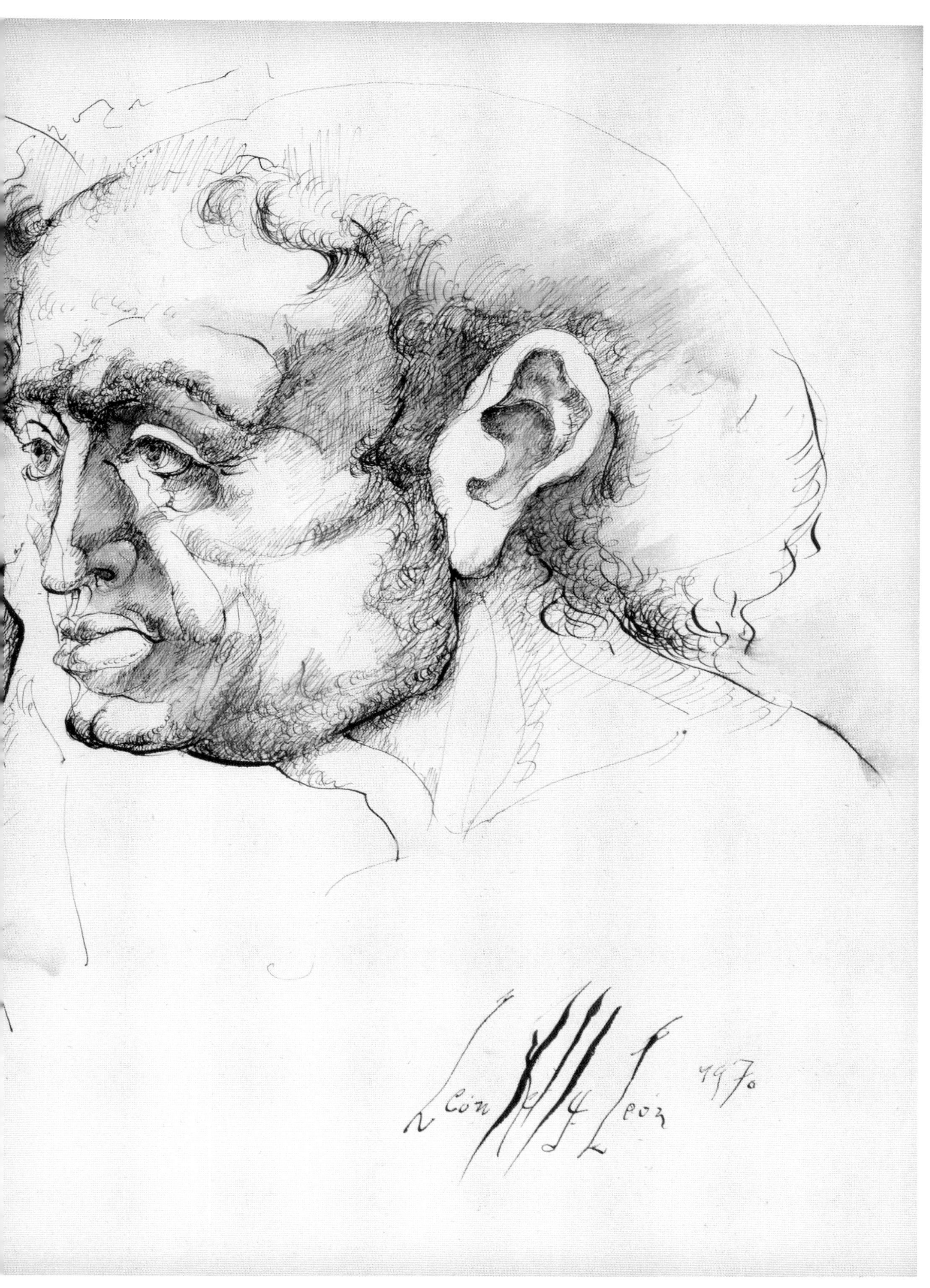

131
Untitled, 1970
Ink, 29 × 40 cm

Works in

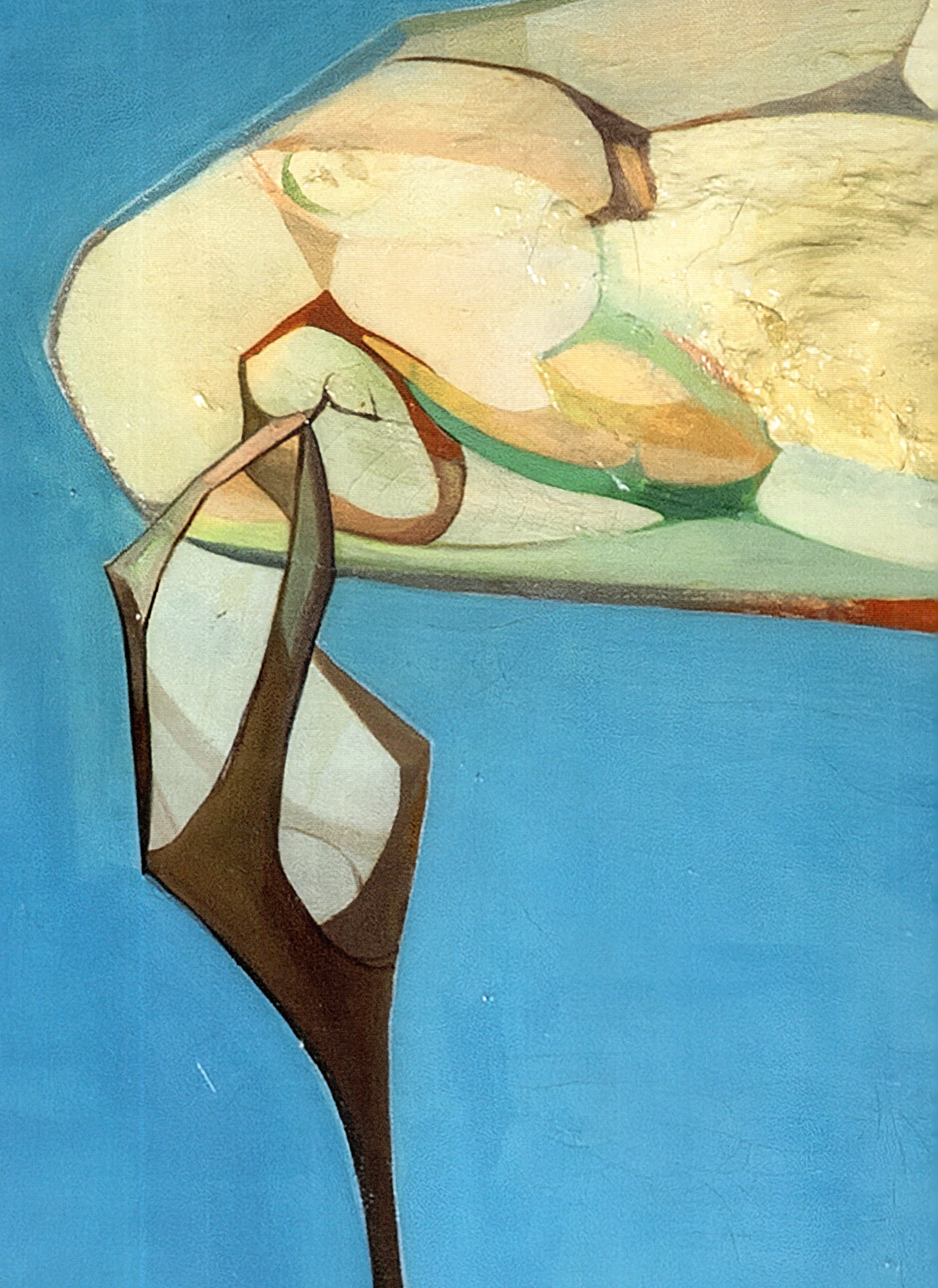

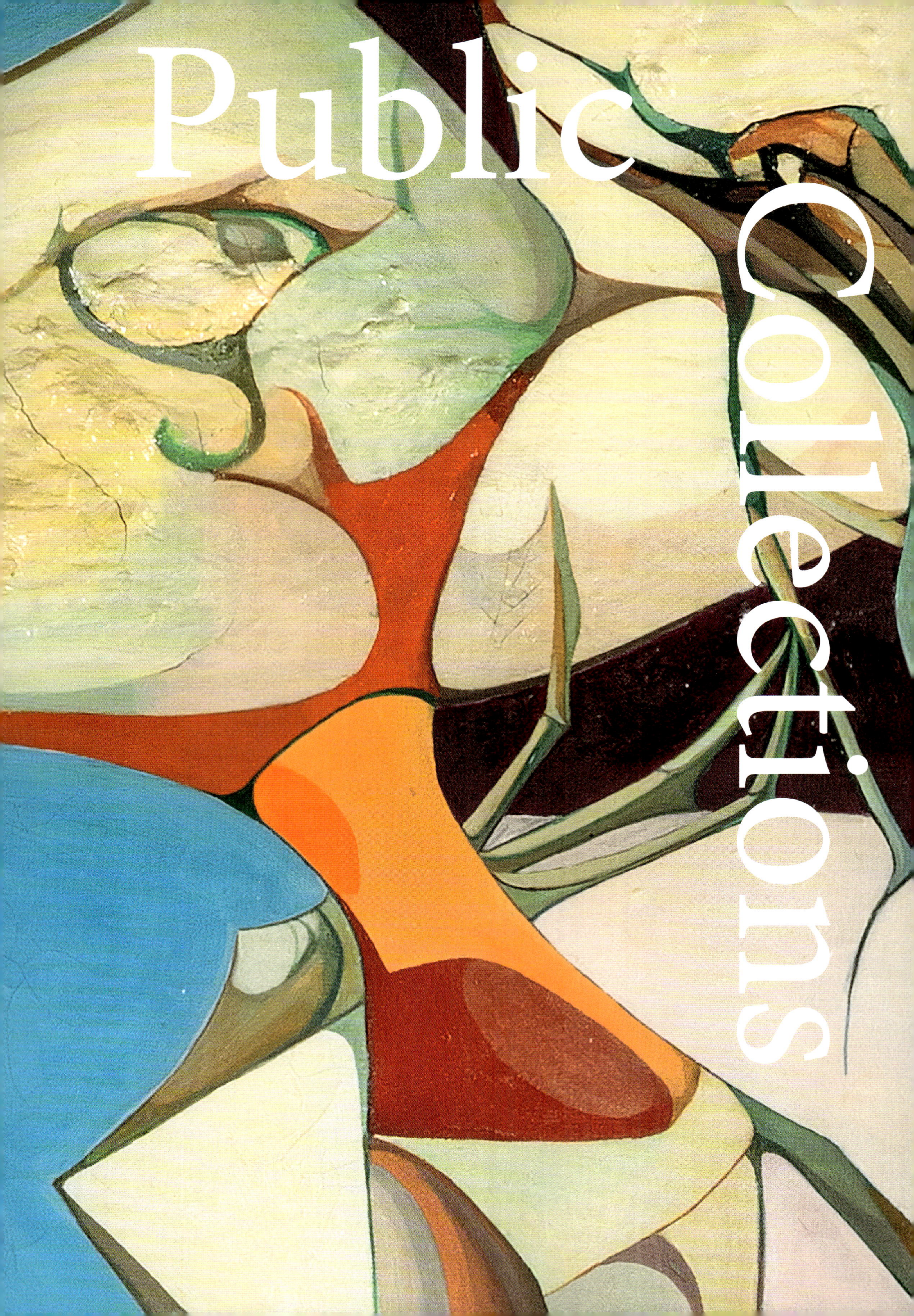
Public
Collections

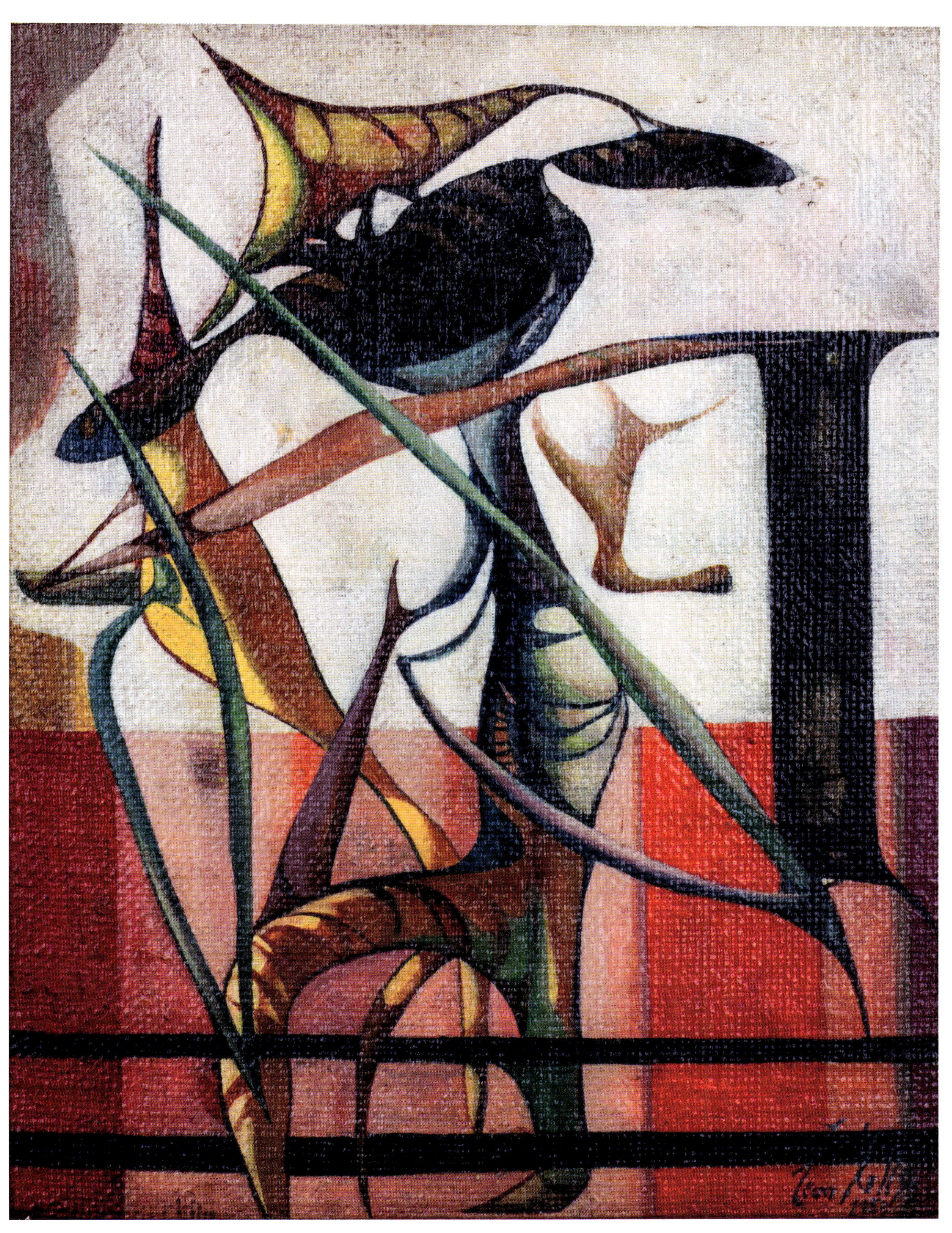

132
The Poet and the Golden Bird, 1953
Oil on canvas, 29 × 23 cm
Tel Aviv Museum of Art
Photo: Tel Aviv Museum of Art/
Margarita Perlin

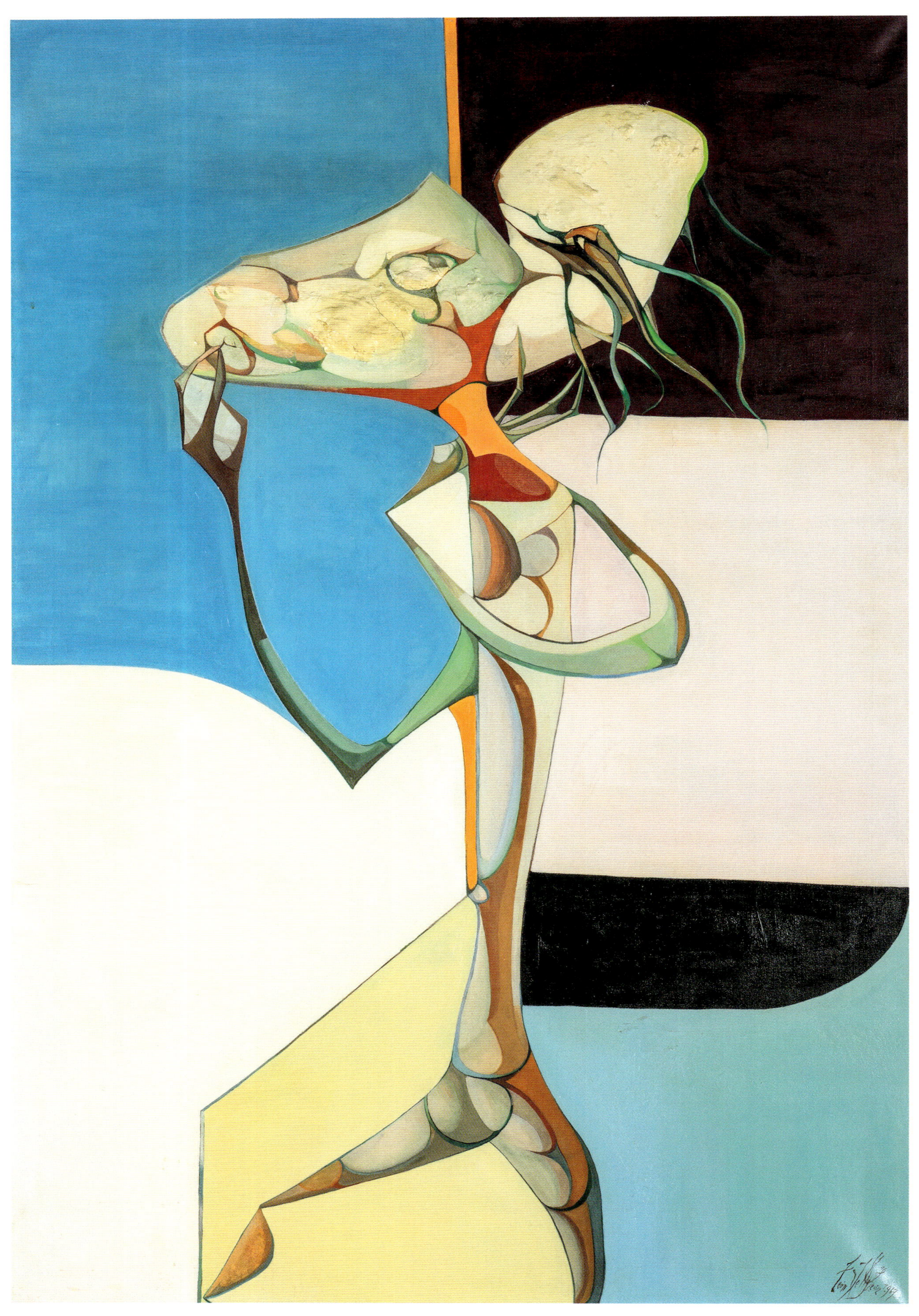

133
Spayed Woman Taking a Lethal Tablet, 1967
Oil and gesso on canvas, 127 × 86 cm
Tel Aviv Museum of Art
Gift of Virginia and Herbert Lust, Greenwich, Connecticut, through AFTAM, 2003
Photo: Tel Aviv Museum of Art/Margarita Perlin

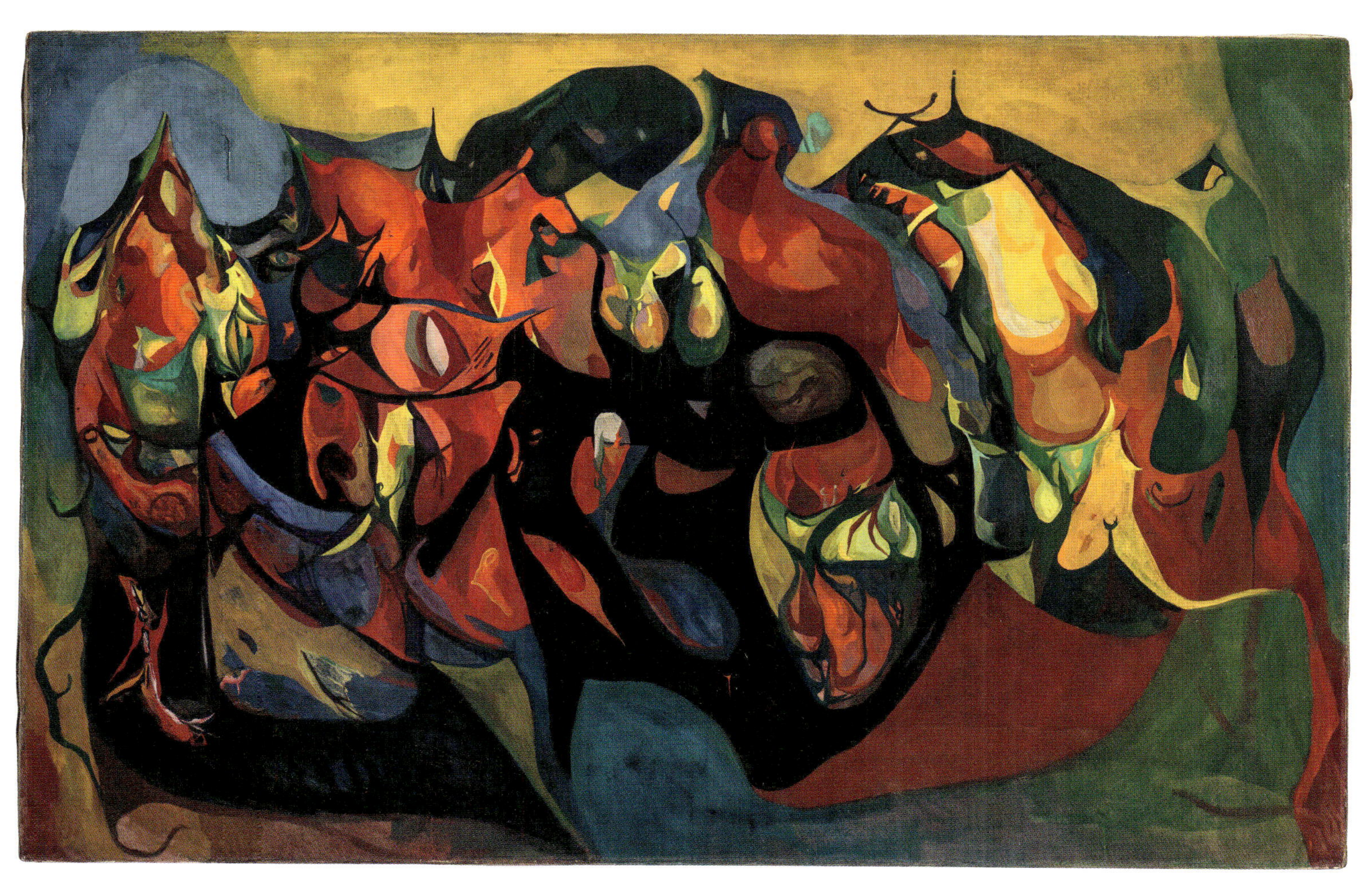

134
Primordial Landscape, 1939–1949
Oil on canvas, 116.2 × 131.3 cm
Philadelphia Museum of Art, Philadelphia
Photo: Philadelphia Museum of Art, Philadelphia

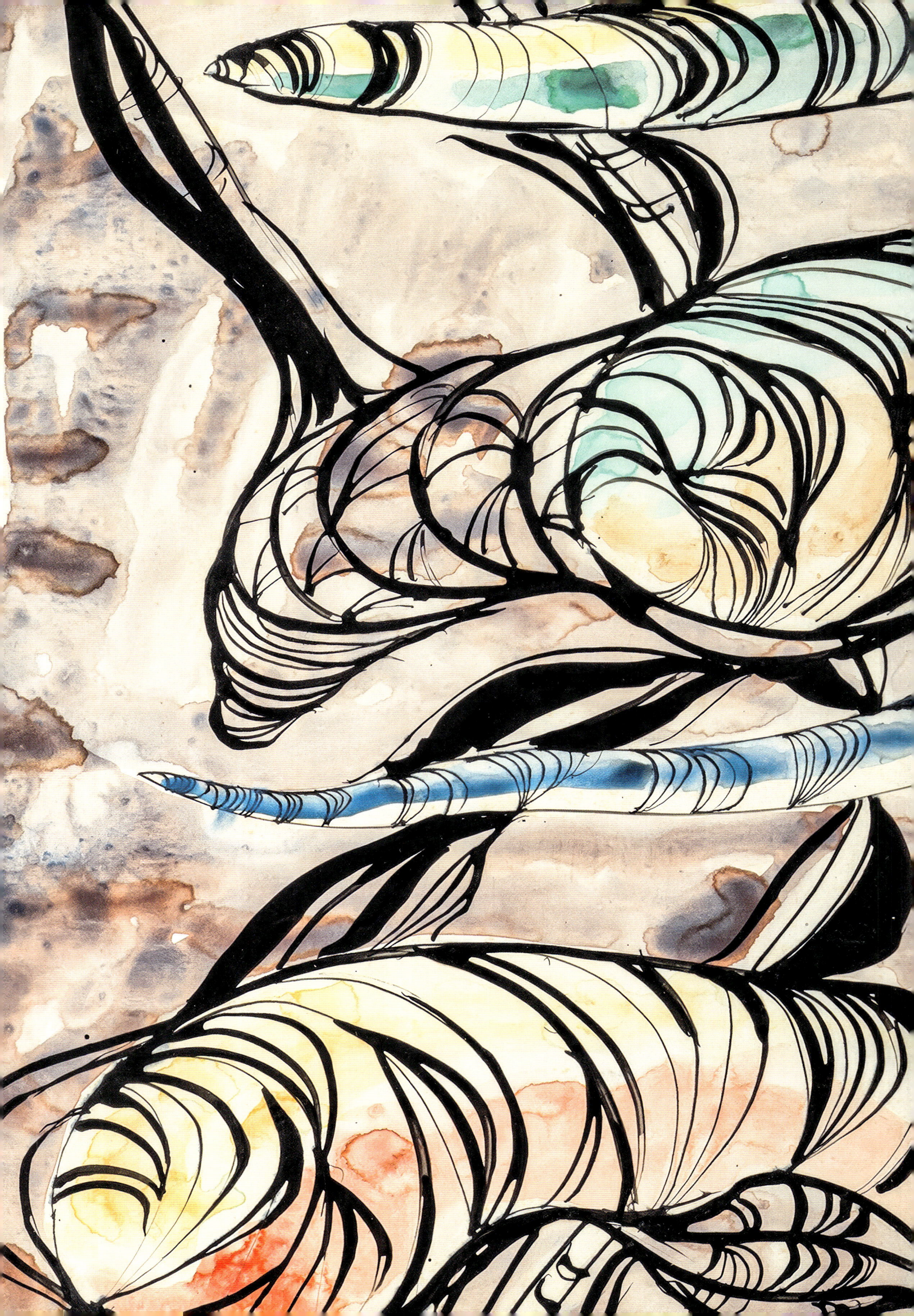

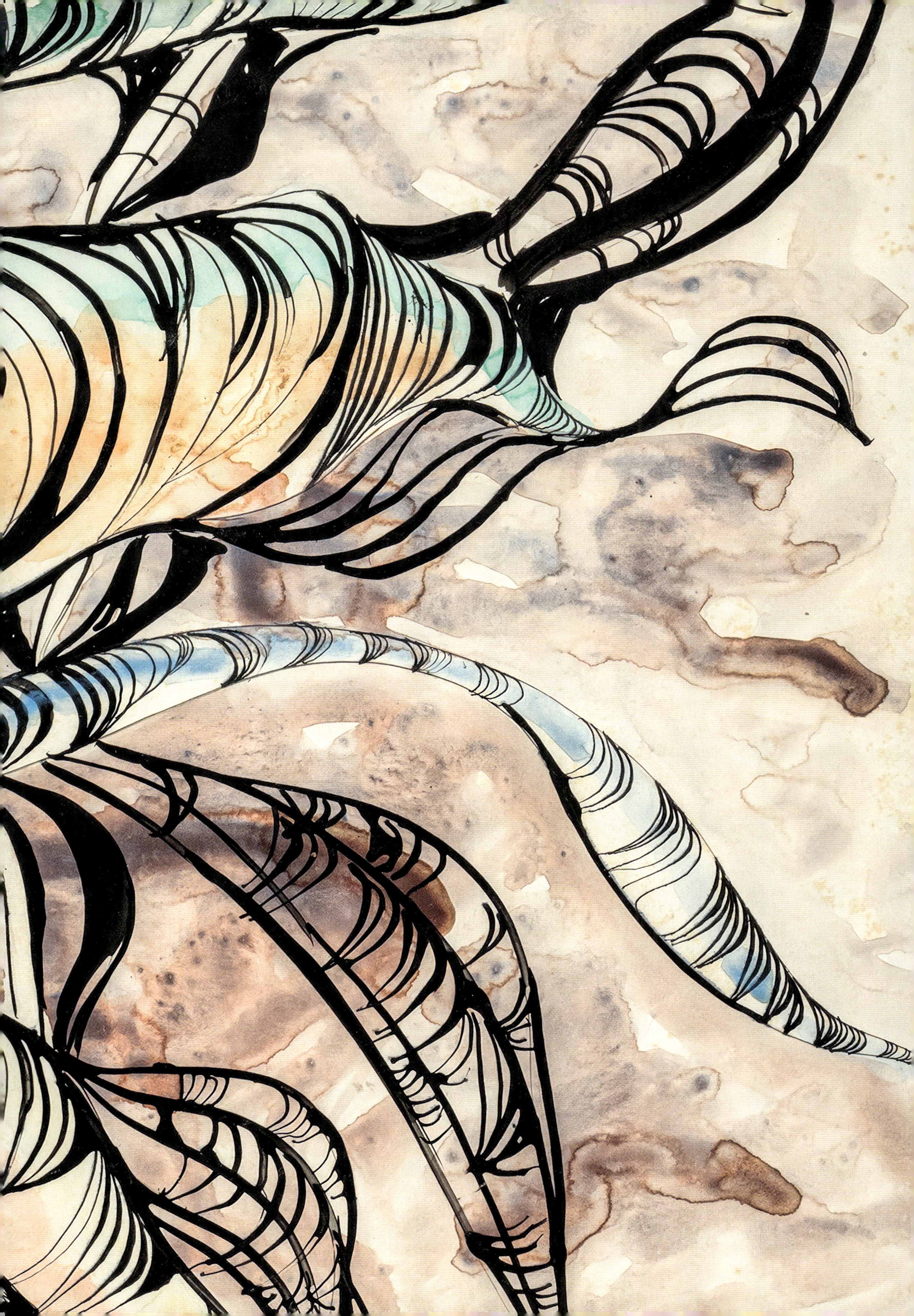

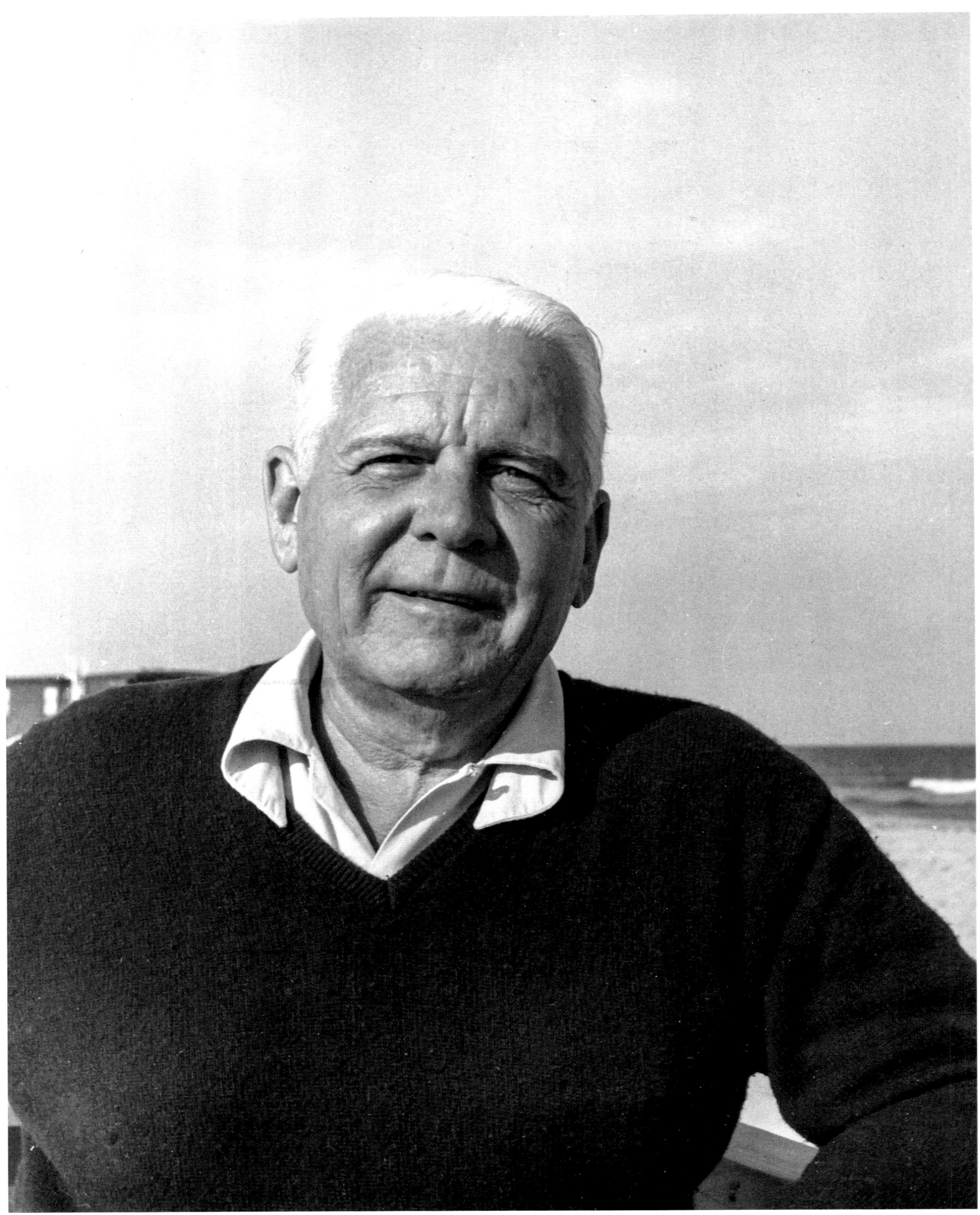

Leon Kelly, source of
photo unknown,
Plewig Collection

Biography

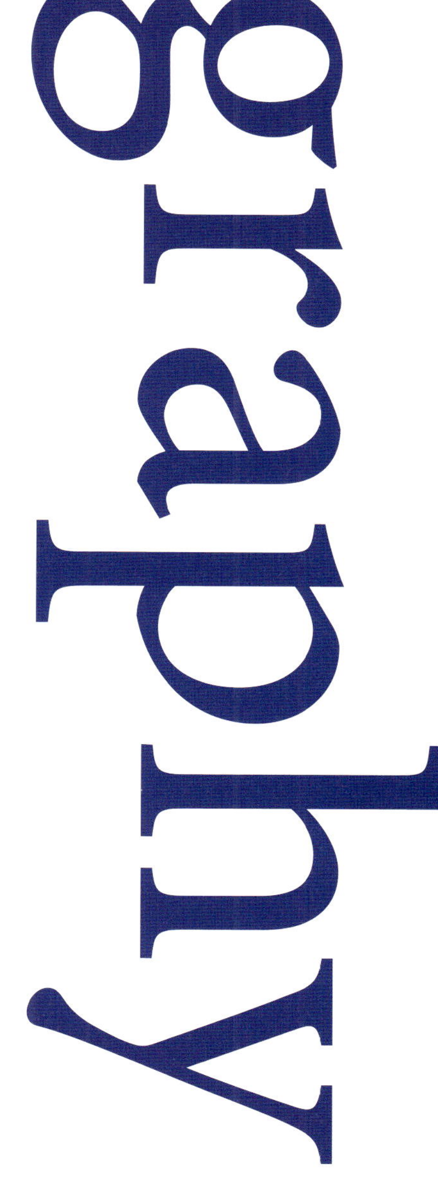

1901
Leon Kelly born in Philadelphia, Pennsylvania, the only child of Pantaleon L. Kelly, the co-owner of a tailoring company, and Elizabeth (née Stevenson).

1902
Kelly's father buys a "rural retreat" and takes Leon there every weekend. In the following years Pantaleon acquires a small collection of paintings and sculpture.

1914
Kelly starts taking private painting lessons with Albert Jean Adolphe, a teacher at the Philadelphia School of Industrial Art.

1917
Kelly begins studying sculpture with Alexander Portnoff.

1920
The family's financial situation worsens by 1920. His father's business collapses and his unhappy marriage ends. Kelly has to work at night. He is allowed to study anatomy during the day at the Philadelphia School of Osteopathy as well as etching with renowned illustrator Earl Horter, whose sizable collection of modern art includes pieces by Brancusi, Matisse, and Cubist painters Picasso and Braque.

1922
Arthur Carles, a colorful and controversial painter who teaches at the Pennsylvania Academy of Fine Arts, is one of the artists associated with Horter. Carles refers to Kelly as "his best student" when the latter enrolls in the Academy.

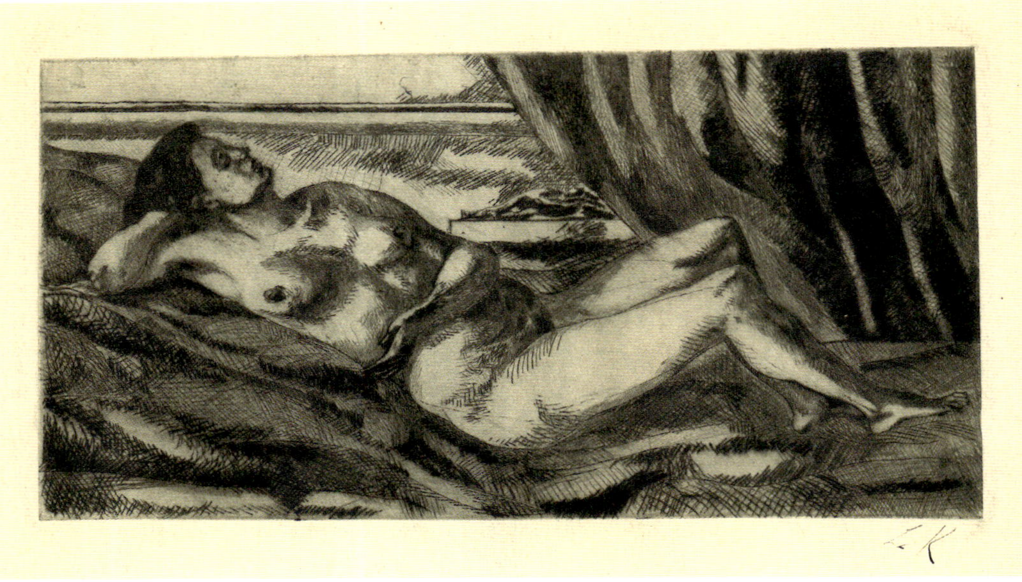

Leon Kelly, *Henriette*, 1937, “5ième” etching, 15.9 × 23.8 cm, Plewig Collection

1925
Receives a Cresson Scholarship and departs for Europe. He lives in Paris, where he meets critic Félix Fénéon, James Joyce, and Henry Miller, among others.

1929
Kelly marries Henriette D’Erfurth, a young Frenchwoman. She is often depicted in works created between 1928 and the beginning of the 1930s.

1930
After the stock market crash, Kelly and Henriette are forced to leave Paris and return to Philadelphia. The severe financial circumstances in Kelly’s life persist, and by the late 1930s, Henriette, who does not speak English, permanently returns to France. Following the divorce settlement, Kelly begins a relationship with Helen Lloyd Horter, a painter from Philadelphia who was also a fellow student at the Academy and the ex-wife of Earl Horter. They marry in 1941.

1940
Helen contacts Julien Levy, a fellow Harvard student of her brother-in-law Paul Vanderbilt, with a proposal for a Kelly drawing exhibition. Levy is a pioneer supporter of surrealism at his 57th street gallery in New York, The Julien Levy Gallery. He is impressed by Kelly’s work and begins to represent him. Levy’s artists include Salvador Dalí, Arshile Gorky, Yves Tanguy, Roberto Matta, Max Ernst, Joseph Cornell, and Marcel Duchamp.

1941
His debut exhibition is held at Philadelphia's Art Alliance. In March 1942, a solo show takes place in New York. The publication of Kelly and Picasso's nude photos in the magazine View in 1943 lead to the United States government banning the publication. The Julien Levy Gallery hosts a second one-man exhibition in 1944.

1942
Kelly leaves Philadelphia and moves to Harvey Cedars, New Jersey, Helen's vacation house on Long Beach Island. Harvey Cedars is a sparsely-populated outpost in the 1940s. His observations of insects, birds, and dragonflies in the garden begin to take shape in the tranquility of this place.

1946
Kelly begins working as a teacher at the Brooklyn Museum School. He discovers their collection of Peruvian textiles, an experience that profoundly alters his work in the following years. He begins researching Peruvian art and civilization.

1950
Kelly frequently lives alone in Harvey Cedars during the 1950s. He is periodically separated from Helen and daughter Paula, due to strains in the marriage.

1953
Kelly travels to North Africa and Spain.

1982
Kelly passes away at his Long Beach Island house.

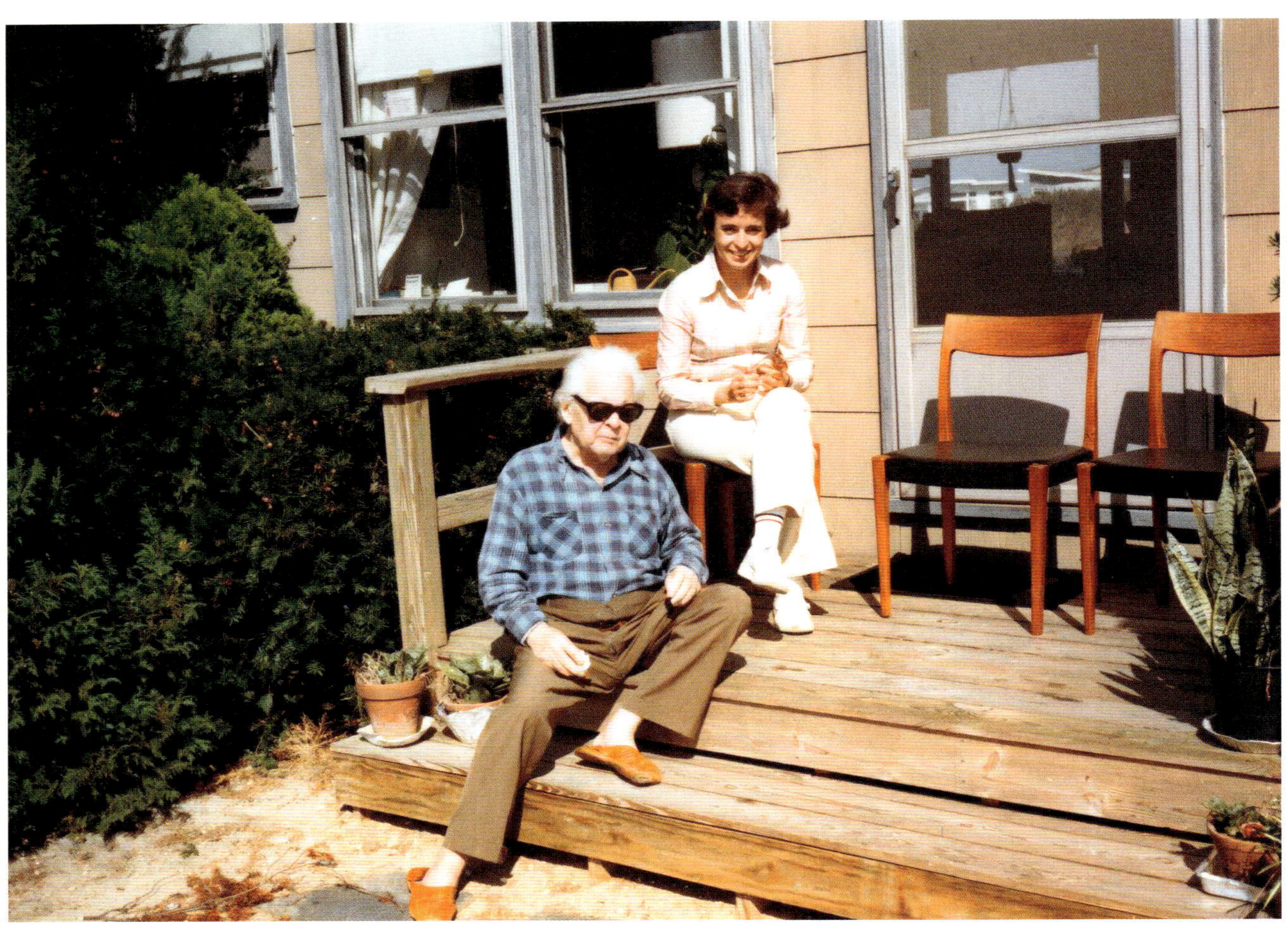

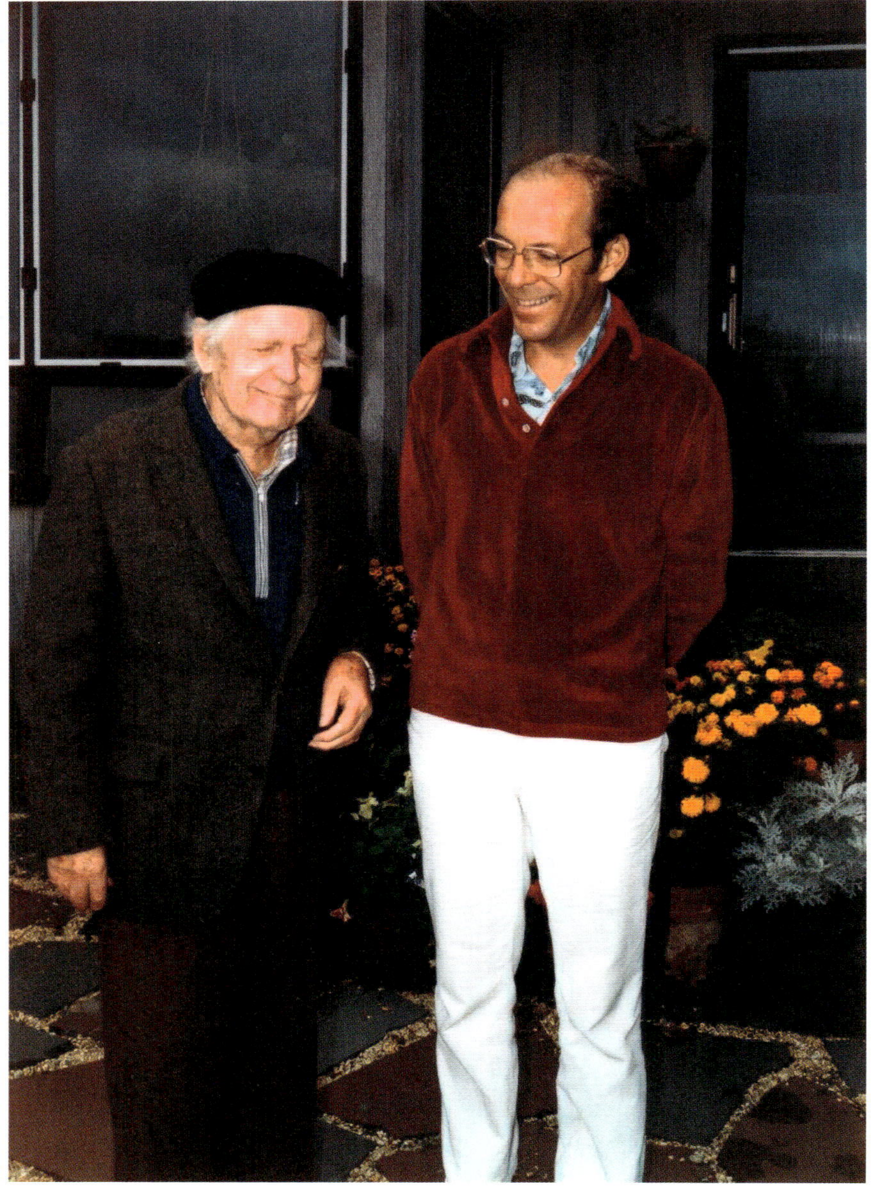

Leon Kelly and Helga, Oceana Dr., 1979
Leon Kelly and Gerd, in front of Oceana Dr., 1980

Authors' Biographies

Gerd Plewig

May 12, 1939	born in Langensalza/Gotha, Germany
1957–1962	medical studies in Hamburg, Graz, Kiel
1967–1982	research fellow, University of Pennsylvania, Philadelphia
1969–1982	dermatology training and staff member, University of Munich
1982–1991	chairman, Department of Dermatology, University of Düsseldorf
1991–2006	chairman, Department of Dermatology, University of Munich

Helga Lincke-Plewig

Feb. 14, 1941	born in Garmisch-Partenkirchen, Germany, née Lincke
1961–1967	medical studies at University of Munich
1969–1972	dermatology training at University of Erlangen
1972–1973	dermatology training at University of Munich
1974–1982	certified dermatologist, active in Munich, Düsseldorf (1982–1991), and Munich (1991–2006)

Uwe Jourdan

Feb. 22, 1964	born in Kaufbeuren, Germany
1984–1986	studies at Ludwig Maximilian University, Munich and apprenticeship as art dealer
1989–1996	publishes various art books
1986–2004	consultant on modern art and antique carpets for Nagel Auctions, Stuttgart
2005–2016 and 2020–2023	CEO Nagel Auctions, Stuttgart

List of

Paintings

1
Landscape, 1920
Oil on cardboard, 20.5 × 25.5 cm
Inv. no. 154, signed l.l., verso title, date, and inv. no. 154

2
Trees Landscape, 1921
Oil on canvas, 25 × 19 cm
Inv. no. 164, signed l.l., verso title, date, and inv. no. 164

3
Landscape and Barn, 1922
Oil on cardboard, 23 × 26.5 cm
Inv. no. 170, signed l.l., verso title, date, and inv. no. 170

4
Seated Nude, 1923
Oil on canvas on cardboard, 21.5 × 18.5 cm
Inv. no. 307, signed u.r., verso title, date, and inv. no. 307

5
Head of a Young Girl, 1924
Oil on canvas on board, 46 × 37.5 cm
Inv. no. 252, monogrammed l.r., verso signed, title, date, and inv. no. 252

6
Old Italian Woman, 1924
Oil on board, 41 × 33 cm
Inv. no. 86, signed l.l., verso signed, title, date, and inv. no. 86

7
Portrait, 1925
Oil on cardboard, 30 × 21.5 cm
Inv. no. 184, signed u.r., verso title, date, and inv. no. 184

8
Landscape with Standing Nude
Oil on cardboard, 23 × 12 cm
Inv. no. 279, verso signed, title, and inv. no. 279

9
Landscape with Seated Bather
Oil on board, 22 × 12 cm
Inv. no. 282, verso signed, title, and inv. no. 282

10
Bather, 1925
Oil on canvas on cardboard, 33 × 24 cm
Inv. no. 191, signed l.l., verso title, date, and inv. no. 191

11
Woman Ironing, 1925
Oil on canvas on cardboard, 46.5 × 38 cm
Inv. no. 238, signed u.r., verso title, date, and inv. no. 238

12
Henriette / The Seamstress, 192(?)
Oil on canvas on cardboard, 48 × 38 cm
Inv. no. 295, signed l.l., verso title, date, and inv. no. 295

13
Head of a Young Girl / Henriette, 1926
Oil on board, 45.5 × 38 cm
Inv. no. 258, monogrammed l.r., verso title, date, and inv. no. 258

14
Head Henriette, 1927
Oil on cardboard, 21 × 15 cm
Inv. no. 286, verso signed, title, date, and inv. no. 286

15
Untitled (Horse), 1940
Oil on canvas, 38 × 50.5 cm
Signed and dated l.r.

16
Autumn Landscape, 1926
Oil on board, 38 × 45.5 cm
Inv. no. 241, signed u.r., verso title, date, and inv. no. 241

17
Autumn Landscape near Paris, 1926
Oil on board, 38 × 45.5 cm
Inv. no. 236, signed u.r., verso title, dated, and inv. no. 236

18
Landscape with Sunset, 1926
Oil on board, 38 × 45.5 cm
Inv. no. 245, signed l.r., verso title, date, and inv. no. 245

19
Portrait of Matthew Sharpe, 1927
Oil on board, 40 × 32 cm
Inv. no. 244, signed u.r., verso title, date, and inv. no. 244

works

20
Portrait of Henriette with a Green Scarf, 1928
Oil on board, 40.5 × 33 cm
Inv. no. 294, signed u.r., verso title, date, and inv. no. 294

21
Bread and a Pear, 1930
Oil on canvas, 26 × 31 cm
Inv. no. 389, signed u.r., verso title, date, and inv. no. 389

22
The Laundress, 1931
Oil on board, 43 × 34 cm
Inv. no. 91, signed and dated u.l., verso title, and inv. no. 91

23
Woman Leading a Child, 1926
Oil on cardboard, 42 × 27.5 cm
Inv. no. 118, signed u.r., verso title, date, and inv. no. 118

24
Femme bagnant son enfant / Woman Bathing, 1929
Oil, 32.5 × 24.5 cm
Inv. no. 77, signed l.l., verso title, date, and inv. no. 77

25
Fruit and Glasses, 1930
Oil on cardboard, 20.5 × 25.5 cm
Inv. no. 146, monogrammed u.l., verso title, date, and inv. no. 146

26
The Abattoir, 1927
Oil on board, 33.5 × 41 cm
Inv. no. 129, signed u.r., verso signed, title, date, and inv. no. 129

27
Portrait Henriette, 1930
Oil on board, 41 × 33 cm
Inv. no. 127, signed mid right, verso title, date, and inv. no. 127

28
A Child Eating Soup, 1930
Oil on canvas on cardboard, 34.5 × 29.5 cm
Inv. no. 231, signed u.r., verso title, date, and inv. no. 231

29
Figure Seated in Doorway, 1930
Oil on canvas on cardboard, 30 × 22.5 cm
Inv. no. 226, verso signed, title, date, and inv. no. 226

30
Henriette in the Doorway, 1930
Oil on board, 41 × 33 cm
Inv. no. 88, signed l.r., verso title, date, and inv. no. 88

31
Man Burning Leaves, 1930
Oil on board, 30 × 18.5 cm
Inv. no. 172, signed l.r., verso signed, title, date, and inv. no. 172

32
Self-Portrait with Dog, 1930
Oil on canvas, 24 × 16.5 cm
Inv. no. 250, verso signed, title, date, and inv. no. 250

33
Untitled (Female Nude), ca. 1966
Oil on board, 24 × 18 cm
Signed u.r.

34
Labor Agitator, 1930
Oil on canvas, 29 × 22 cm
Inv. no. 260, signed l.l., verso title, date, and inv. no. 260

35
Construction of a Garage, 1937
Oil on canvas, 25.5 × 30.5 cm
Inv. no. 7, monogrammed l.r., verso title, date, and inv. no. 165

36
Visit to a Temple, 1938
Oil on canvas, 40.5 × 51 cm
Inv. no. 74, signed l.r., verso title, date, and inv. no. 74

37
Mendicant, 1941
Oil on canvas, 76 × 61 cm
Inv. no. 369, signed and dated l.r., verso title, date, and inv. no. 369

38
Hunter with a Bird, 1949
Oil on canvas, 38 × 20.5 cm
Inv. no. 438, signed l.r., verso title, date, and inv. no. 630, labels Philadelphia Museum of Art and Whitney Museum of American Art

39
The Ritual, 1954
Oil on canvas, 183 × 134 cm
Inv. no. 496, label Whitney Museum of American Art

40
The Solitary Glass, 1961
Oil on canvas, 52 × 66 cm
Inv. no. 594, signed and dated l.r., verso title, date, and inv. no. 594

41
The Levantine Model, 1962
Oil on canvas, 40.5 × 50.5 cm
Inv. no. 619, signed and dated l.l., verso title, date, and inv. no. 619

42
Imaginary Portrait, 1963
Oil on canvas, 23 × 18.5 cm
Inv. no. 630, signed and dated l.r., verso title, date, and inv. no. 630

43
In Memory of Francisco Stamato, 1963
Oil on canvas, 25.5 × 20.5 cm
Inv. no. 629, signed l.r., verso title, date, and inv. no. 629

44
Sylvia in the Levantine Cocoon, 1964
Oil on canvas, 63 × 76 cm
Inv. no. 662, signed and dated l.l., verso title, date, and inv. no. 662

45
Sylvia as a Child, 1966
Oil on canvas, 55 × 46 cm
Inv. no. 673, signed and dated u.l., verso title, date, and inv. no. 673

46
Frightened Child, 1967
Oil on canvas, 61 × 20.5 cm
Inv. no. 690, signed and dated l.r., verso title, date, and inv. no. 690

47
Kneeling Child, 1967
Oil on canvas, 61 × 46 cm
Inv. no. 691, signed and dated u.r., verso title, date, and inv. no. 691

48
Moment of Harmony, 1967
Oil on canvas, 183 × 122 cm
Inv. no. 687, signed and dated l.r., verso title, date, and inv. no. 687

49
Encounter of the adolescent Bather, 1968/69
Oil on canvas, 183 × 135 cm
Inv. no. 696, signed l.r., verso title, date, and inv. no. 696

50
Woman Talking, 1969
Oil on canvas, 66 × 35.5 cm
Inv. no. 700, signed l.r., verso title, date, and inv. no. 700

51
Child Bather at San Vincente Cove, 1970
Oil on canvas, 35.5 × 25.5 cm
Inv. no. 683, signed and dated l.l., verso title and inv. no. 683

Works on Paper

52
Untitled: (Cubistic, standing female nude), ca. 1921
Charcoal and gouache on paper, 96 × 64 cm

53
Untitled: (Heads and Arms), ca. 1922
Ink on paper, 18 × 12.5 cm
Signed l.l., signed l.r.

54
Untitled: (Heads and Arms), ca. 1922
Ink on paper, 18.5 × 13 cm
Signed l.l., signed l.r.

55
Untitled: (Heads, Figures, Anatomy*)*, ca. 1922
Ink on paper, 24.5 × 24 cm
Signed l.l., signed u.l.

56
Untitled: (Heads, Figures, Anatomy), ca. 1922
Ink on paper, 24 × 24.5 cm
Signed l.l., signed u.l.

57
Untitled: (Man with Turban)
Ink on paper, 14 × 9 cm
Signed l.l.

58
Untitled: (Walking Man)
Ink on paper, 14 × 9 cm
Signed l.r.

59
Untitled: (Seated Nude), undated
Ink on paper, 15 × 10 cm
Signed u.l., signed u.r.

60
Untitled: (Horseman)
Ink on paper, 15 × 10 cm
Signed l.r.

61
Untitled: (Nudes)
Ink on paper, 10 × 12.5 cm
Signed l.r.

62
Untitled: (Nudes)
Ink on paper, 10 × 12.5 cm
Signed l.r.

63
Untitled: (Female Nudes)
Ink on paper, 10 × 12.5 cm
Signed l.r.

64
Untitled: (Nudes)
Ink on paper, 10 × 12.5 cm
Signed l.r.

65
Untitled: (Artist and Nude),
Ink on paper, 19 × 14 cm
Signed l.r.

66
Seated Model, 1926
Ink on paper, 27.5 × 18 cm
Signed and dated l.l., verso title

67
Untitled: (Female Nudes)
Ink on paper, 14 × 9 cm
Signed l.r.

68
Untitled: (Female Nudes)
Ink on paper, 14 × 9 cm
Signed l.r.

69
Untitled: (Nude Couple)
Ink on paper, 12 × 10 cm
Signed l.r.

70
Untitled: (Nude Couple)
Ink on paper, 12 × 10 cm
Signed l.l.

71
Untitled: (Nude Figures)
Ink on paper, 19 × 14 cm
Signed l.r.

72
Untitled: (Nude Figures)
Ink on paper, 19 × 14 cm
Signed l.r.

73
Untitled: (group of figures
Ink on paper, 9 × 14 cm
Signed l.r.

74
Untitled: (Group of Figures)
Ink on paper, 9 × 14 cm
Signed l.r.

75
Untitled: (Group of Figures)
Ink on paper, 9 × 14 cm
Signed l.r.

76
Untitled: (Group of Figures)
Ink on paper, 9 × 14 cm
Signed l.r.

77
Untitled: (Group of Figures)
Ink on paper, 9 × 14 cm
Signed l.r.

78
Untitled: (Female Nude), 1928
Ink on paper, 43 × 30 cm
Signed and dated l.r.

79
Untitled: (Seated Nude)
Ink on paper, 30 × 23 cm
Signed l.r.

80
Untitled: (Nude Washing Her Feet),
1929
Ink on paper, 54.5 × 41 cm
Signed and dated l.r.

81
Untitled: (Group of Figures), 1930
Ink on paper, 12 × 14.5 cm
Signed and dated l.r.

82
Untitled: (Group of Figures), 1930
Ink on paper, 12 × 14.5 cm
Signed and dated l.r.

83
Untitled: (Group of Figures), 1930
Ink on paper, 12 × 14.5 cm
Signed and dated l.r.

84
Untitled: (Group of Figures), 1930
Ink on paper, 12 × 14.5 cm
Signed and dated l.r.

85
Untitled: (Man Washing Feet in a Landscape)
Ink and watercolors on paper,
15 × 9.5 cm
Signed l.l.

86
Untitled: (Walking Woman with Hat and Bag)
Watercolors on paper, 17 × 12 cm
Signed l.l.

87
Untitled: (Self-Portrait with Dog),
ca. 1930
Watercolors on paper, 30 × 22.5 cm
Signed l.l.

88
Untitled: (Man Burning Leaves)
Ink on paper, 29 × 17 cm
Signed l.r.

89
Untitled: (Two Men Burning Leaves)
Ink on paper, 29 × 17.5 cm
Signed l.r.

90
Untitled: (Man Working)
Ink on paper, 17 × 13.5 cm
Signed l..r.

91
Untitled: (Nude Figures)
Ink on paper, 13 × 17 cm
Signed u.r.

92
Untitled: (Two Figures), 1930
Ink on paper, 17 × 16 cm
Signed and dated u.r.

93
Untitled: (Standing Figure), ca. 1930
Ink on paper, 18.5 × 13.5 cm
Signed l.r.

94
Untitled: (Standing Figure), ca. 1931
Ink on paper, 18.5 × 13.5 cm
Signed l.r.

95
Untitled: (Horseman Killing Dragon)
Ink and watercolors on paper,
10.5 × 12.5 cm
Signed l.r.

96
Untitled: (Still Life with Flowers and Fruit)
Ink and watercolors on paper,
10 × 11 cm
Signed mid right

97
Untitled: (Seated Woman Reading), 1931
Ink on paper, 55.5 × 42.5 cm
Signed and dated l.r.

98
Untitled: (The Laundress), 1933
Gouache on paper, 60 × 45 cm
Signed and dated l.l.

99
Untitled: (Butcher and Heads)
Charcoal pencil on paper,
22.5 × 18.5 cm
Signed u.l.

100
Untitled: (Two Butchers)
Gouache on paper, 23.5 × 18.5 cm
Signed and dated l.r.

101
Untitled: (Man Walking) 1934
Ink and gouache on paper,
28 × 21 cm
Signed and dated l.r.

102
Untitled: (Male Head)
Gouache on paper, 54.5 × 41.5 cm
Signed l.r.

103
The Rhine Wine Bottle, 1923
Charcoal on paper, 45 × 30 cm
Inv. no. 517, signed and dated l.r., verso signed, title, date, and inv. no. 517

104
Untitled: (Cubes and Balls), 1927
Gouache on paper, 54.5 × 42 cm
Signed and dated l.r.

105
Untitled: (Still Life), 1933
Gouache on paper, 54.5 × 42 cm
Signed and dated l.r.

106
Untitled: (Still Life with Teapot and Figure under a Tree), 1929
Ink on paper, 21 × 13 cm
Signed and dated l.r.

107
Untitled: (Still Life with Teapots and Heads), ca. 1929
Ink on paper, 22 × 13 cm
Signed l.r.

108
Untitled: (Still Lives with Teapot), ca. 1929
Ink on paper, 21 × 13.5 cm
Signed l.r.

109
Untitled: (Venus and Cupido)
Watercolor on paper, 11 × 18 cm
Signed u.r.

110
Untitled: (Two Reclining Figures)
Ink and watercolors on paper,
18.5 × 24 cm
Signed l.r.

111
*Untitled: (*Reclining Nude)
Ink and watercolors on paper,
10 × 12 cm
Signed l.l.

112
Untitled: (study)
Ink and watercolors on paper,
14.5 × 11.5 cm
Signed mid left

113
Franco, 1937
Ink and watercolors on paper,
20 × 15 cm
Signed and dated l.l.

114
Untitled: (Standing Old Man), 1940
Ink on paper, 32 × 24 cm
Signed and dated l.r.

115
Sujet classique représentant le souci d'un parapluie dans le temple
Ink and watercolor on paper,
35.5 × 51 cm
Title l.r.

116
Capullo de gusano de seda
Ink and watercolors on paper,
62 × 46.5 cm
Signed and title l.r.

117
Untitled: (Portrait of a Young Man), 1930
Ink and watercolors on paper,
27 × 20.5 cm
Signed l.r.

118
Untitled: (Portrait of a Young Man with Flower), 1958
Ink on paper, 27 × 20.5 cm
Signed and dated l.l.

119
Untitled: (Portrait of a Woman), 1955
Charcoal on paper, 63.5 × 48 cm
Signed and dated l.r.

120
Untitled: (Nude Figures), 195(?)
Ink on paper, 39 × 28 cm
Signed and dated l.r.

121
Goethe (?) Conversation, etc., 1951
Ink and watercolors on paper,
38 × 31.5 cm
Signed and dated l.l., title l.r.

122
Moon Man, 1956
Pencil on paper, 56 × 48 cm
Inv. no. 494, signed and dated l.r., verso title, date, and inv. no. 494

123
Untitled: (Figure), 1956
Ink on paper, 29 × 22.5 cm
Signed and dated l..r.

124
Untitled: (Standing Figure, Moon Man), 1958
Pencil on paper, 48 × 31 cm
Signed and dated l.r.

125
Untitled: (Figure), 1958
Ink on paper, 34 × 25.5 cm
Signed and dated l.r.

126
Untitled: (Hovering Figure), 1959
Ink and color pencil on paper, 30.5 × 23 cm
Signed and dated l.r.

127
The Insane Mars, 1961
Graphite on paper, 32 × 23.5 cm
Inv. no. 865, signed and dated l.r.

128
Untitled: (Nude Figure), 1968
Charcoal on paper, 77.5 × 57.5 cm
Signed and dated l.l.

129
Mexican Indian Women Looking, 1969
Charcoal pencil, 35 × 27 cm
Signed and dated u.l., verso label Richard Feigen Gallery

130
Untitled: (Two Male Heads), 1970
Watercolor on paper, 29 × 40 cm
Signed and dated l.l.

131
Untitled: (Two Male Heads), 1970
Ink on paper, 29 × 40 cm
Signed and dated l.r.

Details

p. 2: **see fig. 33**

p. 4:“Self-Portrait Trying to Fly…”, photo from 1975, Plewig collection

pp. 6–7: **see fig. 40**

p. 8: **see fig. 126**

p. 11: **see fig. 3**

pp. 12–13: **see fig. 41**

p. 14: **fig. 24**

pp. 18–19: **see fig. 39**

p. 20: **see fig. 56**

pp. 30–31: **see fig. 45**

pp. 40–41: **see fig. 10**

pp. 74–75: **see fig. 37**

pp. 78–79: **see fig. 39**

pp. 88–89: **see fig. 44**

pp. 92–93: **see fig. 45**

pp. 96–97: **see fig. 46**

pp. 100–101: **see fig. 47**

pp. 104–105: **see fig. 48**

pp. 108–109: **see fig. 49**

pp. 112–113: **see fig. 50**

pp. 116–117: **see fig. 51**

pp. 120–121: **see fig. 112**

pp. 152–153: **see fig. 89**

pp. 160–161: **see fig. 95**

pp. 170–171: **see fig. 104**

pp. 184–185: **see fig. 115**

pp. 188–189: **see fig. 118**

pp. 194–195: **see fig. 122**

pp. 204–205: **see fig. 130**

pp. 210–211: **see fig. 133**

pp. 216–217: **see fig. 116**

Works without a date are considered undated.

© all works, the artist's estate, Paula Muller Kelly

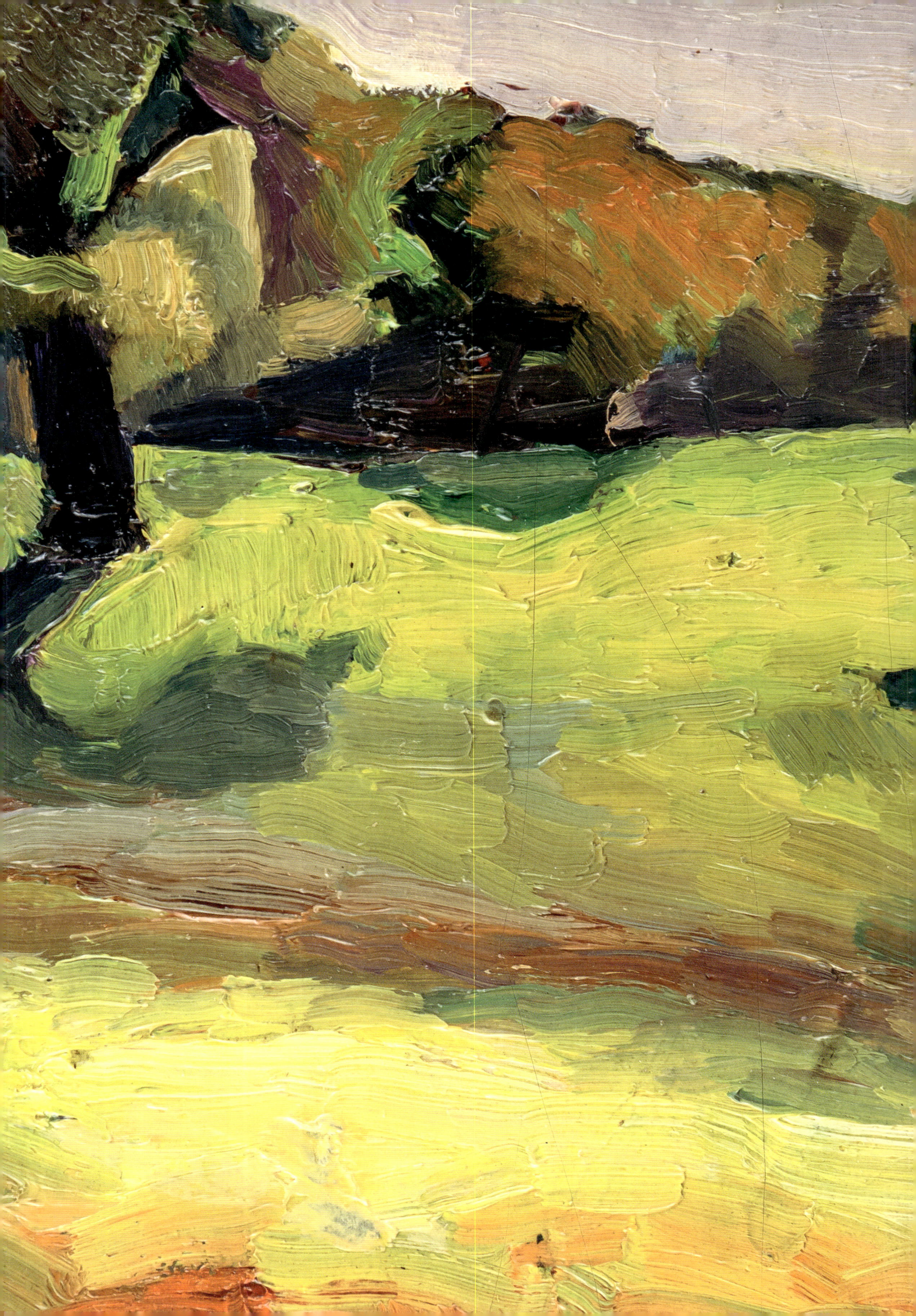

Bibliography

Gerd Plewig, “Leon Kelly,” *Medizin+Kunst, 9*, II. (1997): 8–12.

Leon Kelly: An American Surrealist, Francis M. Naumann Fine Art, LLC. New York, April 16—June 5, 2008. Gratz Gallery, New Hope, Pennsylvania.

Martica Sawin, “This Strange Cosmic Flight of Particles Called Man,” in *Leon Kelly: An American Surrealist*, pp. 1–22.

Christian Busch, “Mehr als nur Glück oder Zufall. Erfolgsfaktor Serendipität.” *Forschung & Lehre*, 31: 5/24 (2024), pp. 370–371.

Serendipity. https://en.wikipedia.org/wiki/Serendipity. The story, the lost camel, the story continues, references.

Sources for “The Art of Leon Kelly in His own Words.” (p. 21)

Leon Kelly: An American Surrealist, Francis M. Naumann Fine Art, LLC. New York, April 16—June 5, 2008. Gratz Gallery, New Hope, Pennsylvania.
Letters and notes by Leon Kelly, Plewig Collection

Sources for “Biography” (p. 219)

Leon Kelly: An American Surrealist, Francis M. Naumann Fine Art, LLC. New York, April 16—June 5, 2008. Gratz Gallery, New Hope, PA 18938.
Wikipedia, 2024

Published by
Hirmer Verlag
Bayerstraße 57–59
80335 Munich, Germany
hirmerpublishers.com

Authors
Gerd Plewig, Uwe Jourdan
Hirmer Project Management
Rainer Arnold
Copyediting and Proofreading
David Sanchez
Layout and Typesetting
Hannes Halder
Prepress and repro
Repromayer, Reutlingen
Printing and binding
Printer Trento
Paper
Garda Art Matt 150 g/m^2
Printed in Italy

Bibliographic information published
by the Deutsche Nationalbibliothek
The Deutsche Nationalbibliothek lists this publication in the Deutsche Nationalbibliografie; detailed bibliographic data is available online at http://www.dnb.de.

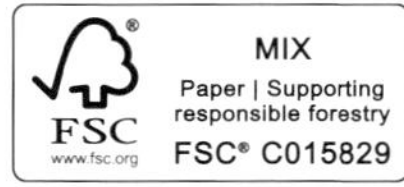

The Gerd and Helga Plewig Collection